BEYOND PROGRAMMING

John Hopkins University
Applied Physics Laboratory Series in Science and Engineering

SERIES EDITOR: John R. Apel

William H. Avery and Chih Wu
Renewable Energy form the Ocean: A Guide to OTEC

Bruce I. Blum
Software Engineering: A Holistic View

R. M. Fristrom
Flame Structures and Processes

Richard A. Henle and Boris W. Kuvshinoff
Desktop Computers: In Perspective

Vincent L. Pisacane and Robert C. Moore (eds.)
Fundamentals of Space Systems

BEYOND PROGRAMMING

To a New Era of Design

Bruce I. Blum

Applied Physics Laboratory
The Johns Hopkins University

New York   *Oxford*
Oxford University Press
1996

Oxford University Press

Oxford   New York
Athens   Auckland   Bangkok   Bombay
Calcutta   Cape Town   Dar es Salaam   Delhi
Florence   Hong Kong   Istanbul   Karachi
Kuala Lumpur   Madras   Madrid   Melbourne
Mexico City   Nairobi   Paris   Singapore
Taipei   Tokyo   Toronto

and associated companies in
Berlin   Ibadan

Published by Oxford University Press, Inc.,
198 Madison Avenue, New York, New York 10016

Library of Congress Cataloging-in-Publication Data
Blum, Bruce I.
Beyond programming: to a new era of design/
Bruce I. Blum.
p. cm. Includes bibliographical references and index.
ISBN 0-19-509160-4
1. Computer software—Development. I. Title.
QA76.76.D47B62 1995 005.1'2'01—dc20 95-6889

9 8 7 6 5 4 3 2 1

Printed in the United States of America
on acid-free paper

To Harriet

PREFACE

Inasmuch as there is a prologue that describes the objectives and structure of this book, I am using this preface to present its goals in a personal context. I begin by observing that I enjoy writing the preface to a book. The preface is the last part that I write; it is a signal that, except for the editor's suggested changes, the book is finished. In this case, the preface is even more satisfying. In a matter of weeks I will retire. After thirty-plus years of work in computing, I am about to try something different. Thus, this book comes at a watershed in my life. As I hope to show, it also comes at a time of fundamental change in the way in which software systems are developed.

In part, the preparation of this book has been an act of closure. It constitutes the fulfillment of my obligation as a government-funded researcher to present coherently the results of my long investigation of the software process. But I am not so self-centered that I would write an entire book just for my own gratification. (If that were my intent, I certainly would have made it shorter!) What new-found wisdom, then, has my research uncovered that justifies this book? Simply stated, it is the observation that we now develop software within a framework of obsolescent concepts. Continued reliance on this framework, moreover, constrains both process improvement and the scope of our applications. I conclude, therefore, that a shift in the software development paradigm is necessary. In the words of the title, I propose that we move *beyond programming*.

What does it mean to move beyond programming? Programming—the preparation of correct and efficient computer instructions for achieving desired ends—is a new concept; it has been with us for fewer than 50 years. Yet programming and program notations have come to dominate much of our thinking about software development. In this book I examine how software will be developed in the next century, and I conclude that the present programming orientation is inappropriate. Programming, as we know it, simply cannot fully exploit software's unique properties. I do have an alternative to offer, and I describe and evaluate this alternative in considerable detail. But to think of this book as a proposal for a particular paradigm would miss the mark entirely. It is concerned with how software engineering *ought* to be organized, with the essential nature of software design, with the conceptual framework that molds our understanding of software, with historical assessments of no longer valid assumptions. Thus, in short, this book seeks to lay the foundation for a 21st century software engineering paradigm, one that emphasizes the *use* of software and not its *construction*.

Paradigm shifts are revolutions. They are not to be undertaken lightly, and they are strongly resisted by those committed to the current paradigm. Often, a generation change is needed before the new paradigm is accepted. Nevertheless, I feel that a shift in our approach to software development is inevitable. Like the child in the fairy tale, it is obvious to me that the emperor is wearing no clothes. Unfortunately, I am not clear about what, in this analogy, the emperor should wear. In what follows I share my view of a software engineering parading in tattered (and sometimes transparent) clothing. I hope to encourage a more critical examination of what we now are doing, to provide a justification for phasing out techniques that emerged as responses to now obsolete technologies, to aid in the identification of the underlying challenges in software development, and to illustrate how the unique properties of automation can be exploited more effectively. But I offer no authoritative description of software engineering's future; there are just too many uncontrollable variables to make that a practical undertaking.

Because I argue that there must be a fundamental change in the way we develop software, this book is directed to the faculty, students, and developers who will bring about that paradigm shift. My hope is that the book will promote thought and serve as a catalyst for change. Of course, I would like all my colleagues to read what I have written; I am confident that they will benefit from reflecting on what is presented in this volume. Finally, I sense that practitioners, whose work is so distorted by today's technology and perceptions, will find the contents interesting and relevant. But, in the final analysis, the principle objective of this book is to engender thought about how software will be developed in the next century.

I note that some readers may find this a strange and frustrating book. Despite its ambitious objective (that of showing why a paradigm shift in software development is unavoidable), it is not dogmatic in the sense of predicting the details of that shift. The book explains why I am convinced that we are following the wrong approach. I also describe an environment that for 14 years has successfully employed an alternative development model. But I do not present my solution as *the* answer; I only assert that it is a proof of concept *and* a "gold standard." That is, my approach works *and*, therefore, other methods ought to perform at least as well or explain why they do not. One of the lessons of this book is that it is easier to discover what is false than to find out what is true. I am content to explain why I believe the present paradigm is flawed and to demonstrate that a viable alternative exists. Therefore, most of this book devotes itself to a critical examination of software engineering and its context. My particular answer, which I readily admit is of significant interest to me, has been included only to illustrate a possible alternative.

A secondary aim of this book is to collect and summarize in one place many of the underlying ideas (outside of computer science) that affect software development. I have been fortunate to have had the opportunity to do considerable reading, and—given the demands on the reader's time—I felt that a concise synthesis of these thoughts would satisfy an unmet need. Obviously, I do not know what the next generation of computer scientists will need to know; nevertheless, I do have a strong sense of the ideas with which they should be familiar. I have elected to focus on the concepts that often are bypassed in a technology-centered education. Indeed, the book leaves out much of what I assume a computer professional already knows or will learn elsewhere. Instead I concentrate on the larger issues, such as the relation of science to technology, the nature of design, and the evolution of software design methods.

Although the material is presented with some repeated themes, there is no unified argument, no spirit of inevitability within my argument. Unfortunately, the foundational concepts do not complement each other; each reader will be forced to resolve many dilemmas on her own. I believe that knowledge is assimilated, not transferred. Therefore, each reader is expected to bring to this book many ideas and insights that are foreign to me, and certainly each reader will add knowledge long after I have left the field. I concentrate on the foundational topics to which the reader may have limited exposure. These topics are complex and diffuse; they are intended to be molded into a reasoned understanding that will guide the reader's future work. My intent is to alter the reader's comprehension of the software process and its scientific and human foundations. I do not present a static collection of facts and opinions; like a software product, the book's value lies in its subsequent use. Thus, even though I argue the validity and efficacy of my particular solution, I expect the reader to develop solutions of his own.

The physical limitations of a book prescribes a hierarchical structure, but the material in a book generally is holistic and integrated. In this case, I have divided the work into three, roughly independent parts. Each addresses a different set of questions: What is the nature of science and scientific knowledge, what are the human dimensions of design, and what is the essence of software engineering? My objective is to have the reader reflect on assertions that often are accepted as fundamental in computer science and software engineering. But the reader may find my presentation too philosophical or obscure. Therefore, she may begin with Part III and use its material as the motivation for continuing on to the other two parts. That is, although reading this book linearly is probably the easiest approach, it is not the only one. If the reader currently has no interest in the problems being addressed, then jump forward (or backward). If I have been correct in my assessment, the material should remain pertinent whenever an interest in it develops.

Now for some personal comments. The title, *Beyond Programming*, evokes a special sense of symmetry for me. I had chosen it to be the title of my first book, and instead it has become the title of my last computer book. (The first book, by the way, had a different title because it was on a very different subject: *Clinical Information Systems*.) Why did I stick with this title for so long? Although I have made much of my living as a programmer, I have never thought that programming was very interesting. For me, the challenge is one of creating a system. Programming is to developing systems as grammar is to writing a novel. A necessary tool to be mastered and used automatically. Yet, most of computer science still considers programming and programming notations to be the central jewels in its crown. If we are to shift paradigms, then we must move away from this historical orientation, one whose justification can be traced back to the problems of computing's early days.

As I will show in the final two chapters, it is possible to develop large and complex information systems without programs. "Ah, yes," the reader retorts, "this is a book about a 4GL. That's what he means." Oh, but I must correct you. This book is not about 4GLs, or a formal specification language, or picture-driven systems analysis, or object-oriented anything. That's why it takes eight chapters before I feel comfortable talking about software. This is a book about a genuine paradigm shift. One that moves us beyond programming and to system design. To be honest, I do not believe that the solution I document in the book's final chapters will have much impact. Many alternatives are possible, and I am not bold enough to claim that I have discovered the only key to the future. Indeed, that is why I have written such a loose book; my goal is to educate rather than to convince. There are many potential solutions, and this book should be seen as a set of questions that will sensitize the reader to the underlying problems and guide him in refining his search for the most appropriate solutions.

Enough about the book; its plan will become clear soon enough. First a brief aside, and then a happy acknowledgement of all those who contributed to it. As the reader already will have noticed, I have found an awkward way to demonstrate my assumption that half the readers will be female. I simply alternate pronoun genders. I have tried to follow the normal standards of technical communication. For example, I made every effort to consistently avoid split infinitives, and my spelling checker has given me the assurance that every word is spelled properly (even when it is not the appropriate word). I have, however, violated one convention. When quoting an author, I have felt free to change the case of the initial letter to conform to the material's grammatical context.

On to the nice part of the preface: the opportunity to thank all those who helped to make the book possible. Because this book comes at the end of a career, I would like to mention many of those who had a significant role in my professional and scientific development. To begin with, I am indebted to the U.S. Navy for the support that they provided me during the last decade. Without it, my final research would not have been possible. My primary support came from the Office of Naval Research, and it was supplemented by IR&D tasks within the Laboratory's Navy Contract. There also were tasks with the Naval Surface Warfare Center and the Air Force Office of Scientific Research. I thank my sponsors for their interest in my work. In particular, I would like to express my gratitude to Ralph Wachter for his continuing demonstrations of confidence in my research. I hope that the results are in some small way worthy of the national investment made in me.

Now to mention where I have worked. I started at the Applied Physics Laboratory of the Johns Hopkins University in 1962. I had just turned 31, my wife was pregnant with our second child, and we agreed it was time to find a job. I stayed at the Laboratory for 5 years, went to industry for 8 years, and returned to the Laboratory to complete this phase of my life. I was fortunate to work with supervisors who were or became friends (Paul Casner, Ned Wharton, Vince Sigillito, Don Williams) in an organization guided by caring directors (Ned Gibson, Alexander "Kossy" Kossiakoff, Carl Bostrom, and Gary Smith). All of these people, as well as the many others whom I have not named explicitly, have made the Laboratory an excellent place to work, an environment that is productive, stimulating, challenging, and effective. Indeed, the completion of this book was made possible by one of the Laboratory's Janney Fellowships.

From 1975 to 1983 I had an interdivisional assignment in the School of Medicine, where I had full-time appointments in Biomedical Engineering under Dick Johns and in Oncology under Al Owens. This experience had a profound effect on my late-blooming development, and three people deserve a special mention: Paul Casner, a long-time personal friend, who found a place for me in the Laboratory and helped me in the transfer to the School of Medicine; Dick Johns, who showed me (by example and displays of confidence) what it meant to work at world-class standards; and Vince Sigillito, who brought me into the Research Center and provided a setting in which I was free to explore the ideas I felt were important.

There were many friends and colleagues who were kind enough to read all or parts of this book and share their comments with me. They are, in alphabetical order, Løve Bhabuta, Subrata Dasgupta, Al Davis, Peter Denning, Batya Friedman, Bob Glass, Bill Harvey, Dave Hurley,

Kari Kuutti, Rachel and Larry Laudan, Manny Lehman, Jacob Mey, Peter Naur, Stan Rifkin, John Sadowsky, Andy Sage, Ben Shneiderman, Jack Smith, John Sommerer, Toomas Timpka, Walter Vincenti, and Dick Walters. I thank them for their interest, help, encouragement, and/or corrective criticism. Attribute the many flaws that remain herein to advice not taken.

As one reads through this book, it should be clear that its preparation would not be possible were it not for the assistance of a modern research library. Through interlibrary loans and transfers, the staff of the Gibson Library promptly provided me with the materials I needed, and I am happy to acknowledge their behind-the-scenes support. Many others contributed to bringing this book to completion. Thanks go to Jeff Robbins and Bill Zobrist, my editors at Oxford, John Apel of APL, who edits the APL series, Dolores Oetting and the other members of the production staff at Oxford, Fay Perry, our group secretary, and the many Laboratory organizations that provided support.

Leaving the best for last, I reserve the final paragraph that I will write as a computer scientist for Harriet. She has provided the right proportions of understanding, sympathy, and reality to make me want to work hard and the proper measures of fun, sensibility, and excitement to keep my compulsions in perspective. Thanks, Harriet; I'm looking forward to spending even more time together.

Columbia, MD   B.I.B

CONTENTS

PART II   ECOLOGICAL DESIGN

BEYOND PROGRAMMING

PROLOGUE

I am a software engineer, and this book seeks an answer to the question, How should we develop and maintain software? I point this out up front because the question may get lost in the search for an answer. The answer, of course, is not straightforward; indeed, it cannot be formulated in a sentence, a paragraph, or even a chapter. Software is quite unlike any other tool. It is a self-realizing design; that is, the design is the product and the product is its design. It took me a long time to recognize this obvious fact, and the implications are startling. Software can be seen as the final step on the path to the elimination of manual manufacture. For example, just as the source code is transformed by a compiler into a target-specific implementation, the computer-created design of a VLSI chip serves as instructions in the automatic fabrication of physical products.

This is not the conventional view of software. By way of calibration, many in the computer science community see software as a formal expression of a desired computation, and they concentrate on building that formal framework. In contrast, the artificial intelligence community focuses on the use of software to express knowledge and reasoning mechanisms. And the primary concern of the software engineering community is the management, definition, and control of the processes, methods, and tools used to create fully compliant, quality software products on time and within budget. Like the blind men seeking to describe the elephant, each orientation is correct and incomplete.

My goal in this book is to build a theory on first principles. Unfortunately, that is an impossible task; one can only build theories on unprovable axioms. And so I must begin by describing and justifying the principles I wish to be accepted without question. Naturally, if I cannot convince the reader of the reasonableness of my assertions, I can hardly expect her to agree with the validity of my conclusions. But how far back must I go? I know the answer I want to give. In fact, I have known that answer for more than a decade. Should I just restate that answer one more time and be done with it? I think not. It is important that I work back to some basic principles that can spawn a family of answers, of which mine will be an instance.

The question, in case the reader has forgotten, is, How should we develop and maintain software? In the early 1980s, when I was making my living developing clinical information systems, I had a clear and simple answer. It was the use of the tools that I had developed. Productivity was 100 lines of quality code per effort day, and the applications were complex and accepted as error free. A very good record, and the answer seemed direct: Do what I do. By the mid 1980s I switched to research in software engineering. This improved my understanding of the process and how my work could be generalized. Roughly the same old answer persisted, but now it took longer to explain. I published my findings in *TEDIUM and the Software Process* (1990) and then went on to reexamine the methods by which others were developing software. This resulted in *Software Engineering: A Holistic View* (1992), the epilogue of which contained the germ of an even more extended answer. Since that time I have written several papers, each of which contains a portion of the complete answer. The present volume is my attempt to organize this material into a cohesive and unified exposition.

Now for the matter of first principles. I have acknowledged that I have a long association with the answer I intend to present. It took root in 1980, and I certainly could not abandon it now. Therefore, I select my first principles so that they necessarily point to my desired conclusions. At first glance this sounds like an admission of dishonesty, but it is not. It is an assertion of openness. Much of what we believe about software development is based on our experience with software development. We learn from our mistakes and improve our processes. I claim that the present approach to software development is based on a faulty model of reality; it ignores the special properties that software affords. Thus, the optimization of the present process places an unnecessary ceiling on productivity and quality. To achieve an order of magnitude improvement in performance, we must break away from our current conception of software as a product to be built and tested. A return to first principles can guide us in the evaluation of alternatives. Even if the reader does not agree with the argument that leads to my specific answer, I would hope that the presentation will develop the insights and skill to arrive at other, and perhaps more promising, answers.

If there are first principles, then they should deepen our understanding of what it is we are trying to do. I have defined software engineering as

> The application of tools, methods, and disciplines to produce
> and maintain an automated solution to a real-world problem.
> (1992a, p. 20)

Much of the software process is devoted to characterizing the real-world problem so that an automated solution can be constructed. Because the problem interacts with its solution, the software product must evolve.

Moreover, because the software operates in a computer, it must be expressed as a formal model of a computation. This need to evolve and to be expressed formally are two of the fundamental characteristics of software. But, rather than build my list of first principles around these two facts, I choose to begin by questioning what we know and how we solve problems. The motivation to do so is based, in part, on my sense that I am shifting the paradigm for "normal" computer science/software engineering. As a result, I can accept little from the present paradigm without being trapped by the arguments that make that paradigm consistent.

The search for first principles is a random walk. Each turn opens many paths, and every selection of direction limits future choices. One is finished when one reaches a distance from which the original question can be addressed with detachment and objectivity. I begin my journey by asking, If I am indeed shifting the paradigm and if the new paradigm will establish the foundations of a new normal computer science, then what is computer science and how is software engineering related to it? The construction of an answer requires an understanding of the philosophy of science, the relationship of science to technology, and the concepts of truth and knowledge. This is the topic of Part I, "Science and Technology." It places computer science and software engineering in a broader context, which is a prerequisite for separating the essential characteristics from those that are the accidental artifacts of historical necessity.

Part II, "Ecological Design," continues this high-level examination. Software engineering is a form of problem solving that depends on human reasoning and culminates in the design of an artifact. Consequently, software engineering is affected by our innate problem-solving mechanisms as well as by the social context for achieving solutions. The solutions to the problems of software engineering are, of course, their designs, and the creation of a design involves the participation of many individuals. Therefore, I review how we perform design in general and, in particular, the design of the applications with which people interact. As with Part I, the discussion builds on philosophical arguments, but the focus is on the human aspects of responding to needs and designing satisfactory responses.

Finally, software engineering is introduced in Part III, "Software Design." The presentation begins with a historical review that helps explain our present approaches. The software process is described, and the characteristics of an essential model are revealed. The principal challenges of software engineering are identified, and the primary design methods are considered in the context of their responses to these challenges. There are some underlying contradictions in the way in which software engineering is conducted, and these tensions are exposed. Once the foundation for the "big answer" has been constructed, the book devotes the final two chapters to an articulation of my response. Chapter 11, "Adaptive Design," updates my answer, first born in 1980 and already documented in *TEDIUM and the Software Process*. It provides a discussion of how software can create an alternative approach to design. Chapter 12, "A Case Study," demonstrates the viability of this approach by means of a fourteen-year evaluation of one major application.

This, then, is the structure of what follows. Ten chapters of introduction leading to two chapters of anticlimactic (and perhaps even unimportant) conclusions. What an odd book! (What an odd author?) When I finished *TEDIUM and the Software Process*, the editor sent it out for review prior to publication. One of the reviewers commented that I offered very convincing arguments but "failed to drive the final nail in the coffin." That was never my purpose. My goal was, and remains, one of expanding perceptions and insights. I aim to educate and extend, not to convince the reader that I am correct. The latter suggests a closed answer, a solution derived from first principles. Yet what I am doing is questioning *all* principles (including those I endorse). And that is why I am comfortable with a book of 10 chapters of introduction and two chapters of conclusions. But this places a burden on the reader.

Norman (1993) writes

> We read too quickly, without questioning or debating the thoughts of the author. But the fault does not lie with the book, the fault lies with the reader.... A book cannot serve reflective thought unless the reader knows how to reason, to reflect upon the material. (p. 47)

I expect the reader to argue with what I have written. As an author I have the advantage of being selective in what I report, of tuning how I present my ideas, of omitting what I choose to consider irrelevant. As a scholar, I have tried to represent the thoughts of others accurately. Nevertheless, I recognize that I am commenting critically on the work of others, many of whom certainly are more intelligent and better read than I am. I offer contradictory theories without identifying those I believe to be correct. I give only brief introductions to complex ideas (along with references for further reading). In fact, the dialectical nature of the book pervades even this prologue, which I open with references to an "answer" that, in the end, I devalue. You see, I do not expect the reader to "learn" my answer but rather to assimilate what I have to say in the creation of his own answer.

This may sound like a difficult assignment, and the reader may wonder if it is worth taking on. Here is the best reason I can offer: After 50 years of computer technology it is time to reexamine the potential role of software in the advancement of human society. This reevaluation occurs within the context of many larger changes that have been brewing for centuries and that are motivated by forces independent of computer and software technology. I certainly do not know what the world will be like in the early 21st century, but it is clear to me that the technology will have moved far beyond programming languages. I look to the past 50 years to understand our present position, and I use that vision to construct a firmer foundation for peering into the future. I believe that what I have to say will be valuable for those who will conduct research in or interact with the computer technology of the next 50 years. I am realistic about the probability of my answer (despite its fourteen-year history) having any impact on the future of computing. I merely offer it as an illustration of what can (and ought to) be done. I recognize that there will be many—some with ideas that I firmly reject—who will claim that their work is the proper response to the questions that I raise. And they may be right where I am wrong. Placing the last nail in the coffin is the wrong metaphor. We are talking about the evolution of ideas and concepts. In every civilization the contributions of an individual will extend beyond that person's mortality, and the ideas assembled in this book are intended to go beyond the narrow answers of the final two chapters. Keep this in mind as you read on. Enjoy the journey, but please don't keep asking, Will we get there soon?

PART I

SCIENCE AND TECHNOLOGY

1

IN THE TRADITION

1.1. The Underlying Thesis

Fifty years ago there were no stored-program binary electronic computers. Indeed, in the mid 1940s *computer* was a job description; the computer was a person. Much has happened in the ensuing half-century. Whereas the motto of the 1950s was "do not bend, spindle, or mutilate," we now have become comfortable with GUI WIMP (i.e., Graphic User Interface; Windows, Icons, Mouse, and Pointers). Whereas computers once were maintained in isolation and viewed through large picture windows, they now are visible office accessories and invisible utilities. Whereas the single computer once was a highly prized resource, modern networks now hide even the machines' geographic locations. Naturally, some of our perceptions have adapted to reflect these changes; however, much of our understanding remains bound to the concepts that flourished during computing's formative years. For example, we have moved beyond thinking of computers as a giant brain (Martin 1993), but we still hold firmly to our faith in computing's scientific foundations.

The purpose of this book is to look forward and speculate about the place of computing in the next fifty years. There are many aspects of computing that make it very different from all other technologies. The development of the microchip has made digital computing ubiquitous; we are largely unaware of the computers in our wrist watches, automobiles, cameras, and household appliances. The field of artificial intelligence (AI) sees the brain as an organ with some functions that can be modeled in a computer, thereby enabling computers to exhibit "intelligent" behavior. Thus, their research seeks to extend the role of computers through applications in which they perform autonomously or act as active assistants. (For some recent overviews of AI see Waldrop 1987; Crevier 1993.) In the domain of information systems, Zuboff (1988) finds that computers can both *automate* (routinize) and *informate*, that is, produce new information that serves as "a voice that symbolically renders events, objects, and processes so that they become visible, knowable, and sharable in a new way" (p. 9). With this new visibility, business improvement can be based on "a fertile interdependence between the human mind and some of its most sophisticated productions" (p. 414). And there are other roles for computing that may improve or threaten society (e.g., Dunlop and Kling 1991).

In this book I explore a different feature of computers: their ability to alter the very concept of design—the design of artifacts and the design of software itself. As I will show, the computer program is not an object; rather, it is the design of an object. It is simply text, but text of a remarkable sort. In the computer, the program text is transformed into an executable sequence of events. These events may operate a robot, lay out a microchip, or process text in a word processor. We long have recognized that we have been moving into an information age in which computers can relieve us of some of the computational tasks that are beyond our human capabilities. Our space program, for example, would have been impossibly complex if there were no computers to perform the calculations. Thus, we have become accustomed to using computers as intellectual extensions just as the earlier industrial revolution showed us how to use machines to overcome humanity's physical limits. But we still design computer programs as if they were mechanical entities. We begin with a statement of requirements and construct a set of programs to satisfy those requirements. In so doing, we fail to exploit the unique features afforded by software; we view the program as a product and not as its design.

Cooley (1988) notes that the word *design* emerged in the 16th century to describe the occupation of designing. Design, of course, had always existed, but now it was being identified as a separate activity. "This recognition can be said to constitute a separation of hand and brain, of manual and intellectual work; and the separation of the conceptual part of work from the labor process. Above all, the term indicated that *designing* was to be separated from *doing*" (p. 197). I see "a new era of design" in which designing is *integrated* with doing, in which the designing *is* the doing. But how can I explain this vision? If, when I say "design" the reader thinks of a white circle, and when I say "do" the reader sees a black square, then how then can the reader comprehend that designing and doing are identical? If I provide an illustration of design as doing, how will the reader be able to separate the specifics of the example from the generalities of the approach? I have struggled long and hard with this problem and finally have come to the conclusion that one must start from first principles and then build up to the illustration. That is why I have written a book rather than one more paper. To accept what I have to say, however, we need to understand computing as it exists at the beginning of the 21st century, not as we came to know it in the middle of the 20th century. Only after the reader has reoriented her sensibilities will this new vision of design seem obvious.

Although this is a book about software development, the first two parts of the book are not concerned with software. There is an intellectual revolution underway that began before there were any computers and that has a momentum independent of computers. Therefore, if we are to employ computers to alter our world—as I am sure we must—then we need to understand something about that greater change and how it affects computing. That is the focus of this first part of the book. It examines science and technology independent of the specifics of computer science and software engineering. It seeks to grasp the nature of science so that we may comprehend the role of computer science. As Naur (1990/1992) puts it,

> If we accept the prestige of science, in some form, to be a decisive part of the common notion of science, it makes sense to pursue the question, what is it in science, or its pursuit, that has led to that high prestige? By such an inquiry we may succeed in finding out at least some of what is characteristic about what is commonly denoted as "science." (p. 50)

Once we agree on the essence of science, we then can determine its relationship to technology. From this we may derive a working appreciation of software engineering and its relation to computer science. Recall that my goal is to alter the process of design, which will restructure software engineering and perhaps even invalidate portions of computer science. The questions are, Is this possible, and, if yes, will we need a new computer science?

1.2. Going Beyond Programming

This is a book about how to develop software. By background, I am a software engineer; that is, I have been paid to develop and maintain systems that rely on software components. Most of the systems I have been involved with have been large: the Ground Data Handling System for Landsat, Navy command and control systems, clinical information systems at Johns Hopkins. Many people have been engaged in each of these projects, and the projects have involved both technical and managerial issues. During the past eight to ten years, I have concentrated on research in software engineering. In parallel with that research, I taught software engineering. In my teaching I described the process *as it now is conducted* and how that process may be improved. In my research, however, I focused the software process as it *ought to be conducted*. The book *Software Engineering: A Holistic View* (Blum 1992a) contains a descriptive model of software engineering—what current practitioners should know about the discipline. This book, on the other hand, constructs a normative model for software development—one that describes how software ought to be developed in the future. Given its objective, *Beyond Programming* cannot be a "how-to" book; it must be one that fosters contemplation and enquiry. Therefore, it is appropriate that it begin by examining the most basic of questions. What are software engineering, computer science, and—in a general sense—science itself?

I have defined software engineering as "the application of tools, methods, and disciplines to produce and maintain an automated solution to a real-world problem" (Blum 1992a, p. 20). The software process is initiated by the need to respond to a real-world problem, but the technology used to create the solution must be expressed as formal models of computation (i.e., as computer programs). Thus, the process may be thought of as one that goes from an informal need (in-the-world) to a formal model (in-the-computer). Moreover, it is this transition from the informal to the formal that constitutes an underlying tension that manifests itself in many ways. I begin from the bottom up and cite what Turski (1985) has to say about formalism.

> The history of advances in programming—the little that there is of it—is the history of successful formalization: by inventing and studying formalism, by extracting rigorous procedures, we progressed from programming in machine code to programming in high level languages (HLLs). Note that before HLLs were sufficiently formalized compilers used to be unreliable and expensive to use, programs could not be ported between machines, and the very use of HLLs was more or less restricted to academia. Observe also that if today a piece of software is still difficult to port it is almost invariably due to a deviation from strict formality. (p. 400)

One can conclude, therefore, that the study of formalism constitutes the core of computer science.

I now add to Turski's observation. The Task Force on the Core of Computer Science (Denning, et al. 1989) has prepared a new intellectual framework for computing. They identify three paradigms for the discipline—theory, abstraction (or modeling), and design—and comment that "the three processes are so intricately intertwined that it is irrational to say that any one is fundamental" (p. 10). They observe that many computing activities do not involve programming, but that "access to the distinctions of any domain is given through language, and that most of the distinctions of computing are embodied in programming notation" (p. 11). This leads to the following short definition.

The discipline of computing is the systematic study of algorithmic processes that describe and transform information: their theory, analysis, design, efficiency, implementation, and application—that describe and transform information. The fundamental question underlying all of computing is, "What can be (efficiently) automated?" (p. 12)

Later, the report notes, "The roots of computing extend deeply into mathematics and engineering. Mathematics imparts analysis to the field; engineering imparts design" (p. 16). Nine subareas are identified, of which "Software Methodology and Engineering" is of principal interest here.

This area deals with the design of programs and large software systems that meet specifications and are safe, secure reliable, and dependable. Fundamental questions include: What are the principles behind the development of programs and programming systems? How does one prove that a program or system meets its specifications? How does one develop specifications that do not omit important cases and can be analyzed for safety? How do software systems evolve through different generations? How can software be designed for understandability and modifiability? (p. 20)

Clearly, there can be no argument that these are all important issues and essential topics for both research and education. But does the description leave anything out? It seems to focus on programs in-the-computer. Is this wrong? I return to Turski's statement.

Logic—a calculus of formal systems—plays an important role in software development from specifications to implementation.... That logic plays no discernible role in descriptive theory formulation—an act always serendipitous and contingent upon invention—should not worry us too much, as long as we do not wish to claim the possession of the philosopher's stone. (p. 400)

Here, again, is the basic tension of the software process. We can rely on logic for what is in-the-computer, but we can only seek the philosopher's stone to comprehend what is in-the-world.

Consider the perspectives of in-the-computer (i.e., that of programming) and in-the-world (i.e., that which is beyond programming). What is in-the-computer is of interest only to the extent that it is difficult to construct. What is in-the-computer is also in-the-world, and its utilitarian evaluation depends on its behavior in-the-world. But there are profound differences in form between what is in-the-computer and in-the-world. The former is stable and formally represented, whereas the latter is dynamic and seldom fully understood.   Naur (1985/1992) observes that programs must change and, therefore, what is needed is a theory of the program, not just a knowledge of program construction.

> Accepting program modifications demanded by changing external circumstances to be an essential part of programming, it is argued that the primary aim of programming is to have the programmers build a theory of the way the matters at hand may be supported by the execution of a program. Such a view leads to a notion of program life that depends on the continued support of the program by programmers having its theory. Further, on this view the notion of a programming method, understood as a set of rules of procedure to be followed by the programmer, is based on invalid assumptions and so has to be rejected. As further consequences of the view, programmers have to be accorded the status of responsible, permanent developers and managers of the activity of which the computer is part, and their education has to emphasize the exercise of theory building, side by side with the acquisition of knowledge of data processing and notations. (p. 48)

Naur draws a distinction between the program, which is an instantiation of a theory, and the theory itself. In general, the theory will not be subject to formal notation. It will contain concepts that guide the interpretation of the program. The theory is valuable because it is more stable than the program; its explanations are valid for whole families of programs. (We will see this argument repeated in Chapter 2 where we discuss theories and their instruments.)

Yet Naur still writes of the program, and I wish to go beyond programming. Today we rely on what I term *technological design*. We perform an analysis in-the-world and specify an artifact (automated or mechanical) that will respond to some identified need. We then fabricate or code a product that satisfies the specification. In software engineering, the specification defines the behavior of what should be in-the-computer, and the process terminates when a correct realization of the specification exists in-the-computer. This design model has been extremely successful. So why look for an alternative? I believe that software has unique features that, once exploited, will permit us to employ a better model, which I call *adaptive design*. Rather than relying on the two-step process of first create a specification in-the-world and then realize that specification in-the-computer, I see a one-step process that permits us to model what goes on in-the-computer as it affects us in-the-world. In this way we go beyond programming (in-the-computer) and concern ourselves only with how the programs behave in-the-world.

Thus, we have a contrast between the careful analysis of what is to be built followed by its construction (i.e., technological design) and the one-step model of continuing response to changing requirements (i.e., design by doing, or adaptive design). With modern technology, both approaches now are feasible, and at least one adaptive design environment has been in use for more than a decade. But how is it possible to have two such different design methods? Is one a refinement of the other, or do they exploit different principles? What are their scientific foundations? Before we can answer these questions, we need a broader understanding of what it means to be scientific and the nature of the relationship between science and technology. The following section establishes a baseline drawn from common perceptions, and the remaining chapters of Part I explore these concepts in detail.

1.3. An Engineering Discipline of Software

Computer technology has always existed in a scientific and engineering environment. The era of the modern, stored-program computer began as the Second World War came to a close, and the computer both affected and was affected by the perceptions of that period. Buoyed by the technological successes that aided in bringing the war to a satisfactory conclusion, a new age of scientific progress was heralded. Reflecting on the cultural values of the modern world, one contemporary recognized "a belief in and approval of 'progress' in this world, a progress which is not necessarily of a unilinear evolutionary kind, but which is somehow cumulative in the way in which science and rational knowledge are cumulative" (Barber 1992, p. 66).

Progress and the growth of scientific knowledge were joined into a causal relationship. Knowledge is cumulative, and the new knowledge empowers. Pure science, which uncovers the fundamental nature of the universe, provides the essential foundations whereby humanity can control its environment. The general framework of this argument remains commonplace. For instance, the Nobel laureate Lederman (1984) observes that, within the scientific community,

> most people acknowledge the most important aspect of science is the cultural one. The need is universal—to give a coherent account of the world and our place in it—and for this purpose our society has cast its lot with the rational explanation of nature.... [There is a quest for] a single and economical law of nature, valid throughout the universe for all time. The quest for such a unified scientific law has been undertaken and advanced

by all nations and all creeds. Indeed, the idea of the unity of science has been a major force in the developing of humanity. (pp. 40-41)

Thus, in and of itself, science may be justified on the basis of its intellectual and social value. Indeed, as we celebrate the 25th anniversary of the first manned landing on the Moon, we recognize that the national and human achievements far exceeded any technological contributions in importance. Yet science offers more than spirituality. There is an economic justification founded on the argument that pure science creates knowledge that subsequently is exploited by technology. This is sometimes referred to as the "linear" model of technology transfer (Price and Bass 1969); science is the prerequisite to progress, and engineering is the application of science.

Kitcher (1993) writes of a model in which the noble goals of science are the attainment of truth through the application of the scientific method. He calls this the "Legend."

Indeed, many advocates of Legend would maintain that science is the pinnacle of human achievement not because of its actual successes but in virtue of the fact that its practice, both in attaining truth and in lapsing into error, is thoroughly informed by reason. Even those whose historical situations lead into making mistakes still do the best they can in the interests of truth, judging reasonably in the light of the available evidence and bowing to whatever new findings expose their concerns. (p. 4)

That is, although some of the *products* of science may be imperfect, the *process* of science represents the highest expression of rationality in mankind.

Certainly, we find our perceptions of computer science and software engineering molded by the concepts just enunciated. For example, the title of this section, "An Engineering Discipline of Software," comes from a paper by Shaw (1990), in which she observes that—although software engineering is not yet a true discipline—it has the potential to become one. Shaw begins by exploring the nature of engineering in general and arrives at a generic definition that might be paraphrased as follows.

Engineering creates cost-effective solutions to practical problems by applying knowledge to building things in the service of mankind.

Thus, engineering exploits scientific knowledge to create useful artifacts. It "relies on codifying scientific knowledge about a technological problem domain in a form that is directly useful to the practitioner, thereby providing answers for questions that commonly occur in practice" (p. 16).

She continues, "Engineering practice enables ordinary practitioners so they can create sophisticated systems that work—unspectacularly, perhaps, but reliably" (p. 16). Although the description may seem to reflect a bias of clever scientist versus pedestrian engineer, her goal really is to distinguish between routine and innovative design (or, more accurately, between precedented and unprecedented designs). Good engineering permits the designer to reuse previous experience, thereby freeing him to concentrate on the application-specific issues.

The chemical engineer, for instance, can reference *Perry's Chemical Engineering Handbook*, but "software engineering lacks the institutionalized mechanisms of a mature engineering discipline for recording and disseminating demonstrably good designs and ways to choose among design alternatives" (p. 16). At issue, then, is how to discover, collect, and represent what the software engineer needs so that she may approach a new assignment as a routine design rather than as an original design.

Shaw proposes a model, shown in Figure 1.1, that relates science to engineering. In this model, solutions begin as ad hoc practice that becomes formalized as it supports effective production. As the demand for the technology grows, a scientific base develops that, in time, becomes sufficiently mature to contribute significantly to commercial practice. Finally, professional engineering emerges with a "sufficient scientific basis to enable a core of educated professionals so they can apply the theory to analysis of problems and synthesis of solutions.... The emergence of an engineering discipline lets technological development pass limits previously imposed by relying on intuition; progress frequently becomes dependent on science as a forcing function" (p. 17).

Shaw validates this engineering discipline development model with the history of both civil engineering and chemical engineering; she then turns to software technology and shows how good software models develop as a result of the interaction between science and engineering. One begins with problems that first are solved by means of ad hoc solutions. The successful solutions ultimately become accepted as folklore. Broadly accepted folklore is codified for broader dissemination, and this codification ultimately is formalized in scientifically based models and theories. These theories are used to improve practice; they also permit the acceptance of newer, more difficult problems. The new problems, in turn, are resolved with ad hoc solutions, and the next iteration of the cycle continues.

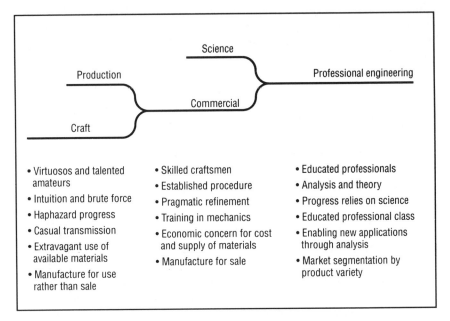

Fig. 1.1. Evolution of an engineering discipline.
Reprinted from Shaw (1990) with permission, ©1990, IEEE.

Because Shaw's model is concerned only with the development of a professional engineering discipline, it depicts science in the reactive role of formalizing and extending practice's ad hoc codification. Figure 1.1, however, does not show science as being driven by practice, and this raises the question of what motivates research in science. Thus, although Shaw does address the specific concerns of the software community and her model does provide useful insights into technology's early "pull" on science, her paper omits a discussion of science's subsequent "push" on technology. In examining the scientific basis for engineering practice, Shaw states, "Engineering practice emerges from commercial practice by exploiting the results of a companion science. The scientific results must be mature and rich enough to model practical problems. They must also be organized in a form that is useful to practitioners" (p. 21). She goes on to observe that, although computer science has some models and theories ready to support practice, their packaging for operational use is deficient. By way of illustrating the successful adoption of theories, Shaw points to the algorithms and data structures introduced in the 1960s, the performance analysis and correctness advances of the 1970s, and the progress in the automation of compiler construction of the 1980s. "It takes a good 20 years from the time that work starts on a theory until it provides serious assistance to routine practice" (p. 21). Given the relative youth of computer science, it is not surprising that few theories now affect practice. Shaw states that the next tasks for the software profession are

> to pick an appropriate mix of short-term, pragmatic, possible, purely empirical contributions that help stabilize commercial practice and

> to invest in long-term efforts to develop and make available basic scientific contributions. (p. 22)

She concludes the paper with a list of five rudimentary steps that will lead to a true engineering discipline: understand the nature of expertise, recognize different ways to get information, encourage routine practice, expect professional specializations, and improve the coupling between science and commercial practice.

It is difficult to argue with this analysis and impossible to fault the five steps that she recommends. Yet it is equally difficult to understand what is meant by science and engineering in the context of computer technology. In the popular view, science uncovers the truths around which we build our technologies. Is this a valid statement? What are the truths of computer science? Are there alternative computer sciences, or are both technological design and adaptive design subject to the same basic principles? Is there an envelope around what can be guided by computer science, and, if yes, how do we address the problems outside the envelope? To answer these questions, I cast a very wide net. Chapter 2 provides a review of the philosophy of science, and Chapter 3 examines the relationship between science and technology. My foundation building uses this analysis of science and technology to establish the context for our principal concerns: computer science and software engineering. In particular, we wish to know (a) what aspects of the technology can be studied scientifically and (b) which areas of computer application are incompatible with scientific investigation. The goal is to produce a unified theory for the development of computer applications, one that may extend beyond our traditional view of what it means to be scientific.

2

THE PHILOSOPHY OF SCIENCE

2.1. Why Study the Philosophy of Science?

This chapter presents an overview of the philosophy of science. Why study this philosophy? Here is my justification. We know that the software process is a transformation from the identification of a need in-the-world into a set of computer programs that operate in-the-computer. The process begins with an idea, a concept, something that may defy a complete description, and it ends with the delivery of a formal model that executes in the computer. As we have seen, there is a fundamental tension in this transformation, a tension between what we want and how we make it work, between the requirements in-the-world and their realization in-the-computer, between the subjective and the objective, the conceptual and the formal. This book seeks to resolve that tension. Science faces a similar problem, and so I start by examining its solutions. Science begins with something very complex and poorly represented—the real world—and its goal is to describe aspects of that reality with theories and models. We know that science is successful. It is reasonable to look, therefore, into its strengths and limitations for insight into resolving the software process' central tension. To gain this insight, I turn to the philosophy of science because it constitutes a kind of meta-science. It examines the nature of science from a theoretical perspective; it helps us appreciate what is knowable and what can be represented formally.

I note at the outset, this is not my area of expertise. Moreover, the philosophers of science have not reached a consensus. Philosophical inquiry is, by its very nature, controversial and argumentative, and the theme of this chapter is the underlying controversies regarding the nature of science and scientific knowledge. If we are to find "scientific foundations," then we must first understand what science is (and is not)—the topic of what follows. I warn the reader that this chapter conforms to truth in labeling; as its title indicates, it literally is about the philosophy of science. There are a few explanatory comments that tie the material to the immediate needs of a software engineer, but this really is a chapter about philosophy. After all, if the reader wishes to develop scientific solutions or to employ them, then she should be familiar with the issues presented here. I recognize that this may seem far from our target interests; nevertheless, to build a foundation for a new era of design, we must move to a vantage point with sufficient separation to accommodate alternative perspectives.

Bechtel (1988a) identifies four areas of philosophy that bear on the philosophy of science:

Logic. The central issue in logic is the evaluation of argument, where an argument is a set of statements that serve as premises for other statements, called conclusions. If whenever the premises are true the conclusions must be true, then the argument is *valid*. There are many logic systems, and a system must be *consistent* (i.e., one cannot have arguments that result in a conclusion being both true and false) and should be *complete* (i.e., the axiom structure permits the derivation of all true statements within the particular domain). Gödel proved that there can be no consistent axiomatization of arithmetic that is complete; moreover, within a complete system, not all conclusions may be *decidable* (i.e., provable as a logical consequence of the premises).

Metaphysics. Metaphysics seeks to determine the fundamental kinds of things that exist and to specify their nature. Of interest here, for example, are the kinds of entities that we can include in scientific theories. Such ontological questions (i.e., questions that relate to being or existence) are fundamental and cannot be resolved by the ordinary observations of empirical investigation. Whereas there are philosophers who believe that the ontology establishes a value-laden context for observation, other philosophers see the metaphysical issues as something that can be avoided.

Epistemology. Epistemology is concerned with the question of what knowledge is and how it is possible. Knowledge often is taken as *justified true belief*, which shifts the argument to a determination of what constitutes justification. Bechtel identifies two approaches to justification. Foundationalists appeal to perceptual beliefs (i.e., sense-data based on personal observation); coherentism appeals to the relationships among beliefs to find justification (e.g., the collection of a set of coherent, noncontradictory beliefs).

Value theory. Bechtel uses this category to cluster domains such as ethics, political philosophy, and aesthetics. The issue then becomes one of establishing norms (i.e., standards that *ought* to be adhered to) for rationally adjudicating questions of value. Because the values normally exist in descriptive claims, it is not clear that normative statements can be rationally defended (e.g., one may not be able to address moral issues rationally in scientific research).

If we disregard value theory, then we see that the philosophy of science rests upon three pillars. Metaphysics is concerned with *"how the world is* (what exists, what is true)," epistemology focuses on "issues surrounding *how we know, believe, infer, how the world is"* (Rey 1983), and logic provides a mechanism for adding to knowledge by means of valid argument. One of the reasons for the philosophical interest in science is that scientific knowledge (especially knowledge of physics) is perceived to be an accurate model of how the world is, which opens the possibility for an epistemology without ambiguity. Logic plays an essential role in this quest. If we begin with value-free observations (i.e., unquestioned truths) and then employ logic, the resulting store of knowledge will represent universal truths (the foundational view). However, if some of our justified true belief is biased by beliefs that cannot be certified as universally true, then logic will institutionalize this belief structure (coherentism). It will become clear as the discussion unfolds that the existence of unbiased beliefs is a central issue in the philosophy of science.

Before continuing, it is important to reemphasize that this chapter presents an understanding of science as described by philosophers. In Part II I examine science as a human institution. The conduct of science can be compared to the flight of the bumblebee; although it can be demonstrated that the aerodynamics of the bumblebee cannot support flight, the insect does not know this and flies anyway. Few scientists feel constrained by logic, metaphysics, and epistemology. Rather, as I shall show, they are guided by their instincts, and they employ heuristics such as model building, approximation, and parsimony. The philosophers of science, on the other hand, study the scientists' actions and characterize what science is and how it ought to be conducted. For the present, I limit the discussion to the essence of science rather than its practice.

2.2. Science in the Early Twentieth Century

The predominant philosophy of science during the first half of the twentieth century was known as *logical positivism*. Its roots were Compte's positivism, which avoided metaphysics and emphasized knowledge based on experience, and the growing faith in the power of formal systems, as embodied in the *Principia Mathematica* (Russell 1903). Many of the founders were physicists and mathematicians who had a strong faith in the ability to model physical phenomena precisely but who also recognized the challenges that relativity theory and quantum mechanics presented to the accepted view of the nature of scientific investigation. Organized in the 1920s, logical positivism has been subjected to considerable criticism. Although most believe that the programme has been soundly refuted (e.g., Chalmers 1982 and Suppe 1974), Bechtel (1988a) observes that "it continues both to set the agenda for many ongoing philosophical discussions and to provide the criteria that many scientists ... use to judge what is good science" (p. 17). It also is of interest to computer scientists because it addresses the central concern of formal representation.

Logical positivism separates the issues of discovery (i.e., how scientists derive hypotheses) from those of justification (i.e., the rational assessment of the scientific hypothesis). The former is accepted as potentially nonlogical (e.g., the "Ah-ha!" of sudden inspiration); justification involves the normative standards by which science may be conducted. "Science that adhered to these standards ... constituted good science that provided knowledge about the world" (Bechtel 1988a, p. 19). The goal is to purge science of the subjective and uncertain so that it may conform to the formal.

One of the major causes of uncertainty can be traced to unclarity in language. Without precision, statements may be ununderstandable; their truth or falsity cannot be determined. One must, therefore, restrict oneself to discourse based on solid principles of meaningfulness. Thus, the meaning of a sentence became the set of conditions that would show that the sentence was true. Because sentences were composed of words (which could be neither true nor false), their meanings had to be analyzed in terms of their roles within sentences. Some sentences could be directly verified through experience (e.g., sensory exposure). Sentences containing theoretical terms (e.g., *soluble*) presented a different challenge. These were linked to identifying sentences that could be tested empirically; if the identifying sentence was true, then the linked sentence also was true (i.e., the statement about the theoretical property was true). Although this mechanism appeared to reduce all sentences to observable verification, it soon was recognized that it would not be possible to verify all sentences, and adjustments to the theory were made.

Of course, the goal of the logical positivists was not simply to make meaningful sentences; it was to explain the phenomena in nature and to predict their occurrence. To accomplish this, they relied on deduction. Given a set of general laws (L_1 through L_n), initial conditions (C_1 through C_n), and an event E to be explained, then

$$L_1, L_2, \ldots L_n$$
$$\underline{C_1, C_2, \ldots C_n}$$
Therefore, E.

In this scheme, the laws play a central role in the explanation; indeed, the explanation requires a complete derivation of the event from the laws and initial conditions. Furthermore, as shown, there is only a temporal difference between prediction and explanation.

Laws, which could be verified empirically, were combined to produce a theory. Just as the theory of Euclidean geometry could be built from a set of primitive terms and postulates (formalized as axioms or laws), the process of axiomatizing theories could bring unity to science. "Astronomy was ... subsumed within physics. Eventually, the Positivists proposed all sciences could be subsumed into one theoretical edifice, that of unified science" (Bechtel 1988a, p. 29). This principle of *theory reduction* presupposes that science is inherently a cumulative process and that the laws of specialized disciplines (e.g., biology or psychology) can be explained in terms of the most basic laws of physics. The fact that we now compartmentalize the scientific disciplines simply reflects the present incompleteness of our understanding.

My description of Logical Positivism has oversimplified and ignored many of the variations and corrections; nevertheless, the essential characteristics should be clear: dependence on sensory experience within a highly controlled vocabulary, the use of deduction to explain events from laws and initial conditions, and a belief in the axiomatic unity of science. These concepts are embodied in the *Received View*, which is shown in Figure 2.1 as it was described in the 1920s. Although there have been many modifications to the view as originally stated, it remains a normative model for science in which there are no uncertainties. Observations are facts, and all inference is based on true statements concerning these facts. Notwithstanding its difficulty to work with, many still consider it an ideal.

2.3. Popper's Correction to Logical Positivism

The primary difficulty with logical positivism was its dependence upon induction. Although events were justified from laws and conditions deductively, the laws themselves were justified inductively (i.e., empirically). The fact that a series of events supports a given hypothesis cannot imply that all future events also will satisfy that hypothesis. Russell gave the example of the inductivist turkey that, after several months on the farm, observes, "I am always fed at 9 a.m." At 9 a.m. of Christmas eve, however, rather than being fed, he was beheaded (cited in Chalmers 1982, p.14). Here is the exception that proves the rule; proves it, that is, to be false. Popper recognized this contradiction in 1920, but he ignored advice to publish it because "I was convinced that my problem ... must have agitated many scientists and philosophers who would surely have reached my rather obvious solution" (Popper 1965, p. 39). His subsequent publication of *The Logic of Scientific Discovery*

(i) The theory is formulated in a first-order mathematical logic with equality, L.

(ii) The nonlogical terms or constants of L are divided into three disjoint classes called *vocabularies*:

- (a) The *logical vocabulary* consisting of logical constants (including mathematical terms).
- (b) The *observation vocabulary*, V_O, containing observation terms.
- (c) The *theoretical vocabulary*, V_T, containing theoretical terms.

(iii) The terms in V_O are interpreted as referring to directly observable physical objects or directly observable attributes of physical objects.

(iv) There is a set of theoretical postulates T whose only nonlogical terms are from V_T.

(v) The terms in V_T are given an *explicit definition* in terms of V_O by *correspondence rules* C—that is, for every term 'F' in V_T, there must be given a definition for it of the following form:

$$(x)(Fx \equiv Ox),$$

Where 'Ox' is an expression of L containing symbols only from V_O and possibly the logical vocabulary.

Fig. 2.1. The Received View as initially presented.
Reprinted from Suppe (1974) with permission, ©1974 University of Chicago Press

(1959) in 1934 provided a necessary correction to the normative theory of science.

Having recognized that one only could *prove* a rule to be false (i.e., *falsify* it), Popper proposed that one should attempt to *disprove* hypotheses. The approach subsequently was described as *conjectures* and *refutations* (see Popper 1965). The scientist begins by making conjectures and then attempts to refute them. If the refutations fail so that the scientist is unable to falsify his hypotheses, then his confidence in their validity has been *corroborated*; that is, the corroborated theory is a candidate for being accepted as a true theory. This substitution of the term corroboration for confirmation

> signals a rejection of the Positivists' attempt to distinguish meaningful from meaningless discourse through the verificationist theory of meaning. Popper ... demarcates scientific from nonscientific discourse in terms of the risk that true scientific theories face of being wrong.... If the theory is true, then certain things cannot happen. If they do happen, then the

theory was not true. This ability to forbid certain things is what gives scientific theories their power. (Bechtel 1988a, p. 34)

Popper suggests that we begin by testing our current theories. Where they already have passed all tests, they should be accepted, but where they have failed in one or more cases, new theories are required. These new theories should satisfy three constraints:

Simplicity. "The new theory should proceed from some *simple, new, and powerful, unifying idea* about some connection or relation (such as gravitational attraction) between hitherto unconnected things (such as planets and apples) or facts (such as inertial and gravitational mass) or new 'theoretical entities' (such as fields and particles" (Popper 1965, p. 241).

Independent testability. In addition to explaining what the theory was designed to explain, it also must have new and testable consequences that lead to the prediction of phenomena.

Third requirement. "We require that the theory should pass some new, and severe, tests" (p. 242).

The more severe the test, the greater the confidence in the theory brought about by the failure to falsify.

Notice the profound change that falsification brings to the positivists' view of progress. For the positivist, knowledge is cumulative, and the process is objective. For Popper, progress comes with bold conjectures that are not refuted. The bolder the conjecture, the greater the potential for progress. Refutations open the way for new conjectures. Progressiveness is dependent upon "change in scientific knowledge," not on reasoning from an "axiomatized deductive system" (1965, p. 221) Thus, Popper replaces the empiricism of establishing truth with an empiricism of falsification. "Statements or systems of statements, in order to be ranked as scientific, must be capable of conflicting with possible, or conceivable, observations" (1965, p. 39). If it cannot be tested, then it cannot be scientific; and testing seeks to find failure, not conformation. (The software engineer will recognize a strong parallel with software testing.)

It would be wrong, however, to interpret Popper's contribution as simply a technical correction to the logical positivists. He was concerned with the growth of human knowledge and the demarcation between science and metaphysics. He tempered his formal reasoning with sensitive exposition that extolled his faith in a science founded in rational argument. For example,

Thus science must begin with myths, and with the criticism of myths; neither with the collection of observations, nor with the invention of experiments, but with the critical discussion of myths, and of magical techniques and practices....

The critical attitude, the tradition of free discussion of theories with the aim of discovering their weak spots so that they may be improved upon, is the attitude of reasonableness, of rationality. It makes far-reaching use of both argument and observation—of observation in the interest of argument, however.... In fact nothing can be justified or proved (outside of mathematics and logic). The demand for rational proofs in science indicates a failure to keep distinct the broad realm of rationality and the narrow realm of rational certainty: it is an untenable, an unreasonable demand. (1965, pp. 50-51.)

By the late 1930s, as war was about to transform Europe, the Received View had been revised, Popperism had been introduced, and the premises for a standard empiricist account of science were available. The most important of the underlying assumptions were *naive realism*, a *universal scientific language*, and the *correspondence of truth*.

These three assumptions between them constitute a picture of science and the world somewhat as follows: there is an external world which can in principle be exhaustively described in scientific language. The scientist, as both observer and language-user, can capture the external facts of the world in propositions that are true if they correspond to the facts and false if they do no not. Science is ideally a linguistic system in which true propositions are in one-to-one relation to facts, including facts that are not directly observed because they involve hidden entities or properties, or past events or far distant events. These hidden events are described in theories, and theories can be inferred from observation, that is, the hidden explanatory mechanism of the world can be discovered from what is open to observation. Man as scientist is regarded as standing apart from the world and able to experiment and theorize about it objectively and dispassionately. (Hesse 1980, p. vii)

This is the portrait of science that emerged from the war; it is what Kitcher calls the Legend. Yet, Hesse followed the above-mentioned description with the sentence, "Almost every assumption underlying this account has been subjected to damaging criticism." The next sections turn to that criticism.

2.4. Epistemological Refinements

Because the Received View, as augmented by Popper's corrections, focused only on justification (and ignored discovery), it was accepted as a formal structure for scientists to organize their hypotheses and validate them objectively (i.e., the foundational view). For many philosophers, however, this division separated the acts of thinking about the scientific problem from those of proving the validity of the concept formalizations. Feyerabend (1970) saw a danger in this excessive emphasis on abstract method and commented that the effort "was soon transformed into problems of a different kind, some of which were no longer related to science at all.... [One] started with the discussion of *simple* cases ... that looked simple when formulated in the language of *Principia Mathematica*. In addition one concentrated on the relation to the evidence, omitting all those properties and aids which arise from the fact that every single statement of science is embedded in a rich theoretical net and chosen to fit this net one way or another" (p. 181).

Yet to a philosopher engaged in epistemology, the study of science remained the key to understanding knowledge. For instance, Popper wrote:

> My interest is not merely in the theory of scientific knowledge, but rather in the theory of knowledge in general. Yet the study of the growth of scientific knowledge is, I believe, the most fruitful way of studying the growth of knowledge in general. For the growth of scientific knowledge may be said to be the growth of ordinary knowledge *writ large*. (1965, p. 216)

Campbell (1974/1987) found in the works of Popper the basis for an evolutionary epistemology based on natural selection. He cites Popper. The aim of falsification "is not to save the lives of untenable systems but, on the contrary, to select the one which is by comparison the fittest, by exposing them all to the fiercest struggle for survival" (Popper 1959, p. 42). "A theory is a tool which we test by applying it, and which we judge as to its fitness by the results of its applications" (Popper 1959, p. 108). Thus, conjectures and refutations is a method of trial and error. Popper observes that the critical difference between the way a scientist and some lower form of life applies trial and error lies in the scientist's critical and constructive approach to error; his ingenuity in building severe tests to refute his theories. For Campbell, these ideas introduced a striking change in the location of the epistemological problem. "Given up is the effort to hold all knowledge in abeyance until the possibility of knowledge is first logically established, until indubital first principles or incorrigible sense data are established upon which to build. Rather, the cumulative achievement of logical analysis is accepted: such grounds are logically unavailable. No nonpresumptive knowledge and no nonpresumptive modes of learning are possible to us" (Campbell 1974/1987, p. 53).

"Human knowledge processes, when examined in continuity with the evolutionary sequence, turn out to involve numerous mechanisms at various levels of substitute functioning, hierarchically related, and with some form of selective retention process at each level" (Campbell 1974/1987, p. 54). Consequently, the evolutionary trial and error process can be applied to "such teleological achievements as embryological growth and wound healing" (p. 55). Campbell identifies 10 process levels going from (1) non-mnemonic problem solving (e.g., paramecium) at the lowest level to (9) cultural cumulation, and, finally, (10) science. "The demarcation of science from the other speculations is that the knowledge claims be testable, and that there be available mechanisms for testing or selecting which are more than social.... What is characteristic of science is that the selective system which weeds out among the variety of conjectures involves deliberate contact with the environment through experiment and quantified prediction, designed so that outcomes quite independent of the preferences of the investigator are possible. It is preeminently this feature that gives science its greater objectivity and its claim to a cumulative increase in the accuracy with which it describes the world" (pp. 70-71).

Campbell goes on to describe "basic" research as being "like biological evolution, opportunistic not only in solutions, but also in problems" (p. 72). He criticizes Popper's "view of the natural selection of scientific theories, [as] a trial and error of mathematical and logical models in competition with each other in the adequacy with which they solve empirical puzzles..." (p. 72). The alternative, he proposes, is a *blind-variation-and-selective-retention* process in which "there are three essentials: (a) Mechanisms for introducing variation; (b) Consistent selection processes; and (c) Mechanisms for preserving and/or propagating the selected variations" (p. 56). The process is blind in that the variations are produced without prior knowledge of which ones, if any, will furnish a selectworthy encounter. There are three essential connotations of "blind":

that the variations emitted be independent of the environmental conditions of the occasion of their occurrence....

that the occurrence of trials individually be uncorrelated with the solution, ... [and]

rejection of the notion that a variation subsequent to an incorrect trial is a "correction" of the previous trial or makes use of the direction of error of the previous one. (p. 57)

This blind variation process, he asserts, permits an evolutionary perspective that, even though it does not rely on the formalisms of logic and mathematics, "is fully compatible with an advocacy of the goals of realism and objectivity in science" (p. 89). The important contribution of this process, states Campbell, is its "effort to root out a prevailing implicit belief in the possibility of 'direct' or 'insightful' creative thought processes" (1960, p. 398).

Both Popper and Campbell recognized the limits of objectivity with respect to sense data. Recall that the logical positivists tried to erect a structure that isolated the subjective through use of observation and theoretical vocabularies. Empiricism depends on value-free observation, and if it can be shown that observations are theory laden, then the truth of an observation will be subject to question. Popper describes an exercise in the late 1930s when he opened a physics lecture with the instruction, "Take pencil and paper; carefully observe, and write down what you have observed." He subsequently commented, "Clearly the instruction 'Observe!' is absurd.... Observation is always selective. It needs a chosen object, a definitive task, an interest, a point of view, a problem" (1965, p. 46). Elsewhere, Popper writes, "We must abandon any approach which starts from sense data and the given [i.e., observation], and replace it by the assumption that all human knowledge is fallible and conjectural. It is a product of trial and error" (1974/1978, p. 116). For Popper the trials ought not be blind; they should be structured so that they may be refuted. Although there may not be objectivity in observation, there is objectivity in criticism. "There is a world of difference between holding a belief, or expecting something, and using human language to *say* so. The difference is that only if spoken out, and thus objectivized, does a belief become criticizable" (1974/1987, p. 120).

Campbell recognizes that not only must observation be interpreted, but also that "science beliefs are radically underjustified [i.e., the same data may be used to justify more than one theory]. The question is thus a matter of which presumptions, not whether or not presumptions" (1974/1987, p. 87). The property of underjustification (or *under-determination*) has a profound impact on the search for a normative framework for science. If observation is theory laden, then empiricism is inherently biased, and one therefore may be forced to rely on descriptive frameworks derived from an analysis of the conduct of science. That is, a theory-laden observation filters the observed phenomena through the theory; it does not capture an objective reality. I close this section with a description of Quine's contributions, and in the following two sections I examine some interpretations of science based on historical experience.

Quine begins by criticizing the logical positivists' distinction between *analytic statements*, which are true by virtue of the words contained in them, and *synthetic statements*, which make empirical claims for which evidence is appropriate. For the logical positivists, the analytic statements—which consisted of theoretic sentences, mathematical propositions, and logical propositions—could be used in developing a science without risk of introducing error. However, Quine claimed that the term *analyticity* can be defined only in terms of other concepts like *meaning*, which then must be defined in terms of analyticity. This circular argument implied that any distinction between analytic and other kinds of sentences was "an unempirical dogma of empiricists, a metaphysical article of faith" (Quine 1961, p. 37). Thus, there is no possibility of a verificationist theory of meaning. As Bechtel describes it, "The terms of our language are interconnected with one another in a vast network, so that we cannot differentiate between those connections in the network that establish the meanings of theoretical terms from those that present empirical findings.... [Quine] contends that we must give up the idea that we can use experience either to confirm or to falsify scientific hypotheses" (1988a, p. 42).

Quine writes, "Language is man-made and the locutions of scientific theory have no meaning but what they acquired by our learning to use them" (1975, p. 74).

> I have urged that we could know the necessary and sufficient stimulatory conditions of every possible act of utterance, in a foreign language, and still not know how to determine what objects the speakers of that language believe in. Now if objective reference is so inaccessible to observation, who is to say on empirical grounds that belief in objects of one or another description is right or wrong? How can there ever be empirical evidence against existential statements? (Quine 1969, p. 11)

Observations will trigger a "verdict on a statement only because the statement is a strand in the verbal network of some elaborate theory" (1969, p. 17). That observation may be consistent with many different networks; moreover, when there are contradictions, they may be accommodated by modifying the network to protect a favored theory.

"Theory is empirically under-determined. Surely even if we had an observational oracle, capable of assigning truth value to every standing observational report expressible in our language, still this would not suffice to adjudicate between a host of possible physical theories, each of them completely in accord with the oracle" (Quine 1975, p. 79). "Terminology aside, what wants recognizing is that a physical theory of radically different form from ours, with nothing even recognizably similar to our quantification or objective reference, might still be empirically equivalent to ours, in the sense of predicting the same episodes of sensory bombardment on the strength of the same past episodes.... [Our science maintains] a manageably narrow spectrum of visible alternatives ... [producing] a tunnel vision ... that has fostered the illusion of there being only one solution to the riddle of the universe" (p. 81). Quine's objective was philosophical: a better understanding of the relation between evidence and scientific theory. By calling to attention the underdetermination of evidence, he shifted the discussion from an abstract view of the objective interpretation of evidence to the "the acquisition of our basic logical habits ... [as] accounted for in our acquisition of grammatical constructs" (p. 78). Where Popper and Campbell justify their enquiry by placing scientific knowledge at the highest level, Quine demonstrates that this knowledge is expressed in a socially determined context (i.e., coherentism). It follows, therefore, that there may be more than one solution to the riddle of the universe, more than one universal law of matter.

How does all this relate to our question about the central tension in the software process? That tension, recall, is brought about by the need to describe a product formally. The product's requirements seldom exist as formal statements, and the highest level formal expression of a product ranges from the specification down to the product's programs. The objective of a formal method is to extend the formal envelope up from the programs to the level of the requirements specification, which raises the issue of what can be presented formally. In the logical positivist view, there are methods for knowing what is true and building on that knowledge. Indeed, the principle of theory reduction implies that there may be some universal theories from which all other theories can be constructed. Popper constrained this view by pointing out that we can only know what is wrong, never what is right. Thus, what we accept as true is what we have failed to show is false.

From the perspective of software engineering, this is the difference between proof of correctness and the testing for errors. (A good test is one that finds an error.) If we seek to employ proofs rather than search for errors, then the problem shifts to one of how to represent what we initially hold as true (e.g., the formal specification). Popper, Campbell, and Quine all point out that the specification will be underdetermined. That is, many different specifications can be developed for the product. (Similarly, the specification itself is underdetermined in that there are many different programs that will be correct with respect to it.) Campbell suggests that—if there is to be progress—our learning should be evolutionary (i.e., driven by blind variation), and Quine observes that objective reference is inaccessible to observation.

So we see that the tension of the software process is related to the dilemma of science. In science, the goal is to find a formal representation for some aspect of reality; in software development, the objective is to go from a need to a formal computational model that responds to it. In both cases, the reality is complex, and we may find only incomplete formal representations for it; but these representations (e.g., the models and theories of science) must be formal if we are to use them. The only alternative, therefore, is to accept the limitations of our theories as we work with them. In the domain of science, this implies that eternal, universal scientific truths may not exist. Of course, we have not yet seen any justification for such an extreme statement, but the arguments of the following sections will bring us closer to that conclusion.

2.5. Science in a Historical Context

The discussion so far has isolated the process of scientific endeavor from its social and historical context. The logical positivists separated the issues of discovery from justification, and, even though Popper used historical precedent to support his ideas, the method of conjectures and refutations also deals with only justification. As just noted, Quine opened the issue of the context in which science is conducted, and, as will be shown later, Kuhn opened a whole new avenue of enquiry into this problem. By way of a segue, recall that the previous section began with Feyerabend's stinging criticism of a formally based empiricism. His essay concluded, "What we must do is to replace the beautiful but useless formal castles in the air by a detailed study of primary sources in the history of science.... It is to be hoped that such a concrete study will return to the subject the excitement and usefulness it once possessed" (1970, p. 183).

The seminal work in the transformation from the "formal castles" to the empirical study of the history of science was Kuhn's *The Structure of Scientific Revolutions* (1970), first published in 1962. After initial training in physics, Kuhn turned to study the history of science, which shattered his preconceptions about the nature of science. His book introduced a new framework for thinking about the character of science, and the remainder of this section details the concepts presented in the first edition.

Rather than finding a process of continuing accumulation and differentiation, Kuhn detected five distinct stages in the growth and evolution of a scientific discipline. The first was immature science, which produced a mature "normal science." This was followed by the stages of crisis (in which the normal science is unable to respond to anomalies and discoveries), revolution (in which competing alternative explanations are offered), and resolution (in which the foundations for a new normal science are accepted). Resolution creates a new normal science, which, in turn, ultimately will be subject to a crisis that culminates in its replacement.

Normal science operates within a *paradigm*. The paradigm may be thought of as a body of knowledge, including theories, methods, tools, and standards, that establishes a framework for the practice of a scientific discipline. Because *The Structure of Scientific Revolutions* was introduced as several of the early major works in cognitive science were being published, there was a strong intuitive sense of what a paradigm might be: it was a kind of collective schema within which a scientific community operated, a context within which ideas could be communicated. Philosophers, however, demand precision, and Kuhn's imprecise definition of *paradigm* exposed him to considerable criticism. Masterman (1970) counted 21 different connotations of the term, and Suppe (1974) commented, "the central concept, 'paradigm,' is used extremely loosely and becomes bloated to the point of being a philosophical analogue to phlogiston [used, in the phlogistic theory of chemistry, to have whatever properties were necessary to explain a given reaction]" (p. 136). As a result, much of Kuhn's later work was devoted to clarification and refinement of the definition of paradigm with specializations such as *theoretical matrix* and *exemplar*. For the purposes of this section, however, the phlogistic use will suffice.

"Normal science, the activity in which most scientists inevitably spend almost all their time, is predicated on the assumption that the scientific community knows what the world is like. Much of the success of the enterprise derives from the community's willingness to defend that assumption, if necessary at considerable cost" (Kuhn 1970, p. 5). The paradigm in which the scientists operate is not, as the logical positivists might assume, a theory that can be postulated as a system of axioms. Neither is it a set of postulates from which observations can be deduced. Rather the paradigm is imprecise, a common schema to be clarified. "Like an accepted judicial decision in the common law, it is an object for further articulation and specification under new or more stringent conditions" (p. 23).

For Kuhn, the scientist's goal is not described in the traditional context of confirming or falsifying theories; rather, it is one of fitting theory to nature. "In the absence of a paradigm or some candidate for paradigm, all of the facts that could possibly pertain to the development of a given science are likely to seem equally relevant" (p. 15). This last comment echoes Einstein's observation, "It is theory which decides what we can observe." It also reflects Quine's comment about the underdetermination of observation. Thus, we need a paradigm to orient a scientific investigation; it provides the vocabulary for understanding what is known and what is to be clarified.

Mopping-up operations are what engage most scientists throughout their careers. They constitute what I am here calling normal science. Closely examined, whether historically or in the contemporary laboratory, that enterprise seems an attempt to force nature into the preformed and relatively inflexible box that the paradigm supplies. No part of the aim of normal science is to call forth new phenomena; indeed those that will not fit in the box are often not seen at all. Nor do scientists normally aim to invent new theories, and they are often intolerant of those invented by others. Instead, normal-scientific research is directed to the articulation of those phenomena and theories that the paradigm already supplies.

Perhaps these are defects. The areas investigated by normal science are, of course, minuscule; the enterprise now under discussion has drastically restricted vision. But those restrictions, born from the confidence in a paradigm, turn out to be essential to the development of science.... When the paradigm is successful, the profession will have solved problems that its members could scarcely have imagined and would never have undertaken without commitment to the paradigm. (pp. 24-25)

Kuhn identifies three classes of problem within a normal science: determination of significant fact, matching facts with theory, and articulation of theory. Work on these problems must be conducted within the paradigm; "to desert the paradigm is to cease practicing the science it defines" (p. 34). Thus, normal science is *puzzle solving*, and the paradigm provides the framework in which the puzzle may be approached. Without a paradigm it is not possible to attack even important problems (e.g., find a cure for cancer). One does not know where to begin or even if a solution is possible, or, putting it more formally, the problem cannot be stated in terms of the conceptual and instrumental tools the paradigm supplies. It is the paradigm that provides the context for understanding the problem and its potential solution. "One of the reasons why normal science seems to progress so rapidly is that its practitioners concentrate on problems that only their own lack of ingenuity should keep them from solving" (p. 37)

Normal science establishes the goals of scientific enquiry. It "is a highly cumulative enterprise, eminently successful in its aim, the steady extension of the scope and precision of scientific knowledge. In all these respects it fits with great precision the most usual image of scientific work. Yet one standard product of the scientific enterprise is missing. Normal science does not aim at novelties of fact or theory and, when successful, finds none" (p. 52). Because all observation is theory laden, the paradigm procedures and applications "restrict the phenomenological field accessible for scientific investigation at any given time" (p. 60-61). Thus, a discovery like x-rays necessitates a paradigm change (and a change in procedures and expectations) for a special segment of the scientific community. The model of that change, or *paradigm shift*, is the scientific revolution of his book's title.

The change process begins with the identification of anomalies and the emergence of new discoveries that challenge the paradigm of normal science. Kuhn illustrates this process in the discovery of oxygen, x-rays, and the Leyden jar. In each case there is "the previous awareness of anomaly, the gradual and simultaneous emergence of both observations and conceptual recognition, and the consequent change of paradigm categories and procedures often accompanied by resistance. There is even evidence that these same characteristics are built into the nature of the perceptual process itself" (p. 62). That is, the paradigm creates a perceptual context for the scientist, and learning is required to accept observations that conflict with previously learned patterns. This is the phase of crisis and the emergence of new scientific theories. In a cumulative view of scientific knowledge, new theories are added to those already learned. But if there is a basic incompatibility between theories (and, as described by Kuhn, the very nature of discovery implies that the new discoveries will not conform to the theories of the existing paradigm), then there will be a struggle for the survival of the "best" paradigm.

How do scientists react to a crisis? "They do not renounce the paradigm that has led them into crisis. They do not, that is, treat anomalies as counterinstances, though in the vocabulary of philosophy of science that is what they are" (p. 77). Instead there is a period of confusion, a blurring of the paradigm. Kuhn illustrates this with two quotations from Pauling. The first from a few months before Heisenberg's paper on matrix mechanics pointed the way to a new quantum theory. "At the moment physics is again terribly confused. In any case, it is too difficult for me, and I wish I had been a movie comedian or something of the sort and had never heard of physics." Five months later he wrote, "Heisenberg's type of mechanics has again given me hope and joy in life" (cited, p. 84). Thus, rather than the smooth transition compatible with a universal model of scientific knowledge, we find that "the transition from a paradigm in crisis to a new one from which a new tradition of normal science can emerge is far from a cumulative process, one achieved by an articulation or extension of the old paradigm. Rather it is a reconstruction of the field from new fundamentals, a reconstruction that changes some of the field's most elementary theoretical generalizations as well as many of its paradigm methods and applications" (p. 84-85).

Clearly, when an established paradigm fails to account for important anomalies it must be replaced. In what sense, however, is this a *revolution*? Kuhn takes the position that all observation is theory laden, and thus the paradigm establishes what can be observed. Normal science, with its wide community of support, already has a paradigm that orients perceptions that are recognized, in part, to be deficient. In response, the crisis has precipitated a new (and competing) paradigm. "When paradigms enter, as they must, into a debate about paradigm choice, their role is necessarily circular. Each group uses its own paradigm to argue in that paradigm's defense.... Yet, whatever its force, the status of the circular argument is only that of persuasion. It cannot be made logically or even probablistically compelling for those who refuse to step inside the circle.... There is no standard higher than the assent of the relevant community" (p. 94). From within the community, this paradigm shift is seen as a revolution. For those outside that community (and therefore lacking the orientation of the old paradigm), however, the shift is accepted as a normal part of the development process. Kuhn calls this phenomena the invisibility of revolution. By the time a new paradigm has been accepted, all evidence of its predecessor will have been removed.

The consequences of a paradigm shift are enormous. The paradigm frames the kinds of questions that can be asked and, in that way, determines the important issues to be addressed. It provides a structure for measurement and interpretation.   When there are competing paradigms, there will be disagreements about the list of problems to be resolved. For example, should a theory of motion explain the cause for the attractive forces between particles of matter? Newton's dynamics was widely rejected because, unlike Aristotle's and Descarte's theories, he simply noted the existence of such forces. With the acceptance of Newton's theories, the question was banished from science until the theory of general relativity reopened the question and offered an answer. This new theory of general relativity, however, could not be interpreted as a refinement of Newton's theories. "To make the transition to Einstein's universe, the whole conceptual web whose strands are space, time, matter, force, and so on, had to be shifted and laid down again on nature whole. Only men who had together undergone or failed to undergo that transformation would be able to discover precisely what they agreed or disagreed about" (p. 149). Each theory offered a different (and conflicting) interpretation of matter and force, and all subsequent observations necessarily would be bound to a particular interpretation.

Like Boring's ambiguous figure (1930), in which one can see either the wife or the mother in law, but never both, the transition between paradigms "must occur all at once (though not necessarily in an instant) or not at all" (Kuhn 1970, p. 151). It took a century before Copernicus' theory was accepted. Priestly never accepted the oxygen theory, Lord Kelvin rejected the electromagnetic theory, and Einstein resisted quantum mechanics. "The transfer of allegiance from paradigm to paradigm is a conversion experience that cannot be forced. Lifelong resistance, particularly from those whose productive careers have committed them to an older tradition of normal science, is not a violation of scientific research standards but an index to the nature of scientific research itself. The source of resistance is the assertion that the older paradigm will ultimately solve all its problems, that nature can be shoved into the box the paradigm provides.... Conversions will occur a few at a time until, after the last holdouts have died, the whole profession will again be practicing under a single, but now different, paradigm" (pp. 151-52).

This movement to the acceptance of a new paradigm is not built upon rational argument. Selection often is based less on past achievement than on future promise. "Something must make at least a few scientists feel that the new proposal is on the right track, and sometimes it is only personal and inarticulate aesthetic considerations that can do that.... [If] a paradigm is ever to triumph it must gain some first supporters, men who will develop it to the point where hardheaded arguments can be produced.... Gradually the number of experiments, instruments, articles, and books based on the paradigm will multiply.... [There will not be] a point at which resistance [to the new paradigm] becomes illogical or scientific ... [but] the man who continues to resist after his whole profession has been converted has *ipso facto* ceased to be a scientist" (pp. 158-59).

Finally, to close out this review of *The Structure of Scientific Revolutions*, what does Kuhn have to say about the progressivity of science. He observes that the term *science* is reserved for fields that do progress in obvious ways, which results in concepts such as "scientific progress" and "scientific objectivity" being in part redundant. (As we have seen, scientific knowledge plays a similar role in epistemology.) There is a clear sense of progress for normal science. The members of the community "can concentrate exclusively upon the subtlest and most esoteric of the phenomena that concern it. Inevitably, that does increase both the effectiveness and the efficiency with which the group as a whole solves problems" (pp. 163-64). Education is optimized to train the scientist in the paradigm. Original sources are not referenced; textbooks extract only what is necessary to know about the paradigm. The scientist sees this training "as leading in a straight line to the discipline's present vantage. In short, he sees it as progress. No alternative is available to him while he remains in the field" (p. 167). Kuhn concludes, "during periods of normal science ... progress seems both obvious and assured. During those periods, however, the scientific community could view the fruits of its work in no other way" (p. 163).

But there are limits to normal science, and "the very existence of science depends upon vesting the power to choose between paradigms" (p. 167). Within a newly established normal science, those who adapted the new paradigm will see the paradigm change as progress. This is, of course, a self-fulfilling perception. The issue that remains is: we know that the scientific community will maximize "the number and precision of the problem solved through paradigm change" (p. 169), but need the acceptance of improving scientific efficiency imply that science is "the one enterprise that draws constantly nearer to some goal set by nature in advance?" (p. 171). Kuhn thinks not.

> The net result of a sequence of such revolutionary selections, separated by periods of normal research, is the wonderfully adapted set of instruments we call modern scientific knowledge. Successive stages in that developmental process are marked by an increase in articulation and specialization. And the entire process may have occurred, as we now suppose biological evolution did, without benefit of a set goal, a permanent fixed scientific truth, of which each stage in the development of scientific knowledge is a better exemplar. (pp. 172-73)

That is, by following Campbell's blind-variation process, a quest for a unified scientific law may never be satisfied.

2.6. Some Other Contributions

Kuhn's goal was to propose a new picture of science and scientific development, in particular scientific progress, grounded in a new historiography (Hoyningen-Huene 1993). Clearly, there is a marked distinction between Kuhn's description of the evolutionary process of science and the positivist/Popperian concern for the justification of theories. These are two sides of the same coin, two projections of a single, holistic universe. Some seek to establish normative models for the conduct of science, while others seek to examine science from within a *weltanschauungen*, a comprehensive conception of the universe and of man's relation to it. These complementary views are the analogues of the two forces that create the central tension in the software process: the need that exists in-the-world and the formal response to the need that exists in-the-computer. In this section I examine the work of some philosophers who explore the nature of science within a larger context. Although it may not be obvious, there is a strong parallel between this topic and the nature of computer science and its application. In both cases we are concerned with what is known, what is knowable, and what can (and cannot) be expressed formally.

I begin again with Feyerabend, whose quotations I used to open the previous two sections. He finds an unhealthy conservatism built into the emphasis on the normative models. He also does not accept Kuhn's view of normal science. Instead, he believes that a single paradigm would be destructive; progress benefits from a plurality of pursuits. In his *Against Method: Outline of an Anarchistic Theory of Knowledge* (1975), Feyerabend writes,

> The idea that science can, and should, be run according to fixed and universal rules, is both unrealistic and pernicious. It is *unrealistic*, for it takes too simple a view of the talents of man and of the circumstances which encourage, or cause, their development. It is *pernicious* for the attempt to enforce the rules is bound to increase our professional qualifications at the expense of our humanity. In addition, the idea is *detrimental to science*, for it neglects the complex physical and historical conditions which influence scientific change. It makes science less adaptable and more dogmatic....
>
> Case studies ... speak *against* the universal validity of any rule. All methodologies have their limitations and the only "rule" that survives is "anything goes." (pp. 295-96)

Thus, Feyerabend dismisses the search for normative models in favor of anarchy. Aristotelianism is a legitimate subject of enquiry if it leads to new suggestions, to looking at things in a new way. One should not constrain the decisions and choices of scientists by the rules laid down by or implicit in the methodologies of science. Although Feyerabend offers the useful observation that it is sometimes necessary to go outside the established order, taken in its extreme, his work fails to address the central question of the philosophy of science, which seeks to show how rational decisions can provide useful guidance.

In contrast, Lakatos adopted the historical perspective to his concern for logical analysis in the justification and evaluation of the scientific enterprise. His philosophical point of view was consistent with that of Popper. Knowledge claims are fallible, there is a fundamental distinction between science and other forms of intellectual activity, the growth of knowledge is the central problem of epistemology, and theories are best understood as sets of statements whose logical contents can be compared. Lakatos saw the appraisal of scientific theories as ultimately a historical and comparative matter, but he offered a historical interpretation that differed from that of Kuhn. Whereas Kuhn believed that a particular scientific community's theories and methods were captured in one paradigm, Lakatos contended that science seldom is dominated by a single paradigm. For him, there was competition among paradigms with advances coming from within a paradigm. He also rejected Kuhn's view of normal science as filling in and further applying the paradigm. Instead, he found a process of theory succession in which new theories replaced old theories while retaining some important features of the old theories.

Lakatos introduced the idea of a *research programme* to provide for this idea of competing successions of theories. The programme was defined by its *hard core* of fundamental assumptions that were immune from refutation. Surrounding this hard core was a *protective belt* of collateral and auxiliary assumptions. Researchers were free to alter the assumptions within the protective belt to accommodate research findings. The hard core, however, must be accepted in its entirely. Thus for example, the Copernican programme required the researcher to accept that the planets revolve around the sun. When Tycho Brahe rejected this assertion, he opted out of the programme (even though it was his observations that established the basis for Kepler's contribution to that programme). Lakatos provided two heuristics for guiding the programme. The *negative heuristic* was simply an injunction against modifying the hard core. There also was a *positive heuristic* comprised of guidelines that instruct the theorist working in the programme. "The positive heuristic consists of a partially articulated set of suggestions or hints on how to change, develop, the 'refutable variants' of the research programme, [and] how to modify, sophisticate, the 'refutable protective belt'" (1970, p. 135). The sequence of theories that constitutes the research programme, therefore, preserves the theories in the hard core and applies the positive heuristics to build on what already exists in the hard core and its protective belt. Neither the hard core nor the heuristics are subject to change, but theories in the protective belt may be refuted and removed.

A research programme is said to be *progressive* if it develops new theories in the protective belt. Those theories must be able to explain everything that their predecessors explained as well as some novel facts (i.e., the product of bold predictions that may be refuted), but the explanation of the novel facts must not have been achieved by ad hoc stratagems (e.g., augmenting a theory with specialized features to account for a specific anomaly). Individual theories are judged with respect to other theories within the same research programme. One research programme is better than its rival only if it both explains everything that its rival explains and also predicts more novel facts than its rival. Because research programmes may have anomalies that cannot be explained by their theories, the ranking of programmes may be imprecise. Research programmes may *degenerate* as well as progress. "In a progressive research programme, theory leads to the discovery of hitherto unknown novel facts. In degenerating programmes, however, theories are fabricated only in order to accommodate known facts" (1978, pp. 5-6).

A programme may progress, then degenerate for an extended period, and then progress again (e.g., a theoretical advance delayed by an immature technology such as Babbage's computational programme not realized until the mid 1940s). Thus, one should not give up on a research programme even when it is degenerating. Indeed, during the early days of a research programme, when the programme may not yet have achieved the success of older programmes, it is reasonable to retain theories even though there are some phenomena that seem to refute them. "One must treat budding programmes leniently: programmes may take decades before they get off the ground and become empirically progressive. Criticism is not a Popperian quick kill, by refutation. Important criticism is always constructive: there is no refutation without a better theory" (1978, p. 6). Thus, a program must be given an opportunity to develop before it should be expected to compete with other programs. Furthermore, even when a programme becomes degenerate, it may be possible to graft that programme into a new endeavor that is progressing. Obviously, Lakatos' research programme is very different from Kuhn's paradigm, and, even though Lakatos relies on the Popperian notion of refutation, falsification is applied subjectively. That is, it is valid only when the research programme is mature.

Toulmin provides a *weltanschauungen* analysis that adds another dimension to the discussion. For him, the function of science is to build up systems of ideas about nature that have some claim to "reality." The systems must be consistent with observations (i.e., the data) and, in the context of the current understanding, be "absolute" and "pleasing to the mind" (1961, p. 115). It is not sufficient for a theory simply to be able to predict; the job of a theory is to specify the expected patterns of behavior and to explain deviations from them. The theory does this by presenting an *ideal of natural order* that specifies a natural course of events that does not require further explanation. For example, "light travels in a straight line." Of course, no phenomena ever realizes the ideal of natural order, and laws are required to explain the deviations from this ideal. Refractory phenomena constitute a deviation from straight-line propagation, which Snell's law accounts for and thus explains. Therefore, a theory contains the ideals of natural order and the laws that account for deviations from that ideal.

The relationship between the ideal of natural order and the phenomena is one of representation. The ideal provides a fresh way of looking at the phenomena. As a method of representation, however, the theory can be neither true nor false; it can be only more or less "fruitful" (1961, p. 57). Moreover, the *scope* of a law is not stated in the formulation of the law itself; it is stated separately, and often it is not known until after the law has been accepted. For instance, some crystalline materials such as Iceland spar do not conform to Snell's law. Thus, we see that laws—which, like pictures and diagrams, are representations—cannot be true or false, but statements of scope—which relate laws to phenomena—are factual assertions that can be true or false.

This presents a hierarchical structure of ideals, laws, and hypotheses in which the lowest level consists of hypotheses whose fruitfulness is still in question. Note that this hierarchy is very different from that of the Received View in which there is a logical pyramid such that lower levels are deduced from higher-level statements. For Toulmin, the hierarchy is established by a *language shift* in which the ideals, laws, and hypotheses are formulated in terms borrowed from earlier usage. "Questions about refractive index will have *meaning* only insofar as Snell's law holds, so in talking about refractive index we have to take the applicability of Snell's law for granted" (1953, p. 80). Therefore, "statements at one level have a meaning only within the scope of those in the level below" (1953, p. 80).

Suppe (1974) summarizes Toulmin's philosophy as follows.

> The theory embodies certain ideals of natural order, which are presumptions about phenomenal behavior which "carry their own understanding" in the sense of not requiring explanation. These presumptions constitute an intellectual frame of thought or *Weltanschauungen* which determines the questions the scientist asks and the assumptions which underlie his theorizing. They even determine or influence what are counted as "facts," and what significance is to be attached to them. If the discovered scope of the theory is such that the theory can explain a large variety of phenomena and answer a substantial proportion of the questions about the phenomena which are counted as important, then the theory is fruitful—for the meantime.... Fruitfulness ... is judged relative to the presumptions and interests of the scientists.... Scientific theories thus are formulated, judged, maintained, and developed relative to a *Weltanschauungen* ... [that] is dynamically evolving, and may change as the theory undergoes development. (pp. 131-32)

There is general acceptance of Toulmin's ideas that the theoretical terms are theory dependent and that theories do provide a mode of representation for phenomena. The major objection to his philosophy is that it is based on *instrumentalism*, according to which descriptions of the world involving observable entities are indeed descriptions of what the world is really like, whereas systems of descriptions based on theoretical concepts really are not descriptions of the world; they are only useful fictions for facilitating calculations. Restating this, instrumentalism asserts that "scientific theories are nothing more than sets of rules for connecting one set of observable phenomena with another, [and] ... it is not the business of science to establish what may exist beyond the realm of observation" (Chalmers 1982, p. 148).

Popper objects very strongly to the instrumentalist view. He cites the illustration of Osiander, who wrote in the preface to Copernicus' *De Revolutionibus*, "There is no need for these hypotheses to be true, or even to be at all like the truth; rather, one thing is sufficient for them—that they should yield calculations which agree with the observations" (cited in Popper 1965, p. 98). In this way Osiander separated the *instrument of calculation* from *a true description of the world*; computation from meaning. Why is this distinction important to Popper? Because without meaning, refutation is impossible; one cannot falsify a syntactically correct representation of a computation. Even though Osiander may have temporarily defused the theological tension, he could not eliminate it. Thus, when Galileo recanted he is said to have tapped the ground beneath him and muttered, "And yet, it moves." Clearly, for Galileo, the theoretical context could not be separated from the computation.

As I bring this discussion of science to a conclusion (in the sense of an ending rather than a consensus), it is clear that I have not presented a unified view of the scientific enterprise. I hope to suggest that there is none. In 1974, Suppe observed:

> The situation today, then, in philosophy of science is this: the Received View has been rejected, but no proposed alternative analysis of theories enjoys widespread acceptance.... For more than fifty years philosophy of science has been engaged in a search for philosophic understanding of scientific theories; today it still is searching. (p. 4)

My reading suggests that this comment remains as valid today as it was twenty years earlier. But there is another explanation. In a recent collection of interviews on the philosophy of science, Callebaut (1993) refers to Locke's distinction between "master-builders" (such as Newton) and "underlaborers" (such as Locke himself) who rest content with "moving some of the rubbish that lies in the way of knowledge" (cited on p. 200). In a review of this book, Fuller (1994) offers the following perspicacious comment:

> One hypothesis is that the positivists were not trying to be underlaborers at all but were in fact using science to promote certain philosophical ends of greater societal importance.... Consider the symbolic function of the natural sciences in the project of "Enlightenment" promoted in our own time by Karl Popper. The idea here is not one of philosophers paving the way for a mounting body of esoteric knowledge. Rather, it is one of extending to all spheres of life the critical attitude that

had motivated scientists to challenge traditional beliefs in the first place. (p. 983)

And so, when the dust finally settles we may find, not truth, but only a critical attitude to what is accepted as truth.

The next section examines some views of knowledge and concludes with some observations relevant to our quest.

2.7. The Structure of Science

Scientific knowledge is accepted as the most refined expression of knowledge. It is described formally and justified rationally. Physics constitutes the purest kind of scientific knowledge in that it can be represented mathematically and reasoned about logically. There are other forms of scientific knowledge, and there are debates regarding whether or not the theories of Marx and Freud constitute science (e.g., Popper 1965). Abrahamsen (1987) presents a specialization hierarchy for the scientific disciplines. There are four levels in this hierarchy. The base contains the physical sciences; on it rests the biological sciences, which support the behavioral sciences, which ultimately support the cultural product domains (i.e., mathematics and engineering science, humanities, and the social sciences). Although her paper is concerned with boundaries within psycholinguistics, her hierarchy implies that biology can be explained by physics and the behavioral sciences can be explained in terms of the biological sciences. (By way of contrast, recall Quine's comment on understanding beliefs from a complete knowledge of the stimulatory conditions of their expression in a foreign language).

Campbell (1969), in reference to the social organization of science (as opposed to scientific knowledge), introduces a *fish-scale model of omniscience* in which knowledge is organized in an overlapping structure that provides comprehensive coverage similar to the protection offered by a fish's scales. He proposes this model as an alternative the clusters of knowledge that characterize the ethnocentrism of disciplines found in most academic settings. The two alternative disciplinary structures are illustrated in Figure 2.2. Campbell's paper, however, does not address the feasibility of such a uniform structure of knowledge; that is, is it possible to organize a universal omniscience with a single vocabulary (and paradigm)? This subject of *interfield theories* (which cross disciplines) has been addressed in some detail by Darden and Maull (1977).

Because it is impossible to separate knowledge from its social context, there has been considerable interest in the sociology of science and of knowledge (e.g., Bloor 1976 and 1981, L. Laudan 1981, and Whitley 1984). But the objective of this section is to draw the

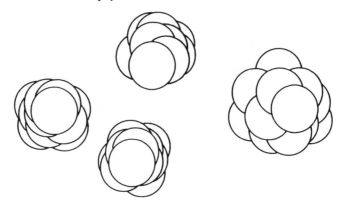

(a) Present situation: Disciplines as clusters of specialties, leaving
interdisciplinary gaps.

(b) Ideal situation: Fish-scale model of omniscience.

Fig. 2.2. Two models of the scientific disciplines.
Reprinted from Campbell (1969) with permission, property of the author.

discussion to a close, not to open new topics. We have seen a universal
recognition of change in scientific theories. Larry Laudan, et al. (1986)
surveyed the theories of change within the philosophy of science and
reported on their areas of agreement and disagreement. As a way of
providing a synthesis, I extract their findings regarding agreement in
Figure 2.3. The results may seem counterintuitive to one who has not
studied the evolving theories of science and scientific knowledge.
According to the Legend and the idealization of scientific knowledge,
there should be certainty and progress; a ratchet-like accumulation of
knowledge. Hesse (1980) points out, however, that natural science is
only *instrumentally progressive*; it is our ability to predict and control
empirical events that continuously improves. But this instrumental

(1)   The most important units for understanding scientific change are large-scale, relatively long-lived conceptual structures which different modelers refer to as "paradigms," "global theories," "research programmes" or "research traditions," and which we, for neutrality term "guiding assumptions."

(2)   Guiding assumptions, once accepted, are rarely if ever abandoned simply because they face empirical difficulties. They tend to endure in spite of negative experimental or observational tests.   In short, negative evidence is less important in the assessment of large-scale theories than is commonly thought. . . .

(3)   Data do not fully determine theory choice, i.e., observations and experiments do not provide a sufficient base for unambiguous choices between sets of guiding assumptions or between rival theories.

(4)   Metaphysical, theological, and other nonscientific factors play an important role in the assessment of scientific theories and guiding assumptions. . . .

(5)   Assessments of guiding assumptions depend as much on judgments about their potential as on their record of performance, . . .

(6)   Scientists do not make absolute judgments about the merits or demerits of a particular set of assumptions or a particular theory, but comparative judgments against extreme rivals.

(7)   There are no neutral observations in science; rather they are all theory-laden. . . .

(8)   The generation of new, and the modification of existing, scientific theories is not a random process; . . .

(9)   Guiding assumptions are never abandoned unless there is a new set available to replace them.

(10) The coexistence of rival sets of guiding assumptions in a science is the rule rather than the exception. Debate about rival sets of assumptions does not alternate with periods of universal assent to one set, but occurs constantly.

(11) A set of guiding principles is always faced with apparent empirical difficulties.

(12) New sets of guiding assumptions are not judged by the same yardstick as well-established sets.

(13) A later set of guiding principles seldom accommodates all the explanatory successes of its predecessors. There are losses as well as gains in the replacement process.

Fig. 2.3. Agreement amongst theories of scientific change.
Reprinted from L. Laudan, et al (1986) with permission, ©1986 D. Reidel

(14)   The technical machinery of confirmation theory and inductive logic has little if any light to shed on theory appraisal.

(15)   The assessment of low-level scientific theories is based in part on the success of the guiding assumptions with which they are associated.

(16)   Theories are always confronted with apparent empirical difficulties, and are never abandoned simply because of those difficulties.

(17)   The solutions given to problems by a scientific theory are often recognized as approximate only when that theory is replaced by a new theory.

Fig. 2.3. (cont.) Agreement amongst theories of scientific change. Reprinted from L. Laudan, et al. (1986) with permission, ©1986 D. Reidel

progress "does not entail convergence of the conceptual framework of theories towards universalizable truth. At best it entails increasing approximation of low-level laws and predictions to the subsequently tested data, and that this approximation takes place in limited domains of data" (p. xi). From the perspective of technology, instrumental progress may be sufficient. But for science to progress, it must bind theory concept to its instruments, which raises questions about the feasibility of realizing a fish-scale model or of satisfying the quest for a unified law of science—the bedrock foundation in Abrahamsen's hierarchy of scientific disciplines.

Here, then, is a pivotal question: If a unified law exists, then we may be able to use it to derive the laws that will, in turn, drive the application of science; but if this law does not exist, then scientific knowledge may not be organized hierarchically, and we must orient our quest for understanding within an alternative structural model of science. Rephrasing the dialectic, Einstein once said, "What interests me is whether God had any choice in the creation of the universe" (cited in Lindley 1993, p. 12); that is, would the laws of nature permit only our kind of universe to happen? He hoped that this was so, and he used the aesthetics of this vision to guide his decisions regarding what is right, elegant, and proper. It was this same aesthetic judgment that led him to reject the implications of quantum mechanics. For example, he wrote, "If you want knowledge of one thing, you have to pay for it with ignorance of something else. There can be, therefore, no perfect knowledge of the kind thought possible in classical physics." (cited in Lindley 1993, p. 74). God does not play dice, declared Einstein; there must be some certainty. Yet, if a unified law exists, how will we know? Empirical justification or aesthetic appeal? This is the central theme of Lindley's *The End of Physics* (1993):

The theory of everything should comprise not just the rules of interaction between particles but also boundary conditions for the application of those rules; it is supposed to dictate, of its own accord, the nature of the universe that the theory of everything will inhabit. (p. 245)

[But] experiments to test fundamental physics are at the point of impossibility, and what is deemed progress now is something very different from what Newton imagined. (p. 255)

Modern physics ... [has] done away with the essential classical ideal of an objective world.... The possibility that we can understand all of the world becomes a logically unattainable goal, because we ourselves are in the world, affecting it at the same time we are trying to stand outside it and apprehend it. (p. 54)

[What] is the use of a theory that looks attractive but contains no additional power of prediction, and makes no statements that can be tested?   Does physics then become a branch of aesthetics? (p. 20)

[If found,] this theory of everything, this myth, will indeed spell the end of physics. It will be the end not because physics has at last been able to explain everything in the universe, but because physics has reached the end of all the things it has the power to explain. (p. 255)

Thus, scientific knowledge, which represents human knowledge *writ large*, has its most "pure" representation in physics, which, by its very nature, can be represented mathematically and reasoned about logically. But physics (or at least particle physics), because of the underdetermination of observation and the difficulty of conducting experiments, seems to be guided by aesthetic rather than empirical considerations (i.e., by the subjective rather than the objective).

We have come full circle. We began the study of science in the expectation that it might provide sound and irrefutable answers, and we end with the realization that it may be the aesthetics of the answer that matter. Of course, every acceptable answer must be consistent with reality; but observation is underdetermined, and many answers will be equally acceptable. Practicing scientists, of course, recognize this, which is why their enterprise is so successful.

How does this relate to the central tension of the software process? Formal representations (e.g., specifications) are merely instruments that have no validity without the theories (i.e., aesthetic world views) that provide their context. This is as true for science, where the world view comes from an interpretation of reality, as it is for software development, where the world view is an interpretation of a need and an appropriate response. The rigor and critical attitude of science are necessary for software development, but they can never be sufficient. The goal of this book is to find the conditions for sufficiency; that is, how can we ensure that the software product does what it must do to satisfy the need (especially when the need is dynamic)? This brief introduction to the philosophy of science holds no hope for the discovery of any preexisting guidelines for computer science. We must design our own science, and its criterion for success will be how well it serves us.

3

DISCOVERY AND DESIGN

3.1. The Relationship Between Science and Technology

This book is about a paradigm shift in the development of software; a move to a new era of design for software (and, for that matter, all manufactured artifacts). The goal of Part I is to lay out the scientific and technological foundations for this new era of design. In the chapter just concluded, we have seen how the Legend of science has become tarnished. During the stored-program computer's brief history, we observe the general perceptions of science and scientific knowledge undergoing a fundamental change. I have focused on the philosophy of science because that tells us something about the theoretical limits of science; it suppresses the details of the day-to-day conduct of science that make it such a successful enterprise.

This reassessment of science, of course, has been independent of the growth of computing; indeed, my examination has been free of any technological considerations. From the perspective of computer science, much of this revolution has gone unnoticed. Many still walk in the pathways first laid out in the era of the Legend; some even try to fit computer science into the framework of the Received View. If the conclusions of Chapter 2 are valid, however, such approaches cannot be sustained indefinitely. Therefore, any response to the evolving understanding of science ultimately must lead to a reexamination of computer science. If we are to shift the software design paradigm, we must expect modifications to the underlying principles embedded in computer science. How will these changes take place? Will there be new scientific findings that alter the technology, or will a shift in the technology modify what the computer scientists study? To gain insight into the answers to these questions, this chapter addresses the relationship between science and technology and, in particular, between computer science and software engineering. As in the previous chapter, I conduct a broadly based, general review.

The traditional relationship between science and engineering normally is described as being causal. Science creates knowledge, and technology consumes knowledge. This has been depicted as an assembly line: "Put money into pure science at the front end of the process. In due time, innovation will come out the other end" (Wise 1985, p. 229). (It also is referred to as the "linear" model, Price and Bass 1969.) In Shaw's (1990) model of the growth of an engineering discipline, science was given a direction by the technology; once mature, the science served to drive the technology. That is, as a technology matured, its ad hoc solutions were extracted and embedded in a body of scientific knowledge, which in time would serve as a forcing function for that technology. In this model, the application of scientific principles empowers engineers and is inherently progressive. Here we have the widely accepted division of labor: Computer scientists develop the knowledge, and software engineers apply that knowledge. This division of assignments is broadly held, and it will suffice to demonstrate its prevalence by citing two illustrations.

Freeman (1980) observes,

> It is important to keep in mind that computer science and software engineering have different objectives that should not be confused.... Computer science is concerned with the scientific study and description of algorithms, programs, the devices that interpret them, and the phenomena surrounding their creation and usage. Software engineering focuses on the application of this scientific knowledge to achieve stated technical, economic, and social goals. (p. 131)

Science discovers knowledge and engineering applies that knowledge.

In their software engineering text, Jensen and Tonies (1979) distinguish between the two orientations as follows.

> The basic difference between the scientist and the engineer lies in their goals. A scientist strives to gain new knowledge about the workings of our universe while the engineer puts that knowledge to work for the needs of mankind. Engineers may not have or need to have total knowledge of the concept they are applying to solve a problem....
>
> It is also important to note that the scientist's training concentrates on the application of the *scientific method* while the engineer's training concentrates on the use of the engineering design process. (pp. 11-12)

They describe engineers as

> basically problem solvers. They are practical people, pragmatists who tackle mundane problems and solve them efficiently and economically. Their solution to a problem may appear complex

or seem to be a trivial bit of inventiveness; however, the solution's simplicity often masks a true work of inspiration and perseverance. (p. 11)

Clearly, one would expect to find contrasts between the activities of those engaged in research (e.g., science) and in design (e.g., engineers). There will be different objectives, measures of success, and training requirements. But are these differences merely attributes of the work setting (i.e., the assignment), or are they indeed representative of an inherent distinction between science and technology? This is the subject of the next two sections.

3.2. Comparing the Engineer and the Scientist

Chapter 2 alluded to the high expectations for science and technology at the close of World War II. Although the principal advances of the war effort relied more on technological improvements than on scientific discovery, the perception was that the accomplishments resulted from the exploitation of scientific knowledge. Because the time between discovery and innovation appeared to be rapidly diminishing, it was assumed that investments in science would lead inevitably to near-term technological rewards. Bush (1947) put it this way.

Basic research leads to new knowledge. It provides scientific capital. It creates the fund from which the practical applications of knowledge must be drawn. New products and new processes do not appear full-grown. They are founded on new principles and new conceptions, which in turn are painstakingly developed by research in the purest realms of science. (pp. 52-53)

Bush had hoped to build "a National Research Foundation supporting the work of modern-day counterparts of everyone from Einstein to the Wright brothers [but what emerged was] ... a National Science Foundation supporting Einsteins only" (Wise 1985, p. 231). Science was tasked to serve as the forcing function for technological progress, and the Legend flourished.

In the 1960s the Department of Defense, which had been spending $300 to $400 million a year for "research," undertook a study to measure the economic benefit of that investment. This effort, called Project Hindsight, selected some twenty weapon systems and compared them with their predecessors of 10 to 20 years earlier (Sherwin and Isenson 1967). In each case, the ratio of performance to cost and the mean time to failure had improved by factors of 2 to 10—clear evidence of technological improvement. The analysts also traced the events that led to that improvement, classifying them as *undirected science, applied science,* and *technology.* Of the 710 events analyzed, only 9% were science events, with only 0.3% classified as undirected science. Of the technology events, 97% were motivated by a DOD need. Only 10% of the events utilized by a successor system had occurred by the time the predecessor was designed; thus the process could be characterized as "the synergistic effect of many innovations, most of them quite modest" (p. 1575). Of course, the study was biased in favor of identifying near-term event effects. When analyzed "on the 50-year or more time scale, undirected science has been of immense value" (p. 1576).

Sherwin and Isenson concluded,

> If Project Hindsight tells us anything about science, it is that it is unusual for random, disconnected fragments of scientific knowledge to find application rapidly. It is, rather, the evaluated, compressed, organized, interpreted, and simplified scientific knowledge that we find to be the most effective connection between the undirected research laboratory and the world of practical affairs. If scientists would see their efforts in undirected science used on a more substantial scale in a time period shorter than 20 years, they must put a bigger fraction of their collective, creative efforts into organizing scientific knowledge expressly for use by society. (p. 1577)

As can be expected, Project Hindsight raised a storm of protest within the scientific community (see Layton 1971), and a subsequent study (TRACES) was undertaken to evaluate the effects of nonmission research on five commercial developments. Using a different method for tracing, it found that 10 years prior to an innovation approximately 90% of the nonmission research had been accomplished (IIT 1968). Although TRACES focused more on the contributions of undirected research, it, like Project Hindsight, operated within a 50-year window.

Price and Bass (1969) reviewed several other studies and observed that the "linear" model was too simple a model. "The role of science in innovation requires focus on the nature and intensity of the dialogue between the scientific and technological communities, rather than the role of the new scientific knowledge as the fountainhead from which innovation springs" (p. 802). They determined that

> Interaction with new knowledge or with persons actively engaged in scientific research is essential.
>
> Innovation typically depends on information for which the requirements cannot be anticipated in definitive terms....

The function of basic research in the innovative process can often be described as meaningful dialogue between the scientific and the technological communities. (p. 804)

Despite this early analysis, the linear model persists. Kline (1985) reported that it "continues to underlie the thinking in many current speeches and much writing" (p. 36); Wise (1985) prepared an extended essay to refute the oversimplified assembly-line model "favored by the policy makers" (p. 229); and Likins (1992) observed that the failure of the linear model raises fundamental questions about the role of government support of research.

Even if there is not a producer-consumer relationship between science and technology, they are clearly different. The historian Layton (1971) calls them mirror-image twins.

While the two communities [in the 19th century] shared many of the same values, they reversed their rank order. In the physical sciences the highest prestige went to the most abstract and general—that is to the mathematical theorists.... In the technology community the successful designer or builder ranked highest, the "mere" theorist the lowest. These differences are inherent in the ends pursued by the two communities: scientists seek to know, technologists to do. These two values influence not only the status of occupational specialists, but the nature of the work done and the "language" in which the work is expressed. (p. 576)

In the 19th century technology was characterized by a problem-solving orientation that relied on the use of relatively informal methods; in part, this reflected the technologists' training. The coupling of science and technology in the 20th century, however, established uniform levels of rigor; it has encouraged "engineers to adopt a self-image based on science" (p. 579). Although the resulting dominance of "engineering science" may have had some deleterious social effects (Layton 1971) and impacted the ability to design effectively (Ferguson 1977, 1992), many of the distinctions between science and technology have vanished. As will be shown in the following section, scientific and technical knowledge are quite similar. The debate on: Is technology applied science? Is the distinction between the two losing its relevance? (See Gutting 1984.)

3.3. Technological Knowledge

Rachael Laudan (1984a) observed that there are three basic reasons why technology change is not treated as knowledge change (analogous to scientific change). First, much of the knowledge is "tacit" and not subject to formal representation; second, the knowledge often is viewed as an application of scientific knowledge; and, third, the complexity of the analytic units makes the study difficult. As a result, science is perceived as "know-what" and technology as "know-how." Yet the process of science is based on technology. (Indeed, science often benefits more from technology than technology does from science.) The difference is not in what is known or how it represented; rather, it is in the goals. Science, which aims at producing descriptive models of phenomena, is a process of discovery and explanation. Technology, on the other hand, is intended to produce useful artifacts; it is a design activity. Discovery is bound to the external phenomena it investigates; design is free to produce solutions within the constraints imposed by the physical environment, the social context, and the current state of knowledge. Although both discovery and design are forms of problem solving, the freedom of design (including the absence of any possibility of verification) affects its conduct.

Design begins with an interpretation of a need and culminates with the construction of an artifact that responds to the need. There is a reliance on subjective judgement. "In specific cases it can be shown that technologists display a plastic, geometrical, and to some extent nonverbal mode of thought that has more in common with that of artists than of philosophers" (Layton 1974, p. 36). In his history of the steamboat and the telegraph, Hindle (1981) points out that both Fulton and Morse had been trained as artists. Morse sought "to discover only enough of the principles involved to design a good, working system. The primary strength he brought to the telegraph was an excellent capability based upon a mind practiced in forming and re-forming multiple elements into varying complexes. This sort of synthetic-spacial thinking is required in its most unalloyed form in painting or in sculpture where analytic, logical, verbal, or arithmetic thinking plays almost no role" (p. 93). Ferguson (1992) refers to the "mind's eye" and observes, "Visual thinking is necessary in engineering. A major portion of engineering information is recorded and transmitted in a visual language that is in effect the *lingua franca* of engineers in the modern world" (p. 41). Henderson (1991) has documented the impact on problem solving and communication when a CAD/CAM device replaces these natural devices. This is the tacit knowledge of technology.

Obviously, the process of design relies heavily on noncomputational problem solving. However, the mind's eye also plays a very important role in a scientist's problem solving. For instance, the Nobel laureate Feynman stated that he saw the letters in Bessel functions in different colors (1988, p. 59). Thus, there is a dimension of our problem solving mechanisms that defies exact representation or easy explanation. We do not think with mathematical or logical precision; nevertheless, science formalizes its conclusions as if we did. Technology also uses formal representations, but its problem solutions are always realized as working artifacts. Science addresses questions identified within a paradigm shared by a focused community, whereas technology responds to a broader audience. "Artifactual design is a social activity directed at a practical set of goals intended to serve human beings in some direct way" (Vincenti 1990, p. 11). Technology's products are evaluated by its intended users. Where science aims at the discovery of universal truths, technology accepts those truths as the boundary conditions for its designs. Of course, the division between the two is not quite so simple. Science relies on design to support its discovery, and technology engages in discovery to improve its designs. Thus, it should not surprise us to find that there is no clear demarcation between the scientific and the technological.

Both science and technology are products of human creativity. At one level there is what Hesse calls instrumental progress; outside this context, however, neither is inherently progressive. We produce and evaluate within a paradigm or a social environment, and the goals and evaluation criteria exist only within that setting. The historian Staudenmaier (1985) observes, "The human fabric is not simply an envelope around a culturally neutral artifact. The values and world views, the intelligence and stupidity, the biases and vested interests of those who design, accept, and maintain a technology are embedded in the technology itself.... Contextualism and the myth of autonomous progress are at odds because the progress myth assumes value-free method divorced from every context and because it assumes one inevitable line of advance hindered only by those who violate the purity of the method and attempt to stop progress thorough value-laden subjective critique" (pp. 165-66).

These words are as valid for science as they are for technology. Barnes (1982) depicts the evolving perception of science and technology in a model, which is partially displayed in Figure 3.1. The model suggests that science and technology differ only to the extent that their objectives differ. As Wise (1985) notes, "Treating science and technology as separate spheres of knowledge, both manmade, appears to fit the historical record better than treating science as revealed knowledge and technology as a collection of artifacts once constructed by trial and error but now constructed by applying science" (p. 244).

Following Wise's orientation, we need to examine how knowledge in science and technology differ. Reference already has been made to tacit knowledge, which typically is gained by training, apprenticeship, and experience. Tacit knowledge is found in both science and technology (e.g., postdoctoral training may be seen as a form of scientific apprenticeship whose goal is to build tacit knowledge, not to accumulate further scientific knowledge).

Institutions Compared	"Bad Old Days"	Present

Forms of Activity	S Discovery
	  Creation of Knowledge
	
	T Application
	  Use of Knowledge
		S Invention
		
		S Invention

Major Resources	S Nature T Science	S Existing science T Existing technology

Major Constraints on Results	S State of nature
	
	T State of technology
		S No single major
		  constraint
		T No single major
		  constraint

Forms of Cognition	S Creative/constructive T Routine/deductive	S Creative/constructive T Creative/constructive

Fig. 3.1. The relationship between science and technology.
Reprinted from Barnes (1982) with permission, ©1982, SAGE.

Beyond this tacit knowledge is a rigorous form of knowledge, generally referred to as *engineering science*. Engineering science is not a substitute for tacit knowledge; it is the scientific analysis of concepts (as opposed to phenomena) of interest to engineers. Vincenti (1990) illustrates this distinction with a series of books on thermodynamics published by a physics professor between 1925 to 1966. Though developed for use by both physics and engineering students, the first books contained only two pages about flow processes and only an elementary discussion of control volume. In 1966 the physics professor coauthored a derivative book with an engineer. Intended for the use in the engineering curricula, it contained a chapter on "Applications of Thermodynamics to Engineering Systems" in which the concept of control volume was introduced.

A subsequent volume, written without the coauthor and again directed to physics students, omitted this material. The discussion of flow control was not useful to physicists, who are interested, for the most part, in understanding and predicting the properties of matter. With nontrivial flows, the physicist needs a level of detail that would be impractical for the engineer, and control-volume analysis would not be of help. Yet, despite the crudeness of the model for analyzing physical phenomena, control-volume analysis creates an excellent conceptual framework for solving the kinds of problems that confront the engineer.

The model is no less "scientific" than those used by physicists. The difference is that the physicists' models provide insight into external phenomena, whereas the engineers' models manage concepts appropriate for the design process (within its economic and reliability constraints). Both physics and engineering science are discovery processes; the former is concerned with the natural phenomena of interest to the scientific community, and the latter concentrates on manmade and natural phenomena as they affect the artifacts to be designed. There is no division between the two categories of knowledge, and both disciplines engage in design. For science, it is design for discovery, and for technology it is discovery for design. Mirror-image twins.

I close the discussion with an examination of how technological knowledge is accumulated. I begin by observing that technological innovation may be free of new scientific input. For instance, Vincenti (1984) illustrated this with a study of flush riveting in American airplanes from 1930 to 1950. During that period, improvements in airplane performance had made the drag caused by rivets enough of a factor to justify their replacement by flush rivets. The potential benefits of the change were broadly recognized, and the transition ultimately was accomplished by a "welling up from below simultaneously throughout the industry" (p. 571). In this instance, many individuals evolved personalized solutions to a shared problem. Standardization came later. By way of contrast, there is the more popular, and less common, model of the inventor who applies technology (or a new scientific discovery) to create a new class of artifact. In both cases, the process begins with the formulation of a problem followed by the generation of new technological knowledge created as the problem is solved.

Rachael Laudan (1984b) identifies four kinds of problems that challenge technologists:

Given by the environment. These problems exist within the environment and have no solutions within the current technology. Such problems are seldom resolved; rather, they often are accommodated by social "fixes" (e.g., society learns to live with the rains that bring floods).

Functional failure. Here the existing technology has been extended beyond what it can support, and a new technology is required.

Extrapolation. Problems are identified for which solutions can be extrapolated from past technological successes.

Imbalances. The relative imbalance between related technologies in a given period are often perceived as technological problems that require improvements to one or more of the interfacing technologies.

Another motivation for change is *presumptive anomaly*, a term introduced by Constant (1980) to describe the result of an analysis that identifies inherent problems in an existing technology. It "occurs in technology, not when the conventional system fails in any absolute or objective sense, but when assumptions derived from science indicate either that under some future conditions the conventional system will fail ... or that a radically different system will do a much better job. No functional failure exists; an anomaly is presumed to exist; hence presumptive anomaly" (p. 15). Finally, Vincenti (1990) identified three problem sources that emerged strictly within a technology: (1) the internal logic of the technology, which mandates how certain things must be done, (2) the internal needs of the design, which includes the context of use, and (3) the need for decreased uncertainty.

Notice that in each of these categories, the problem need originates from either a social context or the existing technology. Science may support technological improvement or the identification of presumptive anomalies, but technology's problem-solving mission resists the acceptance of new scientific knowledge as a solution mechanism in search of a problem; that is, technology exploits scientific knowledge, but it is not driven by it. Vincenti (1990) observes that engineering knowledge usually is taken to mean the knowledge used by the engineers, whereas scientific knowledge is taken to be the knowledge discovered by the scientist. As we have seen, however, there is engineering knowledge that is distinct from scientific knowledge, and the primary difference between the two is in content and intent, not quality or complexity. Vincenti identifies seven knowledge-generating activities in engineering: (1) transfer from science, (2) invention, (3) theoretical engineering research, (4) experimental engineering research, (5) design practice, (6) production, and (7) direct trial. The list would require little modification to become descriptive of the knowledge-generation activities in science. This basic symmetry between the two mirror-image twins is shown in Figure 3.2 taken from Vincenti. It shows a continuum of science and technology with a large domain of shared knowledge that is both created and used by these twins. Notice that replacing the terms *scientists* and *engineers* with, say, *physicists* and *chemists* does not affect the diagram's validity.

3.4. Modeling Reality

The discussion up to this point has been reportorial. I have tried to organize the contributions of philosophers, historians, and the others who have written about science and technology to provide an accurate overview of current thinking. My goal has been to portray the understandings shared by those who have studied these issues in detail.

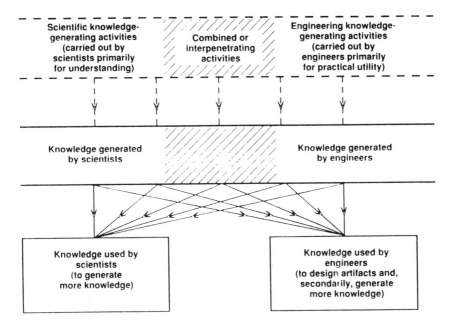

Fig. 3.2. Diagram of knowledge and its generating activities.
Reprinted from Vincenti (1990) with permission, ©1990 Johns Hopkins.

Obviously, I have been selective in my reporting, and often I have been unable to resolve the differences. For example, Kuhn's historical analysis freed science from the formal structure implied by the Received View, but it also opened the philosophy of science to many alternative interpretations and models. For the purposes of this book, it is sufficient to recognize that the perceptions of science that dominated mid-20th century thinking now are difficult to justify, even though there may be no agreement about the replacement model. Similarly, we should recognize that the traditional demarcation between science and technology is less clear than we might have believed several decades earlier.

A careful reading of what has been written since 1960 leaves no doubt about these conclusions. But now I go beyond realm of careful reporting and into the area of personal speculation. In this section I apply what I have documented in the construction of a personal view of science, technology, and reality. I am neither a philosopher nor a historian; I am motivated by a search for a resolution to the central problem of software engineering: how to create a software solution (in-the-computer) to an identified problem (in-the-world). I do not claim that I am correct in my interpretation of science and technology; I only assert that this is what I believe and, moreover, that these beliefs provide the foundation for my approach to resolving the central tension of the software process.

I begin with the assertion that the goal of science is to produce models of reality. These models represent knowledge of the universe (i.e., reality). I recognize that this is only a limited view of science. Rachael Laudan (1984a) observes,

> Traditionally science was thought of as a set of propositions, a collection of theories—a characterization that emphasized its distance and distinctness from technology. More recently, emphasis has been placed on science as an activity, as a process by which scientists come to acquire knowledge. (p. 15)

Churchman (1971) also points out that the view of scientific knowledge as an organized collection of theories is too narrow a concept. "Knowledge is a vital force that makes an enormous difference in the world. Simply to say that it is a storage of sentences is to ignore all that this difference amounts to. In other words, knowledge resides in the user and not in the collection" (p. 10). Clearly, then, the models of which I speak are only a part of the scientific enterprise. Nevertheless, they are the products of the process, and they constitute the most complete description of our perception of reality.

When I speak of models of reality, I do not restrict myself to the narrow instrumental view of formal mathematical or logical models. Theories should be both explanatory and computationally useful (e.g., predictive). There is a mirror-image relationship that ties together the descriptive theory with its instrument; neither image is independent of the other. By convention, most scientific instruments are expressed mathematically. Barwise (1989) offers the following observation about the mathematical formulation and the reality it mimics:

> The axiomatic method says that our theorems are true *if* our axioms are. The modeling method says that our theorems model facts in the domain modeled *if* there is a close enough fit between the model and the domain modeled.... As a philosopher might say, applied mathematics may not guarantee knowledge of facts about the physical world, but it can lead to the next best thing—justified true belief. (p. 847)

That is, there is a distinction between the physical world and our mathematical models of it. The axiomatic method preserves correctness within each model, but the model itself is independent of the facts in the domain modeled. Barwise defines the *Fallacy of Identification* to be the failure to distinguish between some mathematical model and the thing of which it is a model. In other words, the model is not the reality.

Popper (1974/1987) employs a three-level model to distinguish reality from our knowledge of it. "World 1" is the physical world, and "world 2" is the knowledge of "world 1" brought to us through the senses and brain, a form of knowledge that we share with some animals. "But the characteristic thing about specifically human knowledge— *science*—is that it is formulated in a descriptive and argumentative language, and that the problems, theories, and errors which are embedded in this language stand in their own peculiar relations, constituting what I call 'world 3'" (p. 116). For Popper, world 3 is "knowledge *writ large*," and refutation is used to purge the fallacy of identification.

Hoyningen-Huene (1993) describes Kuhn's philosophy in terms of a two-level model. There is the *world-in-itself*, which is unknowable, and hence empirically inaccessible. There also is the "scientist's world" or the world in which scientific work was done. Hoyningen-Huene calls this the *phenomenal world*; it is "a world already perceptually and conceptually subdivided in a certain way" (Kuhn 1970, p. 129). The phenomenal world is an expression of the world-in-itself as filtered by the paradigm of normal science. Scientific revolutions bring new models of the phenomenal world into being, but the world-in-itself remains invariant.

Obviously, there is a distinction between reality, which is unknowable, and our models of it: the human knowledge of world 3, the normal science of the phenomenal world, or the justified true belief of our axiom-derived theorems. My intuition is that we permit our models of reality to be dominated by the tools that we use for model building, thereby constraining us to relatively narrow interpretations of the world-in-itself. For instance, the concept of a hierarchy (along with the associated top-down orientation) permeates our perceptions of reality. Vincenti (1990) finds numerous kinds of hierarchy in engineering. "The relationship between systems and devices is clearly hierarchical. So also is the relationship between problems *for* and problems *within* such technologies" (p. 205). Obviously, physical units, which must interconnect in three-dimensional space, must be decomposable hierarchically. Must the same be true for problems? Ideas? Theories? Simon (1969/1981) would seem to say yes.

> If there are important systems in the world that are complex without being hierarchic, they may to a considerable extent escape our observation and understanding. Analysis of their behavior would involve such detailed knowledge of their elementary parts that it would be beyond our capacities of memory or computation.
> I shall not try to settle which is chicken and which is egg: whether we are able to understand the world because it is

hierarchic or whether it appears hierarchic because those aspects of it which are not elude our understanding and observation. (p. 219)

There are many reasons to favor hierarchical constructions. First, all mathematical models must be developed (or at least proven) in a top-down, hierarchical manner. One starts with the axioms and derives from them theorems, and from those theorems further theorems. There is a logic imposed by the process that does not allow parallelism. Second, all sequential processes can be structured as a hierarchy. In particular, all traces of a time-oriented process define a hierarchy. (That is, even if a process is nondeterministic and asynchronous, every instance of it will produce a hierarchical trace.) Every linear listing without repetition forms a hierarchy (e.g., its outline). Finally, all physical entities can be decomposed hierarchically. Still, hierarchies are relatively rare in nature. The duck-billed platypus illustrates the difficulty we have in defining a hierarchical classification for vertebrates, and the growing use of DNA as a taxonomic analysis tool is generating even more questions regarding species derivation. By way of further example, it is common to subdivide the human body into systems: respiratory, digestive, circulatory, and so on. But these are not independent modules with well-defined interfaces that can be composed to produce an organism. Indeed, some of the most interesting challenges come at the "system" interfaces. Thus, I conclude that we rely on a reductionist approach (also called the separation of concerns) because we lack the tools to express our solutions *holistically*. The resulting dependence on a hierarchical structure for knowledge can hide critical properties of an object being modeled, thereby denying us important information. Fortunately, alternative models are feasible.

For instance, Bechtel (1988a), writing on the philosophy of science from a cognitive perspective, speaks of parallel distributed processing systems (PDP, also known as connectionist systems). These systems are built of very simple units connected to each other; units activate or inhibit each other, and the behavior of the system is determined totally by these local operations. "In PDP systems, the overall task is not the result of performing component tasks that are characterizable from the perspective of the overall cognitive task and so one cannot decompose the system into component cognitive operations in order to explain it" (p. 109). In fact, a PDP system violates the decompositional principle upon which the more traditional mechanistic systems are based. Thus, if the reality of cognition is based on parallel distributed processing, then this property cannot be expressed in hierarchical models of the cognitive tasks. Although mechanistic systems provide useful models of reality, they cannot scale up to create a model of a PDP system, *if that is a valid representation of reality*. I do not assert that the PDP represents a better model of reality. I simply comment that computer technology (with its ability to employ parallel distributed processes) offers an opportunity to explore *holistic* models that can deal with more complexity than the traditional *hierarchical* models. That is, computer technology affords us an opportunity to experiment with new modeling paradigms—a facility that one day may be recognized as its greatest contribution.

In summary, then, even though reality is unknowable, we ought always to pursue richer modeling tools that provide more comprehensive insights. I find the following analogy helpful. Assume the reality we are attempting to model exists in some space of high dimensionality, and we can observe this reality only through projections onto a smaller number of dimensions. The underdetermination of observation will be a consequence of our inability to reconstruct the higher dimensional space from its projection. Moreover, various projections of the same phenomenon might appear different within the lower dimensional observation space; one could expect consistency only within fixed contexts. In this situation, each model would have to consider what was left out (i.e., what could not be represented in the lower dimensioned space) as well as what was being perceived. Thus, to be concrete, we should recognize that every hierarchy is but a one-dimensional projection of reality (i.e., every hierarchy can be transformed into a linear sequence of symbols). This will make us more cautious in our reliance on top-down methods and constraining structures. Furthermore, if we accept *modus tollens* and the principle of refutation, then we can train ourselves to identify what is incorrect (or the context within which it is incorrect). Because we can only be certain about error, we must train ourselves to reduce the model space by ruling out. Finally, if we concede that knowledge always exists within a *context* (i.e., a complex set of preconditions), then we should routinely explore both the nature of the model and the context in which it is valid. As the psychoanalyst Frankl (1985) stated,

> We must remain aware of the fact that as long as absolute truth is not accessible to us (and it never will be), relative truths have to function as mutual collectives. Approaching the one truth from various sides, sometimes in opposite directions, we cannot attain it, but we may at least encircle it. (p. xiii)

3.5. Scientific and Technological Models

The fact that science can provide only imperfect models of reality comes as no surprise; it is consistent with current thinking in the philosophy of science. Now to consider how the scientific models relate to those of technology. To begin with, the technologists' models are perceived to be of a less important sort: less abstract, not as general. In Layton's mirror-image twins metaphor, the scientist seeks to know and the technologist to do. Implicit in this division is the greater honor afforded to the seeker of knowledge. This value judgement is found in the descriptions of computer scientists and software engineers previously quoted from Shaw and from Jensen and Tonies.

This elevation of science has led us to confuse science with technology. Prestigious technology is called science; rigorous methodology is praised as "good science." For instance, in October 1993 the Jet Propulsion Laboratory abandoned its attempts to contact the Mars Observer, thereby ending a decade of commitment by teams of scientific investigators. One billion dollars had been spent, but had any "scientific knowledge" been gained? Not really. The first (and most expensive) phase of the Mars Observer was an instrument-building activity—technology. The second (aborted) phase was to have been one of data collection and scientific discovery. Similarly, each Space Shuttle flight promotes its engineering as science; the 11 billion dollars for the Superconducting Supercollider would have been spent largely on technology for scientific investigation. In contrast, the money allocated for the Human Genome project is used for data gathering and analysis. Does that imply that "genetic engineering" is science, or have the labels simply ceased to retain their meaning? I believe the latter is the case.

The design of a scientific experiment is technology, and the development of a complex device draws upon science. Although mirror-image twins was an appropriate characterization for the communities of science and technology in 19th century America (which was the topic of Layton's 1971 paper), the communities are merging in the 20th century. The demarcation between scientific and nonscientific knowledge also has become murky. Therefore I propose that we accept that much of today's science is, in reality, technology, and vice versa. Thus, it may be more accurate to speak of discovery activities and design activities. The discovery activities are intended to gain knowledge (i.e., building models). That knowledge may be about real-world phenomena, or it may be about human-made artifacts (in which case we call the discovery an invention).

Often, discovery is motivated by a search for knowledge about some real-world phenomena within a human-defined context. There is a continuum from the properties of matter (physics) to the strength of materials (engineering science) to the design of a building (architecture, which combines the technical with the aesthetic). While it may be useful to separate design from discovery, we should recognize that this is an abstraction of convenience. Most activities involve both design (creation) and discovery (learning). The mirror-image twins metaphor implies two views of a single entity: seeking and doing, discovering and designing. Thus, discovery for design adds to our knowledge in the same way as science is perceived to do. That knowledge is not always lasting; as the technology changes (or the paradigms of normal science shift), discovered knowledge can lose its relevance.

This deemphasis of the distinctions between science and technology implies that models used for one may be used for the other. Nevertheless, there remain some important social and policy issues that are predicated on a clear demarcation between science and technology. For instance, to what extent should society support undirected research? That is, should discovery be constrained to operate within a specified design context? Campbell's blind-variation-and-selective-retention would argue against this. Evolution advances knowledge through blind variation. Although undirected research may be costly and wasteful, reliance on directed research restricts science to puzzle solving within the current paradigm. Blindness leads both to new scientific understandings (Kuhn 1970) and new invention (Vincenti 1990), and it would be wrong to constrain it.

Secondly, there is the question of society's obligation to invest in science and technology. If we recognize that much of discovery entails the learning of what already is known (perhaps to be used in different ways), then there is a strong justification for our research universities. At its best, an environment that fosters discovery/design creates practitioners who can excel at discovery/design. There are many who question how well our institutions achieve this ideal (e.g., Runkle 1991, Dijkstra 1989, Parnas 1990, and Denning 1992a), but such self-criticism should not be misconstrued as an abandonment of the goal's validity. The rejection of the linear model that links science and technology does not negate the sound arguments for undirected research and a deep commitment to research-based education.

To return to the central theme. I began by stating that the goal of science is to model reality (i.e., to gain knowledge about the phenomenal world), and I have just asserted that there is no clear division between science and technology, between discovery and design. It follows, therefore, that the goal of science/technology extends to modeling what exists independent of humanity (which includes humanity as a component of the environment) and also to modeling aspects of humanity, such as its artifacts, the process of constructing its artifacts, and so on. By the logic of my argument, we now must model virtually everything. I am not sure that I can accept this challenge, but it will be useful to explore its consequences.

Traditionally, we have taken a narrow view of science and limited it to what could be measured. Falsification requires objectivity, and computational methodology (even more than the scientific method) has come to be the standard by which science is judged. That is why behavioral psychology, which is observable and quantifiable, received such broad acceptance. "Social scientism" sought to extend these tools to provide a comprehensive understanding of human institutions (Matson 1964). This was a period of profound faith in science; a spirit, Staudenmaier (1985) points out, that was captured in the motto of the 1933 Chicago "Century of Progress" International Exposition.

Science Finds, Industry Applies, Man Conforms.

Man is an object to be manipulated, and scientism has the potential to produce the rules for understanding behavior and social institutions. Matson's 1964 book was a cry of protest against this mechanistic view of humanity. The inability of scientism to deliver its promised results has lessened the relevancy of his arguments.

Scientism failed, not because there were no good models of the phenomena and institutions under study, but because the models chosen were too restrictive. Behaviorism could answer some very important questions, but not all (and perhaps not the most important ones). Here again we find a variation of the central tension of the software process: the tension between what we wish to model and the tools available for modeling; what it is important to know and our ability to express that knowledge concretely. Thus, what seems to work for physics may be ineffective for psychology. But the mathematics of physics also can fail us in related technological domains. Reference already has been made to the "mind's eye" (Ferguson 1992) and "synthetic-spacial thinking" (Hindle 1981). Although it is broadly accepted that this is essential knowledge for design and discovery, it is not clear how it can be modeled. Yet, if we do not include such characteristics in our models, then how accurately will our models reflect reality? We are on the horns of a dilemma. We may restrict ourselves to the certainties expressible with mathematics and logic, or we may venture into uncharted waters in the hope of capturing additional properties. There are risks in moving beyond our familiar borders. How we visualize is culturally determined (Deregowsi 1972), and naive models are very persistent (McCloskey 1983). Nevertheless, an excessive dependency on models derived from the laws of physics may mask essential information about the phenomena of interest.

By way of illustration, it is well known that it is possible to produce all colors, including white, by superimposing light projected from three colored sources (red, blue, and green). This basic principle is used in color photography; three superimposed emulsions, each sensitive to one of the three colors, are developed to produce a full-color image. In 1959, however, Land used two different filters to create two separate images of the same subject. He then superimposed the resulting black-and-white transparencies on a screen by projecting them through separate, but identical, yellow beams. Viewers saw the resulting images in full (if unsaturated) color. Land came to "the astonishing conclusion that the rays are not in themselves color-making. Rather they are bearers of information that the eye uses to assign appropriate colors to various objects in an image" (p. 84). Thus, an emphasis on the physical properties of light as demonstrated in the laboratory, although technologically valuable, may provide little insight into human vision (Gibson 1979); that is, the physics of light and color does not explain how people perceive color.

Barwise and Perry (1983) speak of an "ecological realism" that finds meaning in the interaction of living things and their environment.

> It sometimes happens in science that the vocabulary of a particular theory becomes so ingrained that the science starts confusing the empirical data with its theory-laden description. If the categories of theory cut across the grain of actual phenomena, then artificial problems are created, problems whose solutions cannot be given until a new framework is adopted. (p. xi)

Their goal is to produce a theory of linguistic meaning that goes beyond what can be developed with the available modeling tools. For them, the heritage of model theory is a mixed blessing. "The founders of modern logic ... were preoccupied with the language of mathematics. Because of this preoccupation, many assumptions and attitudes about this language were built into the very heart of model theory, and so came to be assumptions about the very nature of language itself" (p. 28).

What we traditionally have viewed as science relies on mathematics. The Received View assumed that all scientific knowledge could be modeled with mathematics and logic; furthermore, what could not be so modeled was not scientific knowledge. But the above-mentioned examples have shown that mathematics and logic have a limited repertoire for modeling what is important. The two-valued logic of T and F is too crude an instrument for capturing the subtleties of reality. Codd (1990) has moved to a three-valued logic for the relational model, and Minsky (1975) long ago decried the limitations of logic.

> Traditional formal logic is a technical tool for discussing either *everything that can be deduced from some data* or *whether a certain consequence can be so deduced*; it cannot discuss at all what *ought* to be deduced under ordinary circumstances....
>
> I cannot state strongly enough my conviction that the preoccupation with Consistency, so valuable for Mathematical Logic, has been incredibly destructive to those working on models of mind.... At the intellect-modeling level it has blocked the fundamental realization that *thinking begins first with*

suggestive but defective plans and images that are slowly (if ever) refined and replaced by better ones. (Minsky 1975, p. 128)

It follows, therefore, that if we seek rich models of reality (i.e., knowledge), we will be forced to go beyond the modeling tools that constitute the greatest investment in our scientific armory.

Figure 3.3 depicts a two-dimensional models-of-reality space. This is not a very elegant model of a model space. It looks like a bounded two-dimensional Euclidean space, but that is not my intent. There is no order nor any sense of closeness; minor modifications to a model may have a major impact on its location within that space. The unsatisfactory nature of this model of models-of-reality illustrates my premise that sometimes one cannot represent a concept clearly. (A weak excuse!) Perhaps if I tried longer, I would have more success. In any case, I trust that the reader now understands what the figure is not meant to imply.

The figure's vertical dimension is one of representation. At the bottom are the *computational* representations that have well-defined syntaxes and operations. The mathematics and logic of traditional science rely on this form of representation. I have labeled the opposite extreme of representation *ideational*, a word intended to convey the ability to capture a concept. There is no strict ordering of representations, and computational representations, of course, do capture concepts. Nevertheless, as I use the terms here: Computational representations must be objective, formal, and unambiguous; ideational representations must not have those properties (i.e., they must be subjective, conceptual, and contain ambiguity). (Notice that ambiguity can be an asset in a representation; it is a form of underdetermination that specifies a class of instantiations that satisfy the representation.) All representations, both computational and ideational, must have a permanent expression. For example, sketches and drawings begin as ideational representations; it is possible that they will be refined into complete drawings, in which case they will be computational representations (i.e., formal and unambiguous).

The horizontal dimension of the figure classifies the phenomena being modeled. To the left are *bound* phenomena, and to the right are *free* phenomena. Bound phenomena provide an external reality against which to test the model. The physical laws of motion are bound to the reality of matter in motion. Free phenomena, on the other hand, lack the ability to provide the feedback necessary to validate the model. For example, processes are free; they may be modeled, but the resulting model will describe how the process *has behaved* in the past, not how it *must behave* in the future. Depending on the representation used, the same phenomena may have models that are bound or free. A bound model, of course, is one that serves as an accurate descriptor/predictor

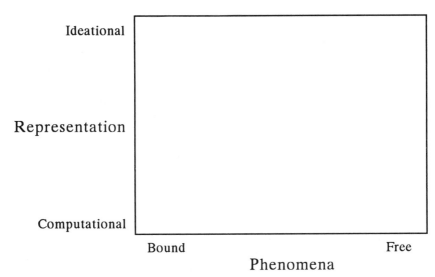

Fig. 3.3. Models-of-reality space.

and that does not impact the phenomena modeled.

Science and art normally are placed at opposite corners of this space. Science relies on computational representations for bound phenomena, and art explores ideational representations (e.g., images, words, sounds) for free phenomena (e.g., thoughts, emotions, sensations). The professionalization of science has boxed the scientific disciplines into the lower left corner, a fact that has led Bickart, an environmental chemist, to define the term *physics envy* as "the belief that employing the mathematical methodology of the physical sciences will enhance the reputation of one's own field." However, as much of the earlier discussion has shown, although this mathematical methodology may be well suited for the phenomena it originally was intended to model, it clearly is limited. Consequently, we must acknowledge that if we restrict ourselves to one corner of this space, there is much that we will not be able to model, and many properties of the phenomena modeled will not be captured. Moreover, we also must recognize that the use of a computational representation does not imply that the model is bound to the phenomena. Consider, for example, Lindley's (1993) earlier questions about the quest for a "theory of everything." What, he asks, "is the use of a theory that looks attractive but contains no additional power of prediction, and makes no statements that can be tested? Does physics then become a branch of aesthetics?" (p. 20) Where in the models-of-reality space would such a theory fit if it could be found?

Thus, we can conclude that science has already escaped from the box in the lower left. Is it possible, then, to cover this models-of-reality space by a fish-scale model of omniscience? I doubt it. To do so would imply that a highly dimensioned reality can be projected onto a plane. Although flat maps approximate small portions of the Earth's surface, a complete representation is not possible within the constraints of two dimensions; information is lost with each projection. Similarly, I believe that reality is far too complex to be portrayed within a uniform structure. At best, we may be able to find deep understanding only within constrained contexts, and we may accept the fact that deep knowledge developed for one class of problems may be of little direct value for a different, if related, class of problems.

We also can ask if this space can be organized according to Abrahamsen's (1987) specialization hierarchy for scientific disciplines, in which the physical sciences act as the foundation for the biological sciences, which, in turn, support the behavioral sciences upon which rest the cultural domains of mathematics, engineering science, the humanities, and the social sciences? Again, I do not think so. Recall Quine's comment that the ability to know everything about the physiology of a speaker of a foreign language will produce no understanding of the speaker's beliefs. True, human beings are made up of atoms, but we have long ago given up Laplace's notion that human behavior is predetermined by the state and organization of those atoms. (As software reengineering has taught us, a complete knowledge of the program's object code provides limited insight into the operation of the program.) Using the high-dimensional space analogy, the physical makeup of an individual and that individual's behavior are but two of many possible projections of a single unified system; information clarified in one projection will be hidden in the other.

The idea of a models-of-reality space opens new territories to exploration. I believe that we have come to rely too heavily on a reductionist approach in which we use the ability to model mathematically as the principal criterion for scientific study. In a holistic universe, science cannot be separated from technology, and art is integrated with technology (and hence, in a more limited way, with science). To deny the role of art in science and technology is to excise the essence of what is human in our search for knowledge. Aristotle observed,

> Now since architecture is an art and is essentially a reasoned state of capacity to make, and there is neither any art that is not such a state nor any such state that is not an art, *art* is identical with a state of capacity to make, involving a true course of reasoning. (From *Nicomachean Ethics*, cited in Layton 1974, p. 33)

Thus, technology is included in Aristotle's term *art*, and design cannot be independent of art. Pye (1978), an architect and industrial designer, points out that "whenever humans design and make a useful thing they invariably expend a great deal of unnecessary and easily avoidable work on it which contributes nothing to its usefulness" (p. 13). Examples are workmanship, design for appearance, and decoration. There is a "pattern of which all men at all times and places have followed: doing useless work on useful things" (p. 13) What is useless, however, is not without value; consider how dreary life would be if it were dominated by "utility." "Of all devices designed for use it may be said that they are intended to get some result which was not there before.... There is a distinction between the result of a device's being and the purpose of it" (p. 15). "The fact that every device when used produces concrete, measurable, objective results, is the only sure basis for a theory of design. Any concept such as 'function' which includes the idea of purpose is bound to have an unsafe foundation; for the purpose leaves commonplace factual affairs like results far behind" (p. 16). "Everything everywhere may be regarded as a component of a system. It is fruitless to consider the action of a thing without considering the system of which it is a component. This fact has a special importance for designers in various fields because they tend to think of things separately and to design them separately" (p. 17). Thus, design—and by extension, all creative activities—merge art and science/technology within the (holistic) context of a larger system. We cannot isolate the "science" and the "art" components of our technology, and we cannot apply scientific knowledge without doing "useless" work.

> No matter how vigorously a "science" of design may be pushed, the successful design of real things in a contingent world will always be based more on art than on science. Unquantifiable judgments and choices are the elements that determine the way a design comes together. Engineering design is simply that kind of process. It always has been; it always will be. (Ferguson 1992, p. 194.)

We may conclude, therefore, that models of reality cannot ignore the models of the upper right corner, those of the free phenomena for which we have only ideational representations. Now to consider the remaining corners of the space. For bound phenomena, the challenge is to find effective representations. Barwise and Perry (1983) have developed a representation for capturing semantics (see also Fodor 1987, Barwise 1989), and Gibson (1979) is working to find richer ways for representing problems in human vision. Although the phenomena characterizations may lack the formality of mathematics, we must study what is important rather than just what can be measured. With diligence and time, representation schemes will be created that improve the computation (and hence the value) of the models of these bound phenomena. Free phenomena for which there exist computational representations offer a very different challenge.

Free phenomena tend to be dynamic, whereas their models tend to be static. For instance, a political model may be able to predict outcomes or preferences accurately. That model, of course, will have been validated for a specific culture within a given time frame, and it will lose its validity as that culture evolves. The model of a free phenomena also may affect the behavior of the phenomena it models. For instance, if the culture accepts the model as a guide for its actions, then the model will direct the behavior as it describes or predicts behavior. This interdependence between the phenomena and its model can be illustrated with a software engineering example. Cost models are based on evaluations of previous experience. The COCOMO model published by Boehm (1981) describes how large software projects were developed in the mid 1970s. If one were to use that model (with its published parameters), it would be possible to structure and manage a software project so that all the cost and schedule goals were met. The result would be, however, the conduct of a software project based on twenty-year-old conventions and technology. The ability to achieve the cost and schedule projections would be the consequence of forcing a free phenomena (i.e., the process of software development) to conform to a fixed model (i.e., program plan derived from the parameters in a 1981 book). As Abdel-Hamid and Madnick (1986) have pointed out, more accurate estimates are not necessarily better estimates and the accuracy of the model as a predictor may be independent of the value of its predictions. Thus, the modeling of free phenomena introduces a perverse kind of fallacy of identification in which *the model becomes the reality*.

The model space shown in Figure 3.3 is undifferentiated. In this book I shall consider only a very special class of model for a very limited domain: that of software engineering. I have entered into this broader discussion for several reasons. First, as I already have made clear, we need to extend beyond our dependence on traditional mathematical models. Second, we should recognize that science and technology—their knowledge and models—are not as different from each other as was previously believed. For any point in the models-of-reality space, the scientist's goal of discovery looks to the left, and the technologist's goal of design looks to the right. In that sense the mirror-image twins have merged, and we end up with complementary views of a single holistic entity. Finally, the figure demonstrates that many of our phenomena are free.

For models of a bound phenomena, we can insist that the model be valid (i.e., that it avoids the fallacy of identification). But there are no phenomena to bind computer science, an extension of mathematics and logic. We can verify that there are no errors in a computer science model, but we can never formally validate the model. There is no "natural direction" for computer science to take because it is independent of all bound phenomena. In his Turing Award Lecture, Hartmanis (1994) observes, "The failure of computer science to conform to the paradigms of physical sciences is often interpreted as immaturity of computer science.... In computer science, results of theory are judged by the insights they reveal.... Do the models conceptualize and capture the aspects computer scientists are interested in, do they yield insights in design problems, do they aid reasoning and communication about relevant problems?" (p. 40).

Thus, computer science can be seen as a set of representations for modeling (and implementing) designs. This is a new and powerful concept; so new and powerful, in fact, that its implications are only beginning to emerge. The goal of this book is to sensitize the reader to the tremendous potential that the freedom of computer technology affords, to illustrate by way of example how we may exploit that potential, and to introduce a new class of relevant problems for computer science to study.

3.6. Science and Free Phenomena

I now turn to the role of science with a free phenomenon, in particular, a science for computer technology. As usual, I begin by casting a wide net. There is a philosophy of technology (Mitcham 1978), but it would not be relevant here. There also is science without technology (e.g., the behavioral and social sciences), and technology independent of science. To add to the complexity, there is no consensus regarding the nature of science. Is science a search for knowledge or a process of problem solving? Is it an aloof observer of Nature or an active factor in the human ecology? Some try to clarify the multiple goals of scientific research by dividing it into two categories: pure and applied. Wright (1978) identifies four viewpoints appropriate for the behavioral sciences. The first, characterized as Baconian (or pure) research, evaluates success only in terms of advances in basic knowledge; the second uses applied research as a starting point for the formulation of basic theories; and the third sees no need for interaction between the pure and applied research.

Wright takes the position that a fourth viewpoint, which fosters the flow of information between the pure and applied scientists, constitutes a very fruitful pattern of interaction. In this case, the applied research studies the reality in an partially controlled, holistic setting, and the pure research examines the reality in the context of a laboratory setting. (Potts (1993) proposes a similar division for software engineering research: the workplace and the laboratory.) These are two different projections of the same phenomena, and the views should complement each other. Yet, as Heisenberg pointed out, the very act of observing affects the phenomena being observed. Furthermore, "social science research changes the phenomena under investigation more than does research in the natural sciences.... Social activity is shaped by culturally shared frameworks of conceptual understanding.... As our concepts and theories are communicated and filter into lay discourse, they reconstitute the very reality they seek to investigate" (Astley 1985, p. 506).

Although it is possible to exclude from science those disciplines that interact with the reality it investigates, we cannot so isolate technology. Its goal is to produce artifacts that are useful to society. Thus, because technology affects science, science cannot be isolated from its social context. Dalbom (1986) considers computerization, which he calls the form of rationalization of our time, the dominating version of the *project of modernity*. "The driving force of this project—the Enlightenment—was a belief of reason, by means of science and technology, to foster progress in all areas of human affairs: knowledge, production, social organization, politics, morals, art, personal happiness, etc." Clearly, there have been successes.   Nevertheless,   he continues, "Positivism in science, mechanization of production, bureaucratization of society, utilitarianism in morals, and nihilistic existentialism are some of the ingredients of our modern, rational world" (p. 17).

Thus, rationality may be necessary, but it is not sufficient. Judgment,   values,   and   humanity—all   of   which   are   inherently subjective—are essential ingredients in the scientific process. The point is not, of course, that one can be trained to understand the proper role of the subjective; rather it is that no technical decisions can be free of the subjective.   The idea of a rational technology is as valid as a pronouncement of the Received View. It is for this reason that I prefer to speak of the processes of discovery and design. Each is a human activity that draws upon our knowledge of reality. A concern for these processes permits us to ignore the complexity of the demarcation between science and technology.

Still, *SCIENCE* has held a very special position in the 20th century. I already have observed that large engineering projects are labeled scientific. Similarly, scholars engaged in the study of free phenomena characterize their quest for truth and understanding as "science." For example, Mitroff (1972) sees a "stereotyped image of science" in the Operations Research Society of America (ORSA) Guidelines published in *Operations Research*:

> Since operations research is a science and the practice of OR
> is to be carried out in a scientific spirit, we shall present the
> relevant characteristics of science....

First, the method of science is open, explicit, ... [and the results] verifiable....

Second, [the] scientific method is objective. (cited p. B-613)

This, retorts Mitroff, is a myth. A fairytale description of science. "It is far from clear that scientists *should be* always unbiased, rational, and unemotional *in their role as scientists.... If the scientist QUA SCIENTIST is not a staunch partisan ADVOCATE for his theories, hypotheses, and positions they may be too readily ignored or not taken seriously by the surrounding scientific community*" (p. B-614). This position is consistent with Lakatos's support for a budding programme. Mitroff also introduces the subjective into science. "It is too simple to say that the process or system of science is either totally objective or totally subjective; it is a highly complicated mixture of the two" (p. B-615). He refers to Hudson's (1966) classification of two kinds of conceptualizers: *convergers*, who are analytical and "parts" oriented, and *divergers*, who are synthetic and "whole systems" oriented. He comments that most scientists tend to converge, most arts and humanities students tend to diverge, and that both types are indispensable for the continued advancement of science.

The science of operations research is similar to that of computer science. Both are involved with the representations used in the creation of models. For operations research, the models are mathematical descriptions of organizational processes; for computer science, they are logical models related to computer operations. In each case, the science centers on the model formalisms; the activity of phenomena modeling is an application of the science. Thus, it might be reasonable to label them fields of philosophy (in the sense of logic) rather than disciplines of science (in the sense of physics). However, both sets of practitioners consider themselves scientists, and we must honor their wishes.

Similarly, there has been considerable discussion of the scientific nature of management information systems (MIS). Can it have a scientific base, and if yes, what should the nature of that science be? Banville and Landry (1989) suggest that the presence of journals, organizational colloquia, and other such manifestations are clear evidence of the desire to have MIS accepted as a scientific discipline. But they find that MIS is "a fragmented field or, to put it in other words, an essentially pluralistic scientific field, especially in view of its vocational character" (p. 58). Consequently, they do not believe that a science based upon a single unifying paradigm would be valid for MIS. "It is now widely recognized that the production of scientific knowledge is an endeavor that is simultaneously cognitive and social" (p. 52). Thus, they reject Kuhn's model of science in favor of Whitley's sociology of science.

Whitley (1984) states that intellectual fields are "the social contexts in which scientists develop distinctive competencies and research skills so that they make sense of their own actions in terms of these collective identities, goals and practices as mediated by leaders of employment organizations and other major social influences" (p. 8). Here we have a shift from epistemology, the knowledge that constitutes science, to sociology, the social context in which the knowledge is discovered and used. Whitley identifies three variables that can be used to stratify intellectual fields: functional dependence, strategic dependence, and strategic task uncertainty. The fact that the intellectual field is based on scientific knowledge is secondary; the classification scheme might be equally valid for other fields, such as the humanities.

Banville and Landry believe that MIS is best characterized as a *fragmented adhocracy* (low strategic dependence, high strategic task uncertainty, and low functional dependence). This model permits many strands of maturation and of progress. Diversity, therefore, is accepted. MIS researchers who seek to find unifying theories, they conclude, "implicitly assume that scientific knowledge has some intrinsic characteristics that distinguish it from other forms of knowledge. So the plea for more unity very often becomes an implicit plea to abide by the standards of good scientific practice and a call for less laxity in the field.... Of course, scientific knowledge must abide by some standards, but these standards are socially defined and redefined with time" (p. 59) Unlike the particle physicists' quest for "a single and economical law of nature," they are comfortable with many independent laws, all tuned to the social and cognitive needs of their communities. Lacking a bound phenomena with which to validate the theories, intellectual appeal comes to dominate observation. Their paper ends with an observation about progress derived from Hesse (1980), "It is pragmatic success that culminates in science, not necessarily the amount of knowledge" (p. 59).

Farhoomand (1987) offers a very different view. He embraces Kuhn's model with its disciplinary matrix of *symbolic generalizations* (e.g., programming languages and diagrammatic techniques), *shared commitments* (e.g., approaches to systems analysis and the taxonomy of DDS), *values* (which for MIS are taken from other disciplines), and *exemplars* (which, despite the growing number of textbooks, remain limited in number for MIS). In this framework, he sees the development of the scientific community to be in its formative stages. The reasons that MIS does not possess a more entrenched scientific community are that its pioneers come from diverse backgrounds, they hold their primary academic affiliation with some other scientific discipline, and they "have historically concentrated on only one aspect of the discipline, i.e., design and development of information systems" (p. 50).

Farhoomand's evaluation of the current state of scientific maturity is based on a content analysis of 536 articles published between 1977 and 1985. He finds a steady movement away from nonempirical work to empirical studies, but he also notes "that there is a large difference between the existing research and what practitioners deem important" (p. 53). He concludes that "MIS will not make significant progress as a *scientific field of study* until it can both explicate its disciplinary matrix through development of its *own theories* and enhance its exemplars so that they can be applied to a wider and more precise set of applications. It is only through well-grounded theories that the discipline will be able to shape its goals and boundaries of its domain structurally, not cosmetically" (p. 55). That is, unlike Banville and Landry, he seeks a unifying paradigm for MIS, perhaps one based on the fundamentals of organizational behavior and organizational theory. "What has mainly hampered scientific progress in the field is *lack of a substantive ideology*" (p. 55). Methodology, however, cannot substitute for the basic MIS theories. Farhoomand concludes his paper,

> Unfortunately, purely empirical research which is not based on solid theoretical foundations, or studies which are primarily preoccupied with technology, will not facilitate reaching this objective [of a mature MIS science]. (p. 55).

Thomas and Tymon (1982) write about this last theme. They assert that "the conventional notions of methodological and scientific rigor that have directed research in the organizational sciences have been deficient as guidance mechanisms. More specifically, ... the hegemony of these notions of rigor has directed energy away from the relevance or usefulness of research and in many cases has encouraged research that is of questionable practical utility" (pp. 345-46). To improve relevancy, they identify five key needs of the practitioners.

Descriptive relevance. The accuracy of research findings in capturing phenomena encountered by the practitioner in an organizational setting.

Goal relevance. The correspondence between the dependent (outcome) variables in a theory and the things the practitioner wishes to influence.

Operational validity. The ability of the practitioner to implement action implications of a theory by manipulating its independent (causal) variables.

Nonobviousness. The degree to which a theory meets or exceeds the complexity of common sense theory already used by a practitioner.

Timeliness.   The requirement that a theory be available to practitioners in time to use it to deal with problems.

The authors note that rigor generally refers to *internal* relationships between the data and the conclusions of a study, and relevance is concerned with the *external* relationships between a study's findings and a practitioner's needs.   "Relevance cannot be assessed without identifying a class of practitioners as potential users" (p. 350).   Thus, paradoxically, we may not be able to make MIS more scientific unless we either make it less relevant or less general.

Astley (1984) comments that "the problem is that different theorists bring different theoretical interests and perspectives to the study of management" (p. 262).   Laboratory experiments are intended, not to be relevant, but to reveal underlying relationships that would otherwise go unnoticed.   "The partial coefficients which proliferate in the academic journals of management science are generated less because of their predictive value in explaining objective reality than because of the support they lend to the abstracted hypotheses which constitute the rarefied world views of analytic perspectives.   It is the production of, and adherence to, ideas *per se* which is important here" (p. 263).   In a section headed "Sophistry," Astley states, "Or to put this rather more abruptly, science is quintessentially a mind game" (p. 256).   "Scientific progress ... does not result from the instrumental acquisition of information about objective reality; it is the product of an essentially subjective process in which administrative scientists seek preeminence for their chosen paradigm *as an end in itself*" (Astley 1985, p. 498, italics added).   "As administrative scientists, we formulate knowledge subjectively through biased, selected observations of everyday managerial practice.... As scientists, we do our job properly only insofar as we are creative in casting phenomena within interpretative frameworks.   The interpretative frameworks, not the observations, contribute to our knowledge" (p. 498). Astley is examining a science of a free phenomena. "Once we relinquish the view that theoretical constructs are direct representations of external reality, language itself becomes the essential subject matter of scientific deliberation.... It is the very embodiment of truth; our knowledge structures are linguistic conventions" (p. 499). "Not only is language, rather than objective fact, the chief product of research, but ambiguous, empirically imprecise language, dominates theorizing.   The maintenance of linguistic ambiguity enhances a theory's conceptual appeal by widening its potential applicability" (p. 501).

Astley makes the point "that our *knowledge* of objective reality is subjectively constructed.   Just as organizational participants subjectively interpret events in order to experience everyday life as meaningful, so administrative scientists superimpose frameworks on empirical observations to render knowledge meaningful" (pp. 509-10).   The importance of the resulting theory (as evaluated by scholars) is unrelated to its ability to predict empirical findings. The appeal of a theory extends beyond the purely intellectual. "Crystallizing theory in attractive images is an important part of scientific writing. Imagery, not the bare reporting of facts, captures the scientific imagination" (p. 503). "Old paradigms fall from grace not because they are wrong but because they are boring" (p. 504). Thus, in administrative science at least, one cannot expect to find discipline-wide agreement about analytic perspectives. Theoretical perspectives do not seem to build cumulatively (which suggests that the MIS model advocated by Banville and Landry might be more accurate than that proposed by Farhoomand). "The problem is that different theorists bring different intentions to the study of administration; they are set on investigating quite different things, interpreting reality through their own conceptual filters, and drawing conclusions that fit their own world views" (p. 505). Whereas the Received View attempted to construct its theories from observational data, administrative science uses data to augment its theories.

> Data can be used effectively as a form of illustration having persuasive appeal for a theoretical interpretation. By contextually grounding abstract terms and theories, we add imagery to them and invite others to employ these terms and theories in interpreting their own research experiences. Empirical documentation, in this case, serves not as a device for verifying a theory's agreement with objective fact, but as rhetorical support in persuading others to adopt a particular world view. Because empirical data is always theory dependent, its main function is to embellish rather than validate the theory from which it was generated. (p. 510)

Administrative science, Astley concludes, "is first and foremost, a theoretical enterprise. Theoretical creativity, rather than information-gathering, drives scientific progress" (p. 510).

Rosenberg (1974), writing a little earlier, examines the scientific premises of information science (a specialization of library science). He comments that most of the research in information science at that time was in the tradition of Newtonian mechanics. "The most important element of this scientific tradition is the belief system based on the notion that behind every phenomenon there is an ultimately discoverable cause or explanation" (p. 264). He observes that the computer has emerged as a cultural phenomena—a way of looking at the world—that he calls the "gestalt of the computer." This has led his field to become dominated by the tools of logic as the human and social sides of information science follow the conventions of behaviorist psychology. Thus, the computer came to take on the character of a powerful mechanist response to human problems. He quotes Matson (1964) to provide a context for his analysis:

> The tragic history of the breaking of the human image parallels the disintegration of the inner sense of identity, the flight from autonomous conduct to automaton behavior, in the modern world.... Out of the wreckage of displaced allegiances and abandoned human values which the mechanization of social science has left in its wake an insurgent movement of reconstruction has steadily been taking form and gaining voice. (cited, p. 265)

As part of the reconstruction activity, Rosenberg asks the question, What is the relationship between man and computer? His response engenders a non-Newtonian view of information science.

Rosenberg observes that new automated technology can create more problems than it solves. To provide a framework for this observation, he introduces Harmon's (1970) concept of the *pathogenic premise*. There are six of these premises; by way of example, the first is:

> The technological imperative that any technology that can be developed, and any knowledge that can be applied, should be.

Harmon claims that this is a pathogenic premise because it is problem generating even as it produces useful consequences. Rosenberg added three more premises to this list (e.g., the premise that useful information is that which can be handled as data). "When we design an information system we have a set of premises in mind, whether implicitly or explicitly. When these premises ... collide with pressing social problems ... the result is most often not a solution of the problem but a proliferation of problems.... The 'gestalt of the computer' and the notion of a mechanistic universe do have their place. But in the search for scientific principles, we should not be misled by our short term success nor can we afford to ignore our obvious failures" (Rosenberg 1974, p. 267). Here is his alternative:

> First, information science must abandon its deterministic approach and must recognize the computer as perhaps an historical accident rather than a scientific organizing principle. We must get out from behind the computer. A more holistic approach is needed. In this the field is perhaps most closely related to a field such as ecology. We must begin to look at the interrelationships between various parts of the information environment. (p. 268)

The choice that Rosenberg offers is between a causal, reductionist view and an interdependent, holistic state. Computer science and technology owe their intellectual roots to the former; the thesis of this book, however, is that the future of computer science—and, indeed, most of technology—rests with the latter. We are in the midst of a transition, and we have many conflicting beliefs. For example, consider the following quotation from Mumford (1964):

> The danger to democracy does not spring from any specific scientific discoveries or electronic inventions.... The danger springs from the fact that, since Francis Bacon and Galileo defined the new methods and objectives of technics, our great physical transformations have been effected by a system that deliberately eliminates the whole human personality, ignores the historic process, overplays the role of abstract intelligence, and makes control over physical nature, ultimately control over man himself, the chief purpose of existence. (p. 6)

The perspective of the 1990s suggests that these may not have been as severe a challenge to democracy as Mumford had feared. Yet much of our policy and scientific enterprise remain consistent with the extract's central assertions. If we seek to model computer science after physics, to make it into a body of knowledge with unifying theories that guide technological advancement, then we will end up confronting a myriad of new problems, each spawned by locally optimized solutions. But the alternative is not without peril. Astley (1985) notes, "Without universal standards to appeal to, appraisers of theory must, by necessity, fall back on particularistic, socially grounded frames of reference, in contrast to purely intellectual ones" (p. 506). How do we deal with the social context? We can continue along the path of reductionism and decompose the social structure to create tools that improve its operation, but, as Dalbom (1986) remarks, such tools simply make tools of their users. Some have examined the social implications of computing (e.g., Kling 1980; Mowshowitz 1981; 1985; Dunlop and Kling 1991), and others have offered noncausal system models (e.g., Mitroff 1983). But ultimately, the design of computer systems remains a human problem-solving activity. Most of our solutions will not be bound to external phenomena, and that provides us both an unprecedented opportunity and a frightening challenge.

The science of computer technology is that of a free phenomena. It is the study of the transformation of ideas into operations. We can apply this science simply to economize and to extend the existing technology, or we may employ it as a catalyst for the integration of fragmented systems (both technological and social). This book favors the path of integration and synthesis. But human limits prevail, and the scope of what I can offer is far narrower than what this chapter may promise. It will suffice to terminate this discussion by proclaiming that in the science of free phenomena, anything goes. We have tools that can identify errors and falsify otherwise appealing theories. Nevertheless, many conflicting, and equally valid, theories will be possible, and there may be no logical criteria for choosing among them. We must be guided by pragmatism, and we must avoid being misled by local maxima. Thus, after all this discussion, we come to the unsettling conclusion that there can be only one rule: In the science of a free phenomenon, there will be no rules.

3.7. A Short Coda

Part I is now complete. What are the scientific and technological foundations for the new era of design? It is not clear. Our goal is to reduce the central tension in the software process: the fact that we start with a need that often is poorly defined and difficult to represent and we must end up with a formal model that executes within a computer. Traditionally, computer science has chosen to concentrate on the formal aspects of the process, but more is needed. I believe that software engineering should cover the entire software process, and that presents a dilemma. Either we have portions of software engineering without a scientific base or we have computer science extending beyond its formal foundations. Obviously, I favor a broader definition of computer science. As we have seen from Part I, computer science is unlike physics in that it can invent itself; it is free.

For a science to be free, of course, implies that it receives its direction from human institutions (as opposed to natural, bound phenomena). To address this component of the software process, Part II turns to the human aspects of design both from a theoretical perspective (e.g., what can be known and how can that knowledge be reused automatically) and a practice orientation (e.g., how have other disciplines addressed design issues and what can software engineering learn from that experience). Once the human dimensions of the problem have been reviewed, Part III confronts the central question of this book: How should we design software in the new era of design?

PART II

ECOLOGICAL DESIGN

4

A FOUNDATION FOR DESIGN

4.1. The Foundation, So Far

The underlying thesis of this book is that, although computing technology, in its relatively short lifetime, has clearly impacted modern economies and cultures, our understanding of software remains rooted in our experience with precomputer technology. It follows, therefore, that if we wish to take advantage of software's unique capabilities, we must begin by reassessing our objectives and constraints. With this renewed understanding serving as a framework, we then can explore alternative paradigms. A revised interpretation is necessary, I assert, because there is a ceiling on the returns available by simply improving the present methods. To attain the level of productivity that software makes possible, we need a new normative model that explains how we *ought* to develop and employ software. Part III identifies one such normative model, called *adaptive design*, and demonstrates its efficacy. Yet this is not a book about adaptive design; it is about the mismatch between software's inherent flexibility and the methods now used in software's construction. If we are to rectify that disjunction, we must abandon our historical assumptions and reexamine the foundations upon which computer science and software engineering rest. The first two parts of the book are devoted to this reappraisal and foundation building.

In Part I, the relationships between science and technology were considered. The discussion was not limited to computers and software. It began by examining the two myths that dominated technological thinking at the time the first digital electronic computers were created; resilient myths that sometimes persist in policy making and academic research. The first myth is that the goal of science is to discover immutable truths about the universe, and the second is that technological advancement depends on the application of this scientific knowledge. These two ideas combine to produce an implicit model of progress: As scientific knowledge accumulates, greater technological advances are enabled. The model is hierarchical. Technological progress follows the discovery of scientific knowledge, and, therefore, technology requires a scientific base to prosper. As we have seen, however, by the mid 1970s there were few historians or philosophers of science who held fast to these beliefs.

There now is a broad consensus that scientific knowledge is contextual (i.e., structured within a paradigm or expressed as guiding assumptions). Observation is underdetermined, and how we interpret what we see depends on the context of the knowledge we seek (i.e., observation is theory based). Knowledge in scientific theories is dual; it consists of the descriptive contextual understanding and a prescriptive instrument. A single instrument may be valid for multiple contextual theories (e.g., Newton's laws continue to be valid for many computations within Einstein's theory of relativity). Thus, science is instrumentally progressive even as the contexts shift. Shifts in context occur because new observations fail to be explained by current theories; they also shift when new contexts, considered to be more technologically or socially important, are introduced. Thus, we find that scientific advancement often comes as a response to a technological challenge.

The differences between science and engineering, and between scientific knowledge and engineering knowledge, turn out to be modest. In each case, there is a continuum, and it is not difficult to contrast extremes. But most knowledge may be applied to either science or technology. As we have seen, the linear model (i.e., science uncovers knowledge for technology to apply) is invalid, and the relative prestige rankings of science and engineering are unjustified. We often label engineering tasks science (e.g., many of the Space Shuttle's activities), and sometimes science is called engineering (e.g., genetic engineering). Thus, I have abandoned these distinctions and speak only of knowledge (which always is valid within some context) and the paired processes of discovery and design.

Discovery and design are like the two faces of Janus. One looks backward onto the existing universe and seeks to improve that vision; the other looks forward into the universe in which we exist (which I shall call the environment) and seeks to improve the environment. Discovery always relies on design, and design depends on discovery. Artifacts created by design alter our environment and add to our discovered knowledge. Moreover, as the environment evolves, contextual changes affect the relevancy of the discovered knowledge. For example, during the 1970s computer science research in text editors was concerned with the command structures for editing text. The shift to text editing by direct manipulation has not invalidated this discovered knowledge, but it has destroyed its relevancy.

This, then, is the first layer of the foundation upon which we shall build a new normative model for software. It establishes the extent to which we may rely upon abstract scientific principles. The second layer in this foundation is that of design. I use the label *ecological design* to denote an extension of the design model that now dominates our thinking about software, a model in which developers employ technological knowledge to construct an artifact that satisfies stated requirements. I call this traditional model, created for and used successfully with hardware projects, *technological design*. Whereas technological design begins with a concern for the technological issues affecting the design and its realization, ecological design begins with the human environment in which design is initiated, conducted, and evaluated. (In Part III I contrast these perspectives as product oriented and problem oriented.) A shift to ecological design implies a reassessment of the methods and techniques deemed essential to technological design. Therefore, the remainder of Part II focuses on the issues affecting design in the human environment.

If ecological design is a new term, its view of design is certainly not unique. As I shall point out, the shift to this enlarged design mission is part of a much larger and more profound intellectual shift that predates the introduction of computer technology. Many of the novel concepts we detect entering into current design practice are driven, explicitly or implicitly, by the force of this greater movement. Therefore, before going on with a discussion of ecological design, I present two separate, but complementary, philosophical sections that, in combination, create a broad conceptual framework for what follows.

4.2. The Rejection of Technical Rationality

Schön (1983) describes the model of Technical Rationality as one in which "professional activity consists in instrumental problem solving made rigorous by the application of scientific theory and technique" (p. 21). As will be discussed in Chapter 6, he rejects this model in favor of "an epistemology of practice implicit in the artistic, intuitive processes which some practitioners do bring to situations of uncertainty, instability, uniqueness, and value conflict" (p. 49). In the previous chapter, Dalbom (1986) echoed a similar sentiment when he implied a causal relationship between a belief in reason and the "mechanization of production, bureaucratization of society, utilitarianism in morals, and nihilistic existentialism" (p. 17). These are but two of many references to a movement away from the certainty of science (normally associated with a Cartesian epistemology) in favor of a more humanistic and pluralistic model.

It is common in architecture to speak of modern and postmodern styles. Both belong to the current century. In intellectual history, however, modernity follows the medieval period, and the shift in thinking just alluded to represents postmodernity (or, if one ascribes to the pendulum theory of history, a return to *pre*modernity). Dalbom dates the beginning of modernity with the Enlightenment, but Toulmin (1990) offers an earlier date. In fact, he finds two distinct origins of modernity. The first he identifies as a literary or humanistic phase beginning in the late 16th century, and the second is the scientific and philosophical phase that arises around 1630. In *Cosmopolis: The Hidden Agenda of Modernity*, Toulmin argues that these two phases have been decontextualized so that the resultant history conforms to an abstract, logically constructed explanation. His book is intended to open a more relevant postmodern enquiry by recontextualizing what has been decontextualized for so long.

Erasumus, Shakespeare, Montaigne, and Bacon are, in Toulmin's view, "Renaissance humanists." They bring with them a humanist skepticism. Unlike Descartes, who later would use skepticism to deny (i.e., his method of systematic doubt), "humanist skeptics took a totally different position: they no more wished to *deny* general philosophical theses than to *assert* them.... The humanists saw philosophical *questions* as reaching beyond the scope of experience in an indefensible way. Faced with abstract, universal, timeless theoretical propositions, they saw no sufficient basis in experience, either for asserting, or for denying them.... Rather, what they had to offer was a new way of understanding human life and motives: like Socrates long ago, and Wittgenstein in our own time, they taught readers to recognize how philosophical theories overreach the limits of human rationality" (p. 29).

The second origin of modernity (what Toulmin calls the Counter-Renaissance) replaced this humanistic skepticism with a universal certainty, and his postmodern (or premodern) programme restores the humanistic diversity. As Toulmin puts it, "We must accept the diversity of views in a spirit of toleration. Tolerating the resulting plurality, ambiguity, or the lack of certainty is no error, let alone a sin. Honest reflection shows that it is part of the price that we must inevitably pay for being human beings, and not gods" (p. 30). References to such a view of skepticism are becoming increasingly common (e.g., Pepper 1942; Kurtz 1992). By way of a visual analogy, consider Boring's wife/mother-in-law in Figure 4.1. It depicts a subject with two mutually contradictory interpretations. Each interpretation is correct, and there exists no higher level view that integrates the two. The picture captures the dilemma of design (science, epistemology, etc.): are there unique, certain truths or only a plurality of competing, incomplete explanations. For the past three centuries, we have been committed to the first understanding, yet today we find a strong force to adopt the second view.

Historical events of the early 17th century provided the context for favoring certainty over plurality. The murder of Henry IV of France, the savagery of the Thirty Years War, the religious intolerance of the counter-reformation, and the associated economic dislocation all created a desire for unambiguous truths. "If skepticism let one down, certainty

Fig. 4.1. My wife and my mother-in-law, W. E. Hill, *Puck*, 1915,
reported in Boring (1930).

was more urgent. It might not be obvious what one was supposed to be
certain about, but *un*certainty had become *un*acceptable" (p. 55). The
foundation had been laid for a retreat from the Renaissance. *"Formal
logic was in, rhetoric was out.... General principles were in, particular cases
were out.... Abstract axioms were in, concrete diversity was out.... The
permanent was in, the transitory was out....* These four changes of
mind—from oral to written, local to general, particular to universal,
timely to timeless—were distinct; but, taken in an historical context, they
had much in common, and their joint outcome exceeded what any of
them would have produced by itself" (pp. 31-34). The result was a shift
from a practical philosophy to a theoretical conception of philosophy,
which is only now shifting back.

It was into this ferment that Descartes' *cogito, ergo sum* established
an epistemology built on certainty, first principles, and a "Mind-Body
dichotomy" that separated the world of (rational) human experience
from the world of (mechanical) natural phenomena. In this way, his
"program for philosophy swept aside the 'reasonable' uncertainties of
16th-century skeptics, in favor of new, mathematical kinds of 'rational'
certainty and truth" (p. 75). What emerged was a Rationalist dream of
a "rational method, a unified science, and an exact language, [which]
unite into a single project" (p. 104). This view represented a
confirmation of Pythagoras' insights regarding the power and elegance

of mathematics.   Scientists were to "find the laws ruling natural phenomena, the better to glorify God, who first created Nature.... Rejecting in both method and spirit Bacon's vision of a humanly fruitful science, Descartes and Newton set out to build mathematical structures, and looked to Science for theological, not technological, dividends" (p. 105).   That is, science was divorced from human needs and not their servant;   there   was   a   commitment   to   a   monistic   view   of   the phenomenological world.

Toulmin goes on to recontextualize the subsequent history, and he concludes that by the early 20th century the Western world was ripe for a shift to a more humanist philosophy.   The shift was delayed by two world wars and a depression, but it finally burst forth in the late 1960s, "a revolution *waiting to happen*" (p. 162).   In the philosophy of science, the seminal event was the publication of Kuhn's *The Structure of Scientific Revolutions*.   "Not everyone saw ... how far it stepped back from the context-free questions of Cartesian rationalism, toward the historic candor of the humanist tradition" (p. 84).   For axiom systems Kuhn substituted paradigms, for a singular method he offered plural explanatory methods, and in place of a formal analysis of a scientific theory he produced a historical analysis of diverse concepts in science taken from different periods.

> Since the 1960s, then, both philosophy and science are back in the intellectual postures of the last generation *before* Descartes. In natural science, the imperial dominion of physics over all other fields has come to an end: ecologists and anthropologists can now look at astronomers and physicists straight in the eye. In philosophy, Descartes' formalist wish ... is now seen to have led the enterprise of philosophy into a dead end. Scientifically and philosophically, that is, we are freed from the exclusively theoretical agenda of rationalism, and can take up again the practical issues sidelined by Descartes' *coup d'état* some 300 years ago. (p. 168)

In conclusion, Toulmin observes that the "dream of *foundationalism*—i.e., the search for a permanent and unique set of authoritative principles for human knowledge—proves to be just a dream" (p. 174). Modernity rested upon two principles: its quest for certainty, and its trust in logical argument built upon a clean slate.   "We need to balance the hope for certainty and clarity in theory with the impossibility of avoiding uncertainty and ambiguity in practice" (p. 175).   "All we can be called upon to do is to take a start *from where we are, at the time we are there* ....   All we are required to do is use our experience critically and discriminatingly, *refining and improving* our inherited ideas, and determining more exactly the limits to their scope" (p. 179).   "The key problem is no longer to ensure that our social and national systems are *stable*; rather, it is to ensure that intellectual and social procedures are more *adaptive*" (p. 185).

4.3. Heidegger's Being-in-the-World

This section complements Toulmin's view of an intellectual revolution in progress by reviewing the ideas of a philosopher whose work is frequently cited by those engaged in design: Martin Heidegger. Winograd and Flores (1986) devote a chapter to his ideas, Bødker (1991b) makes his concept of a breakdown a central theme of her work, and there are many other references. I include this short review of his philosophy for two reasons. First, I introduce his ontology as an alternative to the Cartesian view. Second, I use his philosophy to explain some concepts that reappear throughout Part II, in particular the social determination of objective reality (which we already have noted in the underdetermination of observation).

Heidegger's principal work, *Being and Time*, was published in 1927, and it provides the core of his philosophy. Much has been written since that time, and my limitation to a discussion of only his ideas should not be construed as a measure of their importance in design. In a personal correspondence, Naur points out that my use of Heidegger as a foil to Cartesianism is a historical distortion; in another correspondence, Dasgupta notes that Popper, and not Heidegger, provided the principal philosophic influence on the design theorists of the 1960s and 1970s (e.g., J.C. Jones and Pye). Nevertheless, for the purposes of Part II, Heidegger's ideas offer a convenient set of common references. Having said that, I now must admit that his works are difficult and notoriously hard to translate because he chose to avoid ambiguity by making up many of his own technical terms. Fortunately, Dreyfus (1991) has produced an excellent commentary, and the remainder of this section relies on his interpretation. I use Dreyfus' vocabulary and append some of the equivalent translations frequently found in the design-related literature.

By way of establishing a context for the discussion, recall that Descartes introduced a Mind-Body dualism that separates the rational from the mechanical such that the mechanical could be described rationally; that is, in the Cartesian world subjects contemplate objects. Moreover, in this world it is possible to explain everything in terms of entities that can be taken to be directly intelligible (i.e., understandable as decontextualized objects). Universal explanations are independent of context, and (ideally) may be expressed mathematically. In Chapter 2 we have seen how these ideas evolved into the Received View of logical positivism. The following, called psychological physicalism and presented in 1949, illustrates the consequences of such a logic-based framework.

> All psychological statements which are meaningful, that is to say, which are in principle verifiable, are translatable into propositions which do not involve psychological concepts, but only the concepts of physics. The propositions of psychology are consequently the concepts of physics. Psychology is an integral part of physics. (Cited in Kaplan 1964, p. 22)

In opposition to this kind of decontextualized universalism, Heidegger seeks to make the individual subject somehow dependent upon shared social practices. Rather than having a phenomenological world composed of objects, each with an independent existence that can be described formally, Heidegger depicts humanity's understanding of the world as being framed by what it finds meaningful in its current social and historical context, its *being-in-the-world*.

Since Plato, Western thought has held that everything human beings do that makes sense is rational and can be based on an implicit theory. After Descartes, this theory was seen to be represented in our minds as intentional states and rules for relating the states. Physicalism is one approach to analyzing these intentional states; symbolic information processing is another. Thus, prior to Heidegger, human activity is perceived to result from a holistic network of intentional states (i.e., a tacit belief system). Heidegger reacts to this model by insisting that we return to the phenomenon of everyday human activity (in its social context) to discover the ultimate foundation of intelligibility. This produces a shift from "*epistemological* questions concerning the relation of the knower and the known [to] *ontological* questions concerning what sort of beings we are and how our being is bound up with the intelligibility of the world" (Dreyfus 1991, p. 3).

Heidegger substitutes for a *transcendental* phenomenology with intentionality (i.e., "the way the individual mind is directed at objects by virtue of some mental content that represents them" (Dreyfus 1991, p. 2)) a *hermeneutic* phenomenology. Hermeneutics is the interpretation of texts: sacred, literary, and philosophical. The reading of a text is based on a paradox. One does not know what will be read next, but one cannot read it unless one has an assumed understanding (preunderstanding) of what is to be read. Thus, "meaning is a matter of context; the explanatory procedure provides the arena for understanding" (Palmer 1969, p. 24). For the interpreter to understand the text, "he must preunderstand the subject and the situation before he can enter the horizon of its meaning. Only when he can step into the magic circle of its horizon can the interpreter understand its meaning. This is the mysterious 'hermeneutical circle' without which the meaning of the text cannot emerge" (p. 25). Heidegger "seeks to point out and describe our understanding of being from within that understanding without attempting to make our grasp of entities theoretically clear.... This means that one must always do hermeneutics from within a hermeneutic circle" (Dreyfus 1991, p. 4). "Understanding is conceived not as something to be possessed but rather as a mode or constituent element of being-in-the-world" (Palmer 1969, p. 131). And this contradicts a Cartesian premise; one cannot have a theory of what makes theory possible.

"Heidegger's primary concern is to raise the question of being—to make sense of our ability to make sense of things—and to reawaken in people a feeling for the importance of this very obscure question" (Dreyfus 1991, p. 10). He uses the term *Dasein* for the *way of being* characteristic of all human beings; he is not concerned with "what" a human being is, but rather with its way of being. Only self-interpreting beings exist. "To exist is to take a stand on what is essential about one's being and to be defined by that stand. Thus Dasein is what, in its social activity, it interprets itself to be" (p. 23). It follows, then, that cultures as well as human beings exist. There are no "beliefs" about being, only skills and practices. "An explication of our understanding of being can never be complete because we dwell in it—that is, it is so pervasive as to be both nearest to us and farthest away—and also because there are no beliefs to get clear about" (p. 22). The goal is to arrive at a worked-out understanding of the ontological structures of existence (i.e., of what it is to be Dasein). The design implications of Heidegger's philosophy now begin to emerge. The goal of design is to improve the environment, and this begins within the environment (i.e., within the hermeneutic circle). Understanding design objectives requires an interpretation of the environment (within its social context), and the environment cannot exist without self-interpretation. Although we may discover context-independent laws that facilitate design, their relevance will depend upon the context established by the way of being (i.e., Dasein).

Here, then, is the split between Heidegger and the Cartesian philosophers. The latter hold that understanding is a belief system implicit in the minds of individual subjects. Heidegger, however, "holds that Dasein's shared ways of behaving are not mere facts to be studied *objectively* by a 'scientific' discipline such as anthropology or sociology (although they are that too). Rather, because they contain an understanding of being they must be studied as an *interpretation*" (p. 19). "Our understanding of being is so pervasive in everything we think and do that we can never arrive at a clear presentation of it. Moreover, since it is not a belief system but is embodied in our skills, it is not the sort of thing we could ever get clear about" (p. 32).

To confront this difficulty, Heidegger employs a hermeneutics of everydayness in which Dasein is described "as it is primarily and usually—in its average everydayness" (Heidegger, cited p. 35). It is through Dasein's everyday coping that a phenomenon "shows itself in itself." In contrast to the Cartesian detached inquiries through which the nature of objects is explained, Heidegger holds that it is the human experience that discloses the world and discovers entities in it. "Rather than first perceiving perspectives, then synthesizing the perspectives into objects, and finally assigning these objects a function on the basis of their physical properties, [Heidegger states that] we ordinarily manipulate tools that already have meaning in a world that is organized in terms of purposes. To see this, we must first overcome the traditional interpretation that theory is prior to practice" (pp. 46-47).

"The world is discovered in the everyday activity of Daseining, of being-there—in the activity called existing which is Dasein's way of being-in" (p. 59). In addition to Dasein's way of being-human, there are two other categories of being: *readiness-to-hand* (which Dreyfus translates as *availableness*) and *presence-at-hand* (which Dreyfus translates as *occurrentness*). Equipment (which Heidegger defines as *something-in-order-to*) is available (ready-to-hand), and a piece of equipment is defined in terms of what one uses it for (i.e., its context of use). When the equipment satisfies its definition within its context of use, it tends to disappear. For example, when hammering a nail, one is not aware of the hammer as a distinct entity. Yet if the hammer is too heavy for the task, one becomes aware of the hammer as a distinct entity. It becomes occurrent (present-at-hand). Similarly, if a blind man is given a cane and asked to describe its properties, the cane is occurrent for him. But when he uses the cane in getting around, he focuses on the objects revealed to him by the cane (e.g., curbs and walls) and loses his awareness of the cane itself; the cane now is available for him.

Heidegger calls the user's grasp of his environment in his everyday way of getting around *circumspection*. In contrast to the traditional view of intentionality in which actions can be traced back to mental states, most circumspection does not require deliberate, thematic awareness. It is only when there is a *breakdown* (i.e., when the situation requires deliberate attention) does mental content (i.e., intentionality) arise. The too-heavy hammer is an illustration of a breakdown; there is a shift from hammering to an awareness of the hammer. As we shall see, the world is revealed through breakdowns.

In the traditional approach, representations of objects are purely mental and, therefore, these representations can be analyzed without reference to the world (i.e., decontextualized). For Heidegger, however, even when there is mental content (e.g., rules, beliefs, and desires), it cannot be analyzed as a set of self-contained representations. Deliberative activity is dependent upon Dasein's everyday transparent ways of coping. For example, consider Heidegger's comment on the too-heavy hammer.

Why is it that what we are talking about—the heavy hammer— shows itself differently when our way of talking is thus modified? Not because we are keeping our distance from the manipulation, nor because we are just looking *away* from the equipmental character of this entity, but rather because we are looking at the available [ready-to-hand] thing which we encounter, and looking at it "in a new way" as something occurrent [present-at-hand]. *The understanding of being* by which our concernful dealings with intraworldly entities have been guided *has changed over.* (cited on p. 81)

That is, the hammer's way of being is determined by the context. As an occurrent entity with occurrent properties, we can develop scientific facts about the hammer and how it works. Those facts, however, will be theory laden and they will not describe what a hammer is. (For example, in our culture there is shared sense of what a chair is, but it is impossible to produce a definition of "chairness" that includes all forms of chairs and excludes all forms of nonchairs. See also Wittgenstein (1953) on games.)

To paraphrase Dreyfus, Dasein has four choices in his everyday coping (p. 84). It can simple cope, and if there is a problem, switch to another mode of coping with the available. Second, Dasein can confront its equipment as somehow defective in that context and then try to fix it. Dasein in this case directs itself (intentionally) at independent things whose way of being is *unavailableness* (unready-to-hand). Third, Dasein can decontextualize its object, and what is revealed in occurrentness. Finally, Dasein can just stare without recontextualizing (a kind of holding state), which sometimes is mistakenly taken as an isolated, self-contained subject confronting an isolated, self-contained object (e.g., Descartes' *cogito*).

Thus, we see, the nature of being (other than Dasein) is not inherent in the entity itself, but in the context of some meaningful activity within the world (i.e., the *involvement* of the equipment). For example, when a piece of equipment is found to be missing some element, there can be a transition from the unavailable to the occurrent (i.e., the recognition of something missing leads one to see what else is present-at-hand); moreover, unaffected elements that formerly had the character of available (but that are no longer serviceable) may now reveal themselves in the mode of mere occurrence. "Equipment makes sense only in the context of other equipment; our use of equipment makes sense because our activity has a point" (p. 92). That an activity has a point may suggest intentionality, but "to explain everyday transparent coping we do not need to introduce a mental representation of a goal at all. Activity can be *purposive* without the actor having in mind a *purpose*" (p. 93). For example, skill-based activities such as climbing the stairs and routine social interactions are accomplished without representational states that specify what the action is aimed at accomplishing. (Of course, it always is possible to construct a purposeful model that would create such actions, but such a model is not a prerequisite to Heidegger' explanation.)

"The world, i.e., the interlocking practices, equipment, and skills for using them, which provides the basis for using specific items of equipment, is hidden. It is not disguised, but it is undiscovered. So, like the available, the world has to be revealed by a special technique.... Luckily for the phenomenologist, there are special situations in which the phenomenon of world is forced upon our awareness" (p. 99). These situations are initiated by a breakdown (i.e., a disturbance) and revealed by disclosing (i.e., holistic background coping) and discovering (i.e., dealing in particular circumstances appropriately). Just as our eyes constantly adjust to the light, we are constantly adapting to our situation, an activity Heidegger simply calls *being-in-the-world*.

I illustrate this with a personal story. When my grandson was a toddler learning to talk, he would sit on my lap, point, and ask, "What's this?" Finger, hand, nose, etc. One day he pointed to the small web of flesh between my fingers and asked, "What's this?" Lacking a context, all parts of the body were of equal interest to him. "The-web-of-flesh-between-my-fingers" was too complex an answer, however, to motivate subsequent pointings, and he went on to point to more rewarding objects. Nevertheless, that small breakdown brought about a discovery about my hand that remains with me. Heidegger offers the following explanation:

> Why can I let a pure thing of the world show up at all in bodily presence? Only because the world is already there in thus letting it show up, because letting-it-show-up is but a particular mode of my being-in-the-world and because world means nothing other than what is always already present for the entity in it. I can see a natural thing in its bodily presence only on the basis of this being-in-the-world. (cited, p. 104)

"Heidegger contends that nature can explain only *why* the available works; it cannot make intelligible availableness as a *way of being* because nature cannot explain worldliness" (p. 113). "Things are not encountered as isolated occurrent entities to which we attach isolated predicates" (p. 114). "When theory decontextualizes, it does not *construct* the occurrent [present-at-hand], but, as Heidegger says, it *reveals* the occurrent which was already there in the available [ready-to-hand]" (p. 120). The decontextualization of theory is accomplished by leaving out significance, and once stripped of its context, theory cannot give back meaning. "Facts and rules are, by themselves, meaningless.

To capture what Heidegger calls significance or involvement, they must be *assigned relevance*" (p. 118). Heidegger is concerned with how things are and not with how they work (i.e., understanding and not explaining). There can be no nonsocial Dasein, and the sociability of the culture permits only certain moods, norms, equipment, etc., which "allows in any specific situation an open-ended but limited range of possible activities to show up as sensible" (p. 191).

"Heidegger seems to hold that there can be many systems of practices that support assertions that point out many different incompatible realities. But (1) given any specific criterion of truth, i.e., any specific set of pointing-out practices, at most one system can be right.... And (2) even if a system does succeed in pointing things out as they are, that does not show that the kinds it discovers are the ultimate basis of reality. Reality can be revealed in many ways and none is metaphysically basic" (p. 280). Thus, we are left with a plural realism; it is as if there were criteria of truth that would allow us to see *only* the wife or *only* the mother-in-law but never the ambiguous picture.

What is the relevance of Heidegger philosophy to design? There are clear messages about the situatedness of the environment that is to be affected (i.e., the fact that it is in the world). There also is the concept of breakdowns (disturbances) that make us aware of the otherwise invisible. They are essential for disclosing and discovery, but they should be avoided in ready-to-hand equipment (e.g., the heavy hammer that detracts us from the activity of hammering). Finally, there is the concern for decontextualized knowledge (e.g., scientific theories). For design this manifests itself as a tension between the Cartesian goal of explaining the world with a series of smaller explanations from which a full description can be composed, and Heidegger's sense that no such model is possible; for him, significance and relevance are the primary determinants in selecting theories.

Thus, we are faced with an intellectual dilemma: Can we discover the facts and theories about what makes up the world and then apply them, or must we first understand the environment and the facts and theories appropriate to that understanding (i.e., is design knowledge domain independent or domain determined)? We will explore these issues in the following four chapters. In the process, we will discover that Heidegger's ideas are reflected in a broad variety of theories, including many that may reject his ontology. But, of course, that is not incompatible with a humanist skepticism or a plural realism.

4.4. An Ecological Study of Design

We now are ready to enter into an examination of design. In its broadest context, the goal of design is to alter the environment.

Technological design (i.e., the preparation of design representations for a material artifact to be constructed) has provided the reference model for design in the Modernist period (i.e., the past 300 years). Design also has an aesthetic component, but that normally is isolated from technological design (e.g., design in the art school curriculum, industrial design, and—isolated to a lesser extent—architectural design). In *The Sciences of the Artificial* (1969/1981), Simon extends the concept of design to include any process of changing from an existing state of affairs to a preferred state. The thesis of this book is that the unique properties of software enable a shift from the narrow, technological view of design to an interpretation that integrates the technical, aesthetic, and social (i.e., artificial) components of these separate definitions.

As I have used the term here, *design* is a looking-forward activity in which we consciously alter our environment. We always begin with an understanding of the current environment in which some need has been identified. The object of technological design is to create something (which will become a concrete artifact) that will improve the environment by addressing the need. As we have seen, there is an underlying tension in the design process. The need exists in-the-world, but the design itself must be expressed as a formal model to be realized. This tension can be expressed as the subjective versus the objective, the descriptive versus the prescriptive, the scientific theory versus its instrument, the Heideggerian versus the Cartesian perspective. This tension cannot be avoided; we must live with it and understand it. Confronting the tension permits us to accept what is doable and knowable; avoiding the confrontation will only result in fruitless searches for unobtainable solutions.

We have seen that the power of science lies in its generality (i.e., its decontextualization). The value of arithmetic is that its rules work, *independent* of the nature of the objects being represented. That two apples plus two apples equals four apples, however, tells us nothing about apples. That is a strength, and not a weakness, of arithmetic. But there can be more than one arithmetic (e.g., modulo 2), just as there can be more than one geometry and more than one logic. Which we choose depends on the context of use and not the properties of the phenomenological world. For example, forbidding or allowing parallel lines to meet creates different model systems, but it does not affect the real world. Thus, we must be careful to distinguish between the model of reality and the reality it represents (i.e., what Barwise (1989) calls the Fallacy of Identification). Every model must be abstracted (decontextualized) and will be valid only within a particular context. That is, the decontextualization creates a subset of reality (the context) within which the model is valid. Within this context, the model (or theory) is *closed* in that it always performs in a satisfactory manner. In Kuhn's model, a scientific crisis is precipitated when a scientific model fails to perform as expected. Thus, for every model (and theory), we need to know both how and when to employ the model (i.e., what it does and what its context is).

The philosophical debates summarized in the previous two section have to do with the nature of the phenomenological world. Is it closed or open? Descartes proposed a closed world in which one could begin with a single premise *(cogito sum)* and, by observation and reason, construct a representation of all the objects in the world. Indeed, as physicalism asserted, psychology could be reduced to physics. In contrast, Heidegger offered an open world, one that could be understood only from within the hermeneutic circle; he would not deny the utility of decontextualized models, but he would argue that the composition of such models will not lead to a recontextualization.

And so, before we proceed, we must make a choice. Do we accept the Modernist view, which has advanced us to where we are today, along with its commitment to a closed world that can be explained completely, or do we revert to a humanist skepticism, a plural realism, and an open world? I choose the latter. I believe the fish-scale model of omniscience to be unrealizable and the quest for a unified scientific law to be unachievable. I see the world-in-which-we-are as open and our models of it as being context dependent and closed. Therefore, I take a pragmatic view of our models (and theories): Each is useful in some context. I expect each model to have some formal representation, but I recognize that its context can never be expressed formally. (If the context were formally represented, then it would become part of the model, and the definition of the context would iterate until it ended with either a more comprehensive, but still informal, context or a model of the closed world.)

This is a weak position, and it remains valid even if there is a closed world. I adopt it because it permits me to make practical, utilitarian judgments about the models (facts, theories, etc.) used in design; it acknowledges the role of subjective (and emotion-driven) decision making; and it is tolerant of conflicting theories and apparent logical inconsistencies. For example, Winograd and Flores (1986) construct their new foundation for design from three principle sources: the hermeneutics of Heidegger and Gadamer, the biological investigations of Maturana, and the speech-act theory of Searle. Yet, Dreyfus (1991) points to a basic disagreement between Heidegger and Searle with respect to intentionality (upon which speech-act theory relies). Furthermore, Winograd and Flores illustrate structural adaption in the biological domain with the example of a frog whose optic fibers respond to small moving dark spots, thereby enabling the frog to respond to flies without "seeing" representations of flies (p. 46); despite this example of visual response without seeing, the authors assert, "We are led to a more radical recognition about language and existence: *Nothing exists except through language*" (Winograd and Flores 1986, p. 68). One may complain about the lack of a logical purity, or one may accept their theories within the context for which they are valid. This book embraces the second approach. I examine theories, evade dogma, search for local truths, adopt the practical, and avoid quests that may never be satisfied.

Now that I have explained the orientation for the remainder of this book, we can begin the study of design in its ecological setting (i.e., ecological design). By definition, design takes place in-the-world. In computer science and software engineering, most of the emphasis is on the models (and the methods that guide their use) for creating a software design. Part III will address those models in some detail. What we are concerned with here is the much larger issue of the practice of design (technological, aesthetic, and artificial). This practice occurs in the environment to be altered, and it involves the interactions of people and their environment. At least four roles can be identified: There is the sponsor who seeks to modify the environment, the designer who produces a representation of the modification, the implementor who realizes the representation, and the user who interacts with or is affected by the implementation. A single individual may play all four roles, or there may be multiple individuals playing each role.

It follows, therefore, that we cannot consider the practice of design without first starting with an understanding of people, how they respond to breakdowns (e.g., the discovery of a need), and how they solve problems. These are the topics of Chapters 5 and 6. With this background established, Chapters 7 and 8 turn to the practice of design in its most general form. Part III expands upon that practice as it applies to software and reports on 14 years of experience with a design environment whose approach suggests the framework for "a new era of design."

5

PROBLEM SOLVING

5.1. The Chapter's Unifying Theme

I begin my exploration of ecological design by examining the nature of the individuals engaged in the design process. There are two principal concerns. First, design is a human activity that seeks to alter the human environment. Therefore, an understanding of human behavior in a problem-solving context is essential. In particular, we are interested in the extent the which the proposed solutions are rational (i.e., derivable through the use of clearly stated principles and formalisms) and accurate (i.e., descriptive of solutions that, when available, produce the desired results). Although there may be social and political biases that affect the decisions, the principal focus of this chapter is individual problem solving. How good are people at solving problems? How rational are they, and are there limits to rational analysis? Design depends on the interpretations of those who describe what is needed and those who create the desired products. It is essential that we know where we can be certain and where uncertainty is unavoidable.

The second reason for studying human decision making complements the first; it has to do with the form of the final decision. Recall that the software process begins with an informal recognition of a need (in-the-world) and ends with the formal expression of a response to that need (in-the-computer). One of the products of science (and rational argument) is models of the world (i.e., instruments) that can be expressed in-the-computer. Progress is made as more instruments become available. Although the criterion of relevance may result in the disuse of some of the available instruments, clearly an increase in the number of potentially relevant instruments offers the possibility of improving productivity and/or enlarging the technology's scope (i.e., the class of problems for which the models may be relevant). Therefore, we have a second set of questions to be answered. To what extent are there rational problem-solving mechanisms that can be modeled in the computer, and how may they be modeled? Are some decisions contextually determined, thereby requiring information never available in-the-computer? What are the limits in expressing design knowledge?

This chapter does not provide answers to these questions; I doubt that any consensus answers can be formulated. But I have a less ambitious goal; I intend only to identify the questions and a range of possible answers. When laying the foundation for a new era of design, it is not necessary to solve all the mysteries of the universe; it will suffice simply to produce a set of potential answers and then select one that resists refutation. I make my selection, adaptive design, in Part III, and I use Part II to establish the human context of my solution. In the remainder of this chapter I use the concept of problem solving (and the knowledge used in that process) as a unifying theme. The first section looks at problem solving from the perspective of cognitive science, the second from an ecological perspective, the next two from the perspective of expertise, and the final section from the perspective of complexity. The five sections overlap and sometimes meander into (for me) interesting but (for the reader) secondary sidewaters. I justify this organization because I am as interested in what is not possible as I am in what may be clearly demonstrated. The process of problem solving is holistic, not modular; one learns in layers, and the chapter sections are intended to produce a cumulative impression, one that may reorient the reader's perception of human problem solving and the potential for computer assistance to that activity.

5.2. Human Problem Solving

As soon will be apparent, the title of this section is misleading. Why did I choose a section title that I would tarnish in the very first sentence? Because the section title is also the title of an important book by Newell and Simon (1972), a work that provides an excellent introduction to the symbolic model of human memory, the role of computers in problem solving, and the nature of knowledge in problem solving. I could not resist such a thematic opening.

Human Problem Solving begins, "The aim of this book is to advance our understanding of how humans think. It seeks to do so by putting forth a theory of human problem solving, along with a body of empirical evidence that permits assessment of that theory" (p. 1). The book is a seminal work in cognitive science. By way of background, we already have noted a growing reliance on rigorous scientific methods during the first half of this century. In psychology, this manifested itself as a move from introspection (which subjectively explored the nature of consciousness) to behaviorism (which excluded all that was speculative and that could not be observed directly). In the mid 1950s the paradigm began to shift once more. Works contributing to that shift included Bruner, Goodnow, and Austin, *Study of Thinking* (1956), Miller, "The Magical Number Seven, Plus or Minus Two" (1956), Chomsky, *Syntactic*

Structures (1957), and advances in computing, including the 1954 Dartmouth conference, generally accepted as the beginning of artificial intelligence (AI).

A new paradigm of psychology, cognitive psychology, emerged. It concerned itself with the study of internal processes, conscious or not, that may be inferred by an outside observer on the basis of the organism's behavior. Where the behaviorist was limited to controlling only the stimulus and relating it to a response, the cognitive psychologist chose to study the very process of cognition. In part, this shift was the result of a reaction away from the behaviorist programme; also, in part, it reflected an interest in the new computational technology. If the nervous system was an information processor (and much of the empirical research was consistent with this interpretation), then two implications were clear. The first implication was that "if nervous systems are specially adapted to represent and symbolically transform the world of the organism, then the abstract principles of symbol-manipulation must also apply to it" (Baars 1986, p. 148). Second, it followed that if the information processing computations were discovered, then these computations could be processed in an arbitrary media (i.e., there could be *an* artificial intelligence).

The commitment to this information processing model produced a paradigm shift. Research moved from experimental observations to empirical theories derived from the analysis of verbal protocols. Because cognition (in the sense of thinking, problem solving, or memory) was computational, the proof of a theory was linked to the researcher's ability to demonstrate the theory in a computational model. As Newell and Simon (1972) put it, "The theory performs the task it explains. That is, a good information processing theory of a good human chess player can play good chess; a good theory of how humans create novels will create novels; a good theory of how children read will likewise read and understand" (pp. 10-11). By moving from closed stimulus-response experiments to the more open models of dynamic, history-dependent systems, statistical theory ceased to be of much value. "The theory tends to put a high premium on discovering and describing systems of mechanisms that are *sufficient* to perform the cognitive task under study" (p. 13).

The multidisciplinary nature of the new branch of psychology soon evolved into the field of cognitive science, which overlaps with cognitive psychology, linguistics, philosophy, AI, and neuroscience. "Cognitive science reclaims mentalist constructs like beliefs, desires, intentions, planning and problem-solving.... The study of cognition is to be empiricized not by the strict adherence to behaviorism, but by the use of a new technology; namely, the computer" (Suchman 1988, p. 307). Clearly, this view is at variance with Heidegger's philosophy as described in Chapter 4, and it will be helpful to stake out some common ground before proceeding.   Of particular concern is the acceptance of the information processing model of human cognition.   This, in part, is based on a model of human memory composed of *buffers* for input and output, *short-term memory* with a capacity of seven plus or minus two (or perhaps less), and *long-term memory* with an unbounded capacity.   The contents of memory are organized as *chunks*, which are in turn composed of chunks.   The chunks are organized within long-term memory in a *schema*, which provides access to the chunks that are moved into short-term memory to support processing.   The contents of memory (i.e., chunks) can be expressed symbolically.   This is the essential structure of memory as it was formalized in the mid 1970s. Since then, research has suggested that memory representation is far richer than the schema concept would suggest (Alba and Hasher 1983), that the role of truly unconscious memory is significant (Kihlstrom 1987), that there are memory structures not included in this model (Tulving and Schacter 1990), and that the model addresses only the *how* of memory and not the *why* (Bruce 1985).   Furthermore, the symbolic model of memory does not incorporate the research findings in parallel distributed processing (Rumelhart and McClelland 1986) and some of the recent thoughts in the philosophy of mind (Bechtel 1988b; Goldman 1993).

The model of human memory used in information processing was developed over a period of time through a variety of experiments and empirical studies, and, as will be shown, it is effective for understanding many aspects of human behavior.   The question is, of course, is this a realistic model of the nervous system (i.e., of how the brain works)? Dreyfus, in *What Computers Can't Do* (first published in 1972) led the charge against the possibility of AI achieving its goals.   In the introduction to the third edition (1992), now retitled *What Computers Still Can't Do*, he wrote, "After fifty years of effort, however, it now is clear to all but a few diehards that this attempt to produce general artificial intelligence has failed.... Indeed, what John Haugeland has called Good Old-Fashioned AI (GOFAI) is a paradigm case of what philosophers of science call a degenerating research program" (p. ix). Nevertheless, Newell and his colleagues have pursued a unified theory of cognition and have developed a computer program, SOAR, that builds chunks as it learns from experience (Newell 1990), and Simon and his colleagues have constructed a program, Bacon, that can discover solutions to scientific problems (Langley, Simon, Bradshaw, and Zytkow 1987).   Where do I stand in this debate?

From a biological standpoint, 99% of the human and chimpanzee genetic makeups are identical.   The *Homo* genus emerged only two million years ago, *Homo sapiens* has existed for less than half a million years, and there is less than 100,000 years of human history.   Given the slowness of the evolutionary process and the relatively brief presence of

H. sapiens, I have difficulty is seeing how "intelligence" can be excised from the necessary survival, emotional, and procreational drives mandated by the evolutionary process. For me, the encapsulation of intelligence (except in the sense of, "that's what IQ tests measure") is as practical a charge as the specification of the human components of "walking" (a learned motor skill) or "love" (of parent, of spouse, of sibling, of child, or, if you will forgive me, of country).

My skepticism regarding the isolation of an information processing model for cognition reflects my view of reality. If one accepts a closed world (in the Cartesian, monistic sense), then all true models will complement each other, and it may be possible to build an artificial model of intelligence. However, I accept an open world in which many plural realities exist. The principal criterion for my choice of a model is relevance to the issues I address. Thus, wherever SOAR or Bacon do useful things or provide valuable models, then I accept them; not dogmatically, but pragmatically. Again, this is a weak argument, one that will be useful independent of a validation of SOAR as a unified theory of cognition.

So far in this chapter I have used the most extreme claims of AI. There are, of course, more constrained interpretations of AI. One classic statement is, "If it works, then it isn't AI." In this view, AI approaches new and difficult problems with the understanding that once a solution to the problem is at hand, the "AIness" of the solution disappears. This sense of AI is reflected in the definition of Rich and Knight (1991), AI "is the study of how to make computers do things which, at the moment, people do better" (p. 3). But this is really too broad a view in that it does not exclude algorithmic computations that are poorly matched to the human reasoning capacity (e.g., the computation of Bayesian probabilities). One property common to all AI applications, however, is that they rely on *knowledge*, and perhaps this will serve as a better organizing principle. Gardner (1985) hopes that cognitive science will "explain human knowledge. I am interested in whether questions that intrigued our philosophical ancestors can be decisively answered, instructively reformulated, or permanently scuttled. Today cognitive science holds the key to whether they can be" (p. 6).

Gardner identifies five features or aspects of cognitive science that he holds to be of paramount importance:

> First of all, there is the belief that, in talking about human cognitive activities, it is necessary to speak about mental representations and to posit a level of analysis wholly separate from the biological or neurological, on the one hand, and the sociological or cultural, on the other.
> Second, there is the faith that central to any understanding of the human mind is the electronic computer. Not only are

computers indispensable for carrying out studies of various sorts, but, more crucially, the computer serves as the most viable model of how the human mind functions.

... The third feature of cognitive science is the deliberate decision to de-emphasize certain factors which may be important for cognitive functioning but whose inclusion at this point would unnecessarily complicate the cognitive-scientific enterprise. These factors include the influence of the affective factors or emotions, the contribution of historical or cultural factors, and the role of the background context in which particular actions or thought occur.

As a fourth feature, cognitive scientists harbor the faith that much is to be gained from interdisciplinary studies....

A fifth and somewhat controversial feature is the claim that ... it is unthinkable that cognitive science would exist, let alone assume its current form, had there not been a philosophical tradition dating back to the time of the Greeks. (pp. 6-7)

Gardner's fifth item places cognitive science in a closed world in which, through reason, humanity can derive immutable phenomenological explanations. In contrast, I have accepted the context of an open world in which, even though such explanations may be found, I choose not to seek them. In the closed world, decontextualization produces *generalizations valid in all contexts*. (That is, given that there is a single universal model, reduction can be used to decompose the full model into smaller models, each of which serves as a part of the larger model.) In contrast, in an open world, decontextualization defines the *context within which the generalization is valid*. (Here there are plural realities, and individual models are assumed to be valid only within a specific context; such models may be composed to create larger models only within a common context.) Thus, within a closed world it is appropriate to reduce complexity by restricting the scope of the investigation as Gardner does with his third item. For him, the findings within that restricted context are perceived to be valid for all contexts. In my open-world model, on the other hand, these restrictions establish the context within which the findings are valid.

My reliance on an open-world model also leads me to question the representation of mental states. I believe that the medium used for interpreting the states affects their representation. Most models of internal representation are derived from the analysis of verbal protocols. As a result, the internal representations tend to be expressed symbolically, usually as words or phrases. But in Chapter 4 we have seen that our knowledge of a chair (or of a game) is not something we can explain. Interjections such as "You know," "I mean," and "like" attest to our inability to assign symbols to internal states. Thus, with my view of an open world (and its plural realities), I am able to accept only that some mental states can be expressed symbolically and that some symbolic models of mental representations are relevant.

Hey! What does this have to do with computers and design? The distinction between a closed-world and open-world model is, in its essence, a comment on knowledge and what is *knowable*. In the closed world all knowledge is first formulated as a mental state, and the representations constitute what is *known*. This assertion is exploited in the very powerful AI paradigm in which knowledge is separated from the operations on it. What, then, of knowledge representation within an open-world model? To clarify the ensuing discussion, I begin with a three-level definition in which *data* are the items given to the analyst, *information* is the data organized in a some useful fashion (i.e., data with value added), and *knowledge* is the cumulative experience in the manipulation, exchange, and creation of information.

Machlup (1983) points out that we exchange (i.e., tell and are told) information, but knowledge we possess in the sense of knowing. "The former is a process, the latter a state. Information in the sense of that which is being told *may* be the same as knowledge in the sense of that which is known, but *need not* be the same. That even in everyday parlance people sense a difference can be seen from the fact that in railroad stations, airports, department stores, and large public buildings we expect to find a booth or counter marked *Information* but never one marked *Knowledge*.... On the other hand, we would frown on education programs that fill the student's head with loads of information: We want them to disseminate knowledge of enduring value and to develop a taste or thirst for more knowledge, not just information" (pp. 644-45).

In Machlup's description, information is what is exchanged among knowing individuals, and the individuals' knowledge determines how the information is processed. In a computer model, however, both information and knowledge must be stored as data; one can represent what the designers "know" but not what the computer program "knows." The program can only manipulate the designers' knowledge. Davis, Shrobe, and Szolovitz (1993) identify five distinct roles that a computer-oriented knowledge representation plays.

> First, a knowledge representation is most fundamentally a *surrogate*, a substitute for the thing itself, that is used to enable an entity to determine consequences by thinking rather than acting....
>
> Second, it is a set of ontological commitments, that is, an answer to the question, in what terms should I think about the world?
>
> Third, it is a fragmentary theory of intelligent reasoning expressed in terms of three components: (1) the representation's

fundamental conception of intelligent reasoning, (2) the set of inferences that the representation sanctions, and (3) the set of inferences that it recommends.

Fourth, it is a medium for pragmatically efficient computation, that is, the computational environment in which thinking is accomplished....

Fifth, it is a medium of expression, that is, a language in which we say things about the world. (p. 17)

If one discounts the implications of some of the vocabulary (e.g., thinking and intelligent), then this view of a knowledge representation is compatible with both an open model within a closed world (i.e., with generalized truths valid in all contexts) and a closed model within an open world (i.e., valid only within a given context). The distinction is analogous to that between the search for *an* artificial intelligence and the goal of making computers do things which, at the moment, people do better.

It should be very clear by now that I subscribe to the view of closed models within an open world and that, moreover, my choices will be guided by considerations of utility and practically. As Kitcher (1993) observes, "Truth is very easy to get.... The trouble is that most of the truths ... are boring.... What we want is *significant* truth. Perhaps,... what we want is significance and *not* truth" (p. 94) Goodman (1984) offers a complementary statement, "We are monists, pluralists, or nihilists not quite as the wind blows but as befits the context" (p. 33). Therefore, my dogma (and that of this book) is that of the skeptic. I cannot establish what is true, but I can develop models that I believe to be free of error and that I assert reflect reality within some context. I shall speak of "what we know" (within this context) and seek to represent such knowledge. However, I will avoid words that imply a more ambitious programme (e.g., intelligent, reasoning, thinking, assistant). I am interested in the design of computer-supported artifacts that build on what we know and thereby improve our environments (e.g., workplace, social organizations, ecology). I obviously expect computers to do things that, at the moment, people do better, and I label my approach to design "knowledge based" (i.e., building on previous experience). I exploit the models resulting from research in AI, but I do not restrict myself to any AI paradigm. I see computers as equipment (in the sense of something-in-order-to), and my concern, as well as that of this book, is for the equipment that will make computers more effective (i.e., the equipment for design).

It now is obvious why the section title is misleading. The discussion was not about human problem solving but rather about abstracted models of human problem solving. The message was that the AI paradigm is based upon the assertion that much of the human problem-solving mechanism can be formally replicated in-the-computer. I gave my reasons for skepticism, but I remain open to correction. In any case, I opt for a pragmatic path that exploits everything relevant. In creating software environments that support design, we must draw upon what is known and we must find ways of representing that knowledge. But I do not sense that the AI paradigm can provide the desired solution; indeed, it is not even referenced in Part III. Only humans perform human problem solving, and perhaps we will gain a richer understanding of problem solving if we explore how they do so in-the-world.

5.3. Human Problem Solving in the Real World

In a 1976 conference on Practical Aspects of Memory, Neisser presented a paper titled "Memory: What Are the Important Questions?" in which "he dismissed the work of the past 100 years as largely worthless.... [He felt that] psychologists should adopt an ethological approach, studying human memory in the same way that ethologists study animal behavior. In Neisser's own phrase, memory research should have *ecological validity*. By this he means that it should apply to naturally occurring behavior in the natural context of the real world" (Cohen 1989, p. 2). Neisser subsequently recanted his extreme position and accepted the validity of much of the earlier work, but his rebellion was one of several contemporaneous reactions that moved research away from the controls of a laboratory and into natural settings. This section examines human cognition from an "ecological" perspective. I am concerned with how people solve problems in-the-world, what they do well (and poorly), and how computers may complement the human activity.

One of the early 20th century models of problem solving was developed by Wallas (1926). It was derived from introspective accounts and consisted of four stages:

Preparation, in which the problem is investigated "in all directions."

Incubation, during which there is no conscious thinking of the problem; indeed, such thinking might even be discouraged.

Illumination, which is characterized by the appearance of the "happy idea" or the "Aha!"

Verification, during which the idea is verified using knowledge of the initial problem.

The model relegated the problem solving activity to the unconscious, an approach that seemed consistent with various accounts of how solutions to scientific and mathematical problems seemed suddenly to resolve themselves. Recent work suggests that the role of the unconscious is minimal (Weisberg 1986), and Olton and Johnson (1976) have been unable to duplicate incubation in the laboratory. Olton (1979) nonetheless observes that there is a universal, and unexplained, experience of incubation. "When a person has struggled with a task or problem for a while and seems to be temporarily 'stuck' or in need of new ideas, putting the task aside for a period of time often appears to facilitate one's thinking. Taking a break ... does provide a pause that refreshes, and a thinker seems well advised to take advantage of this" (p. 21).

One of the difficulties in cognitive psychology is that we can only observe the conscious, and even here there is a form of the Heisenberg principle at work: The act of observing affects what is being observed. Olton suggests that incubation may be mistaken for what actually is "'creative worrying' [which] is really a sort of mental time-sharing, when one's attention is devoted primarily to other concerns, but where the person nevertheless manages to devote some conscious attention to the task of interest, albeit in a fragmented and sometime undirected way" (p. 11). He also comments that the break aspect of incubation is similar to the use of a break in the "tip-of-the-tongue" phenomenon, wherein one cannot recall something one knows (e.g., a person's name). In any case, Wallas' introspective model has been discredited, even though no satisfying account for the common experience he called incubation has been proposed.

In contrast to his four-stage model, the information processing models of the 1970s and beyond assume the contents of memory to be expressed symbolically, to be organized in long-term memory in a schema, and to be processed in short-term memory. The processing is described as a search activity that begins with a goal (intention) and continues until the search through the problem space (i.e., knowledge of the problem domain) satisfies the goal (or it is demonstrated that the goal cannot be met). As noted in the quotation from Gardner in the previous section, the information processing model does not address matters of affect such as fatigue or emotion.

Wow! I begin this section by identifying a commonly experienced phenomenon that sixty years of research have failed to explain. But do not be discouraged. Research motivated by the information processing model has generated some very practical insights into problem solving in the real world. For example, memory retention is U-shaped in that the earliest experiences (e.g., a chick bonding) and the most recent experiences are very persistent. This is the source of the joke about medical students—who are exposed to all kinds of rare diseases—that when they hear the sound of hoof-beats, they immediately think of zebras. We also know that a degree of emotional intensity (e.g., commitment) improves learning up to a point, but beyond that point (e.g., during stress) learning is slowed down.

Short-term memory has a very limited capacity, and information processing is limited to what can be managed in short-term memory. Sisson, Schoomaker and Ross (1976) have shown that diagnostic accuracy can be lower when clinicians are provided with too much data than with what appears to be too little data. One way in which people overcome the limitation of short-term memory is to use what Newell and Simon (1972) refer to as external memory (e.g., pencil and paper). Computers also can serve this function. For example, McDonald (1976) demonstrated the efficacy of computer-based protocols (which recommend actions on the basis of standards of care) in reducing the clinicians' information overload. Here the computer acted, not as an "intelligent assistant" to the clinician, but as a preprocessor and integrator of mutually accepted facts and conventions. Thus, for our objective of aiding the design process, there is considerable evidence that the computer can be effective as an organizer, filter, and reporter of what already is known.

Although the models of memory emphasize the symbolic nature of the contents, this representation is incomplete. An early experiment by Sperling (1960) showed that more information is available to an observer than can be expressed explicitly. In Sperling's experiment, subjects looked into a tachistoscope and were shown a 4×3 matrix of randomly selected consonants for 50 milliseconds. Using Miller's magical number, one would not expect subjects to recall more than 7 ± 2 independent items, and the subjects were unable to recall the full matrix. However, if between 150 and 1000 milliseconds after exposure to the matrix, a specific row was identified for the subjects to report, they were successful in listing the contents. Why could the subjects report the contents of any single row but not the full matrix? It seems that the recall of the first few items interferes with the ability to recall the rest. In contrast, computer memory is persistent; there are no restraints regarding the amount of stored information that can be subsequently accessed.

Human memory operates by pattern matching. By way of demonstration, look at the illustration in Figure 5.1. "A seemingly irregular pattern of splodges will on patient inspection transform themselves into a Dalmatian dog. Once seen it becomes impossible to look at the splodges again without seeing the hidden hound" (Thompson 1985, p. 30). That is, memory is trained to perceive a dog, and, once trained, cannot revert to the naive, pre-trained state. Incidently, the photograph originally was intended to demonstrate natural camouflage. "The identifiable outline of a Dalmatian dog disappears when its markings merge in an environment of light and shadow" (Carraher and Thurston 1966, p. 19). These two contexts will affect a naive viewer's reaction to

Fig. 5.1. R.C. James' spotty dog.
From Carraher and Thurston (1966), property of the photographer.

the scene; each observation begins with a different expectation. Nevertheless, the end result will be the same; once trained to recognize a dog, one can never again interpret the picture as a collection of splodges.

The figure brings to mind two important differences between humans and computers. First, a computer program can always be returned to a previous state for reinterpretion; for humans, reassessment requires new learning from the perspective of what already has been learned. The second difference relates to the kinds of patterns that may be processed; whereas people are very good with visual displays, computers excel with numeric structures. Any symbiotic relationship must find a way to match these differences.

As already noted, in the dominant model of human memory the contents of long-term memory are organized in a structure called a *schema*. Schema theory was introduced by Bartlett in 1932 as a way of explaining how people remember stories even though the story may later be reconstructed to make it better fit their knowledge and experience. The theory was neglected until its relevance to the study of human memory became obvious. "Schema theory emphasizes the role of prior knowledge and past experience, claiming that what we remember is influenced by what we already know. According to this theory, the knowledge we have stored in memory is organized as a set of schema, or knowledge structures, which represent the general knowledge about objects, situations, events, or actions that has been acquired from past experience" (Cohen 1989, p. 71).

Studies of how students learn science, for example, show that learners look for meaning and try to construct order even in the absence of complete information (Resnik 1983, Kuhn, Amsel, and O'Loughlin 1988). Students attempt to append new information onto existing knowledge in the schema; if no such structure exists, the information will not be retained. Often, *naive theories* are constructed to bridge between the new facts and existing understanding. In this respect, computers and humans share a similar capability: the ability to organize data (information/knowledge) in complex networks. Unfortunately, few computer systems exploit this potential in any significant way. (Adaptive design does.)

Some of the contents of memory are characterized as mental models, which Johnson-Laird (1983a) states "play a central and unifying role in representing objects, states of affairs, sequences of events, the way the world is, and the social and physiological actions of daily life. They enable individuals to make inferences and predictions, to understand phenomena, to decide what action to take and to control its execution, and, above all, to experience events by proxy" (p. 397). Thus, he views the mental model as a (perhaps incomplete or simplified) working model of the real world that may have been dynamically constructed to guide planning. There is some controversy regarding this view of mental models (see Cohen 1989), but the term has broad acceptance for describing selected aspects of a subject's understanding of the world (e.g., the users' view of a system). Clearly, mental models are captured in computer systems, but often their role is simply descriptive (i.e., they document why the program was designed in such a way). I return to this topic in Chapter 7.

Learning is the process of adding to the schema. Woodworth (1938) described progress in learning as going from chaos, to analysis, to synthesis, and finally to automatization. Rumelhart and Norman (1981) identify three modes of learning:

Accretion. This is the most common mode of learning. New knowledge is added to existing memory schema.

Structuring. This they consider the most important of the models. It entails the formation of new conceptual structures (i.e., new conceptualizations). Because the existing schema no longer suffice, new schema must be formed. As with a paradigm shift, the mode requires great effort and struggle, and it therefore occurs infrequently.

Tuning. This is the slowest mode of learning, but it is the one that transforms mere knowledge into expert performance. It can be characterized as the adjustment of knowledge to a task, typically through practice or experience. Restating this in my vocabulary, as the result of many and various encounters, the learner comes to understand the full context of the knowledge accumulated within a particular domain.

Most computer applications support some form of accretion, but structuring typically requires redesign and/or programming. Tuning, as I discuss in Chapter 8, involves participation by both the system designers and its users.

Of particular interest for us is how people learn science, which can be characterized as a transition from a world of "common sense" to one of model formulation and validation. "As the scientist explores the environment, constructs models as a basis for understanding it, and revises those models as new evidence is generated, so do lay people endeavor to make sense of their environments by processing data and constructing mental models on these data" (D. Kuhn 1989, p. 674). "Common sense," of course, is culturally determined. Our common sense faith in science provides the incentive for moving from naive to formal models. This is a bias of Western cultures; it is not universal.

Horton (1967), for instance, has examined the spiritual thought of traditional cultures in Africa and compared them to the mechanistic thought of modern Western cultures. He showed how the former, no less than the latter, "gave rise to theoretical systems whose basic *raison d'être* was the extension of the magnificent but none the less limited causal vision of everyday commonsense thinking" (Horton 1982, p. 201). Thus, common sense need not be consistent with what we recognize as scientific finding. Indeed, McCloskey (1983) has reported on the persistence of "intuitive physics" in which, despite a knowledge of Newton's laws, subjects believe that moving objects behave otherwise. As Kuhn (1989) explains it, "When theory and evidence are compatible, the two are melded into a single representation of the 'way things are.' When they are discrepant, subjects change strategies for maintaining their alignment—either adjusting the theory, typically without acknowledging having done so, or 'adjusting' the evidence, by ignoring it or attending to it in a selective, distorting manner" (p. 687). Although it is doubtful that computer systems can capture common sense, they can be used to employ the existing formalized knowledge to reduce misinterpretation of the evidence and to lessen the overlooking of known relationships.

Kuhn's remark suggests that individuals may avoid breakdowns by fitting the observations to knowledge by adjusting either the knowledge or the observation. This is a naive mode of accretion, in which the subjects (all children in this context) do not differentiate between knowledge and observation, (i.e., theories and evidence). Because science is culturally valued, one of the goals of education is to instill this distinction. We seek to achieve "the full differentiation and coordination of theories and evidence and the elevation of the theory-evidence interaction to the level of conscious control. It is in these crucial respects that the professional scientist and child as scientist differ" (p. 687). For the scientist, expertise involves a structuring of the schema that extends common sense to include procedural knowledge for reasoning about knowledge and observation. With scientific expertise, the distinction becomes instinctive, obvious, and (therefore) invisible. Just as the splodges of Figure 5.1 will now always depict a dog, the trained scientist will never confuse theory with evidence. The theories become deeply ingrained patterns used in problem solving, patterns that often can be modeled in the computer.

Given a set of learned patterns, the information processing of cognition characterizes problem solving as a search through knowledge within the memory schema. How well does our experience with problem solving in-the-world conform to this representation? In some ways, very well. For example, Elstein and his colleagues (1978) investigated how clinicians perform medical problem solving. They organize the process into the following four-step hypothetico-deductive model.

Cue acquisition. Taking a history, performing a physical examination, reviewing test results, etc.

Hypothesis generation. Retrieving alternative hypotheses of the diagnosis from long term memory.

Cue interpretation. Considering the data in the context of the hypotheses previously generated.

Hypothesis evaluation. Weighing and combining the data to determine which hypotheses are supported or ruled out.

Naturally, the process is iterative.

In analyzing clinicians' actions within the model framework, the researchers find that the generation of early hypotheses has considerable natural force; medical students generate early hypotheses even when asked to withhold judgment. The number of hypotheses is usually around four or five and appears to have an upper bound of six or seven. The generation of hypotheses is based more consistently on single salient clues rather than on combinations of clues. Very few cues seem to be used, and hypothesis selection is biased by recent experience. Also, cue interpretation tend to use three measures: confirm, disconfirm, and noncontributory; the use of a seven-point scale has no greater explanatory power. Finally, researchers note that lack of thoroughness is not as important a cause of error in diagnosis as are problems in integrating and combining information.

In summary, the research suggests humans use a relatively shallow pattern matching mechanism with rapid access to a large store of patterns from which a "best match" can be identified. In contrast, the computer works well with deep models requiring many more than seven plus or minus two variables, but it seems to have a limited facility for storing the kinds of patterns employed in human problem solving. For example, computers have little difficulty in managing multiple clues and measures of fine granularity, but they do have trouble integrating observations not bound to its formal models (e.g., mathematically defined relationships or sets of declarative facts and rules).

Elstein *et al.* describe clinical problem-solving activity as iterations of the hypothetico-deductive cycle until there is a match is made that initiates action. Although the process clearly permits backtracking, it is essentially linear in nature, and the model assumes that the decision will be made from knowledge explicitly available to the clinician. Several recent histiographic studies of invention suggest that when the timeliness of the decision is not critical, the process actually is less well-structured. Gooding (1990) has conducted an analysis of the Faraday's discovery of the electromagnetic motor in 1821. His method attempts to recover situated learning in a material environment (i.e., it tries to use the knowledge and context available to Faraday at the time of the discovery). The goal is to show how Faraday modeled new experience and invented procedures to communicate that novelty, and Gooding constructs maps that represent experiments as an active process within the context of available knowledge.

Using this method, Gooding cannot reconstruct Faraday's actions as a linear process, or even explain it by "reasoning" in the sense of logical problem solving. And herein lies a contradiction. "When reasoning does not resemble this form [of logic]—and situated, practical problem solving does not, without severe distortion, resemble it—then it does not count as reasoning at all" (p. 167). That is, looking forward, he could not establish a logic to explain all of Faraday's actions, but—in retrospect, once the results had been confirmed—he could construct a rational argument that could explain their derivation (something referred to as Whig history: explaining actual outcomes as if they were inevitable). He concludes, "This picture challenges the traditional, Cartesian distinction between mental and material, which has made the 'connection' between thought and talk between the natural and social worlds so mysterious. What connects them is human agency" (p. 196). We cannot hope to model "human agency," but we can devise computer models that support it. Indeed, for the domain of software design, this is what adaptive design accomplishes. But let me return to the topic at hand.

In another investigation of innovation, Gorman and Carlson (1990) examine the cognitive processes of Bell and Edison during the invention of the telephone. They describe invention as a process in which the inventor combines abstract ideas (mental models) with physical objects (mechanical representations) using heuristics. They conclude,

> ... if Bell and Edison are any indication, the innovation process is much better characterized as a recursive activity in which inventors move back and forth between ideas and objects. Inventors may start out with one mental model and modify it after experimenting with different mechanical representations, or they many start out with several mechanical representations and gradually shape a mental model. In both cases, the essence of invention seems to be the dynamic interplay of mental models with mechanical representations. It is hardly a straightforward, linear process moving from conception to realization. (p. 159)

This raises some interesting questions. How like invention is design? How typical are the actions of these three inventors? Is their expertise similar to the expertise found in other domains? How does this experience generate insight into automating support for problem solving?

I offer no answers to these questions. Science progresses when we ask the right answers, and in these foundational chapters I am trying to identify the important questions. There are many conflicting answers, and adaptive design—described and evaluated in Part III—constitutes one such answer. But I do not want to overconstrain the search by the early binding of arbitrary assumptions. We seek a new paradigm for design, one that employs the special characteristics of software. We wish to improve the design process by extending the support provided by software. Therefore, we need to know what people can and cannot do and how computers can and cannot assist them. The goal of Part II is to reshape the solution space, not to narrow it to a single solution. That is the function of Part III.

Where are we now in this journey? Section 5.2 assesses the AI programme and states why I do not believe it offers an appropriate foundation for a new era of design. This section reviews human problem solving in-the-world and compares and contrasts the characters of people and machines. A faint outline is beginning to emerge, one that suggests a division of labor leading to a symbiotic relationship between the human and the computer. Clearly, we do not know what the computer can never do; its potential has only been partially tapped. With our current state of understanding, however, we must assume that the computer can only build on what humans represent as knowledge.

Part I demonstrates that scientific knowledge is not composed of immutable truths; it exists within a context, a set of driving assumptions. Part II investigates the nature of human knowledge: what is known, knowable, and formally representable. Scientific knowledge is a subset of human knowledge, expertise is the richest form of human knowledge, and only formally represented knowledge can be modeled in-the-computer. In establishing a foundation for a new era of design we must understand the relationships among these forms of knowledge. In particular, we need to assess expert knowledge with respect to its formality and to determine which, if any, classes of human knowledge can never be modeled in-the-computer. In pursuit of answers that may identify new questions, I turn now to an examination of expertise.

5.4. The Nature of Expertise

We know that experts have considerable knowledge. For example, in contrast to novices, chess masters consider very few moves at each turn, and their moves are almost always appropriate. Chase and Simon (1973) computed that chess masters acquire approximately 50,000 patterns, with four or five pieces in each pattern. But are those patterns stored and accessed consistent with the information processing model? That is, is the selection of a move the result of a goal-directed search through memory, or is there some other mechanism? I begin by exploring what is meant by expertise.

Glaser and Chi (1988) have highlighted some of its principal characteristics:

> Experts excel mainly in their own domains....
> Experts perceive large meaningful patterns in their domain....
> Experts are fast; they are faster than novices at performing the skills of their domain, and they quickly solve problems with little error....
> Experts have superior short-term and long-term memory....
> Experts see and represent a problem in their domain at a deeper (more principled) level than novices; novices tend to represent a problem at a superficial level....
> Experts spend a great deal of time analyzing a problem qualitatively....
> Experts have strong self-monitoring skills.... (pp. xvii-xx)

Norman (1982) identifies five major (overlapping) characteristics of expert performance.

Smoothness. This is the apparent ease with which a professional performs. The expert seems unhurried and moves gracefully from one action to another.

Automaticity. The expert tends to do the task automatically, without conscious awareness of exactly what is being done. This characteristic is what Glaser and Chi referred to when they spoke of the expert's superior short-term memory: the automaticity of skills frees up resources for greater apparent storage.

Mental effort. As skill increases, mental effort decreases. Tasks seem easier, there is less fatigue, and the need for conscious monitoring diminishes.

Stress. Skills that are automated tend not to deteriorate as much under stress, a fact that distinguishes the amateur from the expert.

Point of view. Norman gives the example of walking: you do not think of leg placement, but rather where you want to go. In a sense, this is the bringing of a skill (motor or intellectual) ready-to-hand and, consequently, invisible unless there is a breakdown.

Norman's description emphasizes the automaticity/invisibility of expertise, properties that are consistent with the five-stage model for skill acquisition developed by Dreyfus and Dreyfus (1986):

Novice. Here "the novice learns to recognize various objective facts and features relevant to the skill and acquires rules for determining actions based upon those facts and features" (p. 21).

Advanced beginner. "Performance improves to a marginally acceptable level only after the novice has considerable experience in coping with real situations" (p. 22). That is, sufficient knowledge has been accreted to permit the process of tuning to begin.

Competence. As the number of context-free and situational elements begin to overload, the individual learns to specialize, often by establishing a hierarchical procedure of decision making. Situations are interpreted as facts, and constellations of facts are seen to lead to conclusions, decisions, or other actions.

Proficiency. The proficient performer moves from a conscious conformance to rules to a deep involvement with and reaction to the task based on intuition or "know-how." *"Intuition or know-how, as we understand it, is neither wild guessing nor supernatural inspiration, but the sort of ability we all use all the time as we go about our everyday tasks"* (p. 29).

Expertise. "An expert generally knows what to do based on mature and practiced understanding. When deeply involved in coping with his environment, he does not see problems in some detached way and work at solving them, nor does he worry about the future and devise plans.... *When things are proceeding normally, experts don't solve problems and don't make decisions; they do what normally works"* (pp. 30-31).

What stands out in the Dreyfus brothers' model is the "progression *from* the analytic behavior of a detached subject, consciously decomposing his environment into recognizable elements, and following abstract rules, *to* involved skilled behavior based on an accumulation of concrete experiences and the unconscious recognition of new situations as similar to whole remembered ones" (p. 35). Their model is intended as a counter the Cartesian view (and the AI programme within it), yet this brief description is compatible with both of the earlier characterizations of expertise. The Dreyfus brothers close their discussion with these observations: "There is more to intelligence than calculative rationality... *Competent performance is rational; proficiency is transrational; experts act arationally"* (p. 36). If this is true (and I believe it is), then expert systems cannot surpass the level of competence. What makes a human expert an expert is the assimilation of intellectual and/or motor skills that are not perceived to be "common."

This is, of course, a cultural assessment. We do not think of ourselves as "expert" readers or spellers, but in a time of limited literacy we would be so viewed; similarly, the stitchery of the 19th century upper-class European women—then viewed as an appropriate social skill—now would be accepted as expert craftsmanship. Placing my stamp on this discussion of expertise: We are all expert in many areas, but where that expertise is shared within the society, the expertise is invisible; it is accepted as an extension of common sense that is instinctive (i.e., requires no rational justification, is arational). Wherever the expertise is rare, it is recognized and generally admired. For the expert, acquired skills are used implicitly, not explicitly. "The best pilots, for example, claim they become a 'part' of the aircraft, anticipating, 'flying ahead of the plane.' Poorer pilots 'keep their heads in the cockpit [i.e., fly by the rules]" (Norman 1982, p. 72).

The nature of expertise also varies with culture. By way of illustration, Suchman (1987) opens her book with a quotation that contrasts the methods of expert Trukese and European navigators. The European begins with a plan (i.e., a course), and the goal is to stay "on course." When unexpected events occur, the plan must be modified.

> The Trukese navigator begins with an objective rather than a plan. He sets off toward the objective and responds to conditions as they arise in an ad hoc fashion. He utilizes information provided by the wind, the waves, the tide and current, the fauna, the stars, the clouds, the sound of the water on the side of the boat, and he steers accordingly. His effort is directed to doing whatever is necessary to reach the objective. If asked, he can point to his objective at any moment, but he cannot describe his course. (Berreman 1966, p. 347)

The European navigator uses knowledge in the form of external memory (i.e., the navigation charts) together with a plan to guide in its use. Expertise here permits the navigator to alter the plans and integrate the knowledge in the external memory. In this way, the planning process has been generalized and can, in theory, be applied to any navigation task. The Trukese navigator, on the other hand, cannot describe the knowledge he uses; he relies on instinct and a deep understanding of a specialized geography. Western thinking has emphasized the formal (e.g., the navigation charts) in favor of the instinctive, and the formal does have the ability to scale up. But when we consider knowledge (i.e., what is "known"), there is a danger that by emphasizing the knowledge that can be represented formally, we may obscure the importance of what is known instinctively.

For example, Dreyfus and Dreyfus (1986) cite the American experience with chicken sexing during the 1930s. For egg production, it is economically desirable to eliminate male chicks as early as possible. It was known that, in Japan, trained "sexers" were able to recognize day-old male chicks, even before their genitals were visibly differentiated. Consequently, Japanese sexers were invited to the United States first to demonstrate their skills and then to train others. During the training, the trainees "watch while an expert takes a box full of assorted chicks as they come from the incubator, picks up the chicks, turns them back side up, takes a quick look, and releases them into two other boxes marked 'pullets' and 'cockerels,' respectively. After three months of apprenticeship trainees are able to begin sorting on their own.... The secret is not in Japanese fingers but in a culture that trusts intuition" (p. 197). That is, where Western culture trusts only what can be written, other cultures place a greater emphasis on what must be learned but cannot be explained.

Brown and Duguid (1992) speak of three kinds of instruction: explicit, tacit, and implicit. Tacit "suggests that this part of understanding is merely hidden, and that once uncovered, can be made explicit.... The implicit is ontologically distinct from the explicit [in] that more explicit instruction will not suffice. Implicit understanding of a praxis is developed in praxis" (p. 170). Thus, it is reasonable to assert that there is much that we know that we cannot represent formally, and that this implicit knowledge is an essential part of our environment.

In addition to establishing our intuitive responses, culture also determines how we see. Deregowski (1972) reports that African children and adults prefer a "split-elephant" drawing (i.e., a top-down view that lays out the legs, back, and head in the form of an elephant-skin rug) to one of a photographically rendered top-view perspective. "In all societies children have an aesthetic preference for drawings of the split type. In most societies this preference is suppressed because the drawings do not convey information about the depicted objects as perspective drawings do. Therefore aesthetic preference is sacrificed on the alter of efficiency in communication" (p. 88).

Similarly, individuals in some cultures have trouble recognizing the contents of a black-and-white photograph. "An analysis of the stimulus dimensions of a typical photograph helps explain how it might be perceived by one not familiar with it. Its strongest contours are its rectangular edges, which constitute its boundaries as a solid thing. Within these edges, the most striking part of the design is the white band around the edge, with its sharp contour where it meets the black-and-grey-mottled area. We have learned to disregard these striking aspects.... Instead, we pay attention to very weak and fuzzy contours and contrasts, which are minor stimuli in terms of any physical scoring of stimulus strength. Doing this has become so familiar to us that we expect these weak stimuli to be equally obvious to others" (Segall, Campbell, and Herskovits 1966, pp. 32-33).

Seeing is not instinctive, it is something that is learned. Sacks (1993) describes the case of Virgil, a fifty-year-old man, blind since early childhood, whose sight was restored and who now had to learn to "see." In one episode Sacks took Virgil to a zoo, where they stopped to see a gorilla. Virgil had difficulty in describing what he saw; he thought it was something like a man, but was unsure and became agitated. Sacks took him to a statue of a gorilla. "His face seemed to light up with comprehension as he felt the statue. 'It's not like a man at all,' he murmured. The statue examined, he opened his eyes, and turned around to the real gorilla standing before him in the enclosure. And now, in a way that would have been impossible before, he described the apes's posture, the way the knuckles touched the ground,..." (p. 68). Forcing Virgil to react visually put him in the position of renouncing all that came easy to him; the sightless examination of the statue associated patterns in much the same way as we recognize a spotty dog in Figure 5.1. Once trained, however, Virgil achieved a sighted perspective for gorillas in a zoo.

Gibson (1979) has proposed an ecological approach to visual perception. In Chapter 3 I described how Land (1959) demonstrated that human perception of color cannot be explained by the three-color composition model. Clearly, the three-color model is derived from sound physics, and the model is the basis for color photography. Despite the theory's relevance, however, it is not a valid model of human visual perception. Gibson points out that humans do not see individual images (i.e., snapshots). Vision occurs in-the-world, and perception develops as a mobile organism adapts within its ecological setting. "Instead of geometric points and lines, then, we have points of observation and lines of locomotion" (Gibson 1979, p. 17).

Gibson shows how animals come to recognize the surfaces that separate substances from the medium in which they live, and he describes what the environment *affords* the animals in the way of terrain, shelter, water, etc. He then introduces a theory of *affordance* "that refers to both the environment and the animal in a way that no existing term does. It implies the complementarity of the animal and the environment.... [The properties of a terrestrial surface]—horizontal, flat, extended, and rigid—would be *physical* properties of a surface if they were measured with the scales and standard units used in physics. As an affordance of support for a species of animal, however, they have to be *relative to the animal*. They are unique for that animal" (p. 127). The theory of affordances can be extended beyond visual perception. "It implies that the 'values' and 'meanings' of things in the environment can be directly perceived.... What other persons afford, comprises the whole realm of social significance for human beings. We pay the closest attention to the optical and acoustic information that specifies what the other person is, invites, threatens, and does" (pp. 127, 128). We see manifestations of this observation in speech-act theory (Searle 1969; Winograd and Flores 1986), in studies of visual imagery in problem solving (Kaufmann 1979, Richardson 1983), and, of course, in the philosophy of Heidegger.

Thus, we find expertise to be arational and based on learned ecological and cultural responses. Is scientific expertise different? That is the question that the next section explores.

5.5. Scientific Expertise

In my examination of foundational issues, we have moved from the idea of invariant, formally represented knowledge to socially determined, implicit knowledge. Recall from Chapter 2 that Popper used the principle of demarcation to separate scientific from nonscientific knowledge. The discussion in that chapter suggested that no such clear demarcation was possible. I now consider the extent to which scientific knowledge, like seeing and intuition, is socially determined.

Suchman (1988) observes, "The commitment to an abstract, disembodied account of cognition ... has led to a view of intelligence that takes it to be first and foremost mental operations and only secondarily, and as a epiphenomenon, the 'execution' of situated actions" (p. 308). She described "situated practice" as a merging of the explicit (e.g., plans) with the implicit (i.e., instinctive reactions). "The purpose of the plan ... [is] to position you in such a way that you have the best possible conditions under which to use those embodied skills on which, in the final analysis, your success depends.... Situated practice comprises moment-by-moment interactions with our environment more or less informed by reference to representations of conditions and of actions,..." (p. 314). Knorr-Cetina and Mulkay (1983) echo this observation. "Reasoned decisions ... are rooted in definitions of the situation which are partly constituted by the perceptions and beliefs of other participants in the situation, and which take into account the crystallized outcome of previous social action. Situational variables, of course, often originate in the larger social context or have other social explanations" (p. 12).

The depth of the effects of these situational variables was demonstrated in a 1977 study reported by Jones (1986). Fifty-one male and female undergraduates, who did not know each other, were paired and asked to make "get acquainted" phone calls. The men were given randomly assigned photographs of the women, and, as might be expected, the men's beliefs concerning their partners appearance led them to act more friendly, openly, and sociably if the picture was attractive than if it was plain. Moreover, women assigned attractive pictures were rated by independent judges as more poised, sociable, gregarious, and self-confident than the women assigned plain photographs. Thus, "the male subjects created a reality that they [the female subjects] then presumably interpreted as independent of their own actions" (p. 43). This kind of result has been replicated in many different experiments, which suggests that interpersonal behavior has a significant situationally determined component.

This situatedness of cognition provides the justification for "a sociological approach to knowledge making [in which] people produce knowledge against the background of their culture's inherited knowledge, their collectively situated purposes, and in the information they receive from natural reality.... Actors are seen to produce and evaluate knowledge against the background of socially transmitted knowledge and according to their goals. The role of the social, in this view, is to prestructure choice, not to preclude choice" (Shapin 1982, pp. 196, 198).

Yet, as Barnes (1983) observes, "The social character of knowledge is still portrayed as an optional extra, or, alternatively, as something which stands in opposition to the character of knowledge as a representation of reality" (p. 20). Barnes' statement reflects the resistance to the changes anticipated by Toulmin (Chapter 4). We see that resistance in cognitive science, computer science, and even in sociology itself. But a reexamination of phenomena in-the-world (i.e., as situated) is providing new insights. By way of illustration, I extract some findings from several ethnomethodological studies of scientific laboratories. Such studies focus on how the participants come to an understanding of the phenomena under investigation; the studies do not address the technical aspects of the decision making.

"According to many of these studies, the 'contents' of scientific research are documents or, in Latour and Woolgar's (1986) terms, 'inscriptions.' Manifestly, what scientists laboriously piece together, pick up in their hands, measure, show to one another, argue about, and circulate to others in their communities are not 'natural objects' independent of cultural processes and literary forms" (Lynch and Woolgar 1988, p. 103). "In the laboratory scientists operate upon (and within) a highly preconstructed artifactual reality.... Nowhere in the laboratory do we find the 'nature' or 'reality' which is so crucial to the descriptive interpretation of inquiry" (Knorr-Cetina 1983, p. 119) "From within scientific inquiry, the focus of many laboratory activities is not texts, but images and displays.... Image surface calculations, reconstructions of events in the test tubes of the lab, and remedial actions designed to transform badly turned-out pictures into showcases of data exemplify the type of work performed when technical images are inspected in the laboratory" (Knorr-Cetina and Amann 1990, pp. 259, 281). "The data *are* and *are not* the things studied *per se*; they are conditions within which 'the things' are addressed in particular instances of shop work.... The data elaborate the action (the 'claim,' the 'reading,' etc.), while themselves being elaborated. The data are inseparable from the situations of their usage" (Lynch 1985, pp. 10-11).

Because of the artisanal nature of scientific experiments, a researcher's competence and the reliability of his/her experiment can only be assessed on the basis of the results obtained. Since, however, the results can be considered valid only if they are obtained from reliable experiments, any assessment is necessarily flawed by circular reasoning. Collins [1985] argues that scientists are able to break this circle of reason by negotiation, the consensual resolution of which depends upon the prior existence of a network of social relations and therefore an institutionalized 'form of life' for the researchers. (Cambrosio and Keating 1988, p. 245)

Knorr-Cetina (1983) refers to the *constructive* nature of scientific activities. "The constructive interpretation is opposed to the conception of scientific investigation as descriptive, a conception which locates the problem in the relation between the products of science and an external nature. In contrast, the constructivist interpretation considers the products of science as first and foremost the result of a process of (reflexive) fabrication. Accordingly, the study of scientific knowledge is primarily seen to involve an investigation of how scientific objects are produced in the laboratory rather than a study of how facts are preserved in scientific statements about nature" (pp. 118-119).

Lynch (1985) refers to "talk about science" as what goes on in laboratory tours and research reports. In contrast, "talking science" is the everyday shop talk of scientists engaged in their practice; this shop talk—characterized as "strange" to non-practitioners—operates within the context of a specialized scientific setting. These ethnomethodological studies implicitly assume that the scientists are experts, that they rely upon their instincts, and that they may proceed arationally (i.e., are unable to justify their rationales fully). Thus "talking science" hones in on the artifacts that confirm their intuitions, and "talk about science" constitutes a formalized (and somewhat abstract) method for validating and describing results. We have seen, in Chapter 2, that observation is underdetermined; now, in Chapter 5, we further acknowledge that modern scientific laboratories distance the objects studied from the reality of which they are a part.

If modern science were not such a successful enterprise, these studies might lead to cynicism. But the fact that science works is a tribute to the human potential. Scientific experts have developed the skills to ferret out what is significant, what is relevant. They construct and validate theories, and modify them as necessary. They are effective in curiosity-driven (i.e., blind) investigations and in strategic (i.e., directed) research. It takes a long time to develop this expertise, and it may not be possible to model. For example, Norman (1982), after citing the previously quoted differences between the best and poorer pilots, asks, "How do we build a science from such observations?" (p. 72). Perhaps we can't; perhaps such a science could operate only in a closed world with models of causality that ignore too many key variables.

In an open world, however, our theories are just models: constructed, used, and abandoned when no longer relevant. As Knorr-Cetina (1983) observes, "The problem-solving model suggests that science is a successful tool for adequately coping with the world, even though we may not want to think of it as correctly representing the world" (p. 135). Expert scientists operate with intuitive models (i.e., Kuhn's paradigm) of what, for them, is normal; when these intuitive models cease to serve as effective representations for the world, science shifts to new models. The time needed to develop new intuitions combined with the strong natural opposition to what is counterintuitive accounts for the paradigm shift's revolutionary character.

5.6. Complex Problem Solving

Where is all this taking us? Recall that the central tension in the software process comes from the fact that we must go from an informally identified need that exists in-the-world to a formal model that operates in-the-computer. If many of the key the problems in-the-world could be defined formally (and the AI programme suggests that this may be possible), then we should concentrate on building the tools that capture and transform that real-world knowledge. That is, we should model the knowledge of the world in-the-computer, and then operate only in the domain of the computer. However, I do not believe this is a feasible approach, and so I look to how people and their machines can operate in partnership.

To understand how that partnership might exist, we need to understand the strengths and weaknesses of each partner as well as the extent to which things are subject to analysis (i.e., are knowable). This chapter is about finding what is knowable, and each of the sections considers some aspect of this quest. The conclusions are that computers and people complement each other and that only a portion of human knowledge can be represented (i.e., many learned and intelligent activities cannot be explained formally). For example, the ethnographic studies of science show that both the instruments and artifacts of science are situated. They exist within a shared understanding; without this situated context, artifacts lose their meaning. If this is so for science, where the bound phenomena under investigation constrain and direct, what does this tell us about the tools for computer science and design?

The objective of design is to alter the environment, and, as we just have seen, we can have only limited knowledge of the environment we intend to change. Returning to the central transformation of the software process (i.e., from an informal need to a formal response), we always have two choices: We can reduce the need to one that is understood and solvable, or we can work with the uncertainty of what is unknowable and adapt the formal solutions to respond to the changing needs.

Psychological studies of problem solving typically employ the first approach (e.g., Weisberg 1980). Virtually all the studies use closed problems (i.e., those with well-defined solutions), and the experiment objective is to provide different information about how the subjects arrive at the solution or how their behavior is affected by the experiment's design. Although this kind of analysis is valuable for understanding human behavior, it is of limited value for our purposes.

In most cases, designers do not confront problems for which neat solutions exists, and the answers seldom will be either obvious or unique. Such problems are variously called ill-structured (Reitman 1965; Simon 1973), complex (Funke 1991), and wicked (Rittel and Webber 1973). Design problems, which aim at altering the environment, are inherently of this sort, and I close this chapter with a characterization of the kinds of problems that confront designers.

Reitman (1965) argued that, although there was too much variety in the types of problems to permit the construction of a meaningful topology, one could classify their initial states and goal states as well-defined or loosely defined. He then characterized ill-structured problems by the number of constraints to the problem that required resolution. He referred to "open" constraints as those with "one or more parameters the value of which are left unspecified as the problem is given to the. problem-solving system from the outside or transmitted within the system over time" (p. 144). Finally, Reitman observed that there are social or community considerations. "To the extent that a problem situation evokes a high level of agreement over a specified community of problem solvers regarding the referents of the attributes in which it is given, the operations that are permitted, and the consequences of those operations, it may be termed unambiguous or well-defined with respect to the community. On the other hand, to the extent that a problem evokes a highly variable set of responses concerning referents of attributes, permissible operations, and their consequences, it may be considered ill-defined or ambiguous with respect to that community" (p. 151). His example of an ill-structured problem was the composition of a fugue. Here the only constraint was the use of a particular musical structure and (implicitly) the rules of tonal structure. Within those constraints the composer must select operators that permit the construction of the composition.

Simon (1973) added to Reitman's analysis by arguing that the problem solver could transform problems that were presented as ill-structured into well-structured problems. "There is merit to the claim that much problem solving effort is directed at structuring problems, and only a fraction of it at solving problems once they are structured" (p. 187). Whereas "Reitman's analysis of the solving of ill-structured problems thus was one of constraint resolution, and the ill-structured problems were taken to be problems which required resolution of a large number of open constraints,... Simon stressed the idea that initially ill-structured problems become well-structured during the solution process" (Voss and Post 1988, p. 262). In his paper, Simon used the construction of a house to illustrate how one can reduce an ill-structured problem by decomposing it hierarchically into smaller, well-structured problems (e.g., constraints on the number of rooms and goals for heating).

This technique has been central to Simon's thought. For example, in 1969 he wrote, "Solving a problem simply means representing it so as to make the solution transparent. If the problem solving could actually be organized in these terms, the issue of representation would be central" (Simon 1969/1981). Recently Kaplan and Simon (1990) extended this idea to the development of insight and commented that "attaining insight requires discovering an effective problem representation, and that performance on insight problems can be predicted from the availability of generators in the search for such a representation" (p. 374).

Here, then, are two basic methods for problem solving employed in the "systems approach." One produces the requirements for a buildable system by closing the open constraints (Reitman), and the other restructures the problem to reuse existing solutions (Simon). Normally, a project employs both methods. In the model of technological design (for which I seek an alternative), we construct a requirements specification that becomes *the* response to a real-world need; product correctness is ensured only to the degree that the specification is closed. Thus, the specification constitutes a closed solution (response) to the problem (need).

Unfortunately, the need often is poorly understood or dynamic. Lehman (1980), for instance, writes of E-Type programs that, once installed, modify their environment and thereby invalidate some of their requirements. I believe that most computer applications are and will continue to be of this type. Therefore, the alternatives to technological design cannot rely on the rational derivation of responses from fixed and closed requirements; rather they must be able to respond to situated interpretations of changing and uncertain needs.

Rittel and Webber (1973) capture this difficulty when they speak of "wicked problems" that cannot be solved; they can only be resolved. They introduced the idea of the wicked problem in the context of the planning problem, but it is also descriptive of the design challenges of the next century. "The classical paradigm of science and engineering—the paradigm that has underlain modern professionalism—is not applicable to the to the problems of open societal systems.... The cognitive and occupational styles of the professions—mimicking the cognitive style of science and the occupational style of engineering—have just not worked on a wide array of social problems. The lay customers are complaining because planners and other professionals have not succeeded in solving the problems they claimed they could solve" (p. 135, page numbers from a 1984 reprint). One senses a defensiveness in their statement, but that just reflects the scientific hopes of 20 years earlier; by now we have a more realistic set of expectations regarding the limits of rationality. Yeh (1991) asserts that system development is a wicked problem, and adaptive design illustrates one approach to achieving solutions and resolutions.

In a wicked problem, "the information needed to *understand* the problem depends upon one's idea for *solving* it. That is to say: in order to *describe* a wicked problem in sufficient detail, one has to develop an exhaustive inventory of all conceivable *solutions* ahead of time. The reason is that every question asking for additional information depends upon the understanding of the problem—and its resolution—at that time.... The formulation of a wicked problem *is* the problem" (Rittel and Webber 1973, pp. 136-137). Thus, the wicked problem is not closeable by either constraint resolution or problem restructuring—every closure sacrifices fidelity with respect to the real problem. "One cannot understand the problem without knowing about its context; one cannot meaningfully search for information without the orientation of a solution concept; one cannot first understand, then solve" (p. 138). Thus, they argue, a second-generation systems approach is needed, one using "an argumentative process in the course of which an image of the problem and of the solution emerges gradually among the participants, as a product of incessant judgment, subject to critical argument" (p. 138).

Rittel and Webber do not define what a wicked problem is, but they do list 10 principal attributes. Among these are the facts that the problems cannot be formulated, they have no stopping rule, their solutions are not true-or-false but rather good-or-bad, the solutions cannot be tested, the problems are unique and one-shot, and every wicked problem can be considered to be a symptom of another problem. Here is an illustration. Otitis media, or ear infection, is a common problem. About 25 million infections are diagnosed each year in the United States, and almost all of them children. The diagnosis is difficult to make, and in only roughly 20% of the cases can it be either diagnosed confidently or ruled out. When it exists, roughly two thirds of the cases are caused by bacteria; the remaining one third are caused by a virus, and therefore do not respond to treatment by antibiotics. The three types of bacteria that cause the vast majority of bacterial otitis have different patterns of resistance to commonly used antibiotics. A definitive diagnosis requires the culturing of a specimen withdrawn by sticking a needle through the ear drum. One safe and inexpensive drug, amoxicillin, has been used so frequently that two of the most common bacterial causes of otitus media have become resistant to it. The alternative antibiotics are more expensive, have a greater potential for allergic reaction, and often are ineffective against one or more of the principal bacteria. Finally, statistical studies indicate that only about one third of the children with acute illness are likely to be helped by antibiotics; often, regardless of cause, the disease goes away by itself.

How should we "solve" this wicked problem? An expert system could read in a microbiology report and identify the most appropriate therapy (including no action). But this requires an invasive procedure and a waiting period. We could adopt the European approach of not prescribing antibiotics until the disease has been present for at least five days, but that would be interpreted as "rationing" in the United States. Or we can continue on our present path, devoting some 15% of the nation's antibiotic prescriptions to this disease as we reduce the bacteria's sensitivity to them. There is no obvious solution; there is no way to modularize or restructure the problem; and indeed, there is no assurance that a solution would be realized even if, as the result of critical argument, we developed a consensus about the goal.

"No fair," the reader may object, "That is *not* a design problem!" But I assert it is. The designer wishes to change the environment. He may elect to draw a boundary around the problem and design only the expert system to recommend therapy as the result of potentially unavailable inputs. This is a closed problem, and it is easily solved. But of what value is that solution in-the-world? Perhaps none. If the designer accepts the responsibility of modifying the environment, then he cannot define an arbitrary context within which his designs will operate.

Unfortunately, this is what we have allowed the traditional systems approach to do; we restrict our solutions to those we know how to build—not to those that we perceive to be the best. As designers, we have come to understand how to solve simple, well-structured problems, and to convert poorly structured problems into well-structured ones. If we are to move beyond this point in the next century, we must learn to solve the complex and wicked problems as well. As I explain in Part III, that is exactly what adaptive design has the potential for doing.

By way of concluding this discussion of human problem solving, explicit knowledge, and the role of context, consider Hunt's (1991) summary of a collection of papers on complex problem solving. He writes, "Historically, psychologists acting as scientists have tried to mimic the physicist's approach to studying complexity, by studying simple systems and then extrapolating the results to complex systems. This approach has a mixed record.... [But] we don't have enough of a theory of system construction to isolate the vital components of complex problems solving for study, if you will, *in vitro* rather than *in vivo*.... The important dimension here is the one between open and closed systems, not between simple and complex systems" (pp. 386, 387). Hunt views a good scientific explanation as one so unambiguous that a robot could use it and a good engineering explanation as one that will be useful in solving a particular problem (i.e., in my words, one that supports a situated interpretation). He concludes his paper as follows:

The direct study of complex problem solving will always be useful, but I think more for gains in engineering than in scientific knowledge. Research on complex problem solving reveals the local knowledge and strategies that are used in those problems. The data on transfer suggest that you learn about how people deal with the problem you are studying, and not about how people deal with complex problems in general....

This is a disturbing conclusion, because it essentially says that we cannot have a science of complex problem solving, simply because all complex problems have local solutions.... However, I do think that we can develop a scientific understanding of how people learn to deal with complexity. The reason is that the principles of learning may be general, whereas the result of learning is specific to the situation in which the learning takes place. (pp. 394, 395)

I concur with this observation. I do not believe that the designer will be able to modularize away complexity; she must learn to deal with it. At best, we can hope to build support environments that facilitate management of the complexity, aid the designer in expressing real-world concepts, and automatically reuse whatever formal knowledge is valid for the given situation.

6

ACTIVITY, REFLECTION, CONTEXT

6.1. A Check Point

We are almost halfway through the book and this part on design ecology, and I have yet to talk about design, no less software engineering. Is this some kind of shaggy dog story? The kind in which the hero climbs mountains in search of the meaning of life only to have the wise man tell him it is, "The wet bird flies at night." I hope not. Here is the basic thesis of the book. Computers offer unprecedented power in creating new tools (equipment), but to achieve their potential we must reconstruct how they are used (i.e., shift the paradigm). The first half of the book concerns the foundations upon which we may reconstruct a new software engineering. In the middle of this century, of course, there would be no question as to what that foundation should be: *science.* But, as I have been trying to show, science and our institutions are in a period of fundamental change. For example, consider what Prigogine, winner of the 1977 Nobel Prize for chemistry, has to say.

> The classical ... view of science was to regard the world as an "object," to try to describe the physical world as if it were being seen from the outside as an object of analysis to which we do not belong...
> The deterministic laws of physics, which were at one point the only acceptable laws, today seem like gross simplifications, nearly a caricature of evolution.... Even in physics, as in sociology, only various possible "scenarios" can be predicted. But it is for this very reason that we are participating in a fascinating adventure in which, in the words of Niels Bohr, we are "both spectators and actors." (1980, pp. xv, xvii)

Thus, in only four decades we have moved from physicalism, which sought to impose a physics model on psychology, to a questioning of the very nature of physics itself. As Holland, a physicist, describes our present situation, "We are in a period of transition between two great world views—the universal machine of the classicists and the new holistic universe whose details we are only beginning to glimpse. The end is not in sight for theoretical physics" (cited in Goldstein 1994, p. 255).

We can ignore this hidden revolution and continue building a computer science. Indeed, we may even be able to ensure that this computer science is complete and consistent. But how well will that computer science serve humanity? That, to me, should be the central issue, and it is the justification for this extended introduction.   If physics, with its external reality to model, is experiencing insecurity, then ought not we question the relevancy of computer science—an abstract mathematical construct?   If there are multiple worlds (i.e., plural realities), then design inherently has great freedom in modifying our world (i.e., environment). How should we do that? The AI approach is to embody computers with intelligent behavior and knowledge so that they can act as agents, assistants, etc. From the discussion of the last chapter, it is not clear that expertise and knowledge can be represented; they are socially constructed. Certainly AI has produced (and will continue to produce) many applications that "make computers do things which, at the moment, people do better." Other paradigms also achieve this end.   Thus, the battle must be fought, not in the alleys of computational dogma, but on the fields of significance and relevance. That is, we must work with many models and select what is, at the time, practical. Although we need not abandon the goal of a unifying science, it is prudent for the near term to behave as if that goal may never be achieved.

Do not confuse my focus on the limitations of science as being in any sense "anti-science." Despite its uncertainties and imperfections, science certainly has served us well. If we wish to continue benefitting from science, however, we must come to understand what it is not as well as what it is. And, if we wish to employ science in support of design—as I believe we must—then we must come to grips with the nature of our environment. Is it "the universal machine of the classicists" or a "new holistic universe whose details we are only beginning to glimpse"? The universal machine is reducible into components, and each component is perceived to contribute to an understanding of the whole. In contrast, the holistic universe permits only abstractions, which must be studied independently. One cannot compose the whole from the abstractions; too much information has been lost in the abstraction process.

I have described these two alternatives as closed and open worlds. The closed world can be decomposed into a hierarchy, but such a reduction is not possible for an open world. At best, we can project aspects of the open world into lower dimensional spaces for study. Each projection establishes a context for the findings, and models produced within one context may not be valid in another context; that is, relevance is context dependent. We see this sense of wholeness in Bruner's (1986) description of human behavior.

> The components of the behavior I am speaking of are not emotions, cognitions, and actions, each in isolation, but aspects of a larger whole that achieves its integration only within a cultural system. Emotion is not usefully isolated from the knowledge of the situation that arouses it. Cognition is not a form of pure knowing to which emotion is added (whether to perturb its clarity or not). And action is a final common path based on what one knows and feels. Indeed, our actions are frequently dedicated to keeping a state of knowledge from being upset (as in "autistic hostility") or to the avoidance of situations that are anticipated to be emotion-arousing.
>
> It seems far more useful to recognize at the start that all three terms represent abstractions, abstractions that have a high theoretical cost. The price we pay for such abstractions in the end is to lose sight of their structural interdependence. At whatever level we look, however detailed the analysis, the three are constituents of a unified whole. (pp. 117-18)

And so we are thrown back to the mind-body problem. Can we separate thought and knowledge from the reality of the physical world? Again, Bruner:

> I am by long persuasion ... a constructivist, and just as I believe that we construct or constitute the world, I believe too that Self is a construction, a result of action and symbolization. Like Clifford Geertz [1973] and Michelle Rosaldo [1984], I think of Self as a text about how one is situated with respect to others and toward the world—a canonical text about powers and skills and dispositions that change as one's situation changes from young to old, from one kind of setting to another. The interpretation of this text *in situ* by an individual *is* his sense of self in that situation. It is composed of expectations, feelings of esteem and power, and so on. (p. 130)

In this chapter I explore the situatedness of the design process. I begin with an overview of activity theory (which is referenced by some of the new design methods), move on to the idea of reflective practice, and then conclude with an examination of bias, error, and the role of the rational.

From the perspective of design, this chapter may seem the most difficult to justify. Chapter 5 deals with human problem solving, and I use that topic to explore what can (and cannot) be modeled in-the-computer. In the end, I argue, expertise exists in-the-world, and it is unlikely that expert behavior can be represented formally. My concern, of course, is for the need that motivates the development of a software product. The better understood and more stable the need, the more likely we will be able to implement a satisfactory response to it. But if the need is situated, dynamic, and not formally describable, then we will have difficulty in designing an appropriate response. In particular, the technological design model may breakdown.

Therefore, this chapter looks at models of learning and problem solving in-the-world (i.e., responding to challenges within the environment). We are interested in the perception of needs and the process of designing responses to them. If we are to shift the paradigm for a new era of design, we must begin with a fresh perspective. We wish to know about both the trees and the forest. Science is our principal source for learning about the trees; an appreciation of the forest, however, requires different insights. That is why this chapter examines how people relate to the world. The relationship creates the context for our problems and their solutions, and no successful theory of design can operate outside that context.

6.2. Activity Theory

Activity theory, briefly, provides a framework (or research programme) for the study of human praxis (i.e., practice) as developmental processes concurrently engaged at both the individual and social levels. Kuutti (1991) notes that it "promises quite a lot—in fact there are opinions which hold that Activity Theory could and should develop towards becoming an 'umbrella' theory for all human and social sciences" (pp. 530-31). With such an endorsement plus the knowledge that the theory is referenced by several current design methods, a discussion clearly is called for. I draw primarily from Wertsch (1981a, 1991), which includes an introduction to Soviet psychology together with some translated references; Engeström (1987), which provides a modern synthesis; and Kuutti (1991), which describes the theory from the perspective of information systems.

Activity theory is a product of Soviet psychology, and—consequently—its theoretical foundations derive from the philosophical system developed by Marx, Engels, and Lenin. To understand the former, one must have some understanding of the latter. Obviously, this is too great a task for such a short section, but a few pages of background will facilitate the comprehension of what follows. Marx was a Hegelian, and therefore I begin with an overview of Hegel's contribution. (For a network that shows the philosophical heritage of activity theory as well as of the design concepts proposed by Winograd and Flores (1986) and by modern logicians, see Raeithel (1991), p. 394.) Kant (1724-1804) demonstrated the inescapable dialectical conflict of metaphysical theses (i.e., contradictions are unavoidable), and Hegel (1770-1831) transformed this doctrine into a new logic of philosophical truth. Every contradiction, for Hegel, is really a disguised relation. Rather than having two conflicting theses about reality: *A* and its mutually exclusive *not-A*, Hegel substitutes *B*, the antithesis, for *not-A* such that the conflict between *A* and *B* resolves itself as the synthesis, *C*. Thus, "contradiction is not a sign of intellectual incoherence, but rather of creativity and insight.... For human beings, there is no end whatever to self-contradiction and, hence, to intellectual development" (Aiken 1956, p. 74-75). The dialectical method, and the resulting intellectual development, are perceived to be progressive: moving towards the Absolute, an unattainable ideal of reason. History, therefore, is a dialectical and a spiritual process: an unfolding or self-development of the Absolute. "Historical change must be read as a continuous struggle toward the spiritual freedom of mankind" (p. 77).

Hegel was an idealist (from the word idea) philosopher, who held that the world is known through the mind, through ideas. In contrast, the empiricists (e.g., Locke, 1632-1704), argued that human beings develop their knowledge of the world only through their senses (i.e., the human brain is a blank sheet at birth). Kant provided an adequate refutation of the blank-sheet approach (e.g., senses can discern the colors of red and blue but not the concept of color) and asserted that humans must have innate facilities, which he called our faculty to reason. Hegel built upon Kant's idealism by adding two central concepts: "Spirit" (*Geist*, roughly the human spirit or its essence) and "the Idea" (*Idee*, thought or reason). Both Spirit and Idea have a history, and human history is the development of the Idea.

Mind actually creates the world. For Hegel this is true in two senses.

1. Since for Hegel "the world" = "knowledge of the world," then as knowledge changes (i.e., as mind develops) so the world changes.

2. Since human beings act in the world on the basis of their knowledge of it, the world becomes increasingly shaped and dominated by reason through human-activity-conducted-on-the-basis-of-reason. (Kitching 1988, p. 15)

Hegel treated reason abstractly; it was what all humans had in common (i.e., universal categories of thought). His philosophy was highly theological, and he thought "spirit" and "mind" an expression of

God. His dialectical process worked through a process of *objectification* (in which ideas were objectified into a material reality, for instance transforming the idea of "shelter" into a house) followed by *alienation* (which results from the mind's inability to accept the objectifications as its products; that is, they are treated as something separate from—alien to—the embodiment of a product of the mind).   "In Hegel, the overcoming of alienation—which is the end, the goal, the culmination of history—consists in mind's total self-understanding.... of, and mastery over, the world" (Kitching 1988, p. 17).

Hegel's concepts of objectification and alienation were soon turned into tools of atheistic thought by the young "left Hegelians" such as Feuerbach (1804-1872). For them, religion was simply a stage in the historical development of the mind. In common with Feuerbach, Marx (1818-1883) accepted Hegel's basic vision of historical progress, reintroduced actual thinking and acting human subjects into the historical process, and embraced the goal of human liberation. Liberation, however, would not occur simply in the realm of thought or reason (i.e., mind); "since human enslavement was a product of human activity, human liberation required a fundamental change in that activity, and that implied ... a fundamental change in human society" (p. 19).

> Whereas in Hegel objectification and alienation are states of "the Idea," are conceived as products of "mind," forms or stages of the self-development of mind in history, for Marx, as for Feuerbach, alienation and objectification are products of human *activity*. Human beings alienate themselves in the very process of filling the world with innumerable objectifications of their activity and creativity. (p. 19)

Thus, Marx "materializes" Hegelian "idealism"; objectification and alienation are converted into states of human beings rather than of "the Idea."   What makes people people is their capacity for conscious creative activity. It is the essence of human beings, Marx believed, that through "creative activity they both transform inanimate nature and they create and transform their own nature.... Since this conscious creative activity is natural to human beings, since it is in their nature to be creative, they do not need any physical compulsion to do it.... [When freed from] physical pressures human beings will produce not only those things which are useful, they will also produce what is beautiful, what satisfies aesthetic standards" (p. 21).   In the early writing of Marx material production is not limited to the production of material objects, it includes everything produced by humans: ideas, values, institutions, language. Kitching states that "this productive faculty of human beings, this conscious creative activity which is unique to them as a form of life, is what is wonderful for Marx about people, and it is this wonder that informs the whole of his early philosophical humanism" (p. 22).

In the later developments of Marx's philosophy, the society of alienated labor becomes "capitalism" and the alienated laborers the "proletariat." The division of labor becomes the main source of conflict; it forces labor to take on the character of a commodity in which there is a disparity between the *use value* (i.e, the value of object produced by the labor) and the *exchange value* (i.e., the value received by the laborer). By the 1920s the philosophy had undergone further evolution as it became the intellectual foundation for the Soviet Union. National pride and a deep commitment to Marxist-Leninist dogma directed investigation into well-defined, approved channels. Among the consequences were the excesses of Lysenko (Broad and Wade 1982) and the suppression of the brilliant work of Vygotsky, whose insights made possible the development of activity theory.

Vygotsky sought to extend psychology in a way that would be Marxist in orientation, consistent with neo-Pavlovian ideas, and still serve as a correction to the earlier ideas of both behaviorism and introspection. "He believed that 'modernization' of the peasant through collectivization and mechanization could be described in the same way as one described the growth of the child from prescientific to scientific thinking.... He believed that the transmission of mind across history is effected by successive mental sharings that assure a passing on of ideas from the more able or advanced to the less so. And the medium in which the transmission occurs is language and its products: literacy, science, technology, literature" (Bruner 1986, p. 74). His *Language and Thought* was first published in 1934, shortly after his death at the age of 38. The book was suppressed in 1936, republished in 1956 (which Newell and Simon (1972) cite as the year cognitive science began) and translated into English in 1962. Vygotsky's thesis embraced the Marxist position that "man was subject to the dialectical play between nature and history, between his qualities as a creature of biology and as a product of human culture. [But] it risked being tagged as 'bourgeois idealism,' for mental activity was given a dangerously dominant place in the system" (p. 71).

Wertsch (1991) identifies three basic themes in Vygotsky's writings: "(a) a reliance on genetic or developmental analysis; (b) a claim that higher mental functioning in the individual derives from social life; and (c) a claim that human activity, on both the social and individual planes, is mediated by tools and signs" (p. 87). The genetic method asserts that it is possible to understand aspects of the mental process only by understanding their origin and the transitions they undergo. There are limits to the study of the static products of development; the genetic transformations will have been buried behind the appearances of "fossilized" forms of behavior. He therefore focused most of his empirical research on the development of the individual (i.e., ontogenesis) and avoided abstract laboratory studies.

Regarding the second theme, he wrote, "Human's psychological nature represents the aggregate of internalized social relations that have become functions for the individual and form the individual's structure" (Vygotsky 1981b, p. 89). In his "general genetic law of cultural behavior," a child's development appears on two planes. On the social plane, it appears between people (the interpsychological category), and within the child it is internalized as an intrapsychological category. This internalization "transforms the process itself and changes its structure and functions.... In their private sphere, [therefore,] human beings retain the function of social interactions" (pp. 163, 164). That is, "there is a close connection, grounded in genetic transitions, between the specific structures and processes of interpsychological and intra-psychological functioning. This, in turn, implies that different forms of interpsychological functioning give rise to related differences in the forms of intrapsychological functioning" (Wertsch 1991, p. 89).

The genetic law of cultural development also claims that a mental function can be applied to social as well as individual forms of activity. Mind can be said to "extend beyond the skin." He describes a *zone of proximal development* which is the difference between the *"actual development level as determined by actual problem solving'* and the higher level of *'potential development as determined thorough problem solving under adult guidance or in collaboration with more capable peers'"* (Wertsch 1991, p. 90, citing Vygotsky, Vygotsky's italics). The zone of proximal development constitutes the difference between what the unaided student can do and what the student can do with tutoring. The zone moves with development, and "good learning" is that which is in advance of development. Thus, learning is not a matter of transferring knowledge; it is a reflective process of development. "The new higher concepts in turn transform the meaning of the lower. The adolescent who has mastered algebraic concepts has gained a vantage point from which he sees arithmetic concepts in a broader perspective" (Vygotsky 1962, p. 115). Therefore, it is as important to measure the level of potential development as it is to measure the actual development; furthermore, instruction should be tied more closely to the level of potential development than to the actual level of development.

The third theme that runs through Vygotsky's work is the claim that higher mental functioning is mediated by tools and signs, in particular, human language as a sign system. The three themes are deeply integrated. Wertsch (1991) writes, "mediation underlies his genetic method because both qualitative and quantitative changes are defined in terms of mediation, and mediation underlies his second theme because it provides the key to formulating the link between interpsychological and intrapsychological functioning" (p. 91). The instruments of mediation are tools and signs. Tools (i.e., technical tools) are externally oriented; they are the means by which human activity can master, and triumph over, nature. Signs (which are psychological tools) "imply and require reflexive mediation, consciousness of one's (or the other persons) procedures.... The essence of psychological tools is that they are originally instruments for co-operative, communicative and self-conscious shaping and controlling of the procedures of using and making technical tools" (Engeström 1987, pp. 60-61). "By being included in the process of behavior, the psychological tool alters the entire flow and structure of mental function" (Vygotsky 1981a, p. 137).

Wertsch (1991) comments that "mediational means are social in two ways that correspond to the two ways noted earlier in which cognition is socially situated. First, mediational means are social in the sense that they are typically used in interpsychological processes.... [Second], they are products of sociocultural evolution and, hence, are inherently situated in sociocultural context" (p. 91). The psychological tools (e.g., language) are not invented by each individual nor inherited by way of instinct. Rather, individuals have access to these tools by virtue of being part of a sociocultural milieu—another way in which mind "goes beyond the skin." "Instead of locating mental functioning in the individual in isolation, Vygotsky locates it in the individual functioning together with a mediational means" (p. 92). Furthermore, *the means used to mediate social interaction are the same means used to mediate the cognitive processes of the individual acting as an independent cognitive agent*" (Wertsch 1981a, p. 190).

This is a good place to conclude the discussion of Vygotsky, the founder of the Soviet cultural-historical school of psychology. Lest the reader believe that this has been an exercise in historiography, I note that these concepts provide the foundation for activity theory, that some of the same higher mental functions recently have been studied in the West under headings such as "executive routine" and "metacognition" in their developed (albeit "fossilized") states, and that Wertsch builds on his findings to construct a model of socially shared cognition. Thus, although Vygotsky's work may be old, it remains quite relevant.

Vygotsky did not dwell on the concept of activity in any detail, and it was his student and collaborator Leontyev who, more than any other, provided the theoretical foundations of activity theory. We find in his writings a profound commitment to what Kitching labels Marx's philosophy of praxis.

> The main conclusion is that man's biologically inherited qualities do not govern his psychic capabilities. Man's capabilities are not virtually contained in the brian. Virtually the brain includes not certain, specifically human capacities of

some form or another, but only *the capacity to form these capacities.*

In other words, biologically inherited qualities constitute only one of the *conditions* in man for the molding of his psychic function and capabilities....

Another condition is the world of objects and phenomena around man created by countless generations of people in their work and struggle. This world also makes man truly human....

The process of mastering and assimilating the world of objects and phenomena created by men during the historical development of society is also the process in which specifically human capabilities and functions are formed in the individual....

Assimilation occurs during the development of the subject's relations with the world. These relations, moreover, do not depend on the subject, or on his consciousness, but are governed by the specific, historical, social conditions in which he lives, and by how his life is molded in these conditions.

That is why the problem of the outlook for the psychic development both of man and mankind is first and foremost one of a just and rational structure of life in human society,....
(Leontyev 1981, pp. 154-55)

Although few today would propose a "rational structure" such as the one that existed in the Soviet Union at the time these words were written, I believe all designers share the sense of responsibility implied in the final paragraph. The contrast that Leontyev makes is between the Western static models of cause and effect (stimulus and response) and the cultural-historical approach within activity theory.

Wertsch (1981b) identifies six central defining features of the contemporary theory of activity. They are (a) activity is analyzed at various levels, (b) activities are motivated and actions are goal directed, (c) activity is mediated, (d) there is an emphasis on developmental or genetic explanation, (e) human activity and the means that mediate it have arisen through social interaction, and (f) internalization (i.e., activities are initially carried out on the external plane—inter-psychological—and are subsequently internalized—intrapsychological). We already have discussed the last four features, and so I now examine the first two.

Leontyev (1981) begins with the stimulus-response formula $(S \rightarrow R)$ and states that we must either accept this two-part scheme of influence "or begin with a three-part scheme that includes a middle link (a 'middle term') to mediate the connections between the other two. This middle link is the subject's activity and its corresponding conditions, goals, and means" (p. 46). Thus we see a dialectic in which a conflict is mediated such that change occurs as the result of the mediation.   That is, rather than having a simple cause-effect relationship, activity theory asserts that development occurs only when contradictions are overcome. The three-part unit by which development can be studied is the activity. Leontyev describes it this way.

> Activity is the nonadditive, molar unit of life for the material, corporeal subject.   In a narrower sense (i.e., on the psychological level) it is the unit of life that is mediated by mental reflection. The real function of this unit is to orient the subject in the world of objects. In other words, activity is not a reaction or aggregate of reactions, but a system with its own structure, its own internal transformations, and its own development. (p. 46)

Activity is analyzed at three levels.   At the highest level is the *activity* itself. The activity constitutes "a minimal meaningful context for individual actions ... [which forms] the basic unit of analysis. [The activity is] ... better defined and more stable than just an arbitrary context ... [and it is] also more manageable than a social system" (Kuutti 1991, p. 531). Each activity is distinguished by its motive (or object), which tells us why the activity exists.   The remaining two levels of analysis are actions and operations. The activity is realized through a sequence of conscious and purposeful *actions*, each of which has a goal. The methods with which an action is accomplished are called *operations*.

Wertsch (1981b) observes that most Western psychologists focus their research on problems that would arise at the level of analysis concerned with operations. The Soviets, in contrast, tend to orient their research around functional criteria at the level of the activity.   For example, in setting up an experiment concerning the recall of a list of words, one might use a set of external pictures or one could store them mentally. Because both these behaviors serve the same functional role, a Soviet psychologist might set up the experiment to detect similarities between these two approaches to solving the problem—a design that might seem, at best, strange to a Western psychologist (pp. 18-19). It is the desire to study activity as a developmental process (in contrast to processes reduced to static, isolated laboratory phenomena) that leads to the choice of activity as the basic unit of analysis.

An activity may be viewed as having a three-level structure. Each activity, with its motive, is composed of a chain of actions, each of which has a specific goal and can employ a set of operations. Kuutti (1991) describes the operations as "well-defined routines used by the subject subconsciously as answers to *conditions* faced during the performing of the action" (p. 534). He presents the relationships as follows:

```
Activity    —   Motive
   ↑↓             ↑↓
Action     —   Goal
   ↑↓             ↑↓
Operation  —   Conditions
```

One reason for the current interest in activities is their flexibility in representing conceptual units. This same property, however, "means that it is in fact impossible to make a general classification of what is an activity, what is an action, etc. because the definition is totally dependent on what are the subject, object, etc. in a particular real situation" (Kuutti 1991, p. 535). For example, if different goals are chosen to carry out an activity, then an alternative chain of actions will be used to realize it. Furthermore, an action involved in an activity in one situation may be considered an activity in another situation. Similarly, what is an operation in one situation may be an action in another. For instance, when learning to drive a car, shifting the gears is a conscious action, but once skilled, it becomes simply an (invisible) operation.

In a way, the granularity of an activity is similar to that of a chunk in the cognitive science model of memory; the difference, of course, is that an activity is always situated in-the-world, whereas the chunk always represents an internal mental state. Both models also employ goals, but the action's goal in activity theory is very different from that of a goal in problem solving search. Because actions are conscious, goal-directed processes, they can be analyzed only in the context of their goals; laboratory studies that analyze structural features independent of the goals (or which construct unrealistic goals), therefore, will be of little value.

To summarize activity theory without reference to its Marxist framework, the activity—the basic unit of analysis—may be thought of as a function. Each function has an objective (motive or object) within some broad context. The context, in part, determines the granularity of the activity. Thus, to use the example of otitis media given in Chapter 5, an individual physician might be engaged in the activity of treating a specific patient and a health policy researcher may view that activity as an action in the activity of establishing guidelines for antibiotic use. Each of these activities motivates the creation of a sequence of goals and subgoals (e.g., review patient history, examine ear, determine therapy), which are carried out as actions. Each action is situated (i.e., in a specific context that helps guide its conduct).

For activity theory, however, the concern is for the activity and not the individual action; the activity motive and not the action situation. In this sense, the activity is "content free"; there may be many alternative sequences of actions that will carry out the activity. The action itself is realized through operations, which may be viewed as routine or internalized (e.g., the physician's reading the patient's medical history). The process, of course, is dynamic. The operations may not be appropriate for the given conditions, and alternative goals (actions) may be required; external processes may affect the activity, thereby altering the goals, etc. In what I have called technological design, we begin with a set of requirements (i.e., goals) and operate at the level of the action in the creation of operational tools. Activity theory suggests that if we are to move to some higher level of design (e.g., the adaptive design of Part III), then we must perform the analysis at the level of the activity and retain the flexibility to experiment with the actions necessary to realize the activity.

A second aspect of activity theory, the role of mediation, may be more difficult to assimilate for a readership accustomed to a cause-effect model. Recall Hegel's dialectic in which historical progress comes from the resolution of contradiction and Vygotsky's zone of proximal development whereby the child learns by being drawn into the zone between what she can do on her own and what she can do with the assistance of her tutor. It is the resolution of contradictions within this zone of proximal development that fosters learning; one neither learns from contradictions that are so obvious that the solution is at hand nor from contradictions that go beyond the ability of the tutor-aided student.

Engeström (1987) refers to this process as *learning by expanding*. It constitutes a sharp contrast to the tradition of learning as the transfer of knowledge (i.e., reactive learning). Engeström describes Norman's (1982) approach to better matching machines to human capabilities as one of designing them to make learning to use them easier—a goal that has broad acceptance in the software industry. But, he continues, "Pleas like this follow the traditional patronizing approach: the poor learners must be helped to cope with the tasks *given* to them. The approach is self-defeating.... It can only be overcome by enabling the users themselves to plan and bring about the qualitative changes (including the design and implementation of technologies) in their contexts" (pp. 2-3). Obviously, such a shift is potentially more easy in the realm of organizational and cultural situations (e.g., restructuring of work) than it is in the domain of technological and mechanical devices; as I shall demonstrate in Part III, however, the unexploited power of computers has the potential for increasing technological flexibility.

To continue, Engeström sees the activity as the gateway to comprehending expansion: internal and external, mental and material. To model the structure of the activity, we first need to have a better understanding of the dialectical method, "a method of grasping the essence of the object by reproducing theoretically the logic of its development, of its 'historic becoming'" (p. 309). The method is both historical and logical. "In dialectical logic, the concrete is an interconnected systemic whole. But the interconnections are not of any arbitrary kind. At the core of the interconnections there are *internal contradictions....* Contradictions become central if we are to handle movement, development and change conceptually" (p. 243). Of course, both Hegel and Marx had a sense of the progress of history (even though they were contradictory senses), and thus there is assumed to be a guide for resolving contradictions in a Marxist context.

If we disregard this perception of an established orientation for choice (as I think we must), we nevertheless must accept two valid aspects of the dialectical method. First, in resolving a contradiction we need to evaluate the full context under consideration, and the activity is the smallest unit with a full context (including its history). Second, the resolution of a contradiction creates something new: an expansion that both affects what we know and adds new knowledge (e.g., algebra makes the student understand arithmetic in a new way). "The motive of this activity is to learn how to acquire skills and knowledge and solve problems *by expanding the tasks into objectively novel activity systems,* resulting eventually not just in acquiring and solving the given, but in creating tasks and problems out of the larger activity context" (p. 135). Notice that the outcome of learning is an activity system—a complex function—and not simply some new actions (each of which satisfies a goal) or operations (each of which constitutes a kind of routine).

Chapter 8 contains some illustrations of the use of activity theory in system design. Therefore I close this discussion with some comparisons with other some previously described alternatives. To begin, notice how Engeström's model is at variance with the information processing model of cognitive science. The former uses contradiction to find new problem solutions; the latter relies on knowledge acquisition and search. The former introduces a middle term to mediate the response (which both inhibits the direct impulse to react and provides and auxiliary responses); the latter restructures the problem to reuse available solutions. Learning for the former is a process of expansion; for the latter, *"assuming learning is invariant* is a useful research strategy for the immediate future" (Langley and Simon 1981, p. 378).

Engeström also critiques the Dreyfus and Dreyfus (1986) model of expertise presented in Chapter 5. He argues that they present a process of internalizing experience, one of contrasting experienced-based intuitive expertise with rule-based analytic expertise. "'Either-or' and 'both-and' are closed and timeless structures. Within them, there is no room for something qualitatively new emerging first as a subordinated mediator between the two poles and being transformed into a determining factor that will eventually change the character of the whole structural configuration. There is no room for thirdness" (Engeström 1987, p. 222). Perhaps more than anything else, it is this thirdness (e.g., contradiction, conflict, dilemma) that differentiates activity theory from the other theories that we have examined.

6.3. Reflection in Practice

Although Marxist epistemology is based on a theory of reflection, that is not the topic of this section. The title is adopted from a book by Schön (1983) that describes how professionals think in practice, and so this section turns to thinking and problem solving in real-world situations by experts. I briefly introduced Schön in Chapter 4 when I referred to what he calls "Technical Rationality," the positivist orientation that, by extension, justifies a claim that professionals can "run society" using scientifically established knowledge and principles. The phrase "run society," by the way, is taken from a 1963 *Daedalus*, whose editors believed that Veblen's sixty-year-old dream "has never been closer to realization" (cited in Schön 1983, p. 6). We know, of course, that it took less than two decades for that restated dream to lose favor; it was discredited by its inability to deliver as promised. "To some critics, the public predicaments of the society began to seem less like problems to be solved through expertise than like dilemmas whose resolution could come about only through moral and political change" (p. 10). Yet, Schön observes, despite the problems of uncertainty, disorder, and indeterminacy, many professionals were effective in producing solutions. Nevertheless, they could not account for their successes. Trained in and committed to "a view of professional knowledge as a hierarchy in which 'general principles' occupy the highest level and 'concrete problem solving' the lowest" (p. 24), professionals had difficulty in describing or teaching "what might be meant by making sense of uncertainty, performing artistically, setting problems, and choosing among competing professional paradigms" (pp. 19-20). That is, they were torn between their commitment to Technical Rationality and what Schön calls *reflection-in-action*, an epistemology of practice that explains the competencies that some practitioners bring to situations of uncertainty, instability, uniqueness, and value conflict. (By way of transition from the previous section, note that activity theory would focus on the dilemma as the motivation for the mediation that expands into a solution.)

Technical Rationality holds that all professions should be taught as engineers still are taught: first the relevant basic and applied science, then the skills of application. One cannot begin application until the necessary skills have been acquired; moreover, because application skills are ambiguous, they constitute a secondary kind of knowledge. Here we have the classic view of the mechanical universe along with its faith in the sanctity of knowledge and its perception of learning as knowledge transfer. "Quite simply, the professions are to give their practical problems to the university, and the university, the unique source of research, is to give back to the professions the new scientific knowledge which it will be their business to apply and test" (p. 36). The alternative is a practice based on "skillful action,", a "knowing more than we can say," a kind of tacit knowledge or "ordinary practical knowledge" that Schön calls *knowing-in-action*.

Knowing-in-action is the means for everyday coping; reflection-in-action hinges on the experience of surprise. "When intuitive performance leads to surprise, pleasing or unwanted, we may respond by reflection-in-action.... Reflection tends to focus interactively on the outcomes of action, the action itself, and the intuitive knowing implicit in the action" (p. 56). That is, it responds to a breakdown by making the ready-to-hand present-at-hand. Schön points out that "as a practice becomes more repetitive and routine, and as knowing-in-practice becomes increasingly tacit and spontaneous, the practitioner may miss important opportunities to think about what he is doing" (p. 61). It is only when something outside the range of ordinary experience occurs that the practitioner "reflects on the phenomena before him, and on the prior understandings which have been implicit in his behavior. He carries out an experiment which serves to generate both a new understanding of the phenomena and a change in the situation" (p. 68). Thus, reflection—the mediation of the experiment—changes both the subject and the object.

Schön developed his understanding of reflection-in-action as the result of protocol analyses of training and problem-solving situations. It is best introduced through one of his illustrations, "design as a reflective conversation with the situation," in which he observes the interactions of an architectural studio master (Quist) and his student (Petra). Petra is given an assignment, and Quist interacts with her to achieve a satisfactory solution. Petra works independently, and Quist operates across the Vygotsky's zone of proximal development so that she may learn the subtitles of design. "Whether Quist and Petra speak in words or drawings, their utterances refer to spatial images which they try to make congruent with one another. As they become more confident that they have achieved congruence of meaning, their dialogue tends to become more elliptical and inscrutable to outsiders" (p. 81). Schön identifies three dimensions of the process as particularly noteworthy.

Design domains. Quist uses an informal language of design that combines drawing with speaking to communicate within the specific problem domain. "Aspiring members of the linguistic community of design learn to detect multiple reference, distinguish particular meanings in context, and use multiple reference as an aid to vision across design domains" (p. 98).

Implications. Every choice, every move, has many branchings that may uncover new problems. "In the designer's conversation with the materials of his design, he can never make a move which had only the effects intended for it. His materials are continually talking back to him, causing him to apprehend unanticipated problems and potentials" (p. 101).

Shifts in stance. Quest views the whole and its parts from different perspectives. "Sometimes he speaks of what 'can' or 'might' happen, and sometimes of what 'should' or 'must' happen. He shifts from a recognition of possibility and freedom of choice to an acceptance of the imperatives which follow from that choice" (p. 101).

Schön presents the design activity as "a global experiment whose results will only be dimly apparent in the early stages of the process" (p. 103).

The process is similar to that of engineering design or the conduct of science. For example, there is the role of visualization, which parallels the mind's eye described by Ferguson (1992) in an engineering context. Quist and Petra speak in a "language about designing" that is similar to the "speaking science" observed by Lynch (1985). The general pattern, however, is not restricted to professional practice. Lave (1988) observed everyday mathematical practice in different settings. "The discussion of money management provided demonstrations that arithmetic in practice is never merely that, but is the product and reflection of multiple relations—of value and belief, of people with each other, and of the conditions for producing and reproducing activity over time" (p. 175). She continues, "Knowledge takes on the character of knowing.... The conception of situation as separate from, and only arbitrarily related to, activity might better be transformed into a concept of dialectically constituted, situated activity.... Procedures for solving problems, as well as their goals, are inherently value-laden.... A problem is a dilemma with which the problem solver is emotionally engaged; conflict is the source of the dilemma. Processes for resolving dilemmas are correspondingly deprived of their assumed universalistic, normative, decontextualized nature. As studies of math in practice have demonstrated, problems generated in conflict can be resolved or abandoned as well as solved, and often have no unique or stable resolution" (p. 175). Thus, what Schön writes about the practice of an expert designer seems also to be true in everyday practice where the expertise is simply that of socially determined common sense.

In all, Schön analyzes six different professional situations. Unsurprisingly, the art of engineering design turns out to be similar to that of architectural design.

When practitioners choose to address new or unique problems that do not fit known categories, their inquiry is ... a design process artistic in nature and fundamentally similar in structure to the reflective conversations [already] analyzed.... And when science-based practitioners try to take account of the larger context of their inquiry, only some elements of which are within their control, they must construct a manageable problem from a problematic situation. In the first kind of case, the practitioner reflects-in-action on puzzling phenomena which are new to him,... In the second, he reflects-in-action on a larger situation that impinges on his activity even though it falls outside what are normally considered the boundaries of a profession. (p. 170)

He describes the process of learning engineering design as follows. At each stage in the process, the students are "confronted with puzzles and problems that did not fit their known categories, yet they had a sense of some kinds of theories (surface chemistry, thermodynamics) that might explain these phenomena. They used their theoretical hunches to guide experiment, but on several occasions their moves led to puzzling outcomes—a process that worked, a stubborn defect—on which they then reflected. Each such reflection gave rise to new experiments and to new phenomena, troublesome or desirable, which led to further reflection and experiment. Unlike Quest, these engineering students were able to make liberal use of research-based theory and technique, but their application of research results were embedded in a reflective conversation with the situation" (p. 176). Schön calls this developing "intuition" or "creativity" *seeing-as*, a sort of similarity pattern matching that Kuhn refers to as "thinking from exemplars."

From these analyses of practice, Schön constructs a structure for reflection-in-action. The process begins as the practitioner attempts to solve the problem as initially set. Typically the problem is unique (i.e., not very close to a problem already solved). The problem must be reframed. Thus, we do not have "problem solving" in the sense of Chapter 5; neither do we have the restructuring of an ill-structured problem. Rather, what we have is professional-level wicked-problem resolution. "Faced with some phenomena that he finds unique, the inquirer nevertheless draws on some element of his familiar repertoire which he treats as exemplar or as generative metaphor for new phenomenon.... Further, as the inquirer reflects on the similarities he has perceived, he formulates new hypotheses. But he tests these hypotheses by experimental actions which also function as moves for shaping the situation and as probes for exploring it" (p. 269). Schön refers to the practitioner's effort to solve the reframed problem as a reflective conversation. "The process spirals through stages of appreciation, action, reappreciation. The unique and uncertain situation comes to be understood through the attempt to change it, and changed through the attempt to understand it" (p. 132). "Through the unintended effects of action [i.e., breakdowns], the situation talks back. The practitioner, reflecting on this back-talk, may find new meanings in the situation which leads him to a new reframing. Thus he judges a problem-setting by the quality and direction of the reflective conversation to which it leads" (p. 134).

The practitioner's expertise exists in both his generalized professional (problem-independent) knowledge and his repertoire of examples, images, understanding of actions. The latter is used in transforming a unique problem into one that is in some way similar or different. "The perception of similarity and difference ... is, as Kuhn says, both logically and psychologically prior to his later articulation of it... It is our capacity to *see-as* and *do-as* that allows us to have a feel for problems that do not fit existing rules. The artistry of a practitioner like Quist hinges on the range and variety of the repertoire that he brings to unfamiliar situations" (p. 140).

Getzels and Csikszentmihalyi (1976) have studied artists at work, and they find a similar process of problem framing. In a laboratory study of still life drawing, they reported that the most highly rated pictures were those in which the student spent considerable work in the early stages composing the still life (i.e., framing the artistic statement prior to its transformation into a finished drawing). Furthermore, in a follow up study, they found that the most successful individuals "tended to be those who had carefully examined a relatively large number of objects before starting to draw, who had taken a relatively long time before arriving at the final structure of their drawings, and who tended to restart their drawings and/or change the arrangement of the objects as they worked" (Weisberg 1986, p. 120). Thus, for the artist, the reflective conversation focuses on the content of the drawing, not its execution.

Dreyfus and Dreyfus (1986) speak of a *deliberative rationality* that "does not seek to analyze the situation into context-free elements but seeks to test and improve whole intuitions" (p. 36). Finally, Agre and Chapman note that "most of the work in using a plan is in determining its relevance to the successive concrete situations that occur during the activity it helps to organize" (cited in Suchman 1988, p. 315). All of this suggests that practice can neither be modularized nor preplanned; it is an iterative activity that depends to a very large extent on the skills and judgment of the practitioner as made occurrent by the situated dilemma.

Schön describes the process as an *on-the-spot experiment*. Not an experiment of the data-collection/hypothesis-rejection form, but one better described as responding to, "What if?" An *exploratory experiment*; "the probing, playful activity by which we get a feel for things. It succeeds when it leads to the discovery of something there" (p. 145). It "consists in the practitioner's conversation with the situation, in the back-talk he elicits and appreciates" (p. 148). "The inquirer's relation to this situation is *transactional*. He shapes the situation, but in conversation with it, so that his own models and appreciations are also shaped by the situation. The phenomena that he seeks to understand are partly of his own making; he is *in* the situation that he seeks to understand" (pp. 150-151). "Doing and thinking are complementary. Doing extends thinking in the tests, moves, and probes of experimental action, and reflection feeds on doing and its results. Each feeds the other, and each sets boundaries for the other" (p. 280).

Clearly, what we see is very different from the problem-solving model of Technical Rationality. We do not start with a body of knowledge and then carry out problem solving by the rational application of that knowledge to the specific problem at hand. Rather, we have a dilemma-resolving dialectical activity that relies on the practitioner's implicit knowledge and repertoire. Formal learning, in the vocabulary of activity theory, creates an armory of operations that enables a solution, and actions are the experiments that reframe the problem into one that has a viable solution. Designs and drawings are what Schön calls *virtual worlds*, they "can function reliably as a context for experiment only insofar as the results of experiment can be transformed to the built world" (p. 159). It is the knowledge, experience, and discipline embodied in the practitioner that permits him to serve as his own tutor, operating within the zone of proximal development, to expand his virtual world such that viable designs for responses to situated problems materialize.

6.4. Closing the Circle

There is an old software engineering saying that goes, "When you are up to your waist in alligators, it's difficult to remember that you came here to drain the swamp." But this is exactly our mission: We are to drain the swamp of prejudice and habit so that we will have a firm foundation for a new era of design. We have almost completed the first part of our investigation into ecological design—the nature of the people affecting and effected by design. Therefore, a short reorientation that shows how I am closing this discussion will be helpful. To begin, this and the previous chapter should be viewed as a single unit. Chapter 5 began with a description of cognitive science and its information processing model of problem solving. Simon is one of the most accomplished spokespersons for that view, and I quote Schön's interpretation of his programme.

Simon believes that all professional practice is centrally concerned with that he calls "design," that is, with the process of "changing existing situations into preferred ones" [Simon 1969/1981, p. 55].... Simon proposes to build a science of design by emulating and extending the optimization methods which have been developed in statistical decision theory and management science.... Once problems are well formed in this way, they can be solved by a calculus of decision.... Although Simon proposes to fill the gap between natural science and design practice with a science of design, his science can be applied only to well-formed problems already extracted from situations of practice. (pp. 46-47)

For Schön, Simon's view of design operates in the closed world of Technical Rationality. All knowledge needed for decision making can be represented formally and processed by a calculus of decision (i.e., the model of information processing). Ill-structured problems can be reformulated as well-structured problems, and properties not explained by this model (e.g., affective factors or emotions) can be temporarily ignored until the basic theory has been constructed. The closed-world model justifies the deferral of "second-order" effects because, in the single-world model, once the key parts of the model are constructed, other portions of the model can be fit in.

The remainder of Chapter 5 questioned the information processing model, first regarding its applicability to problems situated in the real world, then with respect to the nature of expertise, and finally in the context of complex problem solving. The thrust of the criticism was that the information processing model leaves out important considerations. For proponents of that model, however, this is not a problem; they do not claim the model to be complete at this time. By way of illustration, Vera and Simon (1993) reply to critics of their symbolic model of situated action, "We observe that the simulation of the internal part of this process—what goes on inside the head—has proceeded more rapidly than the simulation of sensory, perceptual, and motor processes. But this is a consequence of the greater complexity of the latter, and not a judgment of their lesser importance" (p. 77).

Of course, my orientation is one of plural realism. For me, there are many valid (i.e., relevant and significant) models of important phenomena, and no single model will explain all phenomena. Thus, the information processing model has much to teach us, even if we choose not to commit ourselves to its positivist programme. For example, the information processing model may not explain the automaticity of intuition, but that is no reason not to employ the symbolic model for situations where problem solving is obviously rational.

The present chapter reframed the discourse by shifting to a very different set of premises and implications: Marxism, Soviet psychology, and activity theory. That material was followed by an overview of reflective practice as defined by Schön. Whereas the discussion in Chapter 5 tended to be of the either/or sort (e.g., reasoning by rules vs. intuitive reaction), the interpretations in this chapter tended to emphasize a triad, a dialectic, the role of conflict. The contradiction that initiates the expansion in activity theory also serves as the breakdown that triggers reflection and experimentation.

Both orientations reject the idea that knowledge exists and can be formalized; rather, knowledge is created in response to a situation. Neither do we fit problems to generalized knowledge; instead we apply generalized knowledge to create solutions to unique problems. This orientation opens a wholly new set of questions for philosophers (e.g., What is the nature of scientific knowledge and its demarcation?), psychologists (e.g., How does the social component affect cognition?), sociologists, anthropologists, etc. For designers, who are charged with altering the environment (i.e., changing existing situations into preferred ones), the two central (and reflexive) issues are: (a) What do we know about the environment to be changed? and (b) How does that environment determine what we know?

If we adopt a positivist, closed-world view, then rational change is inherently progressive; whenever our actions are based on solid facts and sound reasoning, progress will be served. But if we reject the positivist philosophy, then progress is uncertain; only change is inevitable. By way of illustration, 19th century American landscape paintings often included smokestacks as symbols of progress, whereas modern social photographers employ smokestacks as a symbol of pollution and industrial decay. Even perceptions of progress change.

If we are, as the title of this book implies, to enter into "a new era of design," then we must be aware of (a) the inevitability of change and (b) the inherent dangers of guiding change by design. In an open-world model, knowledge is developed locally, and it resists integration. Partial models hold promise, but subsequent investigation will ultimately shift the paradigm. For example, consider the following remark about a shift described in these two chapters.

The empiricist assumption that dominated many branches of psychology for decades, the assumption that what we know is a direct reflection of what we can perceive in the physical world, has largely disappeared. In its place is a view that most knowledge is an interpretation of experience, an interpretation based on schemas, often idiosyncratic at least in detail, that both enable and constrain individuals' processes of sense-making. (Resnick 1991, p. 1)

Resnick writes of "challenges to the dominant role of formal logic as an account of human rationality" and of "a sea change in the fields of investigation concerned with human thinking and social functioning. We seem to be in the midst of multiple efforts to merge the social and cognitive, treating them as essential aspects of one another rather than as dimly sketched background or context for a dominantly cognitive or dominantly social science" (p. 3). Cole (1991), in commenting on how children learn in any culture, observes that "systems of knowledge are not 'in' the child's head to begin with. Whatever the mechanisms of their acquisition, they cannot be acquired in a sociocultural vacuum. Hence, if one is to study human cognition as it is encountered in normal human adults, it is necessary to start not with cognitive processes abstracted from their context, but with the structure of activity that provides the functional matrix of and structural constraints on their acquisition" (p. 410). In the previous sentence, one can substitute "design" for "study human cognition, "world" for "adults," and "design" for "cognitive" and end up with an equally valid statement.

Cole continues, "the two analytic categories we label *individual* and *social* are constituted in a unique medium—human culture. It is my impression that a good deal of what gets lumped under the *social* category in the term *socially shared cognition* is actually cultural rather than (or in addition to) social" (p. 411). It follows, therefore, that the effect of the designer will be to alter the culture as he alters the environment (even if he does not realize that was his intention). Just as we cannot separate the technological from the cultural, neither can we separate technological knowledge from knowledge of the culture (i.e., knowledge in-the-world). Whatever knowledge we bring to design has been learned individually, historically, culturally.

This recommends a decentered view of the locus and meaning of learning, in which learning is recognized as a social phenomenon constituted in the experienced, lived-in world, through legitimate peripheral participation in ongoing social practice; the process of changing knowledgeable skill is subsumed in processes of changing identity in and through membership in a community of practitioners; and mastery is an organizational, relational characteristic of communities in practice. (Lave 1991, p. 64)

If, as Lave claims, "learning, thinking, and knowing are relations among people engaged in activity *in, with, and arising from the socially and culturally constructed world*" (p.67), then "changing existing situations into preferred ones" will impact what we think and know. Thus, paradoxically, we find that change is the invariant, not knowledge.

These are just some of the implications of a new era of design. I can offer neither safeguards nor solutions; I can only issue a warning regarding the dangers and responsibilities of design (i.e., the deliberate and conscious altering of the environment). We can never ascertain absolute truth (i.e., certainty of knowledge); nevertheless, we can at least approach it from various sides, sometimes even in opposite directions, perhaps even encircling it (after Frankl 1985). If we think of "truth" as a space containing the knowledge that will guide design, we may never be certain of its contents, but we may be able to recognize its complement. That is, even if we cannot know what is true, we should be able to discern what is false (cf. Popper and refutation). For this reason, I close this first part of the discussion with an overview of human bias and error. I hope that by seeing how people violate the principles of reason and rationality we may gain a better understanding of the role of reason and rationality in design. Moreover, by seeing how people violate normative standards, we may expand the knowledge of ourselves as designers.

6.5. Reason, Bias, and Error

We have seen that human cognition relies on pattern matching (e.g., the spotty dog). Much of what we know is factual and unambiguous. Recall of this factual knowledge may be purely symbolic (e.g., Annapolis is the capital of Maryland), or it may rely on visualization (e.g., Lincoln is looking to the right on the penny). What makes cognition so effective, of course, is the ability to create new facts by deductive inference (e.g., we infer that an elephant eats more than a mouse from known facts regarding the relative sizes of the elephant and the mouse, the relationship between size and food intake, and so on). But inference need not always produce correct facts. For instance, Stevens and Coupe (1978) performed an experiment in which subjects were asked to judge the relative locations of two cities. Without access to a map, the subjects had to rely on inference. Thus, in the case of the direction from Portland, Oregon to Toronto, the subjects tended to guess a north to north east direction, even though Toronto is due east from Portland. Here, the fact that Canada was north of the United States dominated the inference process. Of course, more knowledge of geography (such as that produced by this simple example) will increase the store of facts, thereby yielding better inferences. (It now should be easy to infer the direction from Seattle to Montreal.)

There are, however, many other problems that defy simple inference. For example, assume that there is a diagnostic test for a disease, present in 3% of the population, that produces a positive result in 95% of the cases and a false positive in 10% of the trials. Here we have information about the test result when the presence of the disease is known; we are interested in knowing the probability of the disease being present if a test result is positive. What is that probability? It cannot be inferred (although the falseness of some inferences can be inferred). It requires a computation—Bayes Theorem—that, although very easy, is too large to be managed in short-term memory. The answer, by the way, is 23%.

From this brief introduction, we may conclude that there are many cognitive tasks that we perform effectively and automatically, for example, the recall of facts. There also are tasks that rely on deductive inference, and here performance depends on the knowledge available to support the reasoning. With experience and training, the number of facts increases, and both factual recall and deductive inference improve. Furthermore, from the growth of facts and understanding, inductive inference adds to the rules that may be applied deductively. Finally, we note that for the tasks that exceed human memory capacity, management is possible through recourse to external memory (e.g., pencil and paper or a computer). In the positivist view, all knowledge may be derived from observation-based facts and the use of reason (i.e., deductive inference and computation, perhaps using external memory). Although most people now find flaws in the positivist claim, it nevertheless is true that all formal models have been derived in this manner. Thus, trained individuals can and do behave rationally (at least for some of the time).

But in most complex situations, our cognitive limitations will not permit us to bring to a problem everything we know. According to Simon's theory of *bounded rationality*, we construct simplified models that we use to frame the problem and its solution. The decision maker "behaves rationally with respect to this model, and such behavior is not even approximately optimal with respect to the real world. To predict this behavior, we must understand the way in which this simplified model is constructed, and its construction will certainly be related to his psychological properties as a perceiving, thinking, and learning animal" (Simon 1957, p. 198). That is, within this model, Simon asserts, we are rational; the actual outcome is suboptimal because we aim only to *satisfice*—to arrive at a satisfactory solution.

In an influential paper, Henle (1962) argued that people's deductive reasoning followed the laws of logic (i.e., logic is a normative model for human reasoning). If inferential errors were identified, they could be traced back to an idiosyncratic representation of the problem (e.g., the problem was framed improperly). Since that paper, there have been numerous studies that cast doubt upon his conclusion. For example, consider the following syllogism:

It is important to talk about things that are on our minds.

We spend so much of our time in the kitchen that household problems are on our mind.

Therefore, it is important to talk about household problems.

Training tells us that the syllogism is logically true, but common sense rejects it out of hand. Its contextual invalidity is so strong that we do not bother with a logical interpretation. And that raises the question: Do people reason by logic, or is logic a way of explaining how people reason? The question is central to the task of discovering (and correcting for) patterns of errors and biases. I note that the subject is not without controversy. For example, Cohen (1981) asserts that *irrationality* cannot be demonstrated experimentally. He identifies four categories of research into the defects of cognitive rationality, and shows why each cannot demonstrate irrationality; he then asserts that all future experiments can be assigned to one of these categories. Cohen's concern is that the research into limitations on rationality may lead to an underestimation of people's natural reasoning powers; he calls the manipulated laboratory circumstances that produce biased effects "cognitive illusions". Yet Evans (1989), in his comprehensive treatment of human bias, states that the widespread assumption "that merely framing problems in more realistic terms enhances performance is now known to be oversimplified" (p. 8).

Cheng and Holyoak (1985) propose that "people often reason using neither syntactic, context-free rules of inference, nor memory of specific experiences. Rather, they reason using abstract knowledge structures induced from ordinary life experiences, such as 'permissions,' 'obligations,' and 'causations.' Such knowledge structures are termed *pragmatic reasoning schemas,...* a set of generalized, context sensitive rules which, unlike purely syntactic rules, are defined in terms of classes of goals ... and relationships to these goals" (p. 395). If Cheng and Holyoak are correct, then a simple logical model of reasoning will not suffice.

Rather than attempt to present an overview of bias, I shall focus on two issues of particular concern in design. The first of these is *conformation bias*, the tendency to look for facts that confirm rather than refute a theory. By way of background, Wason introduced a very simple reasoning task in 1960 in which subjects were asked to discover the rule to which the triple "2 4 6" belonged. The subjects would produce test triples, and the experimenter would tell them if the test sample conformed to the rule or not; periodically, the subjects also would offer a tentative hypothesis, and the experimenter would tell them if it was correct or not. The process continued until the rule (which was "any ascending sequence") was discovered or the subject gave up. Subjects had great difficulty with this task. Rather than suggesting triples that might refute a tentative hypothesis, they offered only triples to confirm the working hypothesis. Mahoney (1976) repeated essentially the same experiment with three groups: psychologists, physical scientists, and "relatively uneducated Protestant ministers."

> How did our subjects fare? In a word, poorly. Most of them did not solve the problem. Of those who did, only two were errorless—both were ministers. Consistent with the argument that disconfirmation is a more efficient reasoning strategy, those subjects who used falsifying experiments were substantially more successful. Unfortunately, as with Wason's undergraduate subjects, neither our scientists nor the nonscientists were very prone to using disconfirmation. Over 85 percent of their self-generated experiments were confirmatory.
> ... Contrary to the storybook image, scientists showed a tendency to be more speculative than nonscientists—generating more hypotheses, more quickly, and with fewer experiments per hypothesis! Likewise, they were apparently more tenacious, as reflected by their differential tendency to return to already falsified hypotheses. (pp. 155-56)

Mahoney shows that this kind of behavior by scientists is not atypical; it has been replicated in other experiments.

Wason introduced a related selection task in 1966. Subjects were shown four cards: A D 3 7 and given the rule, "If there is an A on one side of the card, then there is a 3 on the other side of the card." They then were asked to turn over all the cards necessary to see if they conformed to the rule. Two cards should have been turned over: the A for *modus ponens* (that there is a 3 on the other side) and the 7 for *modus tollens* (that there is *not* an A on the other side). Only 15% of the subjects turned over the correct two cards. When the task was later repeated with less abstract materials (i.e., envelopes with the rule that sealed envelopes require a 5 d. stamp, but unsealed envelopes can use a 4 d. stamp), success rose to 80%. Perhaps the naturalness of the setting produced two rules (i.e., 4 d. stamp, then unsealed; sealed, then a 5 d. stamp). In any case, the selection task (and the associated 2 4 6 task) demonstrate that even trained scientists do not look to disconfirm. Evans believes "that the studies associated with confirmation bias reflect not a motivational bias but a set of cognitive failures. Subjects confirm, not because they want to, but because they cannot think of a way to falsify.... [There is] a bias to think about positive rather than negative information" (p. 42). This "positivity bias" arises from the "preconscious heuristic processes that determine the locus of the subjects' attention" (p. 42). For Evans, it is these preconscious heuristics that guide thinking, not the logical analysis of cartesian reasoning. Brehmer (1980) justifies this heuristic ecologically. "In concept learning experiments, the neglect of negative information leads to slow and inefficient learning, but the strategy makes sense when one considers the conditions under which people usually have to learn in the so-called real world" (p. 228). There is a high cognitive cost for attempting to disconfirm what we believe, and we tend to avoid this cost except when confronted by a breakdown.

The second issue is that of judgment under uncertainty (Tversky and Kahneman 1974, Kahneman, Slovic, and Tversky 1982), which is decision making based on statistical reasoning. Brehmer (1980) points out that there is a strong tendency for people to use rules for deterministic tasks even when confronted by a probabilistic task. "For a person with a firm belief in the deterministic character of the world, there is nothing in his experience that would force him to discover that the task is probabilistic and to give up the notion of determinism. To detect the probabilistic nature of the task, the subject clearly has to have the hypothesis that it is probabilistic" (p. 234).

Tversky and Kahneman (1974) observe that people develop heuristics for the subjective assessment of probabilities just as they do for the subjective assessment of physical quantities such as distance or size (e.g., distances are underestimated on a clear day because the estimation heuristic correlates distance with the clarity of the object). They identify three principal heuristics.

> *Representativeness*, which is observed where people must decide if a particular object or event belongs to a general class or process. The reliance on superficial similarity (i.e., representativeness) leads to a bias because it is not influenced by several factors that should affect judgments of probability. For example, there is a tendency to ignore prior probability (base rate) in making judgments. When given short descriptions of individuals and then asked to determine if the person was a lawyer or not, the subjects provided roughly the same assignments when told that the population from which the samples were selected consisted of 70% lawyers or only 30% lawyers. Other illustrations are insensitivity to sample size (e.g., not recognizing that greater variability is found in smaller samples), misconception of chance (e.g., favoring heads in a coin toss when the previous tosses were all tails), and the illusion of validity (i.e., the unwarranted confidence produced by a good fit between the input information and predicted output).

> *Availability*, which is found in situations where people assess the frequency of a class or the probability of an event by the ease with which instances or occurrences can be brought to mind. "Lifelong experience has taught us that, in general, instances of large classes

are recalled better and faster than instances of less frequent classes; that likely occurrences are easier to imagine than unlikely ones; and that the associative connections between events are strengthened when the events frequently co-occur" (Kahneman, Slovic, and Tversky 1982, p. 14). The heuristic developed from that experience, however, results in systematic errors.

Adjustment and anchoring, characterized as the process of producing estimates by starting with an initial value and then making adjustments to yield the final answer. If one starts with a low number in working out a mental estimate of a computation, one tends to yield a lower final answer than if one began with a larger initial number.

Tversky and Kahneman point out that these biases are not attributable to motivational effects such as wishful thinking or the distortion of judgments by payoffs and penalties. "Very few people discover the principles of sampling and regression on their own. Statistical principles are not learned from everyday experience because the relevant instances are not coded appropriately.... The lack of appropriate code also explains why people usually do not detect biases in their judgments of probability" (pp. 18-19). To detect what percentage of one's almost-certain predictions (i.e., probability of 0.9) come true, one would need to keep careful records. The question, then, is how can we overcome these biases? To some degree, reasoning can be taught (Nisbett, Fong, Lehman, and Cheng 1987).

Johnson-Laird (1983b) uses mental models to explain why people make logical errors. He suggests that

the most common cause of difficulty in reasoning for individuals living in a literate society is the limited processing capabilities of working memory.... However, it must be emphasized that there appears to be a spontaneous improvement in reasoning ability as a consequence of practice (with no knowledge of results).... The effect of practice must in part be to increase the efficiency of encoding operations of working memory. Experience with the task may also produce a growing awareness of logical properties of the problems. Some subjects may begin to notice, for example, that two negative premises never yield an interesting valid conclusion. (p. 191)

Thus, rational thinking (i.e., the use of mental logic) is a skill that can be taught. What of probabilistic reasoning? Here is a simple form of Bayes Theorem:

$$P(D|T) = P(D) \cdot P(T|D)/(P(D) \cdot P(T|D) + P(\sim D) \cdot P(T|\sim D))$$

Substitutions from the diagnostic test example given earlier yields the following computation for the probability that, given a positive test result, the disease is present:

$$P(D|T) = (.03)(.95)/((.03)(.95) + (.97)(.10)) = .227$$

I do not believe that the processing capabilities of working memory permit us to perform that computation; instead we rely on the heuristic of adjustment and anchoring. We can be trained to recognize our limitations and biases, and we can learn to use external memory and other tools. But we must accept that people are superb at certain kinds of cognitive activities (some of which may be poorly understood) and very inefficient in the performance of others. The goal of design, of course, is to extend the environment to enhance the human potential; and to do that, the designer must be aware of the human's limitations.

So, within their cognitive constraints, do people think logically? In a review of the selection task, Wason (1983) comments that the differences in performance are not related to the "abstractness" versus the "concreteness" of the experiment design. "What matters is realism however it be achieved. It is not, as Piaget might have supposed, that realistic material enhances logical performance because it enables the individual to be guided by formal operations through matter into some superior world of logical structure. Understanding is related to content [i.e., context within the mental model]" (p. 71). Both logic and probability constitute formal, nominal models of how things should be. Those models are not inherently valid. Nor is their form necessarily appropriate. For instance, most logic accepts the law of the excluded middle, but that is an abstract concept that may not relate to the real world. Probabilistic models may be accurate descriptions of some phenomena, but they do not necessarily provide accurate guidelines for all decision making.

Zukier and Pepitone (1984) identify two orientations: "scientific," which is concerned with general propositions including Bayesian probability, and "clinical," which is concerned with the individual case through the construction of a coherent narrative or case history. Subjects given a problem in one orientation will continue with that orientation and virtually ignore considerations from the other orientation. Thus, when starting with a clinical orientation, the subjects tend to overlook base rate information, and those who consider base rate often miss case-specific factors. In part, this reflects a human inability to manage all the knowledge available; in part, it also indicates that neither model—the scientific nor the clinical—is complete.

Unlike the study of human bias (which identifies imperfections in rational thought), the study of human error focuses on the failure to conceive or carry out an action sequence. There is a vast literature on error from the perspective of system design and human-machine interaction (e.g., Rasmussen, Duncan, and Leplat 1987, Lee, Tillman, and Higgins 1988, Lang 1990, Senders and Moray 1991). Reason (1990) points out that the notions of intention and error are inseparable. "The notion of intention comprises two elements: (a) an expression of the end-state to be attained, and (b) an indication of the means by which it is to be achieved.... Error can *only* be applied to intentional actions. It has no meaning in relation to nonintentional behavior because error types depend critically upon two kinds of failure: the failure of actions to go as intended (slips and lapses) and the failure of intended actions to achieve their desired consequences (mistakes)" (Zukier and Pepitone 1984, pp. 5,7).

Thus, slips and lapses may be thought of as execution failures and mistakes as planning failures.

Whereas *slips* are potentially observable as externalized actions-not-as-planned (slips of the tongue, slips of the pen, slips of action), the term *lapse* is generally reserved for more covert error forms, largely involving failures of memory, that do not necessarily manifest themselves in actual behavior and may only be apparent to the person who experiences them.

Mistakes may be defined as deficiencies or failures in the judgmental and/or inferential processes involved in the selection of an objective or in the specification of the means to achieve it, irrespective of whether or not the actions directed by this decision-scheme run according to plan.

It is evident from this definition that mistakes are likely to be more subtle, more complex and less well understood than slips.... Not only is the quality of the plan open to a diversity of opinion, it is also something that can be judged at two distinct stages: before and after it has been implemented. (p. 9)

Reason organizes the above-mentioned error types within the skill-rule-knowledge framework developed by Rasmussen (1983). That framework consists of three levels of performance corresponding to decreasing levels of familiarity with the environment or task. They are as follows:

Skill-based level, governed by stored patterns and preprogrammed instructions. "Errors at this level are related to the intrinsic variability of force, space or time coordination" (Reason 1990, p. 43).

Rule-based level, governed by stored production rules. "Here, errors are typically associated with the misclassification of situations leading to the application of the wrong rule or with incorrect recall of procedures" (p. 43).

Knowledge-based level, which "comes into play in novel situations for which actions must be planned on-line, using conscious analytical processes and stored knowledge. Errors at this level arise from resource limitations ('bounded rationality') and incomplete or incorrect knowledge" (p. 43). Many of the errors Reason assigns to this level have been described earlier as biases, (e.g., the availability heuristic and confirmation bias)

In this framework, slips and lapses are viewed as skill based, and mistakes are divided into two categories: rule-based mistakes and knowledge-based mistakes. Reason expands this framework into a *generic error-modeling system* (GEMS), which provides the basis for a discussion of error detection and the assessment and reduction of human error risk.

Many of the findings regarding human bias and error have come from analyses of real-world situations (e.g., industrial accidents), but much also has come from the laboratory. Fraser, Smith, and Smith (1992) have cataloged the major error types in the literature and "question whether different experiments should be labelled as describing the same behavior. The fact that boundary conditions may need to be specified in great detail raises concern whether behaviors are being categorized only on surface similarities, not on deeper understanding of cognitive processes.... To make greater progress in the understanding of human error, we need to focus more attention on modeling the cognitive processes that cause particular errors, and on the identification of the contexts in which the processes are likely to be active" (pp. 300-1).

Here we have the cognitive science emphasis on modeling the process "inside the head." The situated activity is recognized as a context. As Bobrow and Norman (1975) put it, "We suggest that descriptions are normally formed to be unambiguous within the context they were first used. That is, a description defines a memory schema relative to a context" (p. 133). Thus, if a production rule contains the entire context, it will be universally valid. Yet there is much in these chapters to question this view. Dreyfus and Dreyfus (1986) might consider expertise as skill based rather than knowledge based, Cole (1991) might place further emphasis on the cultural aspects "outside the head", and activity theory might restructure the issue in an entirely different way.   Perhaps what we see as bias and error is the clash between what humans have gained through coping in-the-world (i.e., everyday experience) and the scientifically founded normative rules for interpreting that experience.

Bruner (1986) comments, "Both science and the humanities have come to be appreciated as artful figments of men's minds, as creations produced by different uses of mind" (p. 44). What we interpret as bias and error may simply be byproducts of the inherent tension between these different uses of mind.

> It is clear that technology makes man's relation to the system he seeks to control abstract and indirect. Both the information he receives and the outcomes he creates are mediated by complex processes that are hidden from direct view. Work thus becomes mental and abstract, rather than physical and concrete. Decision making becomes the very essence of this mental work, for work in the control room of a process plant is similar to that in the board room in that it is a question of selecting actions rather than of performing actions. (Brehmer 1987, pp. 112-13)

In the positivist view (i.e., that of Technical Rationality), a set of potential actions can be defined and classified in advance, and modern design practice holds that those actions should be specified before the system is built.   For those who subscribe to plural realism, this objective—although commendable and desirable—may not be fully achievable.   That is, we may not have the ability to understand all the complexities of the equipment as it will operate in-the-world.   This presents us with a dilemma: Do we limit the extent of the design (a) to what the people can manage or (b) to what the technology can support? Fortunately, the capabilities of both people and technology are dynamic, and it may be possible for the designers to resolve the dilemma by making the equipment the servant of the people and, at the same time, expanding the world of the people to include the equipment.

Technological design operates within the positivist model; equipment is specified to satisfy requirements—to instrument a part of the whole model.   Error and bias, then, become measures of the individual's inability (or unwillingness) to conform to that model.   The ecological study of design moves away from that model and includes people—not as extensions of the equipment—but as creators of the world in which that equipment operates.   It does not deny the validity of technological design; indeed, it depends on it.   It only claims that technological design is not enough, that it does not include the person.

> The "reality" of most of us is constituted roughly in two spheres: that of nature and that of human affairs, the former is more

likely to be structured in the paradigmatic mode of logic and science, the latter in the mode of story and narrative. The latter is centered around the drama of human intentions and their vicissitudes; the first around the equally compelling, equally natural idea of causation. The subjective reality that constitutes an individual's sense of the world is roughly divided into a natural and a human one.

... In practice, we manipulate or operate physically upon *that* which is in the domain of cause and effect; but we interact or try to communicate with *those* who seem governed by intentions. (Bruner 1986, p. 88)

7

THE DESIGN PROCESS

7.1. Finally, an Examination of Design

We have arrived at the last layer of the foundation. I now can begin a systematic analysis of design. As a brief reminder, this really is a book about the development of software applications. My thesis is that we can expect only limited improvement to software application and productivity by working within the current design paradigm (i.e, technological design). I believe that we must shift paradigms to exploit the special characteristics of software. But paradigm shifts are revolutions, and one cannot comprehend any new paradigm by extrapolating from the concepts and methods of the present paradigm. Thus, we must destroy before we can rebuild.

In the physical sciences, the justification for destruction comes from outside the paradigm; phenomena are observed that are at variance with the models of normal science, and new theories are needed to explain them. Computer science and software engineering, however, are formalizations for free phenomena. In a sense, they are self-defining; they establish their own criteria for relevance and evaluation. If we are to replace those criteria, therefore, we must begin *outside* normal computer science. And that is the justification for these first two parts. Part I examines the meaning and limitations of science and provides an interpretation of design: the modification of the environment (or "changing existing conditions into preferred ones"). Part II looks at design from the perspective of those who make and use the designs. I deliberately remain outside the domain of computer science in my search for the knowledge that will be relevant to the subsequent examination of software. Once this knowledge has been assembled, Part III can enter into a less biased consideration of software and its role in the next millennium. Thus, the first two parts construct the context within which a new computer science can be defined, and Part III offers adaptive design as an illustration of what this new computer science can accomplish.

Where are we now in this odyssey? Chapter 1 begins with the traditional view in which the maturity of software engineering as a discipline is related to its utilization of computer science principles. The next two chapters explore the accuracy of this model. Chapter 2 investigates science from a philosophic perspective and finds that few still subscribe to the tenets held to be universal in the early days of computer science. Chapter 3 looks at the relationship between science and technology and reports that the linear model (in which technology is the application of scientific knowledge) is invalid. Indeed, it has become clear that it is difficult to distinguish between science and technology; consequently, a discovery-design orientation is adopted. Discovery seeks to learn about the existing reality (material and cultural); design seeks to gain benefit by altering that reality. Most scientific and technical enterprises engage in both discovery and design (often iteratively).

Chapter 4 opens the present unit on ecological design by exploring the larger context within which the changes noted in Part I are occurring. The next two chapters review issues in cognition. Chapter 5 examines cognition (as human problem solving), first from the perspective of cognitive science, and then from the perspective of what may not be explained by the information processing model. Chapter 6 presents alternative views of cognition and problem solving, views that address the limits to what can be modeled in-the-computer. Finally, I turn to an examination of design.

As with the overview of cognition, I divide this discussion into two chapters. The present chapter focuses on the design process as carried out in other domains. Too often we find software engineers looking to other disciplines (e.g., engineering and architecture) for exemplars that will guide the development of software. This chapter describes how design is conducted in practice, warts and all. The existing models are seen to have shortcomings, difficulties that Part III demonstrates may be overcome by taking advantage of software's special properties. The last chapter of Part II provides a transition from the concern for universal concepts to the specifics of software design. It concentrates on the interactions between people (normally users) and equipment and on how the technology alters the perceptions of needs.

7.2. Design Practice

Earlier I described discovery and design as being like the two faces of Janus: Discovery looks back onto what exists so that it may be understood, and design looks forward to what exists so that it may be improved. I now consider how we conduct design, and two works from the 1960s provide an interesting contrast in how our understanding has changed. A 1963 text on engineering design presented a narrow view of design.

> The art of designing can perhaps be explained on the following lines.
>
> *The designer uses his intellectual ability to apply scientific knowledge to the task of creating the drawings which enable an engineering product to be made in a way that not only meets the stipulated conditions but also permits manufacture by the most economic method.* (Matousek 1963, pp. 3-4)

The author identified three categories of design. Adaptive design would characterize most of the designer's activity; it "demands no special knowledge or skill, and the problems presented are easily solved by a designer with ordinary technical training" (p. 4). Development design, which starts from an existing design and produces a product that differs markedly from the initial product, would require more training and skill. Finally, there was new design, at which few designers would become skilled enough to succeed. Implicit in this overview are the assumptions that the drawing captures the design information, that design is driven by scientific knowledge, and that the process is monotonic. Such a concept of design could taught.

By way of contrast, writing in 1966, Gregory was looking forward to a world of many new projects. "The conscious identification of the design method is quite recent, although precisely when the concept appeared is not certain" (p. 6). He noted that designers were distancing themselves from the drawing board, a trend that was bound to be accelerated by the presence of computers. For him, science was analytic and design constructive. "The end of all design is human satisfaction.... This tendency to disregard the consumer is not only a retreat from the spirit of engineering but it carries the possibility of national disaster. In a competitive world it is the mastery of the market which prevails, and the mastery of the market means design for the consumer" (p. 7). A very modern warning in the light of our current concern for competitiveness and usability (Adler and Winograd 1992a).

In the old—or *formal*—view, routine design is managed as scientifically directed problem solving; in the new—or *contextual*—view, there is an added dimension of nontechnical issues (e.g., human satisfaction). Actually, formal and contextual are far more descriptive terms than old and new, and the formal-contextual dichotomy is not recent.

> In studying man's earliest history ... it is difficult to separate things done for "pure" aesthetic enjoyment from those done for

some real or imagined "practical" purpose....

Paradoxically man's capacity for aesthetic enjoyment may have been his most practical characteristic, for it is at the root of his discovery of the world about him, and it makes him want to live.... Over and over again scientifically important properties of matter and technologically important ways of making and using them have been discovered or developed in an environment which suggests the dominance of aesthetic motivation. (Smith 1970, pp. 497, 498)

In his analysis of the historiography of technology, Staudenmaier (1985) remarks:

Genuine contextualism is rooted in the proposition that technical designs cannot be meaningfully interpreted in abstraction from their human context. The human fabric is not simply an envelope around a culturally neutral artifact. The values and world views, the intelligence and stupidity, the biases and vested interests of those who design, accept, and maintain a technology are embedded in the technology itself.... The specific designs chosen by individuals and institutions necessarily embody specific values. In summary, contextualism and the myth of autonomous progress are at odds because the progress myth assumes a value-free method divorced from every context and because it assumes one inevitable line of advance hindered only by those who violate the purity of the method and attempt to stop progress through value-laden subjective critique. (pp. 165-66)

Formal-contextual, objective-subjective, value-free versus value-laden are but different aspects of the basic tension within design—the decisions regarding *what* the artifact should be and *how* it should be constructed; the distinction between in-the-world and in-the-product. In reporting on a workshop on system design, Rouse and Boff (1987b) identify two schools: the analytical and the artistic. "The analytical school argues that well-done analytical decomposition can make subsequent composition very straight forward, while the artistic school claims that the subtlety and richness of composition is the essence of creative design. To an extent, both these assertions were accepted as correct. The salient issue concerns the appropriate mix of analytical and artistic behaviors" (pp. 47-48). Thus, design involves both "knowing" and "feeling."

Simon (1969/1981) offers an expansive view of design. "Everyone designs who devises courses of action aimed at changing existing situations into preferred ones" (p. 129). He speaks of artificial phenomena and of artifacts whose properties "lie on the thin interface between the natural laws within it and the natural laws without" (p. 131).

> The artificial world is centered precisely on this interface between the inner and outer environments; it is concerned with attaining goals by adapting the former to the latter. The proper study of those who are concerned with the artificial is the way in which that adaption of means to environment is brought about—and central to that is the process of design itself. (p. 132)

> All who use computers in complex ways are using computers to design or to participate in the process of design. Consequently, we as designers, or as designers of the design process, have had to be explicit as never before about what is involved in creating a design and what takes place while the creation is going on....
> The proper study of mankind has been said to be man. But I have argued that man—or at least the intellective component of man—may be relatively simple, that most of the complexity of his behavior may be drawn from man's environment, from man's search for design. If I have made my case, then we can conclude that, in large part, the proper study of mankind is the science of design.... (p. 159)

Although I subscribe to Simon's seminal insights regarding the nature and extent of design, I believe that his particular approach depends too strongly on the laws of nature (within and without); there is no role for culture, art, or humanity. His emphasis is on representing what is known and then reducing design to operations on that knowledge. As a correction to that view, the remainder of this chapter examines the possibilities for explicitness in and the scientific certainty of design.

7.3. Architectural and Industrial Design

Pye, an architect and industrial designer, has written a book on the nature and aesthetics of design (1978), and I begin the analysis with extracts from that most attractive and readable work (reprinted with permission, ⊛1978 Curtis Brown Academic Ltd.).

> The man-made world, our environment, is potentially a work of art, all of it, every bit of it....
> Although the importance of design is realized, the essential

nature of the activity seems not to be understood except by designers, and they have not formulated what they know....

Little is ever said which touches on the fundamental principles of useful design, and what is said is often nonsense. Most of the nonsense probably starts at the point where people begin talking about function as though it were something objective: something of which it could be said that it belonged to a thing. (p. 11)

It seems to be invariably true that those characteristics which lead people to call a design functional are derived from the requirements of economy and not of use. (p. 34)

Whenever humans design and make a useful thing they invariably expend a good deal of unnecessary and easily avoidable work on it that contributes nothing to its usefulness.... These activities: "workmanship," "design for appearance," "decoration," "ornament," "applied art," "embellishment," or what you will, are part of the same pattern of behavior which all men at all times and places have followed: doing useless work on useful things. (p. 13)

When any useful thing is designed the shape of it is in no way imposed on the designer, or determined by any influence outside him, or entailed. His freedom of choosing the shape is a limited freedom, it is true, but there are no limitations so close as to relieve him or the maker of the responsibility for the appearance of what they have done.... All the works of man look as they do from his choice. (p. 14)

The designer always has freedom of choice. That choice is a central issue. Design is done to get results, but the useless work, the freedom of choice about what the thing designed shall look like, matters as much as getting the result and sometimes even more. (p. 90)

There is a distinction between the result of a device's being used and the purpose of it. [For example, the purpose of a cargo ship for the owner is to make money, for the captain it is to be sea worthy, for the designer it is to carry a given load, etc.].... The fact that every device when used produces concrete, measurable, objective results, is the only sure basis for a theory of design. Any concept such as "function" which includes the idea of purpose is bound to be an unsafe foundation; for purpose leaves commonplace factual affairs like results far behind. (pp. 15-16)

All useful devices have got to do useless things no one wants them to do. Who wants a car to get hot? Or wear out its tires? Or make a noise and smell? (p. 13)

When you put energy into a system you can never choose what kind of changes shall take place and what kind of results shall remain. God has already decided those things. All you can do, and that only within limits, is to regulate the amounts of the various changes. This you do by *design*, which is the business of ensuring that at least you get the change you want along with the others you don't want, such as heat, noise, wear, and the rest.... The total of all the results together we may call the "response" of the system to the in-put of energy. (p. 18)

The requirements of use are imperative. If they are not complied with the device does not give the result. The requirements of economy are on a different footing, for the amount of weight given to them is a matter of choice. (p. 34)

The two commonest sources of chance discovery or invention are play and error.... Nearly every device we have has grown out of primary discoveries which simply turned up.... There seems no reason, on first consideration, why a system of forces should not first be invented by reasoning from known principles of mechanics, and then clothed in things. But this does not happen. (pp. 63-64)

Design is not all a matter of problem-solving, neither is it all a matter of art. It is both. The two parts of it are inseparable. (p. 76)

Although Pye was writing to a nontechnical audience, all of the material just extracted is equally valid for software design in-the-world. For example, he describes a style as something that restricts and directs the designer's choices and claims that design without style is an impossibility. The limitations imposed by style may be argued to be "psychologically necessary to nearly all designers. When design gets too easy it becomes too difficult. Styles provide the desired limitations when, as so often, the requirements of use and economy do not impose limitations which are close enough" (p. 35).

Layton (1984) offers a similar view of style in engineering design:

The modern view of design makes it possible to defile style in engineering design. If design consists of a chain of decisions, each influenced by values, then any pattern in this decision-making constitutes a style (or an element in style). Clearly, there can be many different types of style, existing at all levels. The criteria of choice might be aesthetic, economic, social, or intellectual. The use of science, and the manner of its use, also constitutes a stylistic element within design.... In engineering design, the way in which the designer conceptualizes the problem, the way he perceives the choices he has, and the values which he brings to these choices will define an engineering style (or styles). In this sense, engineering design is an art form; it is bound by physical, scientific, and other constraints, but it is an art form all the same. (p. 177)

(Part III examines the role of design style in further detail.)

In 1964 the architect Alexander published *Notes on the Synthesis of Form*, which was hailed as one of the most important books on the art of design. He was concerned that as the problems confronting designers grew in complexity, the "modern designer relies more and more on his position as an 'artist,' on catchwords, personal idiom, and intuition— for all these relieve him of some of the burden of decision, and make his cognitive problems manageable" (p. 10). Although he recognized the limitations of logic in modeling reality, he believed that the use of logical structures to represent design problems had an important consequence: "A logical picture is easier to criticize than a vague picture" (p. 8). And so, his book seeks to establish a formal structure to guide the resolution of design problems.

> The ultimate object of design is form....
> It is based on the idea that every design problem begins with an effort to achieve fitness between two entities: the form in question and its context. The form is the solution to the problem; the context defines the problem. (p. 15)

In his definition of design we find still another representation of the basic dichotomy: formal and contextual, solution and problem, objective and subjective. The rightness of form, for Alexander, depends on "the degree to which it fits the rest of the ensemble.... In the great majority of actual cases, it is necessary for the designer to consider several different divisions of an ensemble, superimposed, at the same time" (p. 16). The designer has control over the form; the context places demands on the form; and "fitness is a relation of mutual acceptability between these two.... We want to put the context and the form into effortless contact or frictionless coexistence" (p. 19).

Observing that it is departures from the norm that stand out, Alexander turns to the negative instances, the *misfits*, that violate fitness.

"We should always expect to see the process of good fit between two entities as a negative process of neutralizing the incongruities, or irritants, or forces, which cause misfit" (p. 24).

> In the case of a real design problem, even our conviction that there is such a thing as fit to be achieved is curiously flimsy and insubstantial. We are searching for some kind of harmony between two intangibles: a form which we have not yet designed, and a context which we cannot properly describe. The only reason we have for thinking that there must be some kind of fit to be achieved between them is that we can detect incongruities, or negative instances of it. The incongruities in an ensemble are the primary data of experience. If we agree to treat fit as the absence of misfits, and to use a list of those potential misfits which are most likely to occur as our criterion for fit, our theory will at least have the same nature as our intuitive conviction that there is a problem to be solved. (pp. 26-27)

Restating this in Heideggerian terms, we recognize the problem because of its breakdowns, and we achieve goodness of fit by means of resolving those breakdowns.

Alexander identifies two types of culture: *unselfconscious*, whose form-making is learned informally, through imitation and correction, and *selfconscious*, whose form-making is taught academically, according to the rules. By way of illustration he points to the Egyptian houses of the Nile, the black houses of the Outer Hebrides, and the hogans of the Navaho. In each case there is an established form, and adjustments are made as misfits are identified. Within the established forms there is change, but the process of change—although continuous—is slow. Change is guided by the context of the existing form, and equilibrium is established before the next cultural change upsets it again. Thus, he argues "that the unselfconscious process has a structure that makes it homeostatic (self-organizing), and that it therefore consistently produces well-fitting forms, even in the face of change.... In a selfconscious culture the homeostatic structure of the process is broken down, so that the production of forms which fail to fit their contexts is not only possible, but likely" (p. 38). Pye observes,

> Change is of the essence of tradition. Our declining civilization has largely lost the conception of tradition as continuous change by small variations—as evolution, in other words—and can produce only fashions which, one after another, appear, live for a little while, and die without issue. At each death another deliberately different fashion is launched and promoted, as sterile as the one before. (Pye 1978, p. 134)

Where Pye is reacting to changing aesthetic styles, Alexander is reflecting on changes brought about by rapid changes in context (e.g., those resulting from technological innovation). In the latter case there is extensive and rapid demand for change, and the feedback responses of an unselfconscious culture cannot suffice. Adjustments to misfits do not have time to reach equilibrium, and, as a consequence, the role of the individual changes. "In the unselfconscious system the individual is no more than an agent.... The selfconscious process is different. The artist's selfconscious recognition of his individuality has deep effect on the process of form-making" (Alexander 1964, pp. 58-59). By freeing the designer from the inhibition of tradition, more questions can be asked, and more answers will be valid. Having thus placed so great a burden on the individual, success in form-making will depend on how well the individual can transcend his inherent incapacities.

Alexander's proposals are, by now, quite familiar to most readers. Complexity is reduced by hierarchical decomposition, the process is divided into the two stages of analysis and synthesis, there is a movement from words to value-free symbols, a level of formal modeling is introduced, misfits are identified for removal, and diagrams are introduced as an aid to problem solving. Formally, the diagram is defined as a hierarchical graph $G(M,L)$ of misfits M and links L such that the links L determine a decomposition especially favorable to the context. This decomposition (which is usually different from the one in the designer's head) is referred to as the *program*.

Analysis begins with the requirements and produces a tree of sets of requirements (i.e., the diagram or program); synthesis is the program's realization. The program or "constructive diagram" thus serves as the bridge between requirements and form. "A constructive diagram, if it is a good one, actually contributes to our understanding of the functional specification which calls it into being.... It offers us a way of probing the context, and a way of searching for form" (pp. 90, 92). Alexander asks how "a process, in which both the requirements and the links between requirements are defined by the designer from things already present in his mind, can possibly have any outcome which is not already present in the designer's mind.... The answer is that, because it concentrates on structure, the process is able to make a coherent and therefore new whole out of incoherent pieces" (p. 110). "Scientists try to identify the components of existing structure. Designers try to shape the components of new structure" (p. 130).

The book concludes with two appendices. The first is a worked example regarding the reorganization of a 600 person village in India. A list M of 141 potential misfits is compiled (e.g., those relating to religion and cast, to social forces, to agriculture), and the links L (i.e., interactions among the items in M) are identified. The graph $G(M,L)$ is constructed by combining the requirements in a hierarchy consisting of four first-level nodes (e.g., one dealing with cattle, bullock carts, and fuel; another with agricultural production, irrigation, and distribution) and 12 second-level nodes. Synthesis follows, during which misfits are resolved and a design for the village evolves. The second appendix contains a mathematical treatment of decomposition that been programmed. Misfits are coded as either 1 or 0.

In the preface to the 1971 paperback edition, Alexander cited the idea of the diagrams (latter called patterns) as the most important discovery of the book. Described only briefly in the text, the diagram is "an abstract pattern of physical relationships which resolves a small system of interacting and conflicting forces, and is independent of all other forces, and of all other possible diagrams" (p. v). The diagrams permit the analysis of relationships one at a time and allow the creation of designs by the fusion of the diagrams; it is the independence of the diagrams that gives them their power. In the book Alexander expended considerable effort on the formal definition of his technique.

But once the book was written, I discovered that it is quite unnecessary to use such a complicated and formal way of getting the independent diagrams.

If you understand the need to create independent diagrams, which resolve, or solve, systems of interacting forces, you will find that you can create, and develop, these diagrams piecemeal, one at a time, in the most natural way, out of your experience of buildings and design, simply by thinking about the forces which occur there and the conflicts between these forces. (pp. v-vi)

Thus, the diagrams provide a mechanism for breaking down a large problem so that it may be examined in smaller pieces; where independence is possible, synthesis permits the systematic elimination of misfits as the design develops. But the process is far from mechanical. "Many readers have focused on the *method which leads to* the creation of the diagrams, not on the *diagrams themselves*, and have even made a cult of following this method.... I reject the whole idea of design methods as a subject of study, since I think it is absurd to separate the study of designing from the practice of design" (p. vi). In a sense, the diagram is the catalyst in a dialectical process that creates an "outcome which is not already present in the designer's mind." That outcome exists in the domain of practice, and it cannot be studied or understood outside the context of practice.

Cuff (1991), an architect, describes the practice of architecture based on ten years of ethnographic research. She notes that there are two views of design: what the architect does, alone, at the drawing board, and the activity of planning environments. Like Simon, she opts for the broader view of design, and her examination includes the contributions of all individuals with a voice in design—the architect, client, engineer, etc. "Design, then, is taking place whenever any of these actors make plans about the future environment.... It is from the context of all their interactions that a building emerges.... 'Design problems in practice' refers to more than design activity in the office; it also means moving a project through the approval process, managing its construction, obtaining the commission in the first place, and so on" (p. 61). Her findings are "readings of the dilemmas practitioners face, and how they resolve them, only to create new dilemmas" (p. 6). She relies on cultural and social analysis, whose perspectives she favors because of "their rejection of positivist notions of the social world, embracing interpretation, meaning in context, interaction, and the quality of the commonplace" (p. 6). Cuff distinguishes between "espoused theory," which is how the architects explain and justify their actions, and "theory-in-use," which is what the architects actually use to guide their actions.

She finds four principle dualities that create tension. First, there is an emphasis on the role of the individual that masks the impact of collective action. Next, design is believed to sprout from a series of independently made decisions rather than emerging as the result of a dynamic social process. Third, design and art are separated from business and management, and finally, the architect is perceived as a generalist even though he must specialize to compete. Schools are guided by the espoused theory, practice by the theory-in-use.

> The dominant belief ... is that design is a kind of problem solving involving problems that can be defined, are determinate, and can be solved. There is a concomitant emphasis on *decision making* as the primary skill an *individual* needs in order to successfully give form to a project. Based in this research, the more accurate description of the necessary skill is not decision making but sense making.... The notion of sense making implies a collective context in which we must make sense of a situation, inherently social, interpret it, and make sense with others through conversation and action in order to reach agreement. (p. 254).

In describing design problems in practice, Cuff identifies six principal characteristics. *Design in the Balance*, in which architecture tries to unite ideologically contradictory forces in the union of art and business. This manifests itself in the tension between quality and cost and the tension between those who do the "design work" (often underpaid) and those responsible for the business end. *Countless Voices*, in which the simplicity of the academic model dissolves in architectural practice. Cuff notes that few projects have less than 10 people involved in the decision making. *Professional Uncertainty* resulting from the dynamics of practice in which the responsibilities, procedures, authority, allegiances, and expertise in a project are ambiguous. When asked about conventions, schedules, assignments, "the answer is, typically, 'It all depends.' The architect's constant litany—that every problem is unique—is an appropriate response to an ambiguous situation" (p. 84).

In spite of this uniqueness, professional knowledge must generalize from one problem to the next. *Perpetual Discovery* arising from the fact that the needed information is never complete and that changes to resolve one problem often affect solutions to other problems. The work-around is to establish a phased development, seek client agreement, and retain flexibility. Design decisions are formed in design conversations, not at the drawing board. The conversations either constrain or provide a foundation for future decisions. The complexity and linked nature of the decisions is "one of the primary reasons why decisions are not simple, and are rarely made directly in meetings" (p. 193). *Surprise Endings*, which suggests an unpredictability of outcome. "Logic indicates that the nature of architect-client interactions precludes clear, exhaustive formulation of needs and requirements, since these develop or become understood through the design process itself" (p. 100). *A Matter of Consequence*, reflecting the high stakes that architects, clients, engineers, and others have at risk in a building venture. Frank Lloyd Wright counseled young architects, "Go as far away as possible from home to build your first buildings. The physician can bury his mistakes, but the architect can only advise the client to plant vines" (cited on p. 106).

Despite these inherent difficulties, it is clear that architecture has produced many examples of excellence. Cuff defines design quality as something measured by the consumers, the participants in the design, and the architectural professions. She selects three examples of high quality projects and identifies seven properties leading to their success. *Quality demands* by both the architect and client. "In excellent projects the client demands an architectural quality that architects themselves are accustomed to demanding from clients" (p. 236). *Simplicity within complexity* (i.e., the response to complexity is not multilayered complexity but simplicity). There is "a dialectic between simplicity and complexity such that the project's success appears to depend on an appropriate blend of each, since too much complexity can overwhelm the potential for excellence and too much simplicity may preclude the rich texture of outstanding work" (p. 237). *Stereovision*, a word used by Cuff to suggest how the different visions of the client and architect combine to make up a single composite. "These perspectives are not the same, and what characterizes excellent projects is that they do not conflict, but complement one another, dovetailing to create a strong bond between two sets of interests" (p. 238). *Open boundaries*, which implies that although the clients and architects establish limits and set goals, the goals are "open-ended and positive, rousing participants to perform to their best ability. Excellent clients demand excellence from their architects and set them a challenge.... If the client in excellent projects is demanding, the architect is principled... [with a] strong architectural concept behind each excellent project" (p. 239). *Flexibility with integrity*, "characterized by both strength of will and flexibility in attitude, by a complex intimacy among actors, by a high level of commitment to the project, and by the embracing of a dynamic situation" (p. 241) Conflict is not avoided, the dynamics and uncertainty are acknowledged, and the participants are willing to accept the risk of giving up what once was thought necessary. *Teamwork with independence* as illustrated by the fact that "excellent projects are designed by a few leaders who, working together, are able to move the project along and coordinate the group of contributors.... When an excellent building is finished, its contributors all claim it as their own" (p. 242). *Exceeding the limits* such that the final buildings goes beyond what was imagined. "It exceeds the expectations of its makers, particularly those of the clients.... There is a sense that the architect read their innermost dreams in order to design a building that captures what they themselves could not articulate" (p. 242).

Cuff notes that there are neither excellent firms nor excellent architects, only excellent projects. The design of these projects is a collective, social activity; one that is neither dominated by a single designer nor by a committee.

> Instead, individual talent, leadership, even genius are important to architecture when they exist in a social context that is conductive to such efforts—a context that consists of other demanding, talented individuals who operate as a team.... The context in which a building is developed is not a static entity but vital, dynamic, and actually formative. The cast of characters, the limits and goals they impose, the power they project, the expectations they hold, the organizations that structure their roles, the conflicts they endure, the intimacy they share, and the respect they are given—all compose a fluctuating constellation utilizing all available human material. It is in this sense that design is a social art, and that the practice of architecture is a culture. (p. 245)

The most overarching observation of her study is that "the production of places is a social process. That is, a very basic task of architectural work is to collect all participants, both in the office and out, to develop a manner of working with them and to interact with them in order to create a design solution. This task, the social process, is significant to the form-giving task of architecture, for it is from this human constellation that the building's final form emerges. The simple but radical proposition is that design itself is a social process" (p. 248).

Both Alexander and Cuff are architects. Writing some 30 years apart from each other, we see in Alexander's work an emphasis on the structuring of information to guide in the organization of what is to be created. There are seminal insights now accepted as commonplace; there also is a concern for how the computer may be used (which we might now view as naive). But beneath the veneer of formalism and method is an understanding that method cannot substitute for experience, that practice cannot be understood without engaging in practice. Writing for today's audience, Cuff takes as her challenge the understanding of practice. She finds the characterization of the hero architect, such as Howard Roark in *The Fountainhead* who opts for individuality over collaboration, to be mythical. Collaboration does not lead to mediocrity; indeed, it is essential when confronting complexity. Design, moreover, is not what is in an individual's head; rather it is something created by the social action of collaboration. Both authors differentiate between the form and the context, the need and the building that responds to it. Alexander wrote in a period dominated by Technical Rationality. Although he sought means to organize the information and apply computation, his diagrams constituted (what we would call today) a mental model that could be transformed into a logical model. In contrast, Cuff builds on the research of the past decades to move beyond the abstractions of design method and into the study of practice. Just as Alexander could produce no simple method for form-fitting, Cuff can only suggest ways to improve education such that it can conform better to practice. That there are excellent buildings is a credit to architecture and the human spirit; that there are also dull (but well-constructed) buildings is simply an acknowledgment of technology's advance.

The process of architecture is dynamic, but once the building exists it is relatively static. Nonarchitectural design (e.g., industrial, graphic, or interior design), on the other hand, is subject to continuing pressure for change. J.C. Jones, an industrial designer, pioneered the development of a systematic design method in the early 1960s.

The method is primarily a means of resolving a conflict that exists between logical analysis and creative thought. The difficulty is that the imagination does not work well unless it is free to alternate between all aspects of the problem, in any order, and at any time, whereas logical analysis breaks down if there is the least departure from the systematic step-by-step sequence. It follows that any design method must permit both kinds of thought to proceed together if any progress is to be made.... Systematic Design is primarily a means of keeping logic and imagination separate by external rather than internal means. The method is:

(1) To leave the mind free to produce ideas, solutions, hunches, guesswork, at any time without being inhibited by practical limitations and without confusing the processes of analysis.

(2) To provide a system of notation which records *every* item of design information outside the memory, keeps design requirements and solutions completely separate from each other, and provides a systematic means of relating solutions to requirements with the least possible compromise. (Jones 1963, p. 11)

Here Jones restates the basic tension in the design process as one between imagination and analysis, what I earlier referred to as the subjective versus the objective, the understanding of what is needed versus the specification of what is to be built. I personally subscribe to his conceptual framework, as I show in Part III. Jones, however, abandoned the subject of design methods "as a blind alley...; [in his recent work] he opposes the radical separation of reason, intuition, and experience within the design system ... and calls for the re-introduction of personal judgment, imagination and what may be called 'artistic sensibility' into design" (Thackara 1988b, p. 29). Jones (1988) seeks to avoid optimization based on function because the functions are not stable; he speaks of adaptable designs and the *un*learning of what we once thought was the case but which is no longer true.

Creative collaboration is perhaps the main challenge of our time. Before computing it was not possible, in principle, at the scale at which we now operate and organize....

Attentiveness to context, not self-expression, is the skill we have to foster, to encourage, to share. In natural evolution inattentiveness is death. So is inability to adapt to what we see happening. The context, not the boss, has to become the manager of what is done, and how. The bosses' role becomes that of designing the meta-process, designing the situation so that designing collaboratively is possible, so that it flows. "It" being the interaction between what everyone is noticing with what everyone is doing. (pp. 224, 225)

Mitchell (1988) describes us as being in a transition from a mechanistic to a post-mechanical design era. "'The Product' as a solely physical entity is an illusion of the mechanical era which can no longer be sustained in an age preoccupied with information. In place of the concept of design as simply a means of producing objects, develops an understanding of designing as a continuous and non-instrumental thought process, a creative act in which everyone, designers and non-designers alike, may participate equally" (p. 214).

7.4. Engineering and System Design

The examples of design in the previous section were taken from situations in which there is a recognized, explicit artistic dimension. Perhaps, this explains their dynamic character: the emphasis on the subjective, the poorly structured processes. As I will show in this section, however, the findings are also representative of engineering and system design. For example, consider what the MIT Committee in Engineering Design reported in 1961.

> The designing engineer who remains on the frontiers of engineering finds himself making only a small fraction of his decisions on the basis of numerical analysis.... This is not to try to belittle the importance of analysis. Everyone recognizes it as an essential tool of the trained engineer. It does not, however, answer all or even a majority of the questions an engineer must answer in a typical design problem, particularly a new one. It seems unlikely that numerical analysis will ever answer more than a small proportion of these questions. The remainder of the questions must be decided on the basis of ad hoc experiment, experience (the art of applying knowledge gained by former experiments on the same or similar problems), logical reasoning and personal preference. The subconscious reasoning process, based on experience, which we call intuition, can play a large part. (cited in Ferguson 1992, p. 165)

Just as Cuff noted a mismatch between what is taught about architecture and its practice, so too have many others described a similar mismatch with respect to engineering education and practice. For example, here is Schön (1983): "In schools of engineering, which have been transformed into schools of engineering science, the engineering scientist tends to place his superior status in the service of values different from those of the engineering professions" (p. 27). Ferguson (1992) adds that with the government "offering apparently unlimited funds for scientific research projects, working knowledge of the material world disappeared from faculty agendas, and the nonverbal, tacit, and intuitive understanding essential to engineering design atrophied" (p. 171).

Ferguson's description of engineering is similar to Cuff's description of architecture. "Engineering design is always a *contingent* process, subject to unforseen complications and influences as the design develops. The precise outcome of the process cannot be deduced from its initial goal. Design is not, as some textbooks would have us believe, a formal, sequential process that can be summarized in a block diagram" (Cuff 1991, p. 37). Petroski (1982) describes the nature of engineering design as "the process of design, in which diverse parts of the 'given-world' of the scientist and the 'made-world' of the engineer are reformed and assembled into something the likes of which Nature had not dreamed, that divorces engineering from science and marries it to art" (p. 8). Finally, Constant (1980), defines engineering design simply as "the process by which technology as social knowledge is transformed into technology as artifact" (p. 24).

To the layperson, the conduct of engineering design seems to be well structured and organized. Rouse and Boff (1987b) note, however, that "if an outside observer were to characterize designers' behaviors, particularly for complex domains such as aircraft design, it is quite likely that such an observer would conclude that chaos is the most appropriate characterization of design teams at work" (p. 49). The sense of order that permits the design to go from requirements to delivery is achieved by the fiction of separating what is done from how it is managed. I explain (Blum 1992a) that design "is poorly structured and opportunistic. Designers seldom channel their thoughts into a given level of detail.... Although design is a continuous process, management must abstract it as a series of discrete events to be monitored and measured" (p. 6). Thus, what we perceive as order is actually only the model of what has been planned. "As images of future work and promises, these charts inject an element of fantasy in their overprecision and create a focus for negotiation between promises and accomplishments.... The effect is an immensely complex and detailed image of the project as logical and fixed. Bucciarelli [1988] argues that all these models miss the point that actual design engineering is a flexible, negotiable process" (Dubinskas 1988b, p. 25).

Sage (1990b) defines design as having four components: It must produce a specification or architecture for a product, it is a creative process, the activity is conceptual in nature, and it must be responsive to the client needs and requirements. Bucciarelli (1988), in his ethnographic study of design at an engineering firm, speaks of two worlds: the "object-world," in which the participant is engaged with the materials of design, and the "process-world," which is the world of dialogue and negotiation. In Sage's taxonomy, the first component exists exclusively in the object-world, and the remaining components operate largely in the process-world. These two worlds employ different dimensions of time. In the object-world, time is measured and flows continuously.

In the process-world, time is not quantified; it operates in starts and stops. In the object-world, it is the object of design that shapes the space; projects typically are organized around the principle functional subsystems. "The aim is to break up the design task so that each participant works within his or her specialty, within a small group, a sub-sub-culture within the firm, and that group's work can be pursued independently of all others" (p. 102). In the process-world, on the other hand, we have the "marketplace where design is negotiated, where ideas are exchanged and decisions made. We leave the world of the designer and his or her primarily solo manipulation of objects, ideas, images and plans and take the broader view" (p. 104). Where time in the object-world is organized in a plan and presented in formal schedules, time in the process-world has a different nature. No one can tell when the design actually started; beginnings and endings are diffuse, and consensus is not possible (or even useful).

"There is a flow to design: hesitating, appearing to sometimes falter, at other times to accelerate out of control, but still directed forward by participants toward the final fixing of ideas, constraints, and values in the material form of an artifact" (p. 110). Decisions are both "hard" (i.e., formal) and "soft" (e.g., a shared agreement). As the design proceeds, the problems change, and the emphasis shifts. Effort is required to ensure that all team members are working on the same problems. Schedules and CPM charts are updated, but it is the process of updating that matters. "They are rarely referred to once the meeting is over. Their construction, their social construction, is what is significant to the design process" (p. 114).

> Ambiguity and uncertainty are essential to design. Attempts to banish them completely are not only doomed to fail but would choke the flow of the design process, bringing it to a lethargic, dispiriting halt. Ambiguity is essential to allow design participants the freedom to maneuver independently within their object-worlds save for ties to others to ensure some degree of consensus....
>
> Uncertainty too is always present. It is what gives life to the process, what makes it the challenge that it is. If design proceeds without it, something is wrong, the process is not designing but copying. (p. 120)

Thus, design may be viewed as a dialectic between two worlds. The object-world with its time of finite duration, its space with sharp organizational boundaries, and its uniformity of time and space; and the process-world with neither beginnings nor endings, only fuzzy diffuse boundaries, a time colored by context, and a space always in flux. Using Cuff's concept of stereovision, successful design comes when these two worlds complement each other and the time of the object-world is sufficiently expansive to accommodate the time of the process-world.

As I have described it, design is characterized by its responses to its underlying tensions: form and context, the artistic and the analytic, the architect and his client, the activity and its management, the object-world and the process-world. Much of the literature in systems engineering focuses on the management aspects, but—as this presentation shows—even the management of systems engineering must extend outside the domain of management (e.g., Sage 1992). And design is the most challenging, critical, and complex component of systems engineering.

> System design is much more complicated than a typical undergraduate textbook might lead one to conclude. Analysis is *not* designers' predominant activity—it is just one of the many tasks involved in the job of design. Also, many people are usually involved in the design of a complex system, and they interact within organizational structures that significantly constrain their discretion or latitude in designing approaches to satisfy system requirements. Organizational constraints are useful to the extent that they foster development of a consistent and coherent product—such constraints are counterproductive when they hinder innovation and foster mediocre incrementalism. (Rouse and Boff 1987b, p. 5)

Rouse and Boff, in their summary of a meeting on the behavioral perspectives on designers, tools, and organizations (1987a), comment that—even though it is difficult to establish exactly who the designers are—the activities of the designers can be organized as four tasks:

> *Formulation*, which includes the activities of (a) defining and/or decomposing the problem and (b) formulating the criteria for evaluation.

> *Understanding*, which involves (c) seeking information, (d) translating information, and (e) representing information.

> *Solution*, consisting of (f) generating interpretations, (g) encouraging intuition, and (h) analogizing.

> *Implementation*, described as the activities of (i) representing, (j) evaluating, and (k) advocating.

The tasks follow in the order presented, but there is feedback. In a sense, this flow may be seen as a canonical design model that is called into play whenever a problem is identified. Thus, for example, if during the solution task, a problem was encountered during analogizing, then the four-step process would be invoked recursively so that the new problem would be formulated, understood, solved, and implemented.

In a paper titled "A Cognitive Theory of Design," Meister (1987) presents a conceptual model of the design process as he thought it ought to be conducted. Following that section, he comments:

> The design process described previously is a highly deliberate one, and it emphasizes logic, deduction, and the application of engineering knowledge. In actual practice, many (if not most) designers deviate from this process in ways that presumably reduce its effectiveness.... It requires actual immersion in design to see instances of the following:
>
> 1. Some of the analyses the designer performs are somewhat unconscious....
>
> 2. The engineer is experience oriented. He will, all other things being equal, try to repeat design approaches and solutions previously found effective....
>
> 3. The engineer is often intuitive in his thinking and fails to fully think through his design solutions.
>
> 4. The criteria which he uses to analyze candidate solutions usually/often do not include behavioral aspects which may result in selection of an inadequate alternative from a human factors standpoint.
>
> 5. The engineer's urge to come to grips with the hardware/software-specific aspect of his design as quickly as possible often causes him to shortchange the analytic aspects that should precede hardware/software design.
>
> 6. When he lacks necessary information, he often does not know where to find it....
>
> 7. As a decision maker, the engineer is as likely as anyone else to deviate from an optimal (e.g., Bayesian) process of making decisions. (pp. 236-37)

The debate, of course, is whether these mismatches between the models of the design process and the designers' activity are an indication of poor designer practice or a poor understanding of the design process.

Nadler (1986), after reviewing the research in the conduct of engineering design, observes that the process selected does affect results and that there are more effective design process models available for use. He identifies seven prescriptive principles for design. The *uniqueness principle* states that each new project is to be seen as starting "fresh," even though the designer may already have experience with as seemingly identical project. The *purposes principle* focuses the designers attention away from What is the problem? and onto What is the purpose of working on the problem? The *solution-after-next principle* places the problem solution in the context of a perfect product rather than as a modification to an existing product. The *systems principle* sensitizes the designer to the fact that the problem actually is part of a system of problems, and the designer must consider related issues and challenges that might—or might not—affect her. The *limited information principle* avoids the traditional approach of trying to learn all about the problem oneself; call in experts as consultants. The *people design principle* fosters the involvement of all stakeholders in the problem; solutions imposed on people can be erroneous and self-defeating. Finally, the *betterment timeline principle* works on the idea of improving it before it breaks. These principles constitute useful checks for guiding design.

7.5. The Individual Designer

I now turn to how the designer actually confronts the challenge of design. Klein (1987) writes, "It seems to me that much of the strength of an experienced designer comes from his ability to recognize the types of problems encountered, to recognize the typical ways of handling such issues, and to recognize the implications of contextual nuances.... The overriding strength of a skilled designer is in knowing what problems are typical and what reactions they call for, along with what problems are unique and what approaches are most promising" (p. 176). Clearly, this is a form of expertise that is developed from practice and not from formal training. Klein notes that his research suggests that analytic methods, although very important, are insufficient. They constitute a substrate which will be employed only as the designer recognizes the problem. Thus he talks about the analytical approach (which is molecular, serial, and context-free) and recognitional approach (which is holistic, parallel, and contextual).

Most design, he asserts, is on ill-defined problems (i.e., not copying). The search for a solution is a process of trial and error. Goal clarification proceeds in parallel with the search for solutions. During the process, there are failures, lessons, and occasional successes. The failures restrict the design space (i.e., resolve misfits), the learning expands the designer's ability, and the successes are worked into the solution. It is expected that the problem may change as the result of the design activity. "Part of the designer's skill is in understanding what the design is really supposed to accomplish. A mistake novices often make is to fixate on the original statement of design criteria" (p. 178). That is, the naive designer violates Nadler's purposes principle.

In his normative model for a theory of design, Meister (1987) writes of the generation of alternative solutions. "The goal is to provide *all* possible design solutions and then to select from among them" (p. 235). He states that the trade off between some alternatives may be performed during analysis, but the final evaluation must concern issues such as performance capability, reliability, feasibility, and the constraints of time, cost, etc. Ultimately, he concludes, a solution considered in some sense the "best" is identified. Compare that model with Klein's (1987) description of how designers "satisfice." "Designers' efforts go into developing at least one effective option. If they can find a typical way to proceed, they are satisfied. If they modify a typical approach or synthesize a new approach, they do so cautiously. Their creativity goes into making a dominant approach work rather than in thinking up new and imaginative untried/risky options" (pp. 180-81). Thus, in contrast to Nadler's solution-after-next principle that seeks to find a solution that will be the most appropriate five years from now, there is a tendency to reduce risk by staying with the familiar.

Rouse and Boff (1987a) note that "new product design is probably much less frequent than design associated with improving or remedying problems with existing products, or modifying existing products for new uses. For example, it is difficult to imagine starting 'from scratch' when designing the next generation of aircraft, diagnostic equipment, or infantry rifle" (pp. 8-9). There are two reasons we do not start from scratch. First, it constitutes a paradigm shift, which deflates the value of our current knowledge; second, systems are composed of subsystems such that innovation always reuses existing subsystem designs (e.g., a revolutionary next-generation aircraft may employ a standard engine design). Thus, we are self-constrained in our designs, unable to conceptualize exhaustive trade-off analyses, and comfortable with solutions that seem to work well if not optimally.

Much of the knowledge used by the designer is derived from his experience in the domain—his expertise. It is tacit, implicit, and context dependent. An excellent designer in one area may only be competent in another. Ideally, one would like the design environment to provide information to the designer that is outside her expertise or to remind her of what might be overlooked due to information overload. (Note that too many reminders in themselves constitute an overload.) Klein

(1987) identifies four categories of design aid: analogues, imagery, research data, and rapid prototyping. The analogues provide information about existing equipment that illustrate the strengths and weaknesses, suggest how the design may be improved, and identify available methods for construction. "The power of analogical predictions is that they can capture the influence of factors that cannot be guessed, let alone be included, in a formal prediction model. For example, if I wanted to predict the reliability of subsystems on an advanced tactical fighter, I could use the operational data for the F-16 and adjust them.... We use the same comparison logic when we set up a control group for an experiment" (p. 182). Case studies act as analogues by sensitizing the readers to the causal implications of different features.

Imagery constitutes a powerful and often-used tool for working out concepts prior to their formal expression as analytical models. This is particularly true for the design of physical entities that will exist in three-dimensional space. Ferguson (1992) observes, "Visual thinking is necessary in engineering. A major portion of engineering information is recorded and transmitted in a visual language that is in effect the *lingua franca* of engineers in the modern world" (p. 41). He cites the "Feynman diagrams" that Feynman developed as an alternative to the complex array of quantum mechanics equations. "Feynman thought that Einstein, in his old age, failed to develop his 'unified theory' because he 'stopped thinking in concrete physical images and became a manipulator of equations' [Dyson 1979, p. 62]" (Ferguson 1992, p. 45). Just as the Feynman diagrams are not the same as the equations, so too must the engineer differ between the visual representations and what they represent.

Ferguson notes that throughout the 19th century the drawing served as a focus for negotiation. As the drawings were elevated in importance, they were no longer considered discretionary; feedback from the shop floor was lost, and authority was transferred to the drawings themselves. We have seen throughout this chapter the importance of socialization in the solution of wicked problems. A drawing or equation can seldom resolve all uncertainty or capture "spirit of the design." Indeed, the drawing and equation express only what is taken to be certain, thereby obscuring what is arbitrary or ambivalent. A true understanding of problems in-the-world can only occur in-the-world. Ferguson comments:

> I was fortunate to learn early that an engineer's intelligent first response to a problem that a worker brings in from the field is "Let's go see." It is not enough to sit at one's desk and listen to an explanation of a difficulty. Nor should the engineer refer immediately to drawings or specifications to see what the authorities say. The engineer and the worker must go together

to the site of the difficulty if they expect to see the problem in the same light. There and only there can the complexities of the real world, the stuff that drawings and formulas ignore, be appreciated. (1992, p. 56).

Returning to Klein's list, there remain the aids of research findings and rapid prototypes. "We would expect that designers would want basic research information in order to conduct evaluations of proposed options. However, in our study of training device designers, research reports and military standards resolved very few of the design questions, and some of these cases were questionable" (Klein 1987, p. 184). Because the reports are underdetermined, designers tend to ignore data that go against their biases or accept information that supports their preferences; that is, the materials are used for justification. Moreover, if the data do not agree with the designers' experience, the research results are rejected. With respect to rapid prototypes, they are perceived to offer an effective means for getting a sense of what is being proposed, for evaluating how the product is being affected by design changes, and for demonstrating how the system will operate.

Yet rapid prototyping can be both a panacea and a problem. Prototypes have "been found, anecdotally at least, to result in people becoming 'wedded' to their initial ideas" (Rouse and Boff 1987b, p. 56). Furthermore, because the prototype is an abstraction that leaves critical features out, it permits an apparent agreement between designers and users even though both groups come to the negotiation with different mental models. This last problem can be overcome when there is a series of evolving prototypes that serves as a catalyst for a continuing dialogue.

I conclude this discussion with a review of three studies of designers in action. Each was a laboratory study, and none produced a finished product. Ballay (1987) conducted an experiment in the design of a device to pay credit card bills through the telephone. Fifty designers, design students, engineers, and draftsmen were involved, 18 of whom became subjects of a detailed protocol analysis, and one subject was studied for over 20 hours. Ballay characterizes design as an ill-defined construction task and notes the important role of visualization.

If a designer has several ideas in mind, he typically cannot evaluate the relationship among them until they are made visible. A drawn external representation is a very important aid to the designer in making spatial inferences. Experienced design teachers find that students who claim to have designed wonderful things "in their heads" usually discover disastrous flaws in their designs when they try to put them on paper....

We have observed that designers do not know many details about what they are going to sketch until part of the sketch is made; "knowing" is in the observing of the external sketch. (pp. 70, 71)

These comments echo earlier remarks about the importance of writing down thoughts so that they may be analyzed (e.g., Alexander in this chapter and Popper in Chapter 2). I believe that short-term memory limits the recognition of interface flaws that become obvious once seen on paper. Ballay states that the sketch is encoded in a representation that becomes part of the designer's memory and of the task environment.

In his study, the activity is observed to be divided into periods of planning and what he terms routine primary processes. In contrast to the primary processes, which are well rehearsed routines, the planning sessions are an "intense combination of reviewing alternatives, reviewing criteria and constraints, and making decisions regarding which processes to employ next" (p. 74). The blocks of time allocated to the primary processes tend to be long (i.e., 20-30 minutes in a 160 minute session), and only 2% of the total time is devoted to planning. The sketches are described as having three dimensions of completeness: *Inclusion*, which is the amount of information in the sketch (i.e., its granularity), *Coherence*, which is the degree to which different pieces of information agree with each other, and *Precision*, or the dimensional refinement the depiction is intended to represent.

The process is described as one of producing a chain of representations. Few sketches start "from scratch," and tracing paper (or CAD workstations) are used to add detail. The sketches are not considered precursors to the final drawing (i.e., not rapid prototypes of the drawing); rather, they are seen as a way to control the information in the early representations of a design solution.

> Through *ex*clusion, *in*coherence, and *im*precision, the designers provide their sketches with enough ambiguity so they can take advantage of inventive opportunities right up to the end of the design process....
> [In assessing the role of the computer, he adds:] At the beginning, it is a tool for individual problem solving, and sketchy representations are appropriate. Toward the end, it becomes a tool for group management or communication, and complete representations are required. (p. 80)

Guindon (1990) performed an analysis of design; the experiment objective was to uncover the structure of the design process (e.g., was it top down?). Three designers, each representing a different style, were identified for observation. These designers were described as being guided by (a) a software design method, (b) past experience with related systems in different problem domains, and (c) a programming paradigm based on a high-level language. The "Lift Control Problem" (a standard abstracted problem used in computer science experiments: Write a program for an elevator controller) was assigned, and the designers were given up to two hours to produce a high-level design solution. For the purposes of this discussion, there are many problems with the experiment. For example, the problem is not ill defined (i.e., all necessary information is in the specification), there is no feedback from implementation, the period of observation is brief, and the goals of the experiment (and thus its design) do not match the context of the present section. Indeed, the participants "commented that in the field, however, they were freer to interrupt design to seek additional information from colleagues, customers, and reference material. For example, Designer 2 frequently wanted to discuss the requirements with the experimenter, as this represented his normal mode of designer-client interactions" (p. 316).

The results of the experiment replicate the findings if Hayes-Roth and Hayes-Roth (1979) in an earlier study, and they warrant repeating here.

[Hayes-Roth and Hayes-Roth] observed that their subjects mixed decisions at various levels of abstraction. For example, the subjects planned low-level (detailed) sequences of errands in the absence of or in violation of a higher lever plan. In the current study, the designers could elaborate partial solutions at arbitrary levels of abstraction in the solution decomposition prior to higher level decomposition. Behaviorally, the observed design process seems best to be characterized as *opportunistic*, to borrow Hayes-Roth and Hayes-Roth's term. (Guindon 1990, p. 326)

Thus, design does not seem to be guided by some higher plan in a top-down fashion; rather it responds to local problems (of differing granularity) opportunistically. These findings, by the way, have been replicated many times, for example, by Visser (1990) for the machining operations of a factory automation cell and by Davies (1991) in an analysis of the program design activity stratified by expertise.

The final experiment is actually an informal exercise I conducted over several years while teaching various graduate software engineering courses (Blum 1989d). Motivated by the benefit one has from learning from one's mistakes or errors (e.g., see Knuth 1989), I suggested that the students keep a log of their errors and changing perceptions as they worked on a simple problem. The problem I proposed was the preparation of an index for a book whose contents happened to be available in machine-sensible form. I already had written a program to produce an index, and the students certainly understood what an index was; therefore, they would be familiar with the problem domain and I with the hidden pitfalls to be discovered while arriving at a solution. I made the project a two-step process. First the students would sketch out the design, and then I would provide some test data for them to implement and test their designs. For me, the task of creating an index was one of reading through the book to identify the important terms, perhaps translating the terms into a standardized vocabulary, entering the terms and page numbers, and then sorting and listing the index. Using the index program I wrote, it takes about a day to produce an index for a book this size. The bulk of the time is spent in scanning through the book, and most of the effort is devoted to issues related to the index contents (e.g., granularity, vocabulary).

It came as a surprise to me, therefore, that the students had fixed on the book's availability in machine-sensible form. Most came up with designs for constructing a concordance—a list of all words used in the book (perhaps without noise words such as the articles). When I provided the class with the test data (a list of the words and phrases to be in the index along with the page numbers), many of the students felt betrayed; the test data implied a data entry-sorting-printing problem, and they were prepared for a much more difficult text analysis problem. Examination of book indexes did not alter their design; it was only when I demanded a working program (and log) that the feedback from producing an implementation resulted in a better understanding of the problem. I repeated the experiment with other classes, but without asking for an implementation. When I asked the students to assess their confidence in their design, there was no correlation between my assessment of the design and their confidence in it. Later, I reduced the experiment to a short questionnaire, but the students soon became so familiar with word processors that they were able to produce an automatic response that nominally solved all index creation problems: Use the tool in the word processor. I stopped with the experiment, but only after it once again confirmed the entrenched commitment to early ideas, the inability to confront problems without any feedback from errors, and the shallowness of understanding even in very common domains. Design is more than the derivation of technical details by using established knowledge and formulae—although that is an essential part of it. It is also the learning by doing, the responding to errors, and the expanding by resolving dilemmas. And, because the learning, responding, and expanding do not cease once a product is delivered, design must be recognized as a continuing activity that is never completed.

7.6. The Challenge

Alexander (1964/1971) closed his introduction with this observation.

> We must face the fact that we are on the brink of times when man may be able to magnify his intellectual and inventive capability, just as in the nineteenth century he used machines to magnify his physical capacity. Again, as then, our innocence is lost. And again, of course, the innocence, once lost, cannot be regained. The loss demands attention, not denial. (p. 11)

The present book seeks to accomplish the goal of magnifying humanity's intellectual and inventive capability in the context of our newly lost innocence regarding the nature of science and the role of culture. The next chapter explores approaches to design that seek to accomplish this goal, and the final chapters of Part III present my vision of how software can affect that goal's achievement.

8

PARTICIPATORY DESIGN

8.1. Evolving Models of Design

The theme of the book now becomes clearer. Design is the conscious modification of the human environment. As with all selfconscious change, there will be benefits—both projected and fortuitous—and deficiencies—both expected and unanticipated. In the modern world, change is unavoidable; thus, if we are to enter into a new era of design, we should seek methods and tools that maximize the benefits as they minimize the deficiencies. Of course, in the real world of systems there will be neither maxima nor minima. Here we can only measure qualitatively, not quantitatively. Consequently, we must rely on collective judgments and accept that any reference points will become obscured by the dynamics of change. Thus, few of our problems will be amenable to a static, rational solution; most will be soft, open, wicked, and, of course, context and domain specific.

This final chapter of Part II explores design in-the-world with particular emphasis on how it affects, and is affected by, the stakeholders. I use the title "Participatory Design" to distinguish this orientation from the historical approach to product development—what I have called "technological design." In technological design, we assume that an object is to be created and, moreover, that the essential description of that object exists in a specification. The design and fabrication activities, therefore, are directed to realizing the specification. How well the specified object fits into the real world is secondary to the design process; the primary criterion for success is the fidelity of the finished product with respect to its specification. We have seen from the previous chapter, however, that this abstract model of technological design seldom exists in practice. Even in architecture, where a building must conform to its drawings, we find excellence associated with flexibility and accommodation. Thus, in reality, technological and participatory design are complementary projections of a single process.

Although I will emphasize computer-based information systems in this chapter, I open the discussion with an examination of a typical hardware-oriented system. Law and Callon (1988) conducted an analysis of a British military aircraft project from its conceptualization in the late 1950s to its cancellation in 1965. From the perspective of the engineers, this was a technological problem involving technological design. Yet, even here, it was not possible to isolate technological decisions.

> It turns out that, when we look at what technologists actually *do*, we find that they pay scant regard to distinctions between technology on the one hand and society, economy, politics, and the rest on the other.... Thus, when they work, they are typically involved in designing and building projects that have *both* technical *and* social content and implications.... Engineers are not just people who sit in drawing offices and design machines; they are also, willy nilly, social activists who design societies or social institutions to fit those machines. Technical manuals or designs for nuclear power stations imply conclusions about the proper structure of society, the nature of social roles, and how these roles should be distributed. (p. 284)

> The sociotechnical process that interest us [the authors] are interactive and emergent; their course and fate are not easily predicted. Yet they are crucially important, for they shape and reshape the modern world. Explanations of social and technical change must avoid three traps.... Social reductionism, the doctrine that relatively stable social categories can explain technical change, and technological reductionism, the converse view, that technological change automatically shapes society, are both one-sided, incomplete, and misleading.... There is a third trap to avoid. This is the notion that the technical and the social evolve as a result of separate processes and only subsequently interact. By contrast, our aim has been to suggest that they are *jointly* created in a single process. (pp. 295-96)

Law and Callon are writing about a technological project in which the social components of change may be described as unselfconscious; that is, the project has no explicit social agenda. Friedman and Kahn (1994) find a similar linking of the technical to the social in computing applications. They state, "We put forth the position that computer technologies are a medium for intensely social activity; and that system design—though technical as an enterprise—involves social activity, and shapes the social infrastructure of the larger society.... Technologies cannot be divorced from a social framework" (p. 65).

The projects of principal concern in this chapter are socially selfconscious; their objective is to alter both the technical and the social.

Examples are decision support systems, computer support for the workplace, and health care applications. In each case there is a deliberate intent to modify the performance of some existing set of tasks and thereby improve functionality, productivity, social well-being, etc. Sonnenwald (1992) identifies three approaches to the design of this class of project. The first is the *rational* approach, in which the problems are subject to closed analysis and solution. We see this in the character-ization of the design task as a "generate-test-refine-remember process" (Silverman and Mezher 1992); if this is the true nature of design, they argue, then knowledge-based tools that generate, test, and remember may be used to assist the process. Sonnenwald's second approach is that of *cognitive engineering*, which "emphasizes individual users' subjective experience with an information system and seeks to develop design methods that will enhance that experience by creating systems more pertinent to users in the context of their domain" (p. 311). Finally, she identifies the *social* approach that "strives to discover relationships between systems and social systems and the causes and effects of these relationships" (p. 311).

Nurminen (1986, 1988) offers an alternative nomenclature for these three approaches. For him there are the *perspectives* of *system* (in which quality is understood in technical terms only), *socio-technical* (where quality is based on both the technical quality and user acceptance), and *humanistic* (which extends beyond the interface to treat all system tasks as social actions performed by human beings). I group these approaches (or perspectives) as three categories of design: *technological* (rational, system), with a dependence on generalized, abstracted knowledge suitable for all applications in the given domain, *interface* (cognitive engineering, socio-technical), with an increased concern for the human aspects of product use: and *participatory* (social, humanistic), with a focus on how the product is perceived in-the-world. These three design approaches are nested such that technological design is an essential component of interface design and interface design is a prerequisite to participatory design.

With this nested model, interest in participatory design can be interpreted as a measure of the success of the other two design types. For example, Friedman (1989) proposes a three-phase model of information systems development based on three levels of technology. At the lowest level is the computer systems core (i.e., the hardware and system software); the second level is the mediating process (e.g., operations, programming, analysis), and the highest level is the use of computer applications in the organization. In his model, costs in a lower level inhibit advances in the upper level(s) (e.g., the high cost of equipment in the 1960s limited advances in interactive system development, which in turn constrained experience with the use of interactive applications). Today we would all agree that equipment cost no longer is a critical factor; therefore, the removal of mediation level barriers permit us to create new applications and to explore new perceptions of computing.

The end result can be understood by taking Kuhn's model of normal science as puzzle solving and adapting it to the dynamics of technological development: Once a technology advances to the point that its initial problems have been solved, its practitioners will either identify new problems within the given paradigm or—if no rewarding new problems can be found—shift to a new paradigm. And this is where we are today: extending the boundaries of normal computer science as we concurrently explore new computer science paradigms. Kuutti (in press) describes our present situation this way, "The differentiation of research approaches clearly has gained new momentum and considerable visibility, with the emergence of a new wave of approaches" (p. 1). However, that new wave is unfocused, and what I label participatory design actually is composed of a spectrum of design approaches that range from a concern for how a product may be made to perform more effectively in a work situation to a desire to use the technology to change (or preserve) the social structure. In what follows I attempt to sort out these overlapping views by starting at the interface, moving outward to the social and cultural agendas, and closing with a model of technology adaptation.

8.2. Human Factors and the Interface

The earliest interest in the psychology of software development was motivated by the need for predictors of programming skill, cognitive models of programming, and scientific models of human-computer interaction. In his *Software Psychology* (1980), Shneiderman provided a foundation for the empirical study of software tasks and addressed human performance issues. The subtitle of his book was *Human Factors in Computer and Information Systems*, and the IEEE tutorial by Curtis (1985) on this subject bore a similar title: *Human Factors in Software Development*. In both cases the authors were working to develop a specialization of the engineering discipline of human factors (or ergonomics).

In their recent review of human factors in human-computer system design, Day and Boyce (1993) begin with the following definition.

> Human factors is: (a) the study of human capabilities and limitations that are relevant to the design of tools, machines, systems, tasks, jobs, and environments, (b) the application of that knowledge to design, and (c) the use of human factors methodologies during design—with the goal of fostering safe, effective, and satisfying human use. (p. 336)

In an engineering context, the human is seen as a component of the system, and the system design must account for the human operators' strengths and weaknesses. Thus, in the Grandjean (1985) text there are chapters on work (heavy, muscular, and skilled), mental activity, fatigue, boredom, and the environment (lighting, noise, and climate). In the text by Wickens (1984) there are chapters on decision making, perception, selection of action, continuous manual control, etc.

Each of these books reports on studies that define an envelope within which the human operators can perform comfortably and outside of which there will be problems. The point is made that an understanding of these limits is an essential key to an effective design. Moreover, such considerations must be evaluated throughout the design process; they cannot be added as a veneer by bringing in human factors specialists once the design is complete. If people are to be actively engaged with the system, then their role must be weighed at every stage of the design process.

This ergonomic model provided the framework for the early studies of human-computer interaction (HCI). There was a hope that an empirical foundation, similar to that used in human factors, could be constructed for computer interaction. For example, in human factors there are two types of activities. "The first is scientific research conducted to obtain information about human capabilities, limitations, and motivations that are relevant to the design of systems.... The second type of activity is practice, i.e., participation in system design, utilizing human factors knowledge and methodologies.... Design involves use of the data available in the human factors scientific and applied literature; however, it is rare that the data are sufficient to provide *all* of the information needed for a specific design problem" (Day and Boyce 1993, p. 340). Thus, for HCI there would be scientific studies to build a knowledge base that could be applied to design problems. As with all engineering applications, not all the knowledge would be available in advance, and some judgment or experimentation would be required during design.

But HCI presented unique problems. For instance, a standard human factors method is task analysis that asks, for the particular task, what must the human operator do, what is the physical setting, what are the possible sequences of correct actions, how is the available information used?

> One of the major difficulties with applying task analysis methodologies to the study of modern computer applications is that many of the tasks users perform are cognitive in nature and have no observable components. In order to apply task analysis to human-computer interaction, it is important to know what the user is thinking as well as what the user is doing. Another

problem with the application of traditional task analysis methods to human-computer interaction is that most usage scenarios are not single-path, linear progressions through observable subtasks. In computer systems, users are often faced with many choices of where to go next from any place in the user interface. (p. 372)

Consequently, it has proven to be to be very difficult to transport the traditional human factors approach to HCI.   Carroll (1991b) comments, "The most sustained, focused, and sophisticated attempts to develop explicit extensions of academic psychology for HCI have had no impact on design practice (Card, Moran, and Newell 1983; Polson and Kieras 1985).   On the other hand, some of the most seminal and momentous user interface design work of the past 25 years made no explicit use of psychology at all (Engelbart and English 1968; Sutherland 1963)" (Carroll 1991b, p. 1). Regarding the attempts to bring critical phenomena into the laboratory for empirical analysis, Carroll continues:

Unfortunately, little of this work produced much insight into the programming process. It was unable to resolve the large issues of the day surrounding the precise meaning and utility of structured programming techniques in producing less errorful and more maintainable code (e.g., Sheppard, Curtis, Milman, and Love 1979). Its failure can be understood in terms of the specificity requirement: The scientific method impels dichotomous contrasts, and this works well only if the required controls are possible and appropriate.   In HCI these requirements are generally not met.   The chaotic and uncontrolled nature of complex activity like programming forced the use of extreme contrasts (structured versus random programs, organized versus random menus) in order to attain statistically significant results. Not surprisingly, such efforts merely confirmed common sense (when they succeeded).   In other cases, complex alternatives were contrasted, amounting to a research design of A versus B with both A and B unknown. (p. 4)

If the empirical studies have not produced formal models of computer interaction that are useful in design, they did, nevertheless, lead to a better understanding of interaction that could be catalogued as rules, standards, and guidelines. For example, Shneiderman (1987) has created a list of Eight Golden Rules of Dialogue Design:

Strive for consistency....
Enable frequent users to use shortcuts....
Offer informative feedback....

Design dialogs to yield closure....
Offer simple error handling....
Permit easy reversal of actions....
Support internal locus of control....
Reduce short-term memory load. (pp. 61-62)

Here we have a set of implicit requirements for all interactive systems. I call these implicit requirements in that they are assumed to be present without explicitly calling them out. They constitute a set of standards for good practice that parallels the implicit requirements of good coding practice (e.g., use informative mnemonics, indent code using white space to separate blocks). The rules are consistent with the results of empirical studies (e.g., the last rule is motivated by models of human memory), but their orientation is that of practice. The rules are not necessarily obvious; they synthesize the results of many studies. They are not natural; they must be learned by naive designers. Once assimilated, the rules become the common sense of expertise: a style that is natural and routine, but not a pattern of behavior that can be subjected to scientific scrutiny.

There also are some guidelines for tailoring product format to the task. In a comparative study of three database query notations (spatial, tabular, and verbal), Boehm-Davis et al. (1989) reported two basic findings. "First, the results support the hypothesis that the nature of the search task to be performed exerts a significant influence on the best form of information to display.... Second, the data indicate that beyond the nature of the search task, performance is affected by stable individual differences in ability to process different forms of information.... Taken as a whole, these data suggest that the nature of the searches likely to be performed on a data base should be considered when the interface is chosen" (pp. 590, 591). That is, the designer should match the user interface to the users' methods for performing the task.

Vessey (1991) has introduced the notion of *cognitive fit* as a theoretical framework for building a taxonomy of task-product matches. She asserts "that complexity in the task environment will be effectively reduced when the problem-solving aids (tools, techniques, and/or problem representations) support the task strategies (methods and processes) required to perform the task.... Problem solving with cognitive fit results in increased problem-solving efficiency and effectiveness" (p. 220). She validates her theory by analyzing the results of studies that examine the performance of graphical and tabular representations in decision making and in empirical studies of performance in spatial and symbolic tasks (Vessey and Galletta 1991). Clearly, the concept of cognitive fit is appealing; nevertheless, even if a taxonomy of tasks existed, it could only serve as a guideline similar to

Shneiderman's Eight Golden Rules. Palvia and Gordon (1992), in their analysis of three modes of decision analysis (table, formula, and tree), observe, "This research points to the continuing need to consider user characteristics in the choice of particular mode" (p. 109).   Thus, individual differences and preferences affect performance as well as format.

Coll, Coll, and Thakur (1994) analyzed the graphs versus table issue using a four-factor experiment that addressed task type, education specialty, display presentation type, and task complexity. Because they consider more data, their findings are more specific: "If, in a proposed MIS, tasks involve working with relationships/trends, then providing a graphing function is of prime importance, especially if the tasks to be performed are complex" (p. 85).   By way of contrast, in Vessey's approach one would analyze the task and, if it were deemed to be spatial, suggest a spatial display such as a graph.

"The goal is to make the interface an extension of the user so its use requires (like a hand or an eye) no conscious attention. The user is empowered to focus his/her entire concentration on the problem at hand" (Coll, Coll, and Thakur 1994, p. 77). That is, we wish to have the computer interface available (ready-to-hand) so that it is invisible (i.e., there are no breakdowns that make us aware of either the interface or the orientation of the material presented by that interface). Perhaps, one way to avoid breakdowns is to employ new technology.   For example, the availability of inexpensive graphic devices has generated considerable interest in visual programming.   Writing from the perspective of end-user computing, Nardi (1993) comments:

> One of the strongest claims to be made about visual programming languages is that they are eminently more "natural" than textual languages—they break through the language barriers (Shu, 1988) and avoid the need to learn syntax, instead revealing semantics through easily understood pictorial means (Myers, 1989). These aspects would certainly represent major advantages for end users if they were true, but there is little support for these claims, which appear to be mostly optimistic appeals to common sense. (pp. 62-63)

Clearly, the ability to perform *direct manipulation* (Shneiderman 1983) has had a profound impact on the user interface, and we have come to understand how it gives rise to the feeling of directness (Hutchins, Hollan, and Norman 1985). And, although it is true that our advances in technology will bring about a host of new interface mechanism (Curtis and Hefley 1994), it is not obvious what the role of visualization will be. Nardi observes, "The essence of visualness lies in exploiting *perceptual* rather than *linguistic* abilities.... Nor are visual depictions always superior to text; it depends on the problem (see Green, Petre, and Bellamy 1991). Sometimes a few words are worth a thousand pictures" (p. 97).

This suggests that the potential of newer, more powerful technologies may not provide the solutions we seek; indeed, waiting for their maturity may only delay the search for effective solutions. Perhaps a more prudent course would be to build on the users' experience with accepted styles. For example, most users of interfaces with windows have come to accept the "look and feel" that has evolved from that first developed at Xerox PARC. Thus, if we adopt the WIMP (i.e., Windows, Icons, Mouse, and Pointers) conventions, we will narrow the cognitive distance between the exposed user and our new system. But Nelson (1990) asserts that this approach fosters bad design. He identifies three mistakes commonly associated with this convention. *Featuritis and clutter* characterized by a screen littered with cryptic junk that leads to having too many separate, unrelated things to know and understand; *Metamorphics* in which the metaphor becomes a dead weight rather than a well-thought-out unifying idea (e.g., of what desktop is the desktop metaphor metaphorically accurate?); and *Add Ketchup* to hide the product behind crypto-social entities such as animated "assistants."

As a complement to Shneiderman's rules for good design, Nelson identifies some observations about bad design—temptations to be avoided.

> Historical accident has kept programmers in control of a field in which most of them have no aptitude: the artistic integration of the mechanisms they work with. It is nice that engineers and programmers and software executives have found a new form of creativity in which to find a sense of personal fulfillment. It is just unfortunate that they have to inflict the results on users. (p. 243)

He notes, "No one seems to be able to recognize *good* design—except users, and that only sometimes" (p. 236), which suggests that value of a system will be found in its use and not in some abstract properties of its technology. Knowing what not to do is essential, but the avoidance of pitfalls is no guarantee of success.

8.3. User-Centered Design

The shift to a more user-centered approach to design occurred in the mid 1980s, and the change is apparent in the contrasting contents of two influential collections published at the time. The first, edited by Baecker and Buxton (1987), focused on the interface: "one of the most poorly understood aspects of any system.... [Its development requires] the skills of the graphic designer and industrial designer, an understanding of organizational dynamics and processes, an understanding of human cognitive, perceptual, and motor skills, a knowledge of display technologies, input devices, interaction techniques, and design methodologies, and an aptitude for elegance in system design" (p. 1). The book collected and annotated a broad body of literature, mostly within the context of a human factors orientation. *User Centered System Design*, edited by Norman and Draper (1986), offered a very different perspective.

> People are so adaptable that they are capable of shouldering the entire burden of accommodation to an artifact, but skillful designers make large parts of this burden vanish by adapting the artifact [e.g., interface] to its users. To understand successful design requires an understanding of the technology, the person, and their mutual interaction.... (p. 1)

Here we see a move from the *machine orientation* with the user as an operator at an interface to the *user orientation* that makes the interface a window through which the user performs the task.

Norman (1993) writes of human-centered and machine-centered views. In the machine-centered view, the designers optimize on the machine's special properties: it is precise, orderly, undistractible, unemotional, and logical. By contrast, then, the user is seen as vague, disorganized, distractible, emotional, and illogical. Clearly, with this dichotomy, the machine can be assigned well-defined tasks, and it will be sure to perform those tasks better than people. By using rigid error-avoidance mechanisms, the machine may become "idiot proof," a 1970's design objective that lead Bannon (1986) to comment, "If we start out with a theory of users that assumes mass idiocy, the likely result is an artifact that is suitable for idiots" (p. 26). The alternative, of course, is a human-centered view that takes advantage of the capabilities of people: They are creative, compliant, attentive to change, resourceful, and their decisions are flexible because they are based on qualitative as well as quantitative assessment, modified by the special circumstances and context. With this set of criteria, we find machines to be dumb, rigid, insensitive to change, unimaginative, and their decisions are consistent because they are based upon quantitative evaluation of numerically specified, context-free variables (after Norman 1993, p. 224).

In *User Centered System Design*, Norman introduced the term *cognitive engineering*: "neither Cognitive Psychology, nor Cognitive Science, nor Human Factors. It is a type of applied Cognitive Science, trying to apply what is known from science to the design and construction of machines" (1986, p. 31). In this paper, Norman begins the development of a theory of action that describes how people actually do things, in particular, how they interact with computers. The theory begins by identifying two entities: the physical system and the user's goals. There is a *gulf of execution* going from the goals to the physical system that is bridged first by establishing the goal, next by forming the intention, and then "by creating plans, action sequences, and interpretations that move the normal description of the goals and intentions closer to the description required by the physical system" (p. 39). A *gulf of evaluation* goes from the physical system to the user. Here the path is from the "output displays of the interface, moving to the perceptual processing of those displays, to its interpretation, and finally, to the evaluation—the comparison of the interpretation of system state with the original goals and intention" (p. 41). All user interaction is composed of iterations of these paired bridgings of the gulfs, and problems may arise when the levels of outcome and intention do not match or when delays in completing the cycle cause some aspects of the intention to be forgotten.

In this model of interaction there are two sides to the interface: the system side and the human side. The designer may change the system side; training can change the user side. The goal is to have the two sides of the interface "close" to each other (thereby reducing the size of the gulfs of execution and evaluation), and here the *conceptual model* plays a key role.

> Think of a conceptual model of the system as providing a scaffolding upon which to build the bridges across the gulfs. The scaffoldings provided by these conceptual models are probably only important during learning and trouble-shooting. But for these situations they are essential.... The problem is to design the system so that, first, it follows a consistent, coherent conceptualization—a design model—and, second, so that the user can develop a mental model of that system—a user model— consistent with the design. (p. 46)

The conceptual model is, of course, a form of mental model. Elsewhere, Norman (1983) states, "In the consideration of mental models we need really consider four different things: the *target system*, the *conceptual model* of that system, the user's *mental model* of the target system, and the *scientist's conceptualization* of that mental model. A system that a person is learning or using is, by definition, the *target system*. A *conceptual model* is invented to provide an appropriate representation of the target system, appropriate in the sense of being accurate, consistent, and complete. Conceptual models are invented by teachers, designers, scientists, and engineers" (p. 7). In the cognitive engineering paper, Norman decomposes the conceptual model into a *design model*, a *user's model*, and a *system image*. Although the vocabulary may have evolved, the basic idea remains the same. The design process is viewed as the designers' refinement of the design model until the system image conforms to the user's model.

Unfortunately, this is easier said than done. Mental models have serious flaws. Norman (1983) describes them as incomplete, unstable, too parsimonious, extra-logical, and not clearly bounded. Moreover, people's abilities to "run" their models are severely limited (p. 8). "A major purpose of a mental model is to enable a user to predict the operation of a target system" (p. 13), and there is great interest in the use of such models for understanding the development tasks (Soloway and Erlich 1984) as well as the design of the human-computer interface and the preparation of training materials (Williges 1987; Kobsa and Wahlster 1989; Ackermann and Tauber 1990; Allen 1990; Tauber and Ackermann 1991). Nevertheless, the construction of user models remains difficult and context sensitive. The user's model changes with exposure to the system, and designers may not be able to anticipate user problems. For example, Camerer, Lowenestein, and Webber (1989) speak of the "curse of knowledge" in economic settings whereby an analyst makes suboptimal decisions by assuming that his competitors share his knowledge. What we know determines what we see (and cannot see).

Even if we acknowledge that we cannot explicitly describe the three conceptual models, we must recognize that they exist. The goal of interface design is to bring these models together so that they do not create breakdowns. For instance, direct manipulation may be interpreted as a mechanism that permits the system image to conform to the user's model of text editing.

> When I use a direct manipulation system—whether for text editing, drawing pictures, or creating and playing games—I do think of myself not as using a computer but as doing the particular task. The computer is, in effect, invisible. The point cannot be overstressed: make the computer invisible. The principle can be applied with any form of interaction, direct or indirect. (Norman 1988, p. 185)

Norman states that a system should be enjoyable to use and should be "deemed useful because it offers powerful tools that the user is able to apply constructively and creatively, with understanding" (1986, p. 49). How can this be accomplished? In *The Psychology Of Everyday Things* (POET), Norman (1988) offers the following prescription:

Design should:

- Make it easy to determine what actions are possible at any moment (make use of constraints).
- Make things visible, including the conceptual model of the system, the alternative actions, and the results of actions.
- Make it easy to evaluate the current state of the system.
- Follow natural mappings between intentions and the required actions; between actions and the resulting effect; and between the information that is visible and the interpretation of the system state.

In other words, make sure that (1) the user can figure out what to do, and (2) the user can tell what is going on....

How does the designer go about the task? As I've argued in POET, the principles are straightforward.

1. Use both knowledge in the world and knowledge in the head.
2. Simplify the structure of the tasks.
3. Make things visible: bridge the gulfs of Execution and Evaluation.
4. Get the mappings right.
5. Exploit the power of constraints, both natural and artificial.
6. Design for error.
7. When all else fails, standardize. (pp. 188-89)

But the POET principles are just an extension of Shneiderman's Golden Rules. Can we be more precise? The evaluation of the users' reaction to the system is called *usability*. Evaluation typically is carried out throughout the development process, and "the data collected from usability tests can be used to improve system design, to ensure that predetermined usability goals are met, and to aid in the development of documentation and training materials for the new system" (Day and Boyce 1993, p. 388). With the technological design model, usability criteria have been included as a part of the requirements specification (e.g., criteria for time to learn, speed of performance, error rates by users, subjective satisfaction).

It now is recognized that interface refinement demands an iterative approach, and there has been some experimentation with specifying the *process* for interface development rather than the characteristics of the *product* to be delivered (Hix, Hartson, Siochi, and Ruppert 1994). Even so, the quantification of usability criteria remains difficult. Nielsen and Levy (1994) have conducted a metaanalysis of usability analyses with respect to the relative importance of user performance and user preference.

There is a strong positive association between users' average task performance and their average subjective satisfaction, and one has a reasonably large chance of success if one chooses between interfaces based solely on users' opinions. Even so, there are still many cases in which users prefer systems that are measurably worse for them, so one should exercise caution. (p. 75)

Thus, we find either that users are not the most effective evaluators of the systems they use or that the quantifiable criteria are poor predictors of usability. If evaluation of the system is difficult, then so to is the design. First, there are technological complexities. Despite the growing number of tools for interface development (e.g., Sullivan and Tyler 1991, Myers 1992a), Brooks (1993) points out that new application domains require new classes of interfaces, and Grudin (1989a) comments that conformance to consistency can be counterproductive. "When user interface consistency becomes our primary concern, our attention is directed away from its proper focus: users and their work" (p. 1164). Therefore, a knowledge of the technology is necessary but not sufficient; to assess usability, one must understand how the system is to be used.

Adler and Winograd (1992b) write of a *usability challenge*: "how best to take advantage of the users' skills in creating the most effective and productive working environment" (p. 3). Here we move from the machine-oriented view of "idiot-proof" systems designed to deskill their users (see Braverman 1974) to a human-oriented view. "The key criterion of a system's usability is the extent to which it supports the potential for people who work with it to understand it, to learn, and to make changes. Design for usability must include design for coping with novelty, design for improvisation, and design for adaption. Usability thus construed assumes a communication dimension" (Adler and Winograd 1992b, p. 7). Thus, design is seen as a dialogue among many parties where "the formal languages of system analysis are foreign and opaque to the users. In their place, designers must develop a variety of other techniques, such as mockups, profession-oriented languages, partial prototypes, and scenarios that provide an extended 'language' for communicating with people who are familiar with the work context and who can best anticipate how the new system might change it" (p. 9). As a result, there is a shift from the design of a product to the "design of the 'learning organization'" (p. 13).

Zuboff (1988) has studied the introduction of automation into the workplace and finds that it provides new capabilities. It *informates* by making hidden information visible thereby empowering workers to utilized their natural capabilities more fully. Salzman (1992) contrasts the choice as follows. "The traditional approach centralizes analysis, decision making, and process adjustment; it automates wherever possible. The alternative approach pushes decision-making and process adjustment responsibilities down to the worker" (p. 91). He notes that there are several factors that favor the widespread acceptance of the second model: competitive pressures, the fact that the direct labor amenable to automation constitutes only 10% of the total product costs, and that integration—with its attendant complexity—requires human attention. Thus, we find that as we extend beyond the interface we move out into the workplace and, therefore, that our decisions at the interface will affect the structure of work. I continue this theme in the next section, but, for now, I limit the discussion to the design of systems as they are used.

In Norman's model of the gulf of execution, he speaks of creating plans, action sequences, and interpretations to bridge between the user's intentions and the description required by the physical system. In her analysis of human-machine communication, Suchman (1987) adds the observation that the selection of these plans will be determined by the situation in which they are to be used.

> The rules and procedures that come into play when we deal with the "unready-to-hand" are not self-contained or foundational, but contingent on and derived from the situated action that the rules and procedures represent.... Situated action, in other words, is not made explicit by rules and procedures. Rather, when situated action becomes in some way problematic, rules and procedures are explicated for purposes of deliberation and the action. (p. 54)

Consistent with much that already has been reported, she comments, "There are no logical formulae for recognizing the intent of some behavior independent of context" (p. 64). She also observes that "there is a profound and persisting asymmetry in interaction between people and machines, due to a disparity in their relative access to the moment-by-moment contingencies that constitute the conditions of situated interaction. Because of the asymmetry of users and machine, interface design is less a project of simulating human communication than of engineering alternatives to interaction's situated properties" (p. 185). That is, one may extend the range of useful machine behavior by understanding the situations of its use and then devising appropriate plans for the anticipated interactions. Suchman illustrates the approach with the design and testing of instructions and messages in a Xerox copying machine. The session involves two users and the data are videotaped and then presented in the form of a four-column tabular display as follows:

The User		The Machine	
Not available to the machine	Available to the machine	Available to the user	Design rationale

In a session with the goal of making two-sided copies, the sequence starts with "Display 1" in the third column and "Selecting the procedure" in the fourth column. The table continues with the dialogue of the two machine users in the first column, for example:

A: (reading) "To access the BDA [Bound Document Aid] pull the latch labelled Bound Document Aid" (Both A and B turn to the machine)
(Points) Right there.
B: (Hands on latch)
A: (reading) "And lift up to the left."
(Looks to B, who struggles with the latch)
"Lift up and to the left."

The dialogue continues until it is lifted and "Raises Document Handler" appears in the second column. This action constitutes an input to the machine, which causes a change to the display available to the user. The new display is listed in column three next to its design rational in column four, and the analysis continues. In this way, the human-machine communication is presented in the central two columns, the situated use (which is not available to the machine) is in the first column, and—parallel to the machine action—the design rationale for the planned action (which is not available to the user) is in the last column. "The design plan defines what constitutes intelligible action by the user insofar as the machine is concerned, and determines what stands as an appropriate machine response" (p. 119). The analysis of sessions such as this establish how well the design plans conform to the users' situated understanding (i.e., their conceptual models).

Of course, this type of anthropological analysis must fit into a much broader context to be of value. Rheinfrank, Hartman, and Wasserman (1992) discuss the concept of "design for usability" they developed for the next generation of Xerox copiers. They contrast *product semantics*, which concentrates on the object's forms and how they are interpreted, and *experimental semantics*, which help "make clear how people and objects participate in the creation of experiences" (p. 17). They speak of the decomposition of an experience as being an "unfolding of meaning," and they produce a "design language" that provides "(1) the means by which designers build meaning into objects, (2) the means by which objects express themselves and their meanings to people, and (3) the means by which people learn to understand and use objects, and engage in experiences associated with objects" (pp. 18-19).

Thus, the product is not viewed as an object with an independent existence; rather it is seen as something situated in the practice of the organization.

> Most of the Xerox design staff [prior to 1980] saw the design of reprographics products as "furniture making" or "cabinet making," where the goal was to conceal functionality wherever possible. Functional areas were revealed only when absolutely necessary. (p. 24)

> One thing designers can do to help people learn is to reveal functionality—through "glass-box" design—rather than to conceal it—through "black-box" design.... A well-designed glass box selectively reveals to people just enough information about "how to use the artifact" and "how the artifact works" for people to accomplish their goals or to do tasks. This selective revelation can be done by allowing the "meaning" of the full experience of using the artifact to unfold gradually according to need, over time, as the artifact is used. (p. 20)

Clearly, such unfolding requires observations of use; it cannot be established by asking the user to speculate about the product's future potential use.

Brown and Duguid (1992), who also are engaged in the development of copiers, outline some principles for design of the workplace (i.e., the setting in which the situations of use will exist). They identify 13 central topics, which they organize into three groups:

> *Design and learning in the workplace.* Learning is seen as a constructive rather than transfer process. "Learning thus viewed draws attention away from the abstract knowledge and cranial processes and focuses it on the praxis and communities in which knowledge takes on significance" (p. 168). Thus, rather than trying to "idiot proof" a system by error avoidance, the focus is on *error repair*. That is, if the designers understand the context of an error, they can prepare a plan with appropriate responses. This reflects what Brown and Newman (1985) describe as "a new global philosophy for interface design: design for the management of trouble" (p. 359).

> *Design and innovation.* Systems are broadly constructed and not seen as narrow responses to specified requirements. They contrast

the *discovering organization*, which "assumes that there is a correct response to any condition it discovers,... [with the] *enacting organization* [that] is proactive and highly interpretive" (p. 175). "In sum, enacting organizations do not simply respond to a changing environment: they involve themselves in generating it" (p. 176).

Design and tools. Three key attributes of tools are identified. First, they are cultural artifacts. Second, tools provide "affordances" (in the sense of Gibson 1979). As Norman (1993) puts it, the affordances of an object refer to its possible functions. "Different technologies afford different operations. That is, they make some things easy to do, others difficult or impossible" (p. 106). Finally, they state, "Tools need to be capable of becoming ready-to-hand.... For members of a community, their tool can disappear as a separate object of observation and simply become an integral part of their practice" (p. 166).

The copier example uses a computer and displays, but the displays are far less complex than those studied by HCI researchers. Nevertheless, the copier example illustrates the trend of moving from a concern for the interface as an independent entity to the consideration of the interface in use. Here is how Carroll (1989a) describes this change in orientation: "It still is the case that HCI research has its principal effect on *discussions* of usability and user-interface design and only a small, derived effect on actual *practice* in the design and development of computer systems and applications" (p. 48). He favors an ecological analysis.

Ecologically responsive empirical analysis of HCI domains takes place *in vivo*: in software shops, more often than in psychological laboratories. It addresses *whole* problems, *whole* situations, when they are still technologically current, when their resolution can still constructively affect the direction of technological evolution. Its principal goal is the discovery of design requirements, not the verification of hypothesized direct empirical contrasts or cognitive descriptions. (p. 65)

Carroll (1991b) is concerned with "the information-processing role played by physical artifacts upon the cognition of the individual—hence the term *cognitive artifact*. [See also Norman 1991] ... The goal is to integrate artifacts into the existing theory of human cognition" (p. 18) He speaks of "taking artifacts seriously" (1989b).

Our consideration of what HCI is and does implies an ontology of *tasks* and *artifacts*, and a basic science that we refer to as the *task-artifact cycle*. People want to engage in certain tasks. In doing so, they make discoveries and incur problems; they experience insight and satisfaction, frustration and failure. Analysis of these tasks is the raw material for the invention of new tools, constrained by technological feasibility. New tools, in turn, alter the tasks for which they were designed, indeed alter the situations in which the tasks occur and even the conditions that cause people to want to engage in tasks. This creates the need for further task analysis, and in time, for the design of further artifacts, and so on. HCI is the study of an ecology of tasks and artifacts. (Carroll and Campbell 1989, p. 248)

Design, which is a superset of HCI, therefore also moves beyond the realization of static requirements and to the ecology of designs in use (i.e., artifacts supporting tasks).

8.4. The Scandinavian Approach

Corbett (1992) observes that "although software is very flexible in theory, in practice it is very difficult to (re)design in order to adapt it.... As a result, the organization typically adapts its job design and local management and planning structures to the software and not vice versa" (p. 137). This implies that, rather than producing tools that serve society, technology has a tendency to transform society until it adapts to the tools. Corbett speaks of a "hard" and "soft" technological determinism where the former "sees technology as possessing an autonomous 'inner logic' that is entirely divorced from the social, cultural, economic, and political context of its development, diffusion, and use. Determinism in its softer form rejects such an assertion. Indeed, the human-centered design tradition, while critical of the way in which Western science and technology has been shaped and developed to the present day, anticipates a more desirable development path shaped by new social arrangements (see Cooley 1987)" (p. 139).

Here we have a tension between society and the technology that serves it. We see a concern for the effectiveness of the support, and there also is the issue of the technology's impact on those who use it. I already have made brief reference to Braverman's *Labor and Monopoly Capital* (1974), which argues that capitalism's pursuit of Taylorist principles leads to the use of technology for worker deskilling. Recent studies suggest that Braverman's fears were overstated (Perrolle 1986, Jirotka, Gilbert, and Luff 1992), but the debate involves more than a political interpretation of technological development (even though, as we shall see, many do approach the problem from a political direction).

There are many nonideological implications of the adoption of a new technology. For example, in reference to advanced manufacturing technology, Corbett finds an element of soft technological determinism, which—if badly managed—will "close off important skill-based organizational and job design options" (p. 160).

By way of further illustration of the social impact of technology, Hirschhorn (1982), in an article titled, "The Soul of a New Worker," begins with a reference to the Three Mile Island catastrophe and the need for flexible systems that permit human intervention. He concludes with the observation, "If unions demand more access to data for their workers, however, they will be entering an area in which the line between management and labor itself becomes an issue" (p. 47). Thus, just as the automobile transformed the American society, economy, and urban structure in the middle of the 20th century, the tools "in the age of the smart machine" (Zuboff 1988) are bound to have a comparable impact on the workplace. The question, then, is what should be the role of the affected social organizations in the specification and selection of these tools?

> There is a world to be lost and a world to be gained. Choices that appear to be merely technical will redefine our lives together at work. This means more than simply contemplating the implications or consequences of a new technology. It means that a powerful technology, such as that represented by the computer, fundamentally reorganizes the infrastructure of our material world. It eliminates former alternatives. It creates new possibilities. It necessitates fresh choices. (Zuboff 1988, p. 5)

We may take either an active or a passive role in that reorganization.

"In Scandinavia we have for two decades been concerned with participation and skill in the design and use of computer-based systems. Collaboration between researchers and trade unions on this theme ... has been based on a strong commitment to the idea of industrial democracy.... This Scandinavian approach might be called a work-oriented design approach. Democratic participation and skill enhancement, not only productivity and product quality, are themselves considered objectives of design" (Ehn 1992, p. 96). Floyd et al. (1989) offer a European interpretation of why this design perception developed in Scandinavia: a strong sense of community, an active labor movement, a commitment to democracy. Naylor (1990), in his description of Swedish Grace, suggests that the beauty of everyday goods is derived from the democratic traditions in the crafts and domestic industries; their products are for everyone rather than a select elite.

Coming from this culture, therefore, it was natural for Nygaard—who played a principal role in the development of Simula—to assess his work from a nontechnological perspective. In 1965, he recognized "that the Simula-based analyses were going to have a strong influence on the working conditions of the employees: job content, work intensity and rhythm, social cooperation patterns were typical examples. The impacts clearly tended to be negative.... The question was unavoidable: Should I continue to support the propagation of a tool that to a large extent was used against whom I wanted to show my solidarity?" (Nygaard 1991, p. 53). He became involved in the Norwegian Iron and Metal Project, started in 1970, whose objective was to plan for the use of data processing in the iron and metal industries. The project soon shifted the planning task from a management to a labor perspective. The "local unions got a new and pivotal role. The task was to create knowledge-building processes locally, and to initiate action relating to the local situation, supported by analyses made by the researchers and working groups of local union members and elected shop stewards. The researchers became consultants and participants in a mutual learning process" (p. 56).

Management did not abdicate their responsibility for setting objectives, defining goals, and establishing constraints, but the labor unions were kept informed and participated in the introduction of new technologies such as computer-based systems. Ehn (1989) describes two other early Scandinavian projects that fostered interest in this approach. DEMOS, which began in 1975, looked at ways for researchers, workers, and their local unions in the Swedish Trade Union Confederation to influence the design and use of computer-based systems in four different enterprises: a daily newspaper, a locomotive repair shop, a metal factory, and a department store.

Although DEMOS and similar projects did not meet their initial expectations, there was a growing sense that the approach was viable. Therefore, it was decided to try to extend the work-oriented approach under study into a union-based effort to design a new technology. As a result, the UTOPIA project was initiated in 1981 to develop new tools for page makeup and image processing in the newspaper industries.

> The idea is that new computer-based tools should be designed as an extension of the traditional practical understanding of tools and materials used within a given craft or profession. Design must therefore be carried out by the common efforts of skilled, experienced users and design professionals. Users possess the needed practical understanding but lack insight into new technical possibilities. The designer must understand the specific labor process that uses a tool. Computer-based tools present special challenges because they are technically complex but, if designed well, can be simple and powerful for the skilled worker. (Ehn 1992, p. 112)

There is nothing radical in the above quotation; it is a programme accepted by all developers of systems with identifiable end users. It is the orientation of the statement that is new: Instead of having management procure a system that will provide the desired functionality (as determined by an independent analysis), the users work with the developers to determine the best way of achieving that functionality.

Participatory design in the context of the Scandinavian approach may be seen to have several dimensions. There is a political dimension concerned with who will participate in the process; the democratic view that those who will be affected by an event should have an opportunity to influence it. Next, there is the technical dimension of how to conduct the process, and here the armory of participatory design—prototypes, simulations, discussion, observation—has a long and independent history (i.e., there is no "PD technology"). Finally, there is the pragmatic dimension.

> Participatory design makes explicit the critical, and inevitable, presence of values in the system development process. To predominant values of product quality and work productivity are added broadened participation and skill development. The premise is that these values are closely related; that the productiveness of our work is tied to the extent of our involvement, and that product quality is a matter of a technology's support for the continually expanding and developing work practices of skilled practitioners. (Suchman, Forward to Schuler and Namioka 1993, p. viii)

Greenbaum and Kyng (1991b) use the term *situated design* and identify its characteristics as follows:

- Computer systems that are created for the workplace need to be designed with *full participation* from the users....
- Computer systems ... should *enhance* workplace skills rather than degrade or rationalize them....
- Computer systems are *tools*, and need to be designed to be under the control of the people using them. They should support work activities, not make them more rigid or rationalized.
- Although computer systems are generally acquired to increase productivity, they also need to be looked at as a means to increase the *quality* of the results....
- The design process is a political one and includes *conflicts* at almost every step of the way. Managers who order the system may be at odds with workers who are going to use it. [If

conflicts are pushed to the side, the] system may be dramatically less useful and continue to create problems.

- And finally, the design process highlights the ... question of how computers are used, which we call the *use situation*, as a fundamental starting point for the design process. (pp. 1-2)

Willcocks and Mason (1989) refer to what I have been calling here the Scandinavian approach as a *soft systems methodology* that "has little to say about physical design. But it does clearly indicate the importance of involving clients, managers, end users, in fact all the important stakeholders, in the *processes* of analyzing what are the existing system(s) and problems therein and agreeing, if possible, [to] the required changes" (p. 76).

There is little in the description of this approach that deviates from the findings of the earlier chapters. Indeed, we may interpret situated/participatory/soft design as just one more expression of the shift from the closed-world view of rationalism (in which problems may be analyzed and generalized independent of context, thereby making completely automated solutions feasible) to the open-world view with its plural realities (in which the context of situated use inevitably creates a region of uncertainty that can be resolved only by the tool's users). Naturally, as we move to an open-world view for design, we should expect to find the methods draw upon other concepts associated with the open-world perspective. For example, Bødker (1991a) notes that activity theory starts with the assertion that human activity is the basic component in purposeful human work. She identifies some of the key points of human activity theory relevant to system design.

- Human activity is always mediated by tools, language, etc. These are made by humans and they *mediate* our relation with what we produce and with other human beings. The artifacts are not as such objects of our activity.
- The ways of doing work, grounded in tradition and shared by a group of workers, we call praxis.... Each individual who holds a praxis continues the praxis, and changes it as well. (p. 552)

Citing Engeström (1987), she goes on to state that "the essence for design may be that practice should not be changed from the outside, but in a collective process by the designers and the workers themselves" (p. 552). In *Through the Interface* (1991b), Bødker applies activity theory to user interface design. "To conduct a certain activity, the person has a repertoire of operations that are applied in conscious actions. While an activity is being carried out, certain shifts in levels of action occur due to conceptualization and operationalization. Each action performed by a human being has not only intentional aspects [i.e., goals of the actions] but also operational aspects [i.e., conditions of the operations]" (p. 47). Design is a process of learning and a social activity. The "design of user interfaces means the conceptualization of former operations as well as the creation of conditions for new operations" (p. 48). To understand the conditions that trigger a certain operation from the repertoire of operations, one must study the product in use and observe how conceptualization takes place in *breakdown situations* (i.e., "situations in which some unarticulated conflict occurs between the assumed conditions for the operations on the one hand, and the actual conditions on the other; between the human reflection of the material conditions, and the actual conditions" (p. 27)). The breakdowns precipitate reflection through which the designer-user team learns about the praxis, thereby allowing them to create interfaces that avoid breakdowns of the sort that make the available (i.e., the invisible ready-to-hand) occurrent (i.e., the visible present-at-hand).

Timpka and his colleagues are working on a method, called action design (Timpka, Hedblom and Holmgren 1991), for developing hypertext applications to aid in the resolution of medical dilemmas. "The focus is on the *pragmatics* of a hypermedia application, not its internal syntax or semantics. What it seems necessary to do is move discussion about hypertext away from design issues (like how links should be marked) and corpus and content issues (how materials should be structured for example). In short, as a basis for hypermedia development it is necessary to study and understand how health care practitioners actually perform their work, and the *context* within which they work" (Timpka and Nyce 1992, p. 1254).

For example, Nyce and Graves (1990) analyzed the knowledge in an expert system designed for medical education and assessed its potential value in a clinical setting. Although the expert system is effective in providing information about the location of a lesion in the central nervous system and is useful as a teaching tool, it does not provide information in a form useful for clinical diagnosis where reasoning is open ended and dialectical. "For neurologists, a lesion represents a significant juxtaposition of various kinds of evidence about complex, dynamic relationships between structure and function. Therefore a lesion is not self-evident and it has to be negotiated through clinical work" (p. 320). It follows that the development of hypertext as a clinical tool will be of little value if it contains medical knowledge without knowledge of the clinical praxis. That is, the representation depends, not on the medical knowledge, but rather on the medical knowledge's situated use.

The need to understand the system's use is obvious, but it remains a difficult task. Kuutti (1991) observes:

Thus far there have been about twenty projects in Finland in which the above methodology [based on Activity Theory] has been employed to develop different work activities. Experience shows that even in this form the methodology is useful. Its conceptual tools—however crude they may still be—evidently help bring out possibilities for development.... Experience shows, however, that the methodology is difficult and laborious to use and needs strong support from the organization and strong commitment on the part of the participants. (pp. 543-44)

We find that participatory design depends more on a mind set than a set of technologies. In their introduction to the special issue of the *Communications of the ACM* devoted to participatory design, Muller, Wildman, and White (1993) present a taxonomy of practices (together with references) that includes ethnographic methods, conferences, prototypes (collaborative, video, low and high tech), mockups, cooperative evaluation, and customization. The collection edited by Schuler and Namioka (1993) contains chapters on ethnographic field methods, cooperative design, contextual inquiry, and a variety of case studies.

Mumford has developed an approach for the Effective Technical and Human Implementation of Computer-based Systems (ETHICS) that has been used and evaluated in several commercial settings. It is a paper-based method with three principal objectives:

1. to enable the future of a new system to play a major role in its design and to assume responsibility for designing the work structure that surrounds the technology....
2. to ensure that new systems are acceptable to users because they both increase user efficiency and job satisfaction.
3. to assist users to become increasingly competent in the management of their own organizational change so that this becomes a shared activity with the technical specialists.... (Mumford 1993, p. 259)

"ETHICS has now been used in many companies by myself and others. Results have been proven positive. Acceptable systems have been created that users like and identify with" (p. 267).

In their study of participatory design's effectiveness, however, Beirne and Ramsay (1992) comment that it is "extremely difficult to reach any informed judgement or conclusions whatsoever on the impact of user-involvement on democracy, or for that matter on efficiency" (p. 93). After analyzing four case studies, they report, "Our research indicates that even the 'best' schemes fall short of the ideal of mutually beneficial change. The findings from our studies paint a far more complex picture of the practice of user-involvement than is usually presented in the literature, and cast serious doubt on the easy assumption that it constitutes a potent force in transforming authority relations" (p. 119)

In conclusion, what I have discussed under the heading of the Scandinavian approach has three dimensions: the political goal of democratizing the workplace, the technical goal of creating a system, and the complementary technical goal of understanding how the system fits into the practice of those who will use it. My overview suggests that much of the effort in participatory design has been in the first and last dimensions and that success has been neither easy nor complete. The method of adaptive design presented in Part III focuses on only the two technical dimensions, and it is shown to be both effective and natural.

8.5. A Model of Computer Technology Adaptation

The central theme of this chapter has been one of making our designed equipment perform its tasks in natural ways, that is, to be usable. Naturally, all equipment has some form of human interaction, but the focus here has been on those systems with complex interfaces as typified by human-computer interaction. The point has been made repeatedly that our primary concern is not the form of the interface but the manner in which it enables the user to carry out the desired tasks. We recognize that science can be of only limited help. Norman (1993) observes, "It is remarkable how little scientific knowledge we have about the factors that underlie motivation, enjoyment, and satisfaction.... In part, this is because the logical, systematic, disembodied intelligence of controlled studies leaves out subjective feelings, emotions, and friendly social interaction.... As a result, we know little about how best to structure tasks and events so as to establish, maintain, and enhance experience" (p. 32). Clearly, the design of usable products is a wicked problem and one not subject to scientific analysis. The goal of product design, especially of products intended to support workplace activities, must combine the technological concerns for performance and efficiency with the subjective issues of adoption, acceptance, and evolution. Every product will affect its users, thereby creating a demand for product changes; the understanding of a technology is not static, and its products must respond to the users' and designers' evolving perceptions. And this fact of continuing change further complicates the process.

In my work in medical informatics (Blum 1986a) I have detected a four-phase model of adaptation for computer technology. First, there is a period of *exploration*. For instance, some of the earliest work in medical applications was done in the laboratory with the processing of biomedical signals (Blum and Duncan 1990). The computational power of the new technology unveiled the potential for exploring traditional concerns in new ways. Although the primary interest was in biological problems (e.g., electrocardiogram or ECG analysis, physiological modeling), the shift in mechanism introduced new classes of problems (e.g., analog-digital conversion, signal processing, and statistical analysis) that had to be resolved before much progress could be made.

Once the foundational studies offered a basis for exploiting a maturing technology, adaptation could move to the second phase of *enablement*. What previously had been impossible to do now became feasible. Thus, for example, there was a shift from the visual examination of the ECG signals to their numerical interpretation; the new questions addressed how computer-processed electrocardiography could complement human interpretation and how the computations could add to our understanding of cardiac function. Gradually, we progressed to the third phase of adaptation: *assimilation* of the technology. Finally, as the new technology becomes integrated into the practice, the users can re-rationalize the praxis and eliminate those accidental processes whose justification lay only in their ability to overcome the constraints of a now-obsolescent technology. The result is the final phase of *restructuring*. Naturally, the technology never stabilizes, and the process iterates.

By way of illustrating this model, in the early 1960s Cormack published the mathematical basics for image reconstruction (exploration). Hounsfield employed Cormack's models in a computerized axial tomography (CAT) instrument introduced in 1972 (enablement). For their contributions, Cormack and Hounsfield were awarded the Nobel Prize in physiology and medicine in 1979 (assimilation). And the subsequent move to nonevasive imaging devices—CAT, magnetic resonance imaging (MRI), sonograms—has altered the practice of diagnostic medicine (restructuring).

The model can also be fit to the use of computers to improve the delivery of care. Obviously, the application of computers will be limited by the technology's maturity, and by the 1960s computers had demonstrated themselves to be effective calculators and processors of simple data structures. These features were well suited to the improvement of the automatic analysis of clinical laboratory data. The basic mechanism had been described by Skeggs in 1957 and implemented in the Sequential Multiple Analyzer (SMA) in 1964 (exploration). Although the SMA proved to be an effective processor of chemical analyses, its results, which were reported on analog strip charts, were difficult to use. Through the application of computer technology, the SMAC replaced the strip charts with computer print outs, and the laboratory processing of specimens now could meet physician demand (enablement).

For example, Mount Sinai Hospital in New York performed 260,000 tests in the entire year of 1965. Once the SMAC was installed, the chemistry department was performing 8,000-10,000 tests per day, and the results were available sooner. Thus, in the clinical laboratory we went from experimentation, to enablement, and then very rapidly to assimilation and ultimately to a restructuring of the role of chemical analysis in medical diagnosis. Whereas a physician in the 1950s would order tests based on the probability that the clinical laboratory could return results in time to affect decisions, today's practitioners have broad batteries of tests available that provide rapid and accurate insight into patient status and physiological function. Indeed, the clinical laboratories have been so efficient that we have shifted from a concern for availability to one about overutilization.

Although the computers of the 1960s were adequate for use in the laboratory, they lacked the mass storage facilities that would enable their use in the hospital wards. Nevertheless, there was early exploration of the use of computers in the delivery of care. An important study by Jydstrup and Gross in 1966 showed that some 25% of a hospital's total cost was for information processing, a task potentially amenable to automation. Lockheed began a collaboration with the El Camino Hospital in California in 1965 to build a hospital information system (HIS) employing the technology they used in missile development.

Lacking a sound domain understanding, however, they ran into difficulties, and in 1971 they sold their interests to Technicon (the developer of the SMA and SMAC). By 1977 it was estimated that twenty-million dollars had been spent on the Technicon Medical Information System (TMIS), and the El Camino Hospital was committed to keep the system only if it proved cost effective. As a result, the system was subjected to several intense evaluations. The final report of an evaluation conducted for the National Center for Health Services Research found:

> The results indicate that the system improved productivity in the medical care departments and caused an overall reduction in patient length-of-stay.... Under the assumption that support department cost increases that were found were not directly caused by TMIS, the system was estimated to be approximately 60 percent self-supporting in 1975. (Coffey 1980, abstract)

That is, the system altered the process and enabled some beneficial outcomes, but it added to costs. To justify retention of the system, another analysis was referenced. It credited TMIS with reducing the rate of increase in length-of-stay and per-diem costs relative to comparable California hospitals (i.e., even if the costs were greater, cost growth would have been worse without TMIS). In actuality, the system had become assimilated, and the cost to remove it would have been too great for the hospital to bear.

The acceptance of the El Camino Hospital HIS was a critical milestone in the introduction of information systems in a patient care setting. TMIS had many features intended to improve care, and its interface was designed to accommodate physician use. By now, most large hospitals have come to install an HIS (the assimilation phase), but such systems have had only a marginal effect on the delivery of care (i.e., they have not led to a restructuring of the process). For instance, in *Clinical Information Systems* (published in 1986) I relied almost exclusively on illustrations taken from systems operating in the mid 1970s. The point that I hoped to make was that in the 1970s we learned how the technology could alter the process and that in the 1980s, with a new generation of relatively inexpensive equipment, we could build on that foundation and start to restructure the process.

As I write in the mid 1990s, I must report that this transition has yet to begin. In a recent paper (1994a) I observe that there are two orientations: an administrative orientation in which the HIS is seen as an institutional tool intended to aid the organization and a clinical orientation in which the technology is viewed as a resource to be used by the health care providers for the improvement of clinical practice. Although there are some systems that display a clinical orientation (e.g., the system analyzed in Chapter 12), the marketplace is dominated by products tailored to meet the administrative requirements of those who purchase them. Thus, until clinicians perceive the technology to be relevant to their needs, they will not create a demand for information systems that support their clinical activities. Unlike the CAT and SMAC technologies, which restructure the process within the existing clinical paradigm, a restructuring of clinical practice for the more effective use of medical information and knowledge involves shifting the decision-making paradigm. And this, of course, explains the resistance to it. Within the current paradigm the benefits are not dramatic, and the revolutionary change needed to improve the outcome entails great risk.

I have used the evolution of medical informatics as an illustration of the changes that are at the heart of this book. My primary goal is to restructure the design process, especially for the design of software, by shifting the paradigm. It is very clear that computers have affected our world and our workplaces. We have gone from a batch-oriented, punch-card technology (with its somber warning of "Do not bend, spindle, or mutilate") to an era of ubiquitous machines that advertise friendliness and encourage personal access. However, I claim that we have only assimilated this technology; we have yet to restructure our workplaces to exploit the technology fully.

Such a restructuring in health care delivery, office work, and design (to give but three examples) is bound to come. The question is, how will the restructuring materialize? Although I cannot offer any authoritative predictions, I am comfortable in claiming that any restructuring must involve a reexamination of the essential activities. Part III concentrates on the essence of software design, and I close this section by considering the role of computers in the workplace (both factory and office). I contrast two views. In the first, we assimilate by adding computer tools within traditional settings, and in the second we restructure by reorganizing the process to exploit the features of a new technology.

I begin by examining the current debate about a "productivity paradox." Skinner (1986) claims, "American manufactures's near-heroic efforts to regain a competitive edge through productivity improvements have been disappointing. Worse, the results of these efforts have been paradoxical. The harder these companies pursue productivity, the more elusive it becomes.... Let me repeat: not only is the productivity approach to manufacturing management not enough (companies cannot cut costs deeply enough to restore competitive vitality); it actually hurts as much as it helps. It is an instinctive response that absorbs managers' minds and diverts them from more effective manufacturing approaches" (pp. 55, 56).

He points out that an emphasis on efficiency can impact quality. Because direct labor costs exceed 10% of sales in only a few industries, relatively small gains are available from labor reduction. In manufacturing there is a "40-40-20" rule whereby 40% of the competitive advantage comes form long-range changes in manufacturing, another 40% comes from major changes in equipment and process technology, and only 20% rests on conventional approaches to productivity improvement. He claims that what is needed is the establishment of strategic objectives such as the determination of markets and quality levels. Once the strategic objectives are in place, production managers can develop and work out the objectives for their individual functions. "Breaking loose from so long-established a mindset [of productivity efficiency] is not easy. It requires a change in culture, habits, instincts, and ways of thinking and reasoning. And it means modifying a set of values that current reward systems and day-to-day operational demands reinforce" (p. 58). He is, of course, writing of a paradigm shift.

Skinner's "40-40-20" rule implies that changes in equipment and process technology can have a significant impact on competitiveness. Our interest here is in how that technology will be used. We begin by observing the central lesson of this chapter that an understanding of the domain of use is essential for the design of effective mechanisms of change. But participation, although necessary, will not be sufficient.

Writing about the adoption of advanced manufacturing technology (ATM), Nadler and Robinson (1987) comment, "For years, many have argued that people will support what they help to create. A corollary, that design and implementation *process* is more critical to the success of an innovation effort that the *product*, has become a cliché, but this may wrongly imply that people simply need some emotional 'ownership' of an innovation in order to accept it.... The point is that the design may be wrong! Furthermore, there is no reason to assume that a solution with advanced technology is automatically good!" (p. 16).

They go on to introduce three psychological gaps that affect the assimilation of ATM. The *value gap* begins with the "altruism myth" that industrial quality-of-life programmes are for the benefit of the workers, which invariably leads to a gap between the intentions of the designers and the managers' and operators' perceptions of reality. The designers must recognize that values change slowly and that new perceptions cannot be imposed from the outside. The *knowledge gap* derives from two other myths: The "know-it-all myth," with its faith in the scientific method, and the "cloning myth," with its assumption that what works in one place will work in another. Finally, there is the *behavior gap*, arising from the "snapshot myth" with its focus on the before-and-after images without any concern for the transition from one to the other.

Nadler and Robinson subscribe to the "minimum critical specification," proposed by Cherns (1977), as a way to defer decisions so that the users can participate in the design and gain a sense of ownership in the product. "The realities of design and implementation at any reasonably complex systems level, such as a new technology, show an endless cycling of both large and small events in both process and product" (p. 19). The key to successful implementation is to address all the concerns—technical and social—throughout the process. "The separation of design, planning, and implementation derives from the historic separation of the people and organizational units carrying out these activities.... Even the activities of 'continued improvement' are usually considered to go on separately, possibly spearheaded by industrial engineers, after implementation of some major change. Another awkward fiction!" (p. 21). Implementation begins with the first rumor of change, planning should never stop, and the process is dynamic and nonterminating. As I have observed in my work with clinical information systems (1992e), there is process at work in which the designers come to learn what the users need and the users come to recognize what the technology can do. The result is a dialectic, an expansion, as perceptions evolve and a restructured solution emerges.

By way of illustrating the role of ATM in a workplace setting, consider the example of Computer-Aided Design (CAD), which has been described in a National Science Foundation report as a technology improvement that "may represent the greatest increase in productivity since electricity" (cited in Salzman 1989, p. 253). Given my model of adaptation, it is reasonable to ask if CAD succeeds by being assimilated into the present paradigm or does it restructure the design process? Salzman (1989) has studied the role of CAD in the automation of design, and he finds that the current software is incapable of fully automating the design process of printed circuit board layout. Thus, CAD does not replace existing tasks. Indeed, he finds that rather than deskilling drafters, the investment in CAD systems has been accompanied by a growth in the number of drafters employed. Although the automated technology can perform the simplest tasks, the more complex still must be performed by the designer.

This limited capability of CAD created a challenge for assimilation. One of the designers interviewed by Salzman observed, "They were trying to get computer operators to do the designers' job. They tried for two years but it just didn't work out" (p. 257). CAD was not a black-box replacement technology that could be installed without some organizational assimilation. "Companies failed because they drastically reorganized their production processes in accordance with the promised or theoretical capabilities of the CAD systems" (p. 257). Clearly an illustration of the pitfalls of faith in the "know-it-all myth."

Design, in general, and routing a board, in particular, is an iterative process; a task of sufficient complexity (at this time) to prohibit a fully automated description. But, by relieving some of the routine work, CAD can change (i.e., restructure) the process.

The change in designing, one CAD designer said, is that

> on a CAD system you approach it (the designing) differently. On the CAD system you collect all the data, then do all the designing. You let the computer hold the data for you, let the computer keep things straight, and you *concentrate on your designing abilities*. (Emphasis added). (p. 26)

Here, then, is the designer's intuition regarding CAD's impact on the design process. But is this the way CAD systems are marketed, or are they sold as the automation of manual activities? Are the investors in CAD looking to restructure the design process thereby exploiting the features of a new technology, or are they simply seeking efficiency improvements through the automation of labor-intensive tasks? And if the latter, will they be loosing more than they gain?

In her analysis of the installation of a CAD/CAM system, Henderson (1991) notes that the mismatch between system and organization led to a loss of communication between the design engineers and the shop floor. The inflexibility of the programs, coupled with the misleading perception of a linear process, disrupted the social mechanisms that ordinarily repair frequently occurring problems. The result was that the introduction of the new technology closed valuable communication avenues and opened the organization to potentially disastrous consequences. There are limits to automation, and its introduction changes the workplace and what is required of its users. Salzman observes, "Paradoxically, the greater the use of the CAD system, the more 'automatic' the designer runs it, the greater is the requirement for more in-depth understanding of what is being designed and how the CAD system works" (1989, p. 260). The CAD system is not a doer-of-work, it is a performer-of-an-action in a human-machine activity. As Norman (1993) states, "The two together—the posers of the machine and the powers of the person—complement one another, leading to the possibility that the combination will be more fruitful and powerful that either alone. If we design things properly, that is" (p. 117). And if, as Nadler and Robinson might add, we accept design as an open-ended, continuing process.

What we have found regarding the assimilation of ATM is also true for the acceptance of information technology (IT) in the office. Indeed, Attewell (in press) detects a "productivity paradox" here as well. He notes that there has been a $154 billion dollar investment in IT in the United States in 1990. "Despite the size of these investments, several careful attempts to measure the payoffs of these technologies have failed to find significant productivity improvements attributable to IT" (p. 2). He accounts for this by noting that there is a tradeoff between quality and productivity with much of the new technology directed to quality-related tasks; unfortunately, many of these tasks (e.g., extensive reformatting of word process documents for "aesthetic" reasons) provide little benefit to the organization. He also finds that many of the savings of IT are absorbed by the cost of the IT infrastructure (e.g., user help organizations, version upgrades).

Finally, Attewell observes that effectiveness is constrained because those who adopt the software are rarely those who actually use it (cf. the administrative and clinical orientations discussed earlier). "All one sees in computerized workplaces is more and more change. The cost of this change needs to be balanced against the promise of productivity gains. But this is unlikely to occur when those who prescribe the changes are not those whose work is primarily affected" (p. 21). This suggests that IT is in the assimilation phase. The new technology's application is imperfect, and its benefits have not been realized fully. Indeed, we may interpret the current trend in downsizing as the attempt to realize cost savings from the assimilation of IT.

There is, however, an alternative use of IT that leads to restructuring. Zuboff (1988) studied the introduction of automation in several organizations and has defined two approaches to using IT. With the conventional orientation to automation, "managers emphasize machine intelligence and managerial control over the knowledge base at the expense of developing knowledge in the operating work force. They use the technology as a fail-safe system to increase their sense of certainty and control over both production and organizational function" (p. 390). As the analysis of this section suggests, there is no guarantee that management will gain much benefit from this approach. The alternative is an "informated" organization that takes advantage of all the information made available to the organization by IT. It "is structured to promote the possibility of useful learning among all members and thus presupposes relations of equality. However, this does not mean that all members are assumed to be identical in their orientations, proclivities, and capacities; rather, the organization legitimates each member's right to learn as much as his or her temperament and talent will allow.... A new division of learning requires another vocabulary—one of colleagues and co-learners, of exploration, experimentation, and innovation. Jobs are comprehensive, tasks are abstractions that depend on insight and synthesis, and power is a roving force that comes to rest as dictated by function and need" (pp. 394, 395).

It is my contention that, in software engineering, we are locked into the assimilation phase. We model the software process as a specialization of technological design; we use Computer-Aided Software Engineering (CASE) to automate manual tasks developed as alternatives to the textual methods of the 1960s and early 1970s; and we remain focused on our technology as if the availability of more powerful features will resolve our problems. Often we address problems from the perspective of the computer rather than that of the problem. We see a similar pattern emerging in the new area of Computer Supported Cooperative Work. For example, Grudin (1989b) has analyzed why groupware applications fail and concludes that most fail because there is a disparity between those who must do the work and those who receive the benefit; one cannot expect full participation if the effort to use a system is greater than the rewards it offers. In the case of electronic mail, he reports, the benefits favor all users; this is not so for digitized voice applications, project management applications, natural language interfaces to databases, and group decision support systems. And yet, the one area of success—electronic mail—depends on a shared culture of use which is being degraded as the technology spreads to those who invent their own models of use (e.g., see the report on being flamed by Seabrook 1994).

Thus, we have two choices. We can address our problems from the perspective of technology, or we can choose the perspective of the technology's users. Exploratory and enabling research will have a natural technological flavor, but assimilation and restructuring always require a user orientation. We can seek replacement technologies that are easy to assimilate (e.g., CAD and CASE models of automating existing manual processes), or we can direct some of our research to the investigation of restructuring technologies. Finally, we can look to improve present practices incrementally, or we can examine our essential goals and establish how technology can best help us to reach them. I assume that by now the reader is familiar with my preference.

8.6. A Closing Observation

We now have completed the first two parts of this book. I have avoided the discussion of computers and programs in all but the present chapter. I am trying to suggest that what we do in computer science is part of a much greater whole. The changes we see in computer science are reflections of (and not motivations for) a set of far more encompassing social transitions. I have identified conflicting world views, and I have reported on a diversity of ideas—some contradictory, some complementary. I hope to expand our insights into the nature of and potential for software design. The bulk of this book asks questions and describes the answers of others; I try be objective, and I avoid critiquing. The result is a work similar to a museum sculpture composed of found objects: aesthetically jarring (at first) and challenging (always). I argue that there are no preexisting logical paths in the domain of computer science; we must rely on our human intuition to decide what that science should be. Part III focuses on this decision. It examines how we have been conducting software development during the past half century and proposes an alternative paradigm better suited to the problems of the next-half century. In looking to the future, we may either construct a new paradigm for software design or extend the present paradigm. The choice is ours; there are no bound phenomena that guide or restrict us.

The material in Parts I and II provides a foundation for making this choice. The parts begin with an examination of science and the possibility of uncovering invariant truths (or knowledge), and they end with an analysis of design from the perspective of human-computer interaction. Mey (1994) distinguishes between *adaptivity*, where the humans adapt themselves to the computer, and *adaptability*, in which the computer is adapted to the human needs. In my presentation of a model of computer technology adaptation, I suggest that the final stage of acceptance, restructuring, involves both adapting the users to the new technology (adaptivity) and the technology to accommodate its users (adaptability). Restructuring is an open-ended process—a dialectical process. It creates a new perception of an activity, one that evolves into a new partnership between the human and his tools. Both adaptivity and adaptability are essential to achieve this outcome. I assert, however, that present design paradigms inhibit adaptability. Thus, we are forced to rely on adaptivity; that is, we are motivated by what we can build and not by what we truly need. Indeed, lacking the feedback from the dialectic, we never even find out what we need. Instead, we become expert at building what we can specify in advance, and if Parts I and II have any lesson at all, it is that we seldom can anticipate our needs in a selfconscious, changing environment. Adaptive design, described and evaluated in the final chapters, offers an alternative that brings adaptivity and adaptability into balance. As Mey puts it, "The blind, mechanical force that makes us *adapt ourselves* to the machine should be replaced by the enlightened, humanizing force of the *adaptable computer*" (1994, p. 27). The goal of this book is to illustrate by example how this may be done.

Adaptive design facilitates discovery during the modification of the human environment (i.e., design). It builds on existing knowledge to create new knowledge. But what does it mean to know, and what are the limits to what can be known? That, of course, has been an underlying theme throughout these first two parts, and I close the foundational discussion with some observations about what is known, how we represent that knowledge, and how the location of that knowledge affects the future of software design. I begin with a quotation from Lord Rayleigh who, in 1884, wrote,

> In science by a fiction as remarkable as any found in law, what once has been published, even though it be in the Russian language, is spoken of as *known*, and it is too often forgotten that the rediscovery in the library may be a more difficult and uncertain process than the first discovery in the laboratory.

He, of course, subscribed to the classical view that all scientific knowledge is descriptive of a single, unified reality. Although errors may be discovered, scientific enquiry provides the most effective means for purifying and adding to that knowledge. Thus, except for transient errors, knowledge reported in the library will be equal in value to knowledge derived from new experiments.

As I have shown, this classical view is under attack, and many of its opponents have long claimed victory. Knowledge is in-the-world; it is socially constructed. Latour (1987) describes the process of science in action. In his account, scientific literature is rhetoric, and laboratory experiments are black boxes embedded in black boxes. Scientific questions are presented as controversies, which, when settled, establish the representations for Nature and thereby produce a sense of stability for Society. Technoscience is presented as a network that connects its concentrated resources in a net that extends everywhere; its legitimacy, to a great degree, is selfproclaimed. That is, there may be profound differences between reality and the technoscience descriptions of reality, but, as lay people, we have no choice but to accept the latter's descriptions.

Elsewhere, Latour (1986) remarks that "insignificant people working only with papers and signs become the most powerful of all.... By working on papers alone, on fragile inscriptions which are immensely less than the things from which they are extracted, it is still possible to dominate things, and all people. What is insignificant for all other cultures becomes the most significant, the only significant aspect of reality. The weakest, by manipulating inscriptions of all sorts obsessively and exclusively, become the strongest" (p. 32). Latour is using hyperbole to make the point that there is a distinction between authoritative written descriptions and the realities they proclaim to represent—a distinction that becomes even more complex when one accepts the presence of contradiction within the knowledge base.

Yet we seem to have no alternative to the modern practices embodied in the technoscience literature. Confronted by such a vast accumulation of knowledge and experience, we must accept many of the claims at face value as we explore our own areas of interest. The problem, of course, not new. It was recognized by Lord Rayleigh and confronted by Bush (1945) in his "As We May Think" article half a century later. "There is a growing mountain of research. But there is increased evidence that we are being bogged down today as specialization extends.... Professionally, our methods of transmitting and reviewing the results of research are generations old and by now are totally inadequate for their purpose" (reprinted in Greif 1988, p. 18). A solution to this retrieval problem, he speculated, was "memex," a device that employed associative search, stored text and image, and preserved links among retrieved nodes. Describing the user's capabilities, he predicted:

> A special button transfers him immediately to the first page of the index. Any given book of his library can thus be called up and consulted with far greater facility than if it were taken from a shelf. As he has several projection positions, he can leave one item in position while he calls up another. He can add marginal notes and comments, taking advantage of one possible type of dry photography, and it could even be arranged so that he can do this by a stylus scheme, such as is now employed in the telautograph seen in railroad waiting rooms, just as though he had the physical page before him. (pp. 30-31)

Bush's memex, of course, is the precursor of hypertext, and hypertext offers a useful metaphor for closing Part II.

Hypertext operates within the closed world of the computer. All that is known must already be represented as knowledge in the database.

To the extent that knowledge is socially constructed outside the computer (i.e., in-the-world), memex (or its hypertext implementation) can provide access to only a finite subset of what is, *in some context*, known.   Many contexts are very broad, and here knowledge-based systems such as hypertext can be of great potential benefit.   But they cannot scale up, first because of the difficulty and cost to represent what we know, and second because of the dynamic character of knowledge—it is nonmonotonic.

Thus, hypertext suggests that there will be a difference between the knowledge inside the computer and its use in-the-world.   This difference constitutes the fundamental quandary of software design where the goal is to build a system that operates *inside* the computer and interfaces with the world *outside* the computer.   We have been successful in doing this with conventional software development practices (i.e., programming) in selected domains.   But I wish to go beyond programming, to a new era of design.   As memex sought to model the world of knowledge *outside* the head so that it would be more effective for processing *inside* the head, I seek to build a model *inside* the computer that depicts its operation *outside* the computer.   That is, I intend to shift the paradigm from one of designing programs that operate in-the-computer to one of designing systems that operate in-the-world.   My dilemma is that what is *inside* the computer is static and subject to logical analysis, and what is *outside* the computer is dynamic and unknowable.   The final part of this book first examines how traditional software engineering has confronted that dilemma and then presents my alternative.

PART III

SOFTWARE DESIGN

9

THE SOFTWARE PROCESS

9.1. A Foundation for Software Design

Now that the foundation has been laid, I can turn to the principal concern of this book: software design. I use the word *design* in its most expansive sense. That is, design is contrasted with discovery; it encompasses all deliberate modifications of the environment, in this case modifications that employ software components. Thus, software design should not be interpreted as a phase in the development of a product—an activity that begins after some prerequisite is complete and that terminates with the acceptance of a work product. The context of software design in Part III is extended to include all aspects of the software process from the design of a response to a real-world need (which ultimately may be expressed as a requirements document) through the design of changes to the product (i.e., lifetime maintenance). This broader use of "design" can be confusing, and the reader may think of software design as the equivalent of the software process. In what follows, the goal is to discover the essential nature of software design, which I also shall refer to as the *software process*.

What of the foundation constructed so laboriously during the first two parts of the book? It is not one of concrete and deep pilings. Rather it is composed of crushed rock. It can support a broad-based model of software design, but it may be unstable when it comes to specifics. The foundation has been chipped from the monolith of Positivism, of Technical Rationality. Its constituents are solid and cohesive models, but they defy unification and resist integration. We interpret them as science, technology, culture, philosophy, cognition, emotion, art; they comprise the plural realities from which we compose human knowledge.

Unfortunately, my description of the foundation holds little promise of broad, general answers. Indeed, it suggests that science may be of limited help to design and that we may never discover the essence of design. That is, we must accept design as a human activity; whatever answers we may find will be valid within narrow domains where knowledge is determined by its context. Thus, Parts I and II prepare us to accept that the study of software design may not be amenable to systematic analysis.

Our objective as software designers is to employ software technology to improve the human environment. We seek instruments to guide us in this endeavor, but we also recognize that such instruments may not exist independent of their use; that is, these instruments cannot be discovered, they must be designed. We are constrained by software's central tension: the environment we wish to modify exists in-the-world and may not be subject to a formal description, whereas the software we create exists in-the-computer and must be represented formally—as models of the real world and as models of computations. We might take solace from our studies of the foundation if they produced formal models of the world that could be represented in the computer or if they demonstrated the existence of an integrating force that would synthesize the individual models. But this does not seem to be the case. There is no independent "design process" that can be discovered and dissected. We must accept the fact that the design process is an ephemeral artifact, a residue of the process's conduct. It provides clues as to what was done, it offers occasional insights into what should not have been done, but it never establishes what ought to be done.

Traditionally, we have made progress by focusing on what could be studied analytically. We designed a science for the models in-the-computer. (Note that I say *designed* rather than *discovered* because there is no computer science in-the-world; like mathematics and logic, it is a human creation.) To resolve the central tension of the software process, we instituted a separation of concerns. The investigation of the real-world environment to be changed is considered to be external to computer science; the study of the models that operate within the computer defines the domain of computer science.

Although the goal of software design is to modify what is outside the computer, a restrictive view of the software process has developed in which the focus is on the quality of the software system inside the computer. Two dimensions of quality normally are considered: the product's conformance to its specified objectives (i.e., correctness) and its ability to satisfy the need identified in-the-world (i.e., validity). Establishing and maintaining correctness can be managed as an abstract, logic-based activity, and this formal perspective has become a central interest of computer science. Assessing validity, on the other hand, is an open, dynamic process that goes well beyond technological considerations. Many software engineers find the domain-specific nature of validity unsettling, and they prefer to work within the envelope of formality and certainty supported by computer science. However, I reject the narrow definition of software engineering as derived from computer science; indeed, I propose to design a new computer science for a software engineering that operates in-the-world.

When I speak of going beyond programming, as I do in the title of this book, I refer to a paradigm shift; a shift from a concern for the models within the computer to a regard for the computer's impact (i.e., how the system affects the environment; its role in-the-world). During the past half-century, we have become proficient in the design of software in the first context (i.e., the preparation of programs that are correct with respect to their specifications), and, within certain technological domains, we also are effective in the second context (e.g., computer systems themselves). But if we are to move out of the box of technology and bring computing power to bear on humanity's deepest problems, then we must learn how to become proactive in design—to understand how computer technology can better serve humanity.

It may be argued that this proactive role ought not be the responsibility of the software engineer. But if not the software engineer, then who? The software engineer is the keeper and builder of the software technology; only he can produce the tools that will enable this shift to materialize. Of course, altering the environment is potentially dangerous, and we must exercise care as we expand the computer's role. But, at the same time, we must acknowledge that the environment is constantly changing and that change is unavoidable. Life-saving medicine increases human populations and thereby stresses local ecologies; technology creates new materials that unbalance the existing decomposition cycles. Where natural change is slow moving and unselfconscious, modern technological change is rapid and selfconscious. We cannot hope to control change; neither can we expect to anticipate all the consequences of our interventions. Therefore, we must be prepared to temper the effects of our technologies through graceful evolution. In Part III I propose a shift away from reacting to computer-supported technologies after they have been installed to a mode of proactive adaptation as the system grows and evolves.

Active, selfconscious change is the heritage of modernity, and we cannot turn back the clock. Yet, we also must be careful to acknowledge technology's limitations. Weizenbaum (1976) saw the progress of the mid 1970s as a forerunner of computing's future role in human domains. "We have very nearly come to the point where almost every genuine human dilemma is seen as a mere paradox, as a merely apparent contradiction that could be untangled by judicious applications of cold logic from a higher standpoint" (p. 13). He wrote that "science has been converted into a slow-acting poison" such that the certainty of scientific knowledge "has virtually delegitimized all other ways of understanding. People viewed the arts, especially literature, as sources of intellectual nourishment and understanding, but today the arts are perceived largely as entertainments" (p. 16).

As the first two parts of this book show, the sacred view of science has diminished in stature. Weizenbaum, however, based his interpretation on a world model that implied the ability to build unified models, and this led him examine what might be left out.

> Without the courage to confront one's inner as well as one's outer worlds, such wholeness [of a person] is impossible to achieve. Instrumental reason alone cannot lead to it. And there precisely is a crucial difference between man and machine: Man, in order to become whole, must be forever an explorer of both his inner and his outer realities. His life is full of risks, but risks he has the courage to accept, because, like the explorer, he learns to trust his own capacities to endure, to overcome. What could it mean to speak of risk, courage, trust, endurance, and overcoming when one speaks of machines? (p. 280)

My intent is to make the machine a better tool for guiding humans in their exploration. Many share this objective, but I sense that they rely on a restrictive, computational model for achieving that end. They seek to write programs (perhaps even what they consider intelligent programs) to achieve that goal. As a result, I see their work as progressing within the paradigm created some 50 years ago. In contrast, I move beyond programming, to a new paradigm that exploits the unique properties of software to create dynamic designs of the world-as-it-may-be. The shift to this new paradigm provides the unifying theme for these final chapters.

9.2. Software Engineering, a Historical Overview

In Chapter 1 I used the paper by Shaw (1990) to open a discussion of software engineering and its maturity as a discipline. We have traveled far and wide since those opening comments, and I now begin a second cycle of examination, this time from an historical perspective. Elsewhere (Blum 1992a) I have described software engineering as "the application of tools, methods, and disciplines to produce and maintain an automated solution to a real world problem" (p. 20). Notice that my definition was careful to avoid the terms *software* and *programming*. It emphases automation's response to the problem, but it does not characterize the response's realization. Software is to software engineering as conductive materials are to electrical engineering; its presence is implicit in the definition of the discipline.

Historically, programming is how we have constructed software. In that sense, programming is like soldering; it may be important to, but it is not descriptive of, electrical engineering. Personally, I find that the idea of programming dominates much of our thinking about software engineering. In what follows I examine why programming has come to exert such a commanding importance and how various researchers see the relationship changing over the next decades.

The history of computer technology is relatively brief, with most of the major advances haven taken place in my adult lifetime. The design of the first stored-program, binary, vacuum-tube electronic computer came into being at the end of the Second World War (1945). Progress was rapid, and by 1951 the commercial UNIVAC I was delivered to the Census Bureau. This was also the year the first text on computing was published (Wilkes, Wheeler, and Gill 1951), and it was the year I graduated college. By the time I finally entered the computing workforce in 1962, the principal high-order languages (HOLs) had been established: COBOL for business applications, FORTRAN for scientific applications, LISP for AI applications, and ALGOL for computer science applications. These languages continue to dominate their application domains with only relatively minor changes. Thus, within 15 years of the invention of the first stored-program computer, families of languages had been developed to hide the details of the machine's operations from the designers. The coders of the 1940s wrote in ones and zeros. Symbolic assembly languages replaced the binary notation with descriptive mnemonics. Next, macros provided a form of chunking in which common processing statements could be reduced to a single statement. And then came the HOLs.

Backus reported on his experience with FORTRAN at the Western Joint Computer Conference in 1957.

A brief case history of one job done with a system seldom gives a good measure of its usefulness, particularly when the selection is made by the authors of the system. Nevertheless, here are the facts about a rather simple but sizable job. The programmer attended a one-day course on FORTRAN and spent some more time referring to the manual. He then programmed the job in four hours, using 47 FORTRAN statements. These were compiled by the 704 in six minutes, producing about 1000 instructions. He ran the program and found the output incorrect. He studied the output and was able to localize his error in a FORTRAN statement he had written. He rewrote the offending statement, recompiled, and found that the resulting program was correct. He estimated that it might have taken three days to code the job by hand, plus an unknown time to debug it, and that no appreciable improvement in speed of execution would have been achieved thereby. (Cited in Bernstein 1966, p. 74)

Here we see one more step away from the mechanisms of the computer and into the problem domain. In this illustration a problem that could be expressed in 47 statements required 1000 instructions to implement. FORTRAN constituted a representation scheme for the problem; a hand-crafted assembly language program might require 1000 statements to detail the operations that the computer had to perform. Yet there was said to be no appreciable difference in performance between the 47-line and the equivalent assembly language implementations. From the perspective of the problem, there was no value added by the compiler that translated the 47 lines into a 1000 instructions, just as the transformation of the mnemonic instructions into binary codes added nothing to the programmer's understanding of his programming task. Clearly, the more compact FORTRAN representation was far superior to the more expansive form of the assembly language. It required less time to write, it focused on the problem to be solved, and it reduced the number of careless errors whose frequency is generally a function of size.

The availability of FORTRAN (and the other HOLs) allowed the designers to work on more complex problems. Freed from having to concentrate in detail on how the computer would carry out its computation, the programmers now could focus on how to express what the computation should be. Of course, the complexity of the problems always grew faster than the technology's ability to manage them. To control the development process, two dimensions of discipline were introduced in the late 1960s. The first can be traced to Dijkstra (1968a) who described the structure of the "THE"-Multiprogramming System in response to a call by the *Communication of the ACM* for papers on "timely research and development efforts". In retrospect, Dijkstra wrote, there had been two major mistakes. First, the designers ignored the potential impact of hardware problems and assumed "a perfect installation," and second, they had given only scant thought to debugging tools. As it turned out, however, each of these initial oversights turned out to be a blessing in the long run.

> I knew by bitter experience that as a result of the irreproducibility of the interrupt moments a program error could present itself misleadingly like an occasional machine malfunctioning. As a result I was terribly afraid. Having fears regarding the possibility of debugging, we decided to be as careful as possible and, prevention being better than cure, to try to prevent most bugs from entering the construction. (p. 342)

Thus, rather than devote much effort to anticipating equipment "pathologies" or building a debugging environment, the team concentrated on writing programs that were correct.

As this line of reasoning matured, the program would come to be viewed as a mathematically correct model of the computation necessary to satisfy the specification.   Rather than "write programs," the programmer would establish a sequence of pre and post conditions and prove that the program's instructions guaranteed the satisfaction of the postconditions whenever the preconditions had been met. This was one aspect of what became known as *structured programming* in the late 1960s and beyond.   The other main component of structured programming involved the avoidance of constructs (such as GOTOs) that made comprehension difficult (Dijkstra 1968b). Although the interest in GOTO-less programs would dominate the discussions, it was the formal aspect of programming that defined the discipline. Gries would later refer to the proof-of-correctness approach as *The Science of Programming* (1981), and the concept remains at the heart of all formal methods of software development. Specifications are seen as formal models of the programs' behavior, and the programs are constructed as proofs of their specifications.

The second meaning of discipline was derived from experience in engineering development. In the late 1960s most programmers (like myself) were trained on the job. Little was taught at the university level, and the relative scarcity of programmers (i.e., those trained to write and debug code) encouraged high turnover rates and strong wills. With the new aerospace and communication technologies finding an increasing dependence on software, the need to manage the development of reliable products inexpensively became a critical factor. In response to this need, the NATO Science Committee organized a conference on software Engineering in Garmisch, Germany, in 1968 (Naur and Randell 1969).

The Garmisch conference was a resounding success. A sense of euphoria arose from the fact that so many people had a common view of the problem and a belief that a solution was possible. A second conference, to meet near Rome, was called for the following year. The following is taken from the Rome report:

> The Garmisch conference was notable for the range of interests and experience represented among its participants.... [They] found commonality in a widespread belief as to the extent and seriousness of the problems facing ... "software engineering." This enabled a very productive series of discussions ... [whose] goal was to identify, classify, and discuss the problems, both technical and managerial, up to and including the type of projects that can only be measured in man-millennia....
>
> [The Rome] conference bore little resemblance to its predecessor. The sense of urgency in the face of common problems was not so apparent as at Garmisch. Instead, a lack of communication between different sections of the participants became, in the editors' opinions at least, a dominant feature. Eventually the seriousness of this communication gap, and the

realization that it was but a reflection of the situation in the real world, caused the gap itself to become a major topic of discussion. (Buxton and Randell 1970, p. 7)

The NATO conferences had established the concept of software engineering, even if they could not determine how its goals could be met. The terms they chose, such as *software engineering* and *software manufacturing*, were intended to provoke thought. They hoped that large software projects could benefit from experience with the organization of engineering efforts and the extension of HOL abstractions.

The acceptance of these two forms of discipline divides the history of computing into two 25-year units. The first, from 1945 to 1970 was a period of learning, experimentation, and foundation building. It witnessed the transition from ad hoc responses to the beginnings of a practice disciplined in the sense of both mathematics and management. By the end of the period the basic formalisms had been established, the technology had shown itself to be cost effective and reliable, and large-scale projects were common. The second period, from 1970 to the present, built on the early insights to establish a framework for addressing the issues confronting software development. Some of the difficulties encountered were accidental in that they were associated with deficiencies in the existing equipment or work environment; others were essential in that they were inherent within the process of software development (and the application of computer technology).

There are, of course, different interpretations of what is essential and what is accidental. And that is the reason this book has devoted so much space to the construction of a foundation for software design. The concern of this book is for the next 25 years, and I wish to interpret that period—not from the perspective of the changes since 1970—but with respect to an abstract process model valid for the early 21st century. Looking forward from today refines the process, and this is what practice-oriented research in software engineering must do to improve the existing technology. Looking back from an idealized, future model, however, is a long-term research responsibility; it provides insight into how the software design process may be improved through restructuring.

It is difficult to review the accomplishments of the period between 1970 and the present. There is too much to report, and we are too close to be objective. Shaw (1990) provides a summary of the major computer science accomplishments of this period, and Glass and Vessey (1992) raise some interesting questions regarding the role of domain in the technology's application. Therefore, rather than offering a careful, technical examination of our advances, I close this section with a lighthearted interpretation of software engineering's evolution. I describe the shifts in software engineering's focus as responses to changes in how we manage the balance between the stimulating, enjoyable aspects of design and the tedious, supporting activities demanded by the process.

This ratio between fun and tedium is depicted in Figure 9.1 for every phase of the software life cycle. The percent of the effort devoted to each phase is given on the left. To make the arithmetic easy, 50% of the effort is shown as maintenance, and the remaining effort is divided according to the "40-20-40" rule. Selling the concept is presented as zero effort; in many cases, of course, it represents the entire effort.

The bar chart on the right depicts an emotional quotient with an undefined scale. Selling the concept is seen to be mostly fun. It represents unconstrained problem solving; speculation about how automation can respond to some problem is almost always enjoyable. As one moves to the statement of requirements and down to the detailed design, the amount of fun diminishes. The analyst must conform to earlier constraints, the problem space becomes more abstract, and there is relatively little feedback. Programming, however, has a very large proportion of fun. That is why it is a hobby. It offers the perception of creating a product; when the product performs in a predictable fashion, there also is a sense of having accomplished something useful. Testing, unfortunately, is as much fun as detailed design. And maintenance is considered to be almost entirely tedium, which is why it is assigned to the most junior people. They don't have enough seniority to complain.

We can use this figure as a framework for explaining the changing orientation of software engineering. During the first period of computer technology, from the early machines to the NATO conferences, there

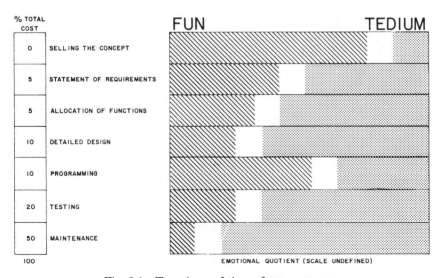

Fig. 9.1. Two views of the software process.

was no programming tradition or scientific base. Hence, the software life cycle tended to optimize fun, and the process frequently flowed directly from selling the concept to programming. Documentation of the requirements, architecture, and design often followed the code's existence.

The correction offered by software engineering in the 1970s was the two types of discipline just described. The emphasis was on the management of the process, and projects were organized so that one could not proceed to the next step until the present step was completed and validated. The rigor of a project discipline provided an effective counter to the casualness caused by the optimization of fun. The formal discipline of programming, however, was popularized without a commitment to models and proofs, and the approach was diluted to simply avoiding GOTOs and limiting program length to what can fit on a single page. These techniques helped reduce cognitive overload and thereby improved the process. As a result, "structured" was accepted as the decade's methodological adjective of choice.

During the 1970s, most large projects involved engineering applications (in which hardware and software developments were integrated), large-scale management information systems (which had well-described objectives), or computer system applications (which relied strongly on algorithms and formal analysis). For such applications the rigid structure of phased development proved to be effective. By the 1980s, however, the technology had advanced to the point that the old methods no longer were suited to the next generation of applications. For example, human-computer interaction introduced a level of uncertainty that made the preparation of specifications difficult and risky. Moreover, the scale and complexity of the new applications extended the period between completion of the requirements, the availability of the implementation, and, above all, the iron test of usage in the field.

Locked into an extended development process with very little feedback from the real world, the designers were forced into a solution based primarily on their understanding of the problem. However closely their understanding matched reality when the project was launched, as development times stretched to 5 or more years, mismatches developed between what had been specified and what was needed. With such extended development cycles, a rigid conformance to the phases listed on the left of Figure 9.1 was no longer feasible. Rapid prototyping and incremental development were popularized as methods for resolving uncertainty, and the spiral model refined the waterfall model to address risk management. Among the technological advances of the 1980s were the use of computer-aided environments to support the process, new representation schemes (such as the object orientation) that improved model building and change, and the use of formalism for better reliability.

Clearly, the solutions of the 1970s were not adequate; but how successful will be those of the 1980s? My thesis is that, although they improve the process, they are locked into a paradigm that limits the effectiveness of software. This is not to suggest that we must find better alternatives before we can resolve the software crisis, because there is no crisis. Consider the number of computers used to bring this book from my fingertips to the reader's eyes; estimate the number of computers used next time you take a trip—the reservation system, the aircraft controls, the management of the airspace, the telephone to call home. If there really was a software crisis, we never could have accomplished all this.

Our sense of frustration is that we would like to do more and to do better. But this is true for science, literature, politics, and our personal lives as well as it is for software development. Like the climbing of Annapurna, the reason that we search for better ways is because they are perceived to be there. We want to get the most out of our technology, and I claim that we cannot do so if we proceed along the current path. The next section describes the traditional view of the software process, and the following section isolates the essence of the process (i.e., the essential properties of every instantiation of the software process). The resulting essential model of the software process establishes the framework for investigating an alternative paradigm, one that can make the technology a better servant of its creators.

9.3. The Traditional Technological Perspective

Earlier I introduced a canonical problem-solving model consisting of five steps: What, How, Do it, Test, and Use (Blum 1992a). This model is the basis of scientific research (Hypothesis formulation, Experiment design, Experiment, Analysis, Report or revise hypothesis) and bridge building (Requirements determination, Design, Build, Certify, and Use). When, in the early days of software engineering, it was agreed that an engineering discipline was needed, a natural first step was to structure the software development process in accordance with this generic flow as it already was being used elsewhere in system development. Royce (1970) is credited with being the first to recognizing the need for this orientation. Figure 9.2 contains the waterfall diagram as it was subsequently depicted by Boehm (1976).

The diagram can be interpreted as an expansion of the canonical problem-solving model. Each phase within the Boehm diagram also employs this canonical model. The *what* is defined as the input to the step (except the first, which must define the requirements for the system). The *how* and *do it* activities are named in the upper box, and the type of *test* is named in the pentagon below the box. The output

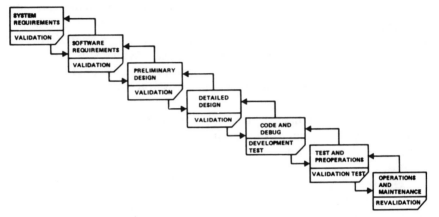

Fig. 9.2. Boehm's 1976 software life cycle model.
Reprinted from Boehm (1976) with permission, ©1976, IEEE.

(*use*) of the step becomes the input to the next step (except, of course, for the last step). The Boehm diagram assumes that there will be lessons learned from later steps that will modify earlier decisions. Consequently, feedback is shown with backward-pointing arrows. To reduce the diagram's complexity, feedback is usually shown only to the previous level, but feedback to any previous phase is always permitted. The waterfall life cycle has the following beneficial properties:

> Phases are organized in a logical fashion. Steps that cannot proceed until higher level decisions have been made must await those decisions. Thus, *detailed design* awaits *preliminary design*, and *code and debug* is delayed until *detailed design* is complete.

> Each phase includes some review process, and product acceptance is required before the output can be used. In this way, the process is organized to reduce the number of errors passed on from one step to the next.

> The process is iterative. Although the basic flow is top down, it is recognized that problems encountered at lower level steps will affect decisions made at a higher level. One goal of management is to limit the iteration to the lowest active levels by ensuring that the highest level decisions have been thoroughly analyzed.

The fact that the waterfall flow conforms to the canonical model implies that it is a natural way of approaching the problem. The difficulty, of course, is that it is not always possible to know "what" the project is to provide. There are changes in perceptions, needs, and technology that become ever more important as the duration of the project extends, and excessive feedback disrupts the basic flow.

The need to manage change was recognized in the 1970s. In his description of the software development process, Royce (1970) described preliminary program design in a section labeled "Do It Twice." He wrote:

> After documentation, the second most important criterion for success revolves around whether the product is totally original. If the computer program in question is being developed for the first time, arrange matters so that the version finally delivered to the customer for operational deployment is actually the second version insofar as critical design/operations areas are concerned. (p. 7)

Using simulation where today we might use a prototype, Royce continues,

> the point of all this ... is that questions of timing, storage, etc. which are otherwise matters of judgment, can now be studied with precision. Without the simulation the project manager is at the mercy of human judgment. With the simulation he can at least perform experimental tests of some key hypotheses and scope down what remains for human judgment, which in the area of computer program design (as in the estimation of takeoff gross weight, costs to complete, or the daily double) is invariably and seriously optimistic. (p. 7)

In *The Mythical Man-Month*, Brooks (1975) echoes these sentiments. In a chapter called "Plan to Throw One Away," he writes,

> In most projects, the first system built is barely usable. It may be too slow, too big, awkward to use, or all three. There is no alternative but to start again, smarting but smarter, and build a redesigned version in which these problems are solved....
>
> The management question, therefore, is not *whether* to build a pilot system and throw it away. You *will* do that. The only question is whether to plan in advance to build a throwaway, or to promise to deliver the throwaway to the customer. Seen this way, the answer is much clearer. (p. 116)

Both these references recognize that when the systems are new, the first implementations are contaminated by artifacts of the learning process. The delivery of a maintainable system requires the removal of these artifacts. As development times extended and the complexity of projects grew, it was recognized that all the learning could not be completed prior to product delivery. In response to the acceptance of unavoidable uncertainty, two refinements of the basic flow were introduced. The first is incremental or evolutionary development (e.g., Mills, Linger, Dyer, and Quinnan 1980, Gilb 1988) in which the process is layered into small incremental steps (each organized with an informal waterfall flow) that permit iterations of doing and learning, thereby allowing changes in direction as the project continues. The second is the use of prototypes, most generally for requirements refinement. This is best illustrated in Figure 9.3, which shows the spiral model described by Boehm (1988). Here the process is represented as a series of learning cycles, each beginning with a risk assessment to identify those areas of greatest uncertainty that may affect the project. Prototypes are expected to offer insight into these problems, thereby reducing risk. This cycle of risk assessment, prototype construction, evaluation, and formalization of lessons learned continues until a low-risk requirements document exists.

In Figure 9.3 four prototypes are constructed, but the number of cycles need not be fixed; it is a function of the developers' uncertainty, and it is

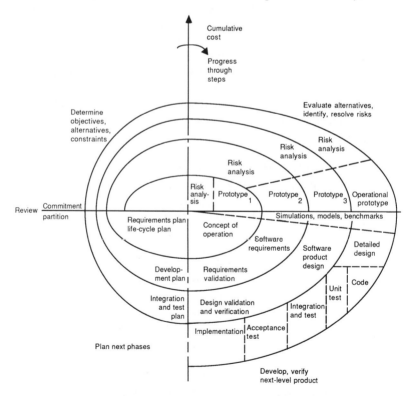

Fig. 9.3. The spiral model of software development and enhancement. Reprinted from Boehm (1988) with permission, ©1988, IEEE.

possible to experiment with more than one prototype concurrently. Once the requirements are defined, the figure shows that the traditional phased flow will be used for system implementation. Even with its use of prototypes, however, the spiral model remains a variation of the traditional model of technological design: First we specify what is to be built, and then we build it. The prototypes serve to improve confidence in the requirements before implementation begins. Incremental development, on the other hand, can be adaptable. The method supported by Gilb (1988) assumes the existence of an open architecture, and the understanding of the needs can be reassessed after the delivery of each increment. Brooks (1987) refers to this as growing rather than building systems. As Royce (1990) has shown, one can combine the multiple-deliverable principle of incremental development with a requirements-first process model.

The process models described in this section can be characterized as variations of a two-step process that first specifies and then implements all or part of the system. In contrast, I propose a one-step process that combines design and implementation. Its description is the topic of the next section.

9.4. The Essential Software Process

The two-step technological model of design begins by defining what is to be built. This is how (in theory at least) we construct buildings and bridges. We plan ahead, and only when we are satisfied that we know what is needed do we begin the actual construction; the costs for making changes once a commitment has been made are prohibitive. The description of what the project is to produce normally is documented as a requirements specification, and there are a variety of methods for determining those requirements (Davis 1993). The requirements specifications may be interpreted from several perspectives, and in what follows I identify three requirements classification schemes. The schemes overlap, and there may be additional categorizations. The existence of so many subgroupings implies that any analysis of the role of requirements specifications will vary among project types.

The most common division of requirements is with respect to the system properties they specify. Two categories normally are identified:

Functional. These define the functional capabilities that the product is to provide. With software, this is sometimes referred to as the behavior of the system, and this behavior can be specified formally. (In systems engineering, behavior takes on a slightly different meaning.) With software, logical models may be used to demonstrate that the functional requirements have been meet.

Nonfunctional. These define constraints that the product must satisfy. With software, they are descriptive properties of the completed system that can be evaluated (e.g., processing time, resource utilization). The software engineer can model the nonfunctional properties of a system, but, from a software perspective, the nonfunctional requirements are not subject to the same logical inspection as is the system's behavior.

The software requirements specification establishes a set of implementations that will respond to a particular need. It employs generality without regard for efficiency. The design reduces that generality until there is a single product optimized for a particular environment (Zave and Schell 1986). Logic may be used to ensure that the design decisions are correct with respect to the functional requirements; because the nonfunctional requirements are not subject to logical analysis, the software engineer must rely on analytic tools to predict or assess their satisfaction.

A second classification scheme organizes the requirements according to their relative importance. Three levels are defined.

Essential. These requirements specify all the properties of the target system that must be delivered for the system to be acceptable. The essential requirements are never complete (Lehman, Stenning, and Turski 1984); completeness would overspecify and thereby constrain the freedom of design.

Derived. These specify system features derived from the essential requirements. The derived requirements are never explicitly included in the requirements specification, but there is seldom a distinct boundary between the essential and derived requirements.

Implicit. These requirements are assumed to be a byproduct of "sound engineering practice." Because there are too many such practices to specify explicitly, only those that demand particular attention are elevated to the level of essential requirements.

In a sense, the implicit requirements exist for all projects of a class, the essential requirements constitute those called out in the specification, and the derived requirements surface during the design activity. To illustrate this stratification, consider an accounting system with the essential requirement that it print out tax forms. The specification of the particular formats might be a derived requirement, and the fact that an audit trail and recovery procedures are necessary might be an implicit requirement. Depending on the situation, however, any of these derived or implicit requirements could be included in the essential category. The point is that not all requirements are essential. In fact, the selection of which requirements are to be considered essential is a subjective matter. The decision often is affected by the state of understanding at the time the specification is documented.

The final categorization scheme qualifies the character of each requirement. Two types of requirement are identified:

Closed. Closed requirements are well defined and stable. Often there is an existing domain notation that can be used to express the requirements. For example, mathematical notation is used in engineering applications. Most hardware products expect closed requirements before initiating the final construction. Because of the precision of the specification, the greatest uncertainty normally is with respect to the construction of a product that satisfies the requirements.

Open. Open requirements are poorly understood and dynamic. Often these requirements specify product properties that are routinely achieved with the current technology. A typical example is the naive use of an existing technology in a new domain. With open requirements, the greatest uncertainty is with regard to the specified product's ability to meet the expectations in a real-world setting.

The categories of closed and open are somewhat like Lehman's (1980) *S*-Type and *E*-Type programs, but they are not defined as precisely. Few applications will fall into just one category, and most complex products will contain components with closed and open requirements. Thus I treat openness and closedness as qualitative measures.

In a traditional requirements specification, there is a clear distinction between the functional and nonfunctional requirements, but the specification identifies only the essential requirements. Distinctions among the essential, derived or implicit requirements are matters of subjective choice; assignments are determined more by project-level dynamics than by product-specific needs. The technological view also makes no distinctions regarding the character of the individual requirements; all functional requirements are specified as if they were closed because only closed requirements can be specified. But the differences in character between a closed and an open requirement are so great that no process model can be satisfactory for both. The artificial closure of an open requirement creates problems, and the orientation of the project should be based on an assessment of the specification's character: closed or open.

Throughout the early 1970s, most large projects were perceived to have closed requirements, and the two-step model of technological design provided a satisfactory fit. As projects became more complex, their requirements became more open. This openness can exist in two senses: We do not know what the product should do, and, secondly, once the product exists it changes our understanding of what should be done. Prototypes for requirements refinement are effective for closing the first type of openness, but they do not address the second. If we accept, as I think we must, that our products must evolve, then a two-step process that fixes the initial point for evolution will be inflexible. What we need is a specification approach that allows the design to adapt as the external requirements change. I call this one-step process *adaptive design*.

To understand how adaptive design works, we must return to the analysis of the software process. I begin by reducing the essence of the waterfall model to the three basic transformations shown in Figure 9.4.

From the need in the real world to a problem statement that identifies a software solution for that need. This is the definition of what is to be done (e.g., the requirements specification).

From the problem statement to a detailed implementation statement that can be transformed into an operational system. This transformation includes the bulk of the waterfall activity. It encompasses the definition of how to build the software, its building, and its testing. The implementation statement includes the design descriptions, the source code, and the testing materials.

From the implementation statement to a system that will satisfy the real-world need. This requires equipment, procedures, people, etc. It represents the embedding of the software product within its operational environment.

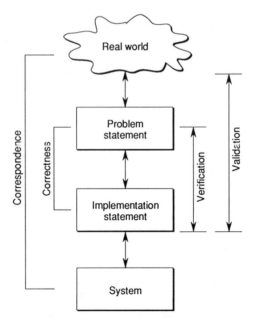

Fig. 9.4. The essence of the waterfall model.

The composite transformation is one from a need to a software product that satisfies that need. Naturally, after the system is installed in the real world, the environment is modified, thereby altering the appropriateness of the original problem statement and consequently generating new software requirements. Thus, the figure represents only the trace of one path in an iterative process.

The figure also displays two quality measures for the system and the processes used to evaluate them. *Correspondence* measures how well the delivered system corresponds to the needs of the operational environment. *Validation* is the activity used to predict correspondence; true correspondence cannot be determined until the system is operational, and, even then, its determination can be difficult and controversial. Unlike correspondence, *correctness* can be, and, indeed, must be, established formally. Correctness measures the consistency of a product with respect to its specification. *Verification* is the exercise of determining correctness. Notice that correctness is always objective. Given a specification and a product, it should be possible to determine if the product precisely satisfies the requirements of the specification by verification. Validation, however, is always subjective; if the evaluation criteria could be detailed and formalized, they would have been included in the specification. As Boehm (1984) puts it, these quality activities answer the following questions:

Verification. "Am I building the product right?"
Validation. "Am I building the right product?"

Validation begins as soon as the project starts, but verification can begin only after a specification has been accepted. Verification and validation are independent of each other. It is possible to have a product that corresponds but is incorrect (for example, a necessary report is part of the delivered product when a different, and useless, report is described in the specification). A product also may be correct but not correspond (for example, after years of waiting, a system is delivered that satisfies the initial design statement but no longer reflects current operating practices). Finally, observe that unless the specification provides a framework for a formal assessment, only validation is possible.

For problems with closed requirements, there will be high confidence in the problem statement and the principal risks will be associated with verifying that the product is correct (i.e., the requirement's closure already implies that I am "building the right product.") Here the two-step model works, and formal methods are effective. A far more interesting case, however, is when the requirements are open. To gain insight into the problems of dealing with open requirements, I abstract the previous model to produce the essential software process model depicted in Figure 9.5. It shows the software process as two modeling activities.

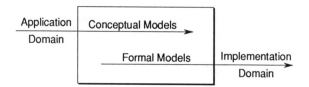

Fig. 9.5. The essential software process.

Conceptual modeling represents the first design activity: the one that establishes a software-realizable response to the application need. The orientation of the conceptual model is that of the domain as tempered by the demands of the design process; although software concepts are modeled, the intent of the model is to be understandable to the sponsors and users. *Formal modeling*, on the other hand, is formal in the sense of mathematics and logic. It is more than just precise and unambiguous; it is desirable that the representation scheme be machine processible for error identification. Computer programs are formal models of computation; their specifications (when they exist) also are formal models.

The essential software process thus may be decomposed into three transformations:

From the need in the application domain to a conceptual model that describes a software product responding to that need (T_1: $N \rightarrow C$).

From the conceptual model to a formal model that prescribes the essential properties of the software product (T_2: $C \rightarrow F$).

From the formal model to an implementation that is correct with respect to the formal model (T_3: $F \rightarrow I$).

Each of these transformations is one to many, and the design process is concerned with the selection of an element (i.e., $c \in C$) that satisfies the mapping and is perceived to be in some way the best. For transformations T_1 and T_2 there is no concept of correctness; the only concern is one of validity: Will the target software product respond effectively to the identified need? Application domain formalisms may be used to assess validity, but they only can refute design assumptions (i.e., they only can "prove" invalidity). Because T_3 begins with a formal model, one can demonstrate (i.e., rigorously "prove") the correctness of all designs *with respect to the formal model*. Of course, if the higher level model is neither formal nor sound, then correctness cannot be determined. Because of our confidence with compiler technology, we always assert that the object code is correct with respect to the source code; much of the interest in formal methods is derived from a desire to support the derivation of designs from their specifications automatically and correctly.

In the two-step process, T_1 and T_2 are combined as a single transformation that produces a specification $f \in F$; the second design step employs T_3 to realize the implementation $i \in I$. Because validity and correctness are independent of each other, we must assess our confidence in the validity of f when assigning risks to the two design activities. For hardware developments we assume a high confidence, which is why we employ the technological design model. (Indeed, it would not be possible to fabricate the product without this assumption.) But for a software product with uncertain (i.e., open) requirements, one cannot assert that f will be valid; naturally, if f is invalid, then i will be invalid. For such products the composite transformation (T: N → I) permits the assessment of the implementation i without binding i to some intermediate specification f. Although the one-step process is not possible with hardware, adaptive design can be implemented for software.

We see, therefore, that the software process can be interpreted in two different ways. It can be seen as the transformation from a need to a product (T: N → I) or—once a specification f has been derived—as an implementation activity (T_3: F → I). The scientific foundations of software engineering normally are concerned with activities that can be managed formally (e.g., the recording of f and the conduct of T_3). When T_1 and T_2 are considered within computer science, it usually is in the domain of computer technology (e.g., communications, compilers, operating systems, and database systems). When software engineering addresses a domain outside of computer technology, it generally adopts a pragmatic or domain-independent approach. For example, fourth-generation languages provide comprehensive support for a subset of problems using ad hoc tools and methods, and the entity-relationship model has received broad acceptance even though it captures only a portion of the database conceptual model. When we restrict software engineering to T_3, we exclude complications; T_3 is a closed (and logical) process that can be studied independent of an application domain. Although this generality advances development within the technology domain, it does not address many of the real world needs.

This, then, is our dilemma. T_3 exists within a logical framework that is subject to a formal (i.e., scientific) analysis, but T, which is the transformation of central interest to us, is independent of many of the logical constraints associated with T_3 (i.e., it is in-the-world). What I call traditional software engineering, with its emphasis on programming methodology, builds upon the scientific foundations for T_3, which for open problems is necessary but not sufficient. Notice that f in T_3 serves as a set of axioms in a theory; if the axioms are changed, the correctness of the entire theory will be in question. Therefore, f cannot adapt unless there is a way to ensure that the changes in f' do not invalidate the correctness of i with respect to f'. Adaptive design offers a way out of this dilemma. Rather than working with T_3 as a *build-to* document, adaptive design operates at the level of T and treats the specification as an *as-built* description. It accomplishes this by using an environment with the following properties:

> The environment supports conceptual modeling (i.e., $T_1: N \rightarrow C$). This implies that its representation scheme formally expresses application domain (as opposed to implementation domain, or programming) concepts.

> It provides automated support for the transformation of the conceptual model into an implementation (i.e., $T_2 \circ T_3: C \rightarrow I$). The generated product feeds back the implementation consequences of the conceptual design. That is, the effect of every design decision in the conceptual model is made clear by experimenting with its implementation.

> Because the product will evolve, the environment maintains a complete and accurate description of the conceptual model (i.e., the as-built documentation) together with the realization (i.e., the implementation) derived from it.

There are several methods for building such an environment. The operational approach uses executable specifications to validate the conceptual model (Zave 1984). Megaprogramming uses simulations to experiment with the behavior of large systems made up of preexisting components; its conceptual models employ domain architectures to establish the relationships among these components (Wiederhold, Wegner, and Ceri 1992). The domain-specific software architecture (DSSA) approach creates a general architecture within which objects may be customized to produce the desired system (F. Hayes-Roth et al. 1992, Tracz 1994, B. Hayes-Roth et al. in press). Finally, products such as STATEMATE permit experimentation with potential designs (Harel, et al. 1990, Harel 1992). Chapter 11 describes how I implement adaptive design. For the purposes of the present discussion, however, it is important to recognize the one-step, as-built specification model of adaptive design as an alternative to the traditional two-step model of technological design.

In summary, the essential software process involves two classes of analysis. The first looks out to the problem space (conceptual modeling) and the second focuses on the implementation space (formal modeling). In earlier decades, there was the perception that the needs could be defined accurately (i.e., the requirements were closed), and the conceptual models were in fact quite close to the formal models (e.g., engineering applications that could be described effectively in FORTRAN). As we move to more open problems (open both in initial understanding and change over time), the gulf between the expression of the concept and its formal representation widens. We have two choices. We can continue to rely on the two-step model with its notion of a build-to specification. The two major deficiencies of this model are, first, that the special role of the specification inhibits iteration and refinement, and second, that the cognitive distance between the conceptual and formal models can act as a deterrent to problem understanding.

The alternative that I propose is to create expressive representations for the problem domain that can be transformed automatically into an implementation. Here the conceptual model of the product will constitute an as-built specification, and it can adapt as the domain requirements evolve. In my implementation of this approach, the representation scheme makes C and F isomorphic and the transformation T_3 is automated, thereby reducing the transformation T to the process of conceptual modeling, T_1. This is not a particularly new idea; in fact, this is exactly what a "draw" program does. The challenge, of course, lies in the ability to find a rich representation scheme for the target domain and to establish how representations appropriate for that domain can be mapped into computer instructions.

This, then, is the paradigm shift I propose. We should move from our historic interest in modeling the *product* in favor of a concern for modeling solutions to the *problem*. This implies a migration from build-to specifications (together with their realizations as programs) to the use of as-built specifications that describe evolving responses to problem-space needs. That is, we should go from the characterization of solutions in-the-computer to solutions in-the-world. Clearly, such a shift goes *beyond programming*. Clearly, too, such a shift will not be easy and cannot be phased in.

As shown in Figure 9.6, the product and problem orientations begin with different intentions and end with different goals. The current product-oriented paradigm is a two-step process in which the design begins after a specification exists; its goal is to create a set of programs to satisfy that specification. In the product-oriented paradigm (i.e., the technological design model), software engineering is considered a subset of systems engineering, and the initial phase begins after the requirements are allocated between the automated and nonautomated components of the system. In the problem-oriented paradigm, on the other hand, the process begins with the identification of a need together with a response (i.e., the problem solution), and the process concludes with the completion of the solution's

	Product Oriented	Problem Oriented
Top	System Specification	Solution Identification
Bottom	System Implementation	Solution Design

Fig. 9.6. Two software paradigms.

design, which of course includes both functional and performance decisions. The two orientations create different products: one produces stable systems, and the other establishes adaptive solutions. Although both types of products are necessary, the next section demonstrates that the need for adaptive solutions is growing.

9.5. Looking to the Future

The previous section introduces an essential model for the software process and identifies an alternative paradigm for software development better suited to the open problems of the next quarter century. This section speculates about the future of software development in the next millennium. I see the following trends:

Open requirements. As already noted, requirements may be placed on a scale that ranges from closed (i.e., well understood) to open (i.e., uncertain or changing). The tradition of software engineering, as exemplified by the importance it places on the requirements specification, has focused on closed requirements. Most prototypes are seen as tools to validate the requirements specification before design begins. But there is a growing recognition that the requirements are not always clear and that viable systems are subject to considerable change. The importance and scope of software maintenance has been recognized, and few now expect complete and stable requirements.

Reuse. Software development long has benefitted from reuse at the level of the program library and concept formalization (e.g., the reuse of mathematical libraries and the hiding of input/output macros within the syntax of the FORTRAN WRITE statements). Although there is considerable interest in reuse at finer levels of granularity using traditional and object-oriented technologies (Biggerstaff and Perlis 1989), I believe that the reuse of the 1990s will have a different character. There already is an enormous investment in software, and there is little likelihood that that software can ever be replaced. It would be too costly to reprogram, and few understand exactly what the current systems do. Thus, despite their imperfections, we must learn to reuse key portions of the available (legacy) systems. The present move to open architectures provides a framework for easing the reuse of application components and sharing reusable facilities (e.g., windowing environments).

Integration. Whereas the systems of the 1970s were independent and complete, few new comparable projects can be expected; the resources no longer are available for such large-scale developments. Moreover, as our systems grow in size and complexity, they interact with other large systems. Thus, a key challenge of the 1990s is the integration of new and existing systems. Rather than starting with a specification for a complete system to be built, systems will rely increasingly on the resources of other systems; boundaries between systems will become obscured. The software engineer will be expected to provide new functionality by using (reusing) existing resources. Development, maintenance, and integration will be viewed as aspects of a unified, long-lived process.

Diversity in computational models.   Through the 1970s there were divisions that separated the tools and computational models used to develop systems. Symbolic, numerical, and database systems were managed independently, and it was difficult to adapt the tools and environments used in one domain to another. This no longer is the case. What once was called an "AI environment" now is a workstation; frames, objects, and abstract data types represent variations of a common concept. Although problems in interoperability remain, the software engineer has many more tools available and there is the perception that, once a problem is understood, an appropriate solution can be realized. The concern is for integrating the parts of the solution rather than finding a language or environment that will support a complete solution.

If this analysis is valid, then the systems of the early 21st century will be composed of existing and new components, implemented with a variety of languages and environments. The software systems, like the organizations and societies that they serve, will be dynamic and evolve. The software engineer will not be asked to design and build a new system; instead, he will be expected to exploit existing systems to create new functionality and to augment existing environments to enhance their functionality. Closed requirements for systems will be rare, and new developments to replace existing systems rarer still. But is this a valid analysis? Let me compare it to the views of two highly regarded researchers.

I begin with Brooks (1987), whose "No Silver Bullet" has already been cited. The subtitle of that paper is "Essence and Accidents of Software Engineering." Following Aristotle, Brooks divides the difficulties of software technology "into *essence*, the difficulties inherent in the nature of software, and *accidents*, those difficulties that today attend its production but are not inherent" (p. 11). He then goes on to define the essence of a software entity as a construct of interlocking concepts. Using italics for emphasis, he concludes:

I believe the hard part of building software to be the specification, design, and testing of this conceptual construct, not the labor of representing it and testing the fidelity of the representation. We still make syntax errors, to be sure; but they are fuzz compared with the conceptual errors in most systems. (p. 11)

The negation in the title comes from this observation:

If, as I believe, the conceptual components of the task are now taking most of the time, then no amount of activity on the task components that are merely the expression of the concepts can give large productivity gains. (p. 16)

After arguing that the main accomplishments of the past (e.g., high-order languages, time sharing, and integrated environments) corrected accidental difficulties, he goes on to claim that most "hopes for the silver" (e.g., Ada, object-oriented programming, AI, and graphical programming) are limited to the task components of the software process and, therefore, cannot produce significant improvements. In closing, Brooks identifies four "promising attacks on the conceptual essence," which are reuse (with integration), two methods for closing requirements (prototyping and incremental development), and the nurturing of great designers. Each provides insights into the building of the conceptual construct. Thus, his argument suggests that as computer costs fall and as the systems become more powerful, the technological barriers will become less critical. Rather, the challenge is seen to be one of exploiting our experience in-the-world. And this is a human, knowledge-based task that technology can support but not assume.

Belady (1991) offers a slightly different perspective for understanding the software industry of this decade. In his analysis of software technology evolution, he describes a transition from the classification of software by function (i.e., system and application programs) to one in which software is organized by type. The first type is a made up of standardized components (Type A software), and the second type integrates these components to produce a smoothly functional, domain-specific system (Type B software). The Type B software also is called the Integrator's "glue." In the argument presented by Brooks, the Type A software would represent what can be bought rather than built (i.e., reused), and the Type B software would constitute an expression of the conceptual construct. The designers who build the Type B software must know what is to be reused, must learn—by prototyping or iteration—what is needed, and must apply their experience in creating the domain-specific system.

Belady concludes his paper with this comment.

This world [of large system development] is undergoing a shift in mission that will utterly transform the software engineering discipline. Because integration is the key to creating large, complex computer systems, software engineers must become application system designers, and ones with significant hardware and application expertise at that. These designers must take an often staggering number of components, many of which are themselves quite large, and combine and recombine them into the integrated networked super-applications of tomorrow. (p. 8)

Notice that neither Brooks nor Belady speaks of technological solutions. The task is one of understanding the domain need, knowing the tools available to produce a response to the need, and then constructing that response. The construction, however, is not presented in terms of programming (object oriented or otherwise); it is a process of integration and iteration. Belady notes the role of application expertise; when the requirements are open, not even great designers can produce a valid response to a need if they do not understand the environment in which the need exists.

Although Brooks, Belady, and Blum share a common sense of what the future may bring, there are significant differences. For example, Brooks (1987) describes the "conceptual construct" as the key to effective design. But that construct is not the same as what I call the conceptual model. For Brooks, "The essence of a software entity is a construct of interlocking concepts: data sets, relationships among data items, algorithms, and invocations of functions. This essence is abstract in that such a conceptual construct is the same under many different representations" (p. 11). For me, however, the constructs in the conceptual model should be domain actions, representations of domain surrogates, application procedures. Where Brooks sees constructs from the perspective of the solution's implementation, my constructs are defined external to the computer and in the domain of use. Although I strongly subscribe to his analysis, I am not certain that the essential difficulties he describes for the computer-oriented constructs necessarily will also be essential difficulties for the constructs of the application domain. Once we shift the paradigm from the product to the problem, the statement of the problem has been changed, and silver bullets again become possible.

Finally, a brief remark concerning Belady's model with components and the glue to create domain-specific applications. Although I believe that this is an effective way to gain insight, to build prototypes, and to create simulations, I sense that the coarse granularity of large (perhaps parameterized) modules will degrade efficiency. For example, Unix offers many tools that can be linked together to perform nonstandard tasks with little initial effort. However, as the problems get to be complex, it is recognized that this pragmatic approach does not scale up efficiently. Certainly we should formalize and reuse processes and functions; I only suggest that we should identify the features at a lower level of granularity and learn to integrate them for reuse and improved efficiency. I do not believe that either Brooks or Belady would argue with these observations.

Indeed, a recent comment by Brooks on object-oriented programming (OOP) is consistent with my criticism.

> The fundamental hope for OOP is that it permits one to move up a level by building a set of objects for the domain of discourse of the particular application area, hence allowing one to program within the intellectual context and using the elementary concepts of the particular application area. Most of today's programming languages are general-purpose and work a level below this. (Cited in Denning and Dargan 1994, p. 59)

Reverting to the early FORTRAN example, this quotation suggests a hope that the use of OOP will provide a domain-oriented language that permits designers to express solutions effectively and compactly—in 47 lines rather than 1000 lines. Such a representation scheme would permit the designers to focus on the problem to be solved rather than the complexities of the solution's realization, which is the goal of adaptive design.

9.6. Exploiting Software's Unique Properties

The central theme of this chapter is that we have derived our models of software engineering from our experience with hardware engineering. We rely on a two-step process model, and we introduce the specification as a way to separate our thinking about the problem from our thinking about its implementation. This approach employs an architect metaphor in which the architect works with models and drawings until the client is satisfied that the proposed building will satisfy her objectives. Once the plans are accepted, construction begins, and—because changes are very expensive—modifications are discouraged. As we have seen in Chapter 7, that is not how architects really work; it is recognized that there will be some degree of openness throughout the process. In more dynamic applications, such as those with open requirements, a sculptor metaphor is more appropriate. The sculptor works with the materials and adjusts his goals as he interacts with the process. Although the process begins with sketches and analysis, fidelity to the initial goals is relatively unimportant. The process stops when the object is aesthetically pleasing, and the object's delivery constitutes its as-built specification. Of course, software, unlike a sculpture, is never complete, and so the process of sculpting never ends.

One cannot apply the sculpture metaphor to conventional constructive activities (e.g., buildings, bridges, airplanes), but the unique qualities of software permit us to employ the sculptor metaphor to software deign as well as to the design of automatically fabricated objects (e.g., VLSI circuits). Software has (at least) five characteristics that distinguish it from hardware.

Software is a design. It is wrong to consider the program code a product; it is simply the most detailed expression of the design. Like the rest of the design, the program is only text, and its linkage with higher level text should be maintained. When using a program design language (PDL), for example, one expects the structure of the final source program to follow that of the PDL.

Software manufacture is cost free. The conversion of a design in the form of a source program into an implementation in the form of an object program has essentially no cost. Paradoxically, the specify-first model was intended to reduce the cost impact of changes, even though with software there is no cost for change.

Software design is machine processible. Virtually all of a software specification and design is expressed in a textual form that can be managed as software. This includes both the design and its realization. Where the text is informal (e.g., text descriptions), it can be treated only as passive knowledge. On the other hand, where the design objects are stated formally, they can be manipulated and transformed by other software.

Software can be exercised locally. Each software module constitutes a formal model of computation. Given the proper context and state, it can be exercised independent of the whole. This implies that software can be very tolerant of incompleteness. Moreover, once the desired properties of some software object have been certified, the object is available for use in all settings that conform to its constraints.

Software is dynamic. As a design that expresses a specified problem solution, software evolves with improvements in the knowledge of the problem and the efficacy of the solution. Experience with the software enhances the understanding of the initial problem and sows the seeds for subsequent refinement.

Two important points need to be made before continuing. First, there is a difference between the software design and the software product that represents a correct and valid design. The requirements to which the software responds are dynamic, and so too will be the software design. The software implementation, however, must be a stable instantiation of a tested design; it can be replaced only with other instantiations of a tested design. That is, we must distinguish between a dynamic design (which is incomplete, incorrect, and/or invalid most of the time) and the static operational software system (which will have satisfied the correctness and validity criteria before acceptance for operational use). Second, there is a difference between the process of creating a correct and valid implementation and the management of that process. For the purposes of management, a waterfall-type flow may be appropriate. Indeed, for projects with both hardware and software it may even be highly desirable. However, one should be careful to separate the concern for how we carry out the process from how we manage it.

Today, few environments take advantage of these special features of software. Indeed, I assert that our programming-dominated view of the process hides the potential of its unique properties. I believe that if environments exploited these extraordinary characteristics, the software process would change radically. Design would no longer be considered an activity that culminates in the decision to write code; the code would be part of the design, and the design could be tested operationally. The developers would be free to alter the design as they experiment with the completed code. The process would emphasize the design activities, and the cost of realizing the designs would be considered a necessary overhead expense. Emphasis would be placed on capturing experience for reuse, and iteration would concentrate on those areas with the greatest uncertainty. By maintaining the entire as-built design as an integrated knowledge base, designers would have access to a complete and unified design. Modifications to one portion of the design would extend automatically to all affected design objects. In this way, we would move from the architect's sequential processes of first specify, then build to the interactive and iterative activity of system sculpture. System development would become an ongoing, adaptive process of sculpting responses to humanity's need.

Here, then, is the challenge that confronts us. Can we reorganize software development so that it is problem oriented, uses a one-step process model, maintains as-built specifications, and exploits software's unique properties? Chapter 10 examines the methods currently used for software design, and Chapter 11 describes an alternative that I call adaptive design.

10

DESIGN METHODS

10.1. Adaptive Design in Context

The previous chapter on the software process introduced two contrasting orientations: problem and product. Both orientations have the same objective: the efficient and effective creation of an automated response to a real-world problem. They differ only in the methods and tools used to achieve that end. In the product-oriented model, the difficulty of realizing a solution is accepted as the critical path. Thus, the approach applies the principle of separation of concerns and divides the process into two discrete activities: first establish the essential requirements of what is needed, and then build a product that will satisfy those requirements.

As already noted, this model is appropriate when the requirements are stable or if the complexity of development is so great that a fixed specification is necessary to reduce risk. In contrast, the problem-oriented model is valuable for real-world problems with open requirements (open both in the sense of initial uncertainty and of operational change). Unfortunately, it can be implemented only for domains in which the technology is relatively mature. For example, military applications that push the limits of technology have open requirements (i.e., they begin with uncertainty and are subject to modification as potential adversaries develop responses to newly introduced capabilities). In this domain, however, the technology may be too complex for development without frozen requirements. In other domains, such as interactive information systems, the technological challenges are sufficiently well understood to permit a problem-oriented approach with its one-step process model.

The adaptive design paradigm proposed in this book is problem oriented. The instantiation I describe in the next two chapters creates interactive information systems. In principle, there is no reason why the adaptive design model may not be used for complex, real-time military applications; the fact that it has not been so used is a function of our knowledge of that domain and not a limitation of the paradigm. There always will be a fuzzy boundary about the technology that separates what we can and cannot do.   At that boundary, we must rely on experimentation and hacking to gain understanding.

For example, Simon (1969/1981) observes that "the main route open to the development and improvement of time-sharing systems was to build them to see how they behaved.... Perhaps theory could have anticipated these experiments and made them unnecessary. In fact, it didn't" (p. 25).   Once the structure of a time-sharing system was understood, reliability and efficiency demanded more formal analysis, and the two-step process of development was used. Because the system requirements were relatively stable, this product-orientation proved adequate.   For the applications that used the time-sharing system, however, many of the requirements were open.   Here, several alternatives were possible: Learn to live within the product-oriented model by adapting work to the software and restricting requests for changes to what can be accomplished easily, abandon the central resources in favor of personal computers and commercial tools that foster individual support over organizational integration and sharing, or work toward flexibility by installing systems with end-user capabilities (e.g., report writing and ad hoc search). As I will show, adaptive design provides one more alternative, one that optimizes the match between fixed resources and changing needs.

In the previous chapter I emphasize the role of adaptive design in constructing and evolving conceptual models. I now seek to bind that vision to the formalisms of computer science. I build upon what I have reported already. For instance, Part II on ecological design establishes that artifacts should perform useful functions (where utility is determined by the users in the context of their goals); that learning about the users' situated needs requires observation and interaction rather than abstract analysis; and that—in the domain of human activity—scientific analysis may have limited value because clarity and stability are such rare phenomena.

This concern for the domain of use provides the framework for adaptive design, but it does not address the product-creation aspect of the paradigm. The implementation of computer artifacts requires a set of skills best characterized as the formal development of the computational models that constitute the product. For example, if a time-sharing system provides every desired user feature but lacks the robustness expected of a resource, it would be considered a poor system. It is the abstract, formal models of time-sharing systems (which are, of course, themselves abstract, formal models) that has led to the reliability and subsequent acceptance of time-sharing. The question is, How do we combine the informality that exists in-the-world with the formality that must be present in-the-computer?

Software relies on formality, and conceptual models must describe target products in-the-world. Therefore, adaptive design seeks to put a domain-oriented face on its formality. This introduces a family of new technical (and formal) problems driven by the need to express domain concepts within a formal representation scheme that is conceptual on the outside, but formal on the inside. Given such a scheme, what the designer perceives as conceptual, the environment will process as formal. When interacting with the conceptual model, the designer can sculpt the intended response to the need; when working in the domain of the underlying formalisms, the environment can transform the conceptual model into an efficient implementation.

Notice that this pursuit of an expressive representation scheme is very different from the objective of a CASE tool or software engineering environment (SEE). The CASE and SEE approach is to improve productivity by automating portions of the current software process; their goal is to refine the product-oriented process. In contrast, adaptive design seeks to move to a new era of design in which the essential process is automated. It goes beyond improving the present process, and it certainly goes beyond the kind of programming that CASE and SEE support.

From a traditional perspective, however, there is something paradoxical about adaptive design: It builds on existing formalisms but rejects existing software design methods. Let me clarify this apparent contradiction. The rules for operating with formalisms are reasonably well understood within computer science. What distinguishes the various types of formalisms from each other are the objects they are intended to represent. Historically, the earliest formalisms were created to represent models of computation and computer operations. These were the first of the programming languages. Since then formalisms have been introduced for assessing complexity, specifying abstract properties, and representing data and knowledge.

Adaptive design pushes this trend one step further to the description of a target system in-the-world. I defer until Chapter 11 any discussion of how this is accomplished, but I note here that this change in representation allows fundamental changes in method. Indeed, it is the desire to change the methods that is the motivation for the new representation scheme. It might, therefore, seem most logical to begin the discussion with a description of the new methods, but that proves to be very difficult to do. One of the complications of a paradigm shift is that those who are conversant with the old paradigm will try to understand the new paradigm in the old vocabulary. Consequently, the reader will tend to interpret a description of adaptive design's methods as specializations of commonly used methods in the product-oriented approach. To help overcome this barrier, the remainder of this chapter discusses the existing software methods. My intent is to explain how the present methods approach their objectives, how they complement each other, and how the methods are evolving.

10.2. Methodological Dilemmas

A method provides a set of rules and guidelines that establishes a routine sequence of activities for accomplishing some task. It provides a direction for activity, it suggests paths for progressing from step to step within the method, it offers a model for organizing knowledge, and it constrains the activity. The method imposes a style in the sense that Pye (1978) defines the term; it restricts and directs the designer's choices. We cannot design without some reliance on a method, whether it be maximize-fun-by-hacking or some more disciplined approach. No single method can support the design process fully, and designers must be proficient with several methods. Some methods will be domain specific (e.g., a performance analysis method); most will be standardized within the development and user communities to permit sharing and to encourage communication. The methods of interest for software development fall into two groups: those that seek to model aspects of the software as a response to some need, and those that guide the programming activity. Some methods are suitable for both goals. Because I am not interested in the task of programming, I shall consider only methods of the first type.

There are many methods. There also are different types of products, components, phases in the development process, and views of how software should be developed. Each project will use more than one method, and it is seldom that the methods used will share the same philosophical and logical orientation. Any incompatibility among methods within a project constitutes a methodological dilemma. The fact that successful project completions are routine implies that these dilemmas are resolved routinely. But this resolution seldom is selfconscious. By way of contrast, Mitroff and Mason (1981) describe a method they call *dialectical pragmatism* for resolving dilemmas in social situations; for instance, they might organize people into groups with shared, but opposing, views, and then set up a situation in which the groups are encouraged to synthesize a solution. Here, the awareness of the difference is used to lead to a resolution. In software engineering, however, we tend to ignore the existence of methodological dilemmas.

Software development methods are treated as products of the technology: rational, theory based, disciplined, and inherently integratable. We are encouraged to overlook contradiction and to accommodate diversity. Often, the motivation for the move to a new method is based on novelty or popularity (e.g., the move from "structured" to "object-oriented" analysis-design-programming). Indeed, the use of methods is so fluid that it is almost impossible to evaluate the impact of changes (Fenton 1993). Although the methods are intended to guide activities within the software process, there is a general recognition that the "existing models of the software development process do not provide enough insight into actual development processes to guide research on the most effective development technologies" Curtis, Krasner, Shen, and Iscoe 1987, p. 103). As a result, we often rely on management techniques to stabilize the process, thereby establishing the foundation for evaluating the improvement interventions (Humphrey 1989). That is, although we accept methods as a way to rationalize our approach to software development, we seldom approach methodology rationally.

In practice, perhaps the most common technique used by individuals to resolve the methodological dilemma is to "personalize" the method.

> Experienced designers—instead of following the rules and procedures of Structured Analysis—pick and choose among the various formalisms given in the method, adapt them for their own purposes, and integrate them into their own design processes. By using the tools in their own way and very often together with other, supplementary tools, the designers avoid or compensate for some of the method's deficiencies and limitations, especially with respect to describing the user-interface and the human-computer interaction. (Bansler and Bødker 1993, p. 189)

Although this pragmatic approach may be appropriate in some circumstances, it is not one to be recommended. A tool is intended to support a method (Musa 1983), and the method provides a context for the use of the tool and the interpretation of its products. Without a shared context, communication is compromised; without assuming a commitment to use a method, research in software methodology is trivialized.

The widespread failure to follow methods carefully should not be taken as a criticism of the software engineer's discipline; rather, it should be seen as a reflection of contradictions inherent within the process itself. Earlier I wrote of the central tension of the software process. That tension can manifest itself in many forms. For example, here are some of the many competing goals we find within the software process; the list is somewhat arbitrary, and it easily could be longer.

> *Problem and product.* I have used this contrast to characterize the underlying dilemma of software design. The process begins with a conceptual understanding of a need and concludes with the delivery of a formal, operational response to that need. That is, it begins with a problem and ends with a product. This places the designers in the dilemma of viewing their task as either one of looking out to the dynamic problem or stabilizing a solution within a requirements specification and then creating a product to satisfy that specification.

Lehman (1980) draws a distinction between *S*-Type programming (which develops programs that are correct in the mathematical sense to a fixed specification) and *E*-Type programming (which develops programs for use in the real world). In (1994) he states that for *E*-Type programs *"correctness* is meaningless" (p. 6); that is, the specification is not an invariant in the process.

Validity and correctness.   These are two independent quality attributes, and most methods favor a temporal division of their confirmation. That is, once we establish validity, the focus is on correctness. For example, in the LST model of the software process, the process begins with the assumption of a valid theory. All models of that theory must be correct, and each iteration of the process begins with a correct and valid theory. In this context, the validity obligation within an iteration restricts itself to the rejection of correct models that introduce permissive, but invalid behaviors (Lehman, Stenning, and Turski 1984). As we have seen, however, correctness is relative to the fixed criteria of the specification, and validity is subject of the dynamics and uncertainty of the problem space.

Formality and comprehension.   Clearly, the software process must produce formal models. However, where there is a poor cognitive fit between the concept and the formal model, the assessment of validity suffers and productivity is impaired. By way of illustration, the 1957 report on FORTRAN demonstrated how a change in the formal representation scheme improved comprehension, thereby reducing what would have been a 1000-statement problem to a 47-statement problem. When assembly language provided the only formal expression for solving the problem, the available formalism obscured the true nature of the problem. Too often, we rely on the perceived expressiveness of informality and tolerate formalisms that degrade comprehension. For example, Denning (1991) observes that the formal models of work based on extensions of the principles of Taylor biased the management of work, and he extends this analogy to models of software development. What we seek, of course, is a scheme that is both formal and that captures the concepts of interest.

Fun and tedium.   This is the tension between what people enjoy doing versus what must be done. Clearly, creativity is enhanced as we move to fun, while thoroughness and accuracy involve tedium. Often the context of work affects perceptions of fun and tedium. For instance, in Chapter 8 reference was made to the time spent on the unnecessary reformatting of reports, a task that would have been strongly resisted prior to the introduction of word processing.

Management and development. Management abstracts a project as a discrete model with events, and it associates development status with event status (Blum 1992a); in contrast, developers operate opportunistically and often find the events artificial. It follows, then, that one may model a management view of the process (Osterweil 1987), but not the process itself.

Hardware and software development models. The initial lack of experience in software development led to the adapting the technological design methods of hardware to software. This metaphor constrains experimentation and leads to invalid analogies such as that "code and debug" is a form of "fabrication," and that the "detailed design specification" is a kind of "engineering drawing." This affects both the conduct and management of development activities. We must gain the confidence to overcome our successful heritage (based on the hardware model) and exploit the unique properties of software.

Tradition and change. The software process is a socially determined activity, and its structure has evolved over time. All change entails risk, and management's first responsibility is to control risk. Where the risk is low, moves to a new technology (e.g., minicomputers and personal computers) and investments in ancillary tools (e.g., CASE, SEE, and developer training) are favored. In contrast, a paradigm shift implies social restructuring with a high risk (see Zuboff 1988). Thus, we must manage the tension between incremental, but minor changes, and the need for a fundamental restructuring.

Those who develop and analyze methods naturally recognize, and must respond to, these tensions. Each method begins with some (often implicit) model of the process and identifies a subset of activities to be supported. Although there is a general consensus that all design depends on domain understanding, most researchers hope to make their design methods domain independent so that they may be used in many different settings. That is, they wish to study *generic design* (Goel and Pirolli 1989). Dasgupta (1991), for instance, has undertaken a very ambitious programme to "construct a theory of the design process—an explanatory model—that (a) can serve to clarify and enhance our understanding of how computer systems are, or can be, designed; and (b) consequently, provides a theoretical basis for building methods and computer-aided tools for the design of such systems" (p. xiv). He hopes to establish a relationship between design, on the one hand, and mathematics and science, on the other. Naturally, if the relationship can be established, then our knowledge of the latter would permit the development of automated tools to support the former.

It should be clear from the earlier discussion that adaptive design also establishes such a relationship (albeit a far less formal one than that envisioned by Dasgupta). Nevertheless, even with automated support, there remains the problem of how to uncover the domain-specific information that must be formalized during the design activity. This aspect of the process engages those who request or will use the system, which introduces a class of problems that transcends the technology.

Bloomfield (1992) comments that there is a "tendency toward a proliferation of methodologies within the area of information systems.... [but] the root of the problem facing systems developers does not lie so much in the lack of the right method but, rather, [in the] sociologically impoverished views of management, and above all their own practices.... [The designers] are heterogenious engineers, simultaneously engineering or exercising control over people and artifacts. Given this we can suggest that if the development of information systems in organizations runs into difficulties it may not be because the so-called technical specialists have ignored vital social factors among users but that the assumptions about the social already inherent in their various approaches are flawed" (p. 204). That is, in the domain of social activity, the designers are not trained to recognize what they see.

Because both design and system interaction involve social processes, information system development itself must be seen as social action. Hirschheim, Klein, and Newman (1991) pursue this thesis with the examination of four case studies and modestly conclude that "our perspective is more of a *descriptive* tool that a *prescriptive* one. Its strength lies in its ability to describe and 'make sense' of the systems development process" (p. 603). Illustrations of the failure to adopt a social action perspective include the manipulation of users to achieve consensus and the evaluation of system success based solely on technical criteria. They regard their strategy an alternative to that proposed by DeMarco (1978):

> Political problems aren't going to go away and they won't be "solved." The most we can hope for is to limit the effect of disruption due to politics. Structured analysis approaches this objective by making analysis procedures more formal. (p. 13)

Here is the dilemma of the separation of concerns as proposed by DeMarco in the 1970s. Can we draw a boundary around the problem to exclude all but the technical issues? If not, does that imply that the system development process must resolve all of the sponsoring organization's political conflicts? In part, of course, it depends upon the system to be designed. If the system is well defined and stable, a rational definition of the design is recommended. For open and dynamic problems, on the other hand, participative design may offer a better path to the settlement of outstanding issues affecting design. Incidently, the data-flow diagram, as a tool, may be useful in either situation.

Checkland (1981) distinguishes between methods based on work in "hard" and "soft" systems. In a hard system, "problems can be expressed as the search for an efficient means of reaching a defined objective or goal; once goals or objectives are defined, then systematic appraisal of alternatives, helped by various techniques, enables the problem (now one of selection) to be solved" (Checkland, cited by Miles 1985, p. 57). The hard systems tradition assumes that the world is made up of systems that can be identified and examined, and that this reality may be approached systematically.

Miles (1985) points out that the hard systems paradigm embodies a means-end schema, and that the analyst must conform to this means-end schema. In contrast, he claims, programmers are concerned only with means and not ends. "One of the continuing frustrations of the programmer's lot is that at a later point someone, frequently the analyst, comes along and changes the ends" (p. 62). The proposed alternative is to move to a "soft systems paradigm" that recognizes that imposed solutions may be invalid and that the analyst can proceed in the absence of a definition (Checkland and Scholes 1990). Indeed, Couger (1990) points out that delaying the convergence on a solution permits more alternatives and solutions to be generated and evaluated, which often leads to a better and more creative solution. Such an approach, of course, defers issues of correctness.

Olerup (1991) explores the dilemma by contrasting the formal information systems development method proposed by Langefors (1966) with Alexander's (1964/1971) approach to architectural design.

> The Langeforsian approach is goal-directed while Alexander's approach is oriented towards removing misfits. Despite differences in subject matter, the two approaches are similar in many respects, which suggests that they have both been influenced by a movement towards rationality in design.... Since the essential feature of a[n Alexanderian] systems-fit approach is design as an ongoing process, having procedural rationality and involving active participation, such an approach is appropriate when design problems are not well understood. Goal-centered approaches [such as those of Langefors] have been successful in well-understood situations but not when design situations are not well understood. (p. 24)

He goes on to point out that much work remains and that both approaches are "far from being well understood." Thus there is no synthesis, only alternatives that seem to be merging.

Olerup's use of architecture as a foil to the formal approach to software development is very different from my use of the architect metaphor in contrast to the sculptor metaphor of the previous chapter. For me, architecture (and the manual construction of any large, technical product) requires a two-step process, which I seek to avoid. Nevertheless, architecture has become a powerful metaphor for those seeking alternatives to the present design process. For example, Denning and Dargan (1994) seek a discipline for software development and claim

> that the missing discipline is neither software engineering nor software design, but software architecture.... [We also claim] that an ontology of design is needed to bring the two fields together; neither has such now. (An ontology is a conceptual framework for interpreting the world in terms of recurrent actions.) Software engineers see design as a process of gathering requirements into a formal specification and then organizing the software production process, and the software, to meet specifications efficiently and economically. Software designers see design as a collection of practices that can only be verbalized as aphorisms and rules of thumb; design is satisfactory only when a client says it is. (pp. 56-57)

They use the architect's blueprint as I use the sculptor's work-in-progress. "Working from sketches and interviews, the architect must come to understand the interest of the client including form, function, social relations, styles of those who will use the building, efficiency, and affordability. This understanding is manifested in the blueprint. The same blueprint conveys sufficient information that the building contractor can calculate the time, materials, and costs to assemble the structure.... At present, the fields of software design and engineering have no method of mapping analogous to the blueprint" (pp. 59-60).

> The key to transforming software design and engineering into a single discipline is the development of a method of mapping that would be simultaneously intelligible to clients, designers, and engineers. The function of a map is to enable the parties to navigate the territory depicted by the map and to coordinate their actions. (p. 60)

As I will demonstrate in the next chapter, adaptive design utilizes such a map (i.e., the conceptual model). Moreover, because the environment

I use also automates the implementation process, the "blueprint" becomes an as-built specification, and the behavior of the system becomes simultaneously intelligible by allowing the clients, designers, and engineers to experiment with it.

Although Denning, Dargan, and I share a common interpretation of the need, we offer different interpretations of the solution.   Their method is based on a language/action approach to design (Erickson 1993) derived from the earlier work of Winograd and Flores (1986). "All design embodies an ontology, a set of constitutive distinctions, of the domain in which design is an intervention.... The ontology in which we are designing is one of action happening through language" (Flores, Graves, Hartfield, and Winograd 1988, p. 171).   For Denning and Dargan (1994), the "discipline of software architecture would be capable of training its practitioners to systematically fulfill promises to build and install software systems that are judged useful and dependable by their customers" (p. 62), and language plays a central role in the mapping of that understanding.   The goal is shifted from one of "meeting specs" to that of "satisfying the customer."   Denning (1992c) reframes "the question 'What is software quality?' to 'How do we satisfy the customers of our software?'" (p. 13).

One can distinguish three levels at which a customer can declare satisfaction:

1. *All basic promises were fulfilled....*
2. *No negative consequences were produced....*
3. *The customer is delighted.* (pp. 13-14)

Even though we may accept this reframing as intuitively obvious, it is less clear how our traditional methods and tools can guide us. That is, the current state of the technology leaves us only with agreement about the nature of the problem and "aphorisms and rules of thumb" for its solution.

Lehman (1994) starts with a similar observation about quality: "The criterion of *E*-Type acceptability is *user satisfaction* with each program execution" (p. 6). In an earlier paper he defines an uncertainty principle for computer application:

The outcome, in the real world, of software system operation is inherently uncertain with the precise area of uncertainty also not knowable. (1991, p. 248).

This uncertainty can be reduced only by learning through feedback. Denning (1992b) notes that such feedback operates within a network.

Work is a closed-loop process in which a performer completes actions leading to the satisfaction of a customer's or client's request. In carrying out the work agreed to, a performer becomes the customer of others, who agree in turn to take on pieces of work. In this way a network of performers and customers comes into play for the fulfillment of the original request. (p. 314)

Medina-Mora, Winograd, Flores, and Flores (1992) build on this model in their exploration of management technology.

Floyd (1991) writes of closing the software development process.

The viability of a design decision is determined through its evaluation. Where feedback is permitted from the evaluation to the design process, we have *closure*, the results of design again forming the basis for its further development. Successful design is marked by a stabilization of the web of design decisions through revisions. (p. 88)

Lehman builds on this closed-loop concept by dividing the software process into two parts: the forward path elements of design and development and the feedback paths. He concludes that, in general, "changes to forward path elements of the software process cannot be expected to produce major global improvement unless accompanied by commensurate change to related feedback mechanisms. Software process improvement must therefore be pursued in the context of the total process domain" (1994, p. 8). He credits the following innovations with representing successful feedback: inspection, reviews, prototyping, incremental and evolutionary development, and software process measurement. He argues, moreover, that most current process modeling approaches tend to divert attention from, and even hide, global process activities and properties, and even more importantly, "feedback effects." That is, the local improvement from the use of a method may be of limited benefit from the total process, or global, point of view. For instance, I believe that the use of CASE tools primarily for the creation of attractive diagrams (which prove difficult to maintain and change) can act as a barrier to learning and refinement.

How do we currently manage this feedback when there is an operational system that must be modified to accommodate what has been learned? Denning and Dargan (1994) interviewed the designers of several award-winning software packages. "All the designers said they did not pay much attention to software engineering methodology. Several said that the internal structure of their code is ugly and is not well modularized. When fixing bugs they make patches; when the system gets too patchy, they declare the next version and reengineer it completely" (p. 61). This is a modification of what Brooks (1975) referred to as throwing one away. It is an expensive recognition that the learning artifacts can be removed only through clarifying the acquired knowledge within a new system. In an analysis of the impact of modern methods on the maintenance of information systems (IS), Dekieva (1992) came to the following conclusions.

> This study provides no evidence that modern IS analysis methodologies decreases the overall time and cost of maintenance. However, the times spent on various maintenance activities do change. Systems developed with modern methodologies are apparently more reliable and require repairs less frequently.... After the first year it [the maintenance effort] grows and surpasses the time required to maintain systems developed with traditional systems. (pp. 370-71)

What happens is that the maintenance team must respond to more complex requests for changes. When "traditional" development methods had been used, changes were made by patching, and the scope of the accepted change requests was functionally constrained. The use of modern methods creates better structures that enable more complex changes. But the technology still restricts the amount of change that can be tolerated. "Larger numbers of changes are requested, but a lower number of changes is implemented" (p. 371). In maintenance we can observe the essential role of feedback in the process, but we also see how the technology restricts the extent of the responses to the feedback. Our choices seem to be to patch, to select a few of the many requests, or to reengineer and throw the old one away. As I will show in the final chapters, there is a better alternative.

It seems that the discussion of software design methods has brought us back to the subject of the previous chapter: the software process. Either I am poorly organized or the topic is not easily compartmentalized (or both). Let me justify my meanderings by claiming that one cannot understand the parts without a knowledge of the whole, and vice versa. Greenbaum and Mathiassen (1987) have a report whose title speaks for itself, "Zen and the Art of Teaching Systems Development." The field is just not neat, and rational explanations hide as much as they describe. Although the development process involves a great deal of documentation, Glass, Vessey, and Conger (1992) have analyzed the tasks within the process and conclude that they contain more intellectual than clerical activity.

When engaged in intellectual activity, the designers must develop goals and make choices. In a frequently cited study, Weinberg and Schulman (1974) showed how products varied with different optimizing objectives (i.e., completion time, program size, data space used, program clarity, and user-friendly output). Even though each group was able to rank first for its given objective, it suffered by comparison with respect to the other criteria. Thus, early interpretations of the goals (and their context) will have profound impacts on the resultant products. Marca and McGowan (1993) suggest that the designers' world view leads them to favor different specification approaches, which will lead to different designs, and Kumar and Bjørn-Anderson (1990) have studied variations due to national or cultural biases. The obvious conclusion is that, as a human enterprise, software design will be subject to considerable variability and spontaneity.

Despite all these conflicts and contradictions, we still develop complex and reliable systems routinely, and we use methods to support that endeavor. So, perhaps it is best to accept the fact that the methodological dilemmas are unavoidable and unresolvable and to conclude, therefore, that we can use the principle of "separation of concerns" to hide the need for synthesis. In their analysis of the human and organizational issues in information systems development, Hornby, et al. (1992) assess the current state:

> To summarize, our findings suggest that no single method covers all phases of the life-cycle. Coverage of human and organizational issues is patchy in the mainstream technical methods. Users of the methods may get a prompt to consider an issue but little guidance on how to do it.... Methods explicitly covering the human and organizational issues are very much in minority usage. Analysts do not use methods according to the idealized descriptions contained in their manuals ... Furthermore, analysts do not generally consider human issues to be their responsibility and, even when they do, they tend to rate them fairly low on their list of priorities. (p. 166)

Thus, I acknowledge the limitations of the current design methods and restrict the subsequent analysis to an examination of their technical properties.

10.3. A Taxonomy of Design Methods

To provide a context for the analysis of the software design methods, I shall construct a taxonomy for them. Although a taxonomy is defined to be either the study of the general principles of scientific classification or an orderly classification of plants and animals according to their presumed natural relationships, the word has been used for categorizations of methods for user interface design (Bødker 1991b) and requirements analysis (Davis 1988). I follow in this tradition. My taxonomy employs a framework with two dimensions. First, I consider the goal of the method. Methods that concentrate on producing a better understanding of the problem and its proposed solution are called *problem-oriented* methods, and those that center on the correct transformation from a formal specification into a maintainable implementation are called *product-oriented* methods. Many methods will claim to support both orientations, and I make somewhat arbitrary decisions in my assignments. The intent is to establish a general pattern, not to describe specific methods.

A problem-oriented method lacks all criteria for establishing correctness. Its users can apply domain formalisms to determine (1) what is consistent with previously accepted assertions and (2) what is clearly in error. But these are domain formalisms, and they relate only to what should be in the specification. For methods with a formal model (e.g., a software requirements specification), the modelers may reason about the correctness of their solution with respect to that formal model. The more powerful the formal model, the better the tools for reasoning about correctness. Because problem-oriented methods have no formal models for the proposed solution, they can only reason about the validity and consistency of their models. (For example, one can process a data-flow diagram to discover syntactic errors automatically, but evaluations of the diagram's validity will be subjective.)

It follows, therefore, that problem-oriented methods will exhibit properties in a form tailored to human comprehension. They capture and record concepts. Their value lies in their ability to describe, to reduce detail (i.e., to abstract), to communicate, and to document accepted decisions. Product-oriented methods, when formal, add to these features the ability to reason logically about the model and its extensions. Because the software process always culminates in the creation of a formal model, formal models are a necessary part of the process. Clearly, it is to our advantage to have formal models as early in the process as possible. A potential shortcoming of the formal model is that it may not help the designers reason about validity. Thus, a problem-oriented method, when dealing with an open problem, may have limited use for a formal model, whereas the same method, when applied to a closed problem, may find formal models most effective. And this suggests the second dimension of the framework matrix: type of model—conceptual or formal.

Conceptual models often reference domain formalisms, and most conceptual models have some degree of formality (if only syntactic). In some cases the conceptual and formal models are isomorphic. As these terms are used in the framework, they relate only to the software product to be created. Conceptual (descriptive) models offer guidelines for design decisions and validation; formal (prescriptive) models establish criteria for acceptance and correctness. The conceptual models describe an external reality, and the formal models prescribe the behavior of the software product being developed. The matrix in Figure 10.1 identifies the four method categories to be considered.

Briefly, the characteristics of these four categories are as follows:

Quadrant I methods are concerned with developing an understanding of the problem to be solved (i.e., how the identified need will be addressed) and expressing solutions in a form that can be reasoned about by domain specialists. Database conceptual models, such as the entity-relationship model, are instances of this category.

Quadrant II methods help transform nonimplementation concepts into implementation decisions. Techniques, such as structured design, that guide in the modularization of a system illustrate this category. They transform an unstructured conceptual model of a system into a collection of implementable units with their interfaces.

Quadrant III methods aim at representing properties of the problem to be solved in ways that facilitate reasoning about both the problem and its solution. Instances of these methods include problem-oriented programming languages (e.g., the use of FORTRAN for a small computational problem) and formal methods for abstract problems (e.g., the use of a formalism for reasoning about the security of an operating system).

Quadrant IV methods are used to create correct implementation units, typically called modules. Examples include programs, packages, and objects.

If one were to create this matrix a decade earlier, there is little doubt that one of the dimensions would be labeled data-structure oriented versus data-flow oriented. This was how the methods were categorized at the time. Thus, the reader should be aware that my classification is somewhat arbitrary, and many alternatives are possible.

	Problem Oriented	Product Oriented
Conceptual	I	II
Formal	III	IV

Fig. 10.1. Matrix of method categories.

10.4. A Brief Survey of Design Methods

The most cohesive way to classify the methods is to identify representative samples in the context of their development. In what follows, I summarize the principal characteristics only briefly. Elsewhere (Blum 1992a) I provide more complete explanations illustrated with a common example. I begin with the description by Dijkstra (1968a) of his experience with "THE"-Multiprogramming System. Concerned with being able to isolate faults in the program from problems with the equipment, he chose to design the system "in such a way that its logical soundness can be proved a priori and its implementation can admit to exhaustive testing" (p. 432). His method employed *levels of abstraction*, in which the system design was described in layers such that higher levels could use the services of lower levels, but lower levels could not access higher levels. The lowest level was implemented first, and it provided a *virtual machine* for the implementation of the next level. The process continued until the highest level was completed.

Whereas the levels of abstraction could be called a bottom-up technique, *stepwise refinement*, introduced by Wirth (1971), represented a top-down technique. Originally described in a pedagogic illustration of the programming process, the method was quickly adopted as a standard approach for procedural abstraction. One constructs a graph of the target program and defers the detailing of selected nodes as refinement steps. Here was an alternative to dealing with one big program (or system); one worked in units of manageable size and abstracted potentially large processes as procedures for later development. The technique paralleled how hardware was decomposed into components, which in turn were further decomposed, until the units were simple enough to be designed and fabricated. The process, at the system level, also is called *functional decomposition*.

Both these methods deal with the issue of how to divide a large unit into smaller parts, which may be constructed, tested, and subsequently combined. I call this issue *modularization*, and, as I will explain, it is a major consideration in many design methods. For example, Stevens, Myers, and Constantine (1974) defined the term *structured design* as a "set of proposed general program design considerations and techniques for making coding, debugging, and modification easier, faster, and less expensive by reducing complexity" (p. 115). The work represented the culmination of almost a decade of research by Constantine, who "observed that programs that were the easiest to implement and change were those composed of simple, independent modules" (p. 116). The concepts of *coupling* and *cohesion* were introduced to assess the internal structure of and connections between modules, and the *structure chart*—along with a set of design guidelines for its use—were employed to depict the relationships among the modules in a system.

At about the same time, Parnas (1972a) described a different criterion for decomposing systems based on the principle of *information hiding*. Two alternative modularizations were offered for a simple application. The first utilized the criterion of well-defined interfaces (as advocated in structured design), and the second was guided by the principle of information hiding (derived, in part, from Dijkstra's levels of abstraction). Although both worked well, the first proved difficult to maintain; changes often affected all the modules. On the other hand, "every module in the second decomposition is characterized by its knowledge of a design decision which it hides from all others. Its interface or definition was chosen to reveal as little as possible about its inner workings" (p. 1056). In part, the difference between the two modularization approaches was that the first was based on a pragmatic reaction to operational experience, whereas the second was working toward an underlying formalism for modularization.

I already have mentioned Dijkstra's paper about levels of abstraction. His most dramatic impact on software production, however, came as the result of a letter to the editor published earlier in that year, "Go To Statement Considered Harmful" (1968b). The immediate result was a debate on GOTO-less programs and the concept of *structured programming*. Often lost in this discussion was the rationale for the elimination of GOTOs: one could reason better about the dynamics of the program's execution if one localized the scope of control. In his letter, Dijkstra identified Hoare and Wirth as the earliest proponents of restricting the use of the GOTO, and these three computer scientists led the way in linking the creation of programs to the mathematical principles of the programming languages that expressed them. Labeled *proofs of correctness*, the approach looks to the assertions that are assumed to be true before and after a sequence of operations and then chooses operations so one can prove that, if the preconditions are true and the process terminates, then the postconditions will be true. In effect, one writes the program by selecting a sequence of assertions and then providing the operations that will guarantee each outcome (i.e., each intermediate postcondition). The annotated program is actually the proof; one does not first write a program and then prove it to be correct (see Gries 1981).

The concept of formal proofs implied a concern for the notations used in specifications. As we have seen, without formality, there is no concept of correctness. In another paper, Parnas (1972b) described a technique for software module specification. The goals of this scheme bear repeating:

1. The specification must provide to the intended user *all* the information that he will need to use the program correctly, *and nothing more*.

2. The specification must provide to the implementer, *all* the information about the intended use that he needs to complete the program, and *no additional information*; in particular, no information about the structure of the calling program should be conveyed. (p. 330)

Two additional goals were (3) that the scheme should be formal, so that machine testing for consistency would be possible, and (4) that the specification should be understandable by user and implementer alike. He illustrated his approach with a module for processing a stack.

All that you need to know about a stack in order to use it is specified there. There are countless possible implementations (including a large number of sensible ones). The implementation should be free to vary without changing the using programs. If the programs assume no more about a stack than is stated above, that will be true. (p. 332)

Liskov and Zilles (1975) included Parnas' example in their review of specification techniques for data abstraction. They described their goal this way, "What we are looking for is a process which establishes that a program correctly implements a *concept* which exists in someone's mind" (p. 7). The concept they used in their illustration was the stack, and five different techniques were described. Their description of the *algebraic specification* has become accepted widely as a model for the *abstract data type*.

As we see, by the first half of the 1970s computer science had established the principles of proofs of correctness (based on the use of preconditions and postconditions), information hiding (best described as the first two of Parnas's specification goals), alternatives for procedural abstraction (both top down and bottom up), data abstraction, and an enumeration of properties for a good (and formal) specification. The next major thrust came in the form of alternatives to the text-based requirements documentation. The adjective of choice for the 1970s was "structured," and several variations of *structured analysis* were introduced (Ross and Schoman 1977, DeMarco 1978, Gane and Sarson 1979). The form that employed the data-flow diagram—derived from the notation of structured design—came to dominate the workplace. As described by DeMarco (1978), the purpose of the data-flow diagram (DFD) "was to *divide the system into pieces* in such a way that the pieces were reasonably independent, and to *declare the interfaces among the pieces*" (p. 95). This approach to functional decomposition paralleled Wirth's stepwise refinement except that, whereas the DFD modeled the application domain using a descriptive notation, stepwise refinement operated in the formal domain of a programming language. DeMarco relied on the modeler's intuition. "With a DFD, you have the opportunity to absorb the information in parallel; not to *read it*, but to *see it*" (p. 95).

By the mid 1970s, there was a broad acceptance of the fact that one of the greatest barriers to effective system development was the inability to establish valid requirements, and, moreover, that the concept of a textual requirements document was deeply flawed. Teichroew and Hershey (1977) wrote, "It is widely accepted that documentation is a weak link in system development in general and in logical system design in particular" (p. 43). They proposed a computer-aided documentation technique, PSL/PSA, that would maintain and produce portions of the project documentation. Here, a conceptual model was formalized and analyzed for deficiencies (e.g., incompleteness and inconsistency). Unfortunately, the conceptual model was not bound to the subsequent formal models. Thus, the automated records served as a nonintegrated adjunct to the delivered system; one could change the conceptual model without affecting the formal model and vice versa. Most CASE tools still share this deficiency.

Given the cost of computing in this time period, it is not surprising that there were relatively few attempts to develop automated tools to support the process. Most techniques aimed at developing richer conceptual models through the use of diagrammatic conventions. For instance, Chen (1976) introduced an appealing notation, the entity-relationship model (ERM), for analyzing information systems. Derived from work in semantic data modeling, whose origins can be traced to concepts developed within the artificial intelligence community (see Hull and King 1987; Peckham and Maryanski 1988), the ERM achieved broad and rapid acceptance. In fact, the ongoing series of annual international ERM conferences began five years after the initial paper's publication. Clearly, the software community was sensitive to the difficulty of conceptual modeling and was responsive to pragmatic, intuitive alternatives to the written word. Many other diagramming techniques were introduced, but only a few, such as the state-transition diagram (STD) and the Petri net (see Murata 1989), gained broad acceptance.

As already noted, structured analysis was a method for functional decomposition; data were documented in the context of how they flowed from process to process (i.e., as process interfaces). Others, however, believed that more effective conceptual models could be developed if one modeled the structure of the data rather than its flow—hence the distinction between the data-structure and data-flow orientations. Warnier developed methods for the logical construction of programs (1975) and the logical construction of systems (1981). The latter work began with the following principle.

Any collection of data constitutes a set in the sense defined and utilized in mathematical theory.

Once this axiom is accepted, every set of data in a system should be precisely defined.

Then, the various sets related to a particular problem can be manipulated through classical logical operations in order to comply with the needs that arise during the data organization. (p. 1)

That is, if one could define the data used by an organization, the use of that data could be derived logically from the definitions. One rationale for this data-structure orientation was that the structure of an organization's data was more stable than the procedures carried out by the organization. Therefore, a data-structure oriented conceptual model would be a more accurate description of the problem domain; it also would be less subject to change (and therefore easier to modify).

Jackson (1975) introduced a variation of this data-structure theme in his program design methodology, which is called JSP. The program, he noted, is a transformation from an input to an output. If one modeled the structure of the input and the output, then one could use those models to determine the best structure for the program. Where the input and output data structures were similar, the structure of the program could be composed from them; methods also were given to deal with structure clashes. JSP introduced a formal (and diagrammatic) notation, and the method was rigorous enough so that, for certain applications, different designers would produce equivalent programs for the same problem.

The Jackson System Development method (JSD), introduced some time later, used the same diagrams, but in a very different way (Jackson 1982). In JSD, one models the relevant properties of the application domain (i.e., the real world) and then derives the software structure from that model. One begins by identifying the entities of interest and the actions on them (an idea also used with an object orientation). Each entity is modeled as a sequential process, and then the individual processes are joined together into a network. Additional processes (e.g., produce a report) may be added to the network, and finally the network is converted into a control hierarchy for implementation. The result is a system design whose structure conforms to that of the external reality.

The models produced by JSD sometimes are considered operational in that they provide a mechanism to reason about the behavior of the system in a given state (Zave 1984). Another way of employing formality is through the use of a formal specification language (see Cohen, Harwood, and Jackson 1986). By way of illustration, the Vienna Development Method (VDM), developed during the 1970s at the IBM Vienna Research Laboratories, is based on denotational semantics, often used for programming language definition (Jones 1980). As its name suggests, VDM provides both formal notations and methods for their use. A model-based approach, it models the input, output, and state of the system as well as the operations and functions that manipulate the data. As with the proof of correctness assertions, all operations are defined in the context of their preconditions and postconditions. There is more than a decade of operational experience with VDM, and—although it takes time to train the development team—the projects are characterized by low error rates and high productivity (Bjørner 1987).

The origins of object-oriented programming (OOP) also can be traced back to the late 1960s and early 1970s. Many of the basic principles were explored by Dahl and Nygaard in Simula 67 and subsequently extended by the efforts of Kay, Goldberg, and Ingalls in the development of Smalltalk-76 and Smalltalk-80. Today, for a language to qualify as an OOP language, it is expected to support four properties: information hiding, data abstraction, dynamic binding, and inheritance. Meyer (1988) describes OOP in the context of modularization with a shift in the focus of design. "Ask not what the system does; ask WHAT it does it to." (p. 50). In a sense, this suggests a data-structure orientation, except that here we are concerned with implementation units (i.e., modules) and not conceptual models.

OOP modularizes by identifying the data (i.e., the object, which is defined by a class within an inheritance structure) and binds the operations to the object. In contrast, the procedural view organizes the module as a control structure for statement sequences and then declares the data structures necessary for processing. In OOP, information hiding establishes how modules interact with each other, data abstraction provides the framework for defining the objects and the operations on them, dynamic binding permits polymorphism and the run-time creation of objects (i.e., instances of a class), and inheritance reduces complexity by eliminating redundancy. The key contribution of OOP, of course, is that this modularization approach is supported by the language and run-time environment.

The apparent benefits of OOP quickly lead to other methods based on the concept of an object. Object-oriented design (OOD) was popularized by Booch in the early 1980s. At the time, his primary interest was the Ada programming language, which supported abstract data types. He believed software engineering with Ada required new design methods to exploit Ada's encapsulation features (Booch 1983). In a later paper Booch (1986) described the goal of OOD as follows: "Each module in the system denotes an object or class of objects from the problem space" (p. 213). His diagrammatic notation was designed to map these objects into Ada program packages.

The initial focus of Booch's OOD was the establishment of new criteria for the organization of the system structure into modules. His method was not comprehensive; he advocated the use of techniques such as structured analysis prior to the initialization of the OOD activity. In time, Booch (1991) came to develop a more comprehensive set of methods, which ceased to rely on the properties of Ada. There are, of course, many other proponents of OOD; some describe methods for building conceptual models of a system that may be implemented using any modern programming language, and others concentrate on the development of applications using an OOP.

Methods also were introduced to apply the object-oriented paradigm to analysis, and it will be instructive to examine the object-oriented analysis (OOA) proposed by Coad and Yourdon (1991). Yourdon was one of the initial developers and advocates of structured analysis and structured design. Indeed, he was instrumental in its widespread acceptance. His early view of structured analysis was that of functional decomposition. One identified processes and their interfaces and depicted these relationships in DFDs. Descriptions of the data in the flow were preserved in a data dictionary, and—once the functions had been reduced to a manageable size—the processes were described in *minispecs*. Over time, however, Yourdon's view of structured analysis changed. As the method was adapted to meet the demands of real-time systems, environmental and behavioral models were introduced that relied on DFDs, the ERM, events, and STDs (Ward and Mellor 1985, 1986).

Soon after this, Yourdon (1989) wrote a book presenting what he called "modern structured analysis." He abandoned many of his earlier ideas and augmented his method with other modeling techniques, such as the ERM and STD. His intent was to create better models of the external reality, even if this obscured the purity of the initial structured analysis approach. One year later, Yourdon coauthered a book on OOA, which abandoned the tenets of structured analysis in favor of a new, five-step process: (1) identify the classes and objects, (2) determine their structure, (3) organize the classes and objects into subjects (which reduces the clutter of diagrams), (4) define the attributes (i.e., the class and object internal structures), and (5) define the services (i.e., the operations on the classes and objects). The idea of functional decomposition had been subsumed by the goal of modeling real-world objects, and a method for structuring modules had evolved into a guideline for requirements analysis. For a comparative study of OOA and OOD methods, see van der Goor, Hong, and Brinkkemper (1992).

How can one bring order to this complex interplay of concepts? In the mid 1970s, when DeMarco and Yourdon first were disseminating their methods for systems analysis and design, there seemed to be two alternatives. One could focus on either the data flow or on the data structure within what were, at the time, predominately information system applications. The method creators were reacting to a poorly managed, document-driven environment in which diagrammatic conventions reduced the volume and improved both understanding and communication. As the technology advanced and the applications grew in complexity, these solutions of the 1970s evolved. In his overview of JSD, Cameron (1986) describes and contrasts the design alternatives in terms of decomposition and composition.

> The idea of top-down decomposition (or stepwise refinement) is to develop software by successive decomposition....
> The difficulty is this. That first box marked "system" is largely unknown, yet the first decomposition is a commitment to a system structure; the commitment has to be made from a position of ignorance. This dilemma is repeated at successive levels; the designer's ignorance decreases only as the decisions become less critical....
> The alternative is to develop software by composition. Instead of starting with a single box marked "system" we start with a blank piece of paper. Each increment added is precisely defined; an increment is any abstraction of the whole, not necessarily just a component of the whole; part of the system may have to be restructured, repackaged, or transformed in order to compose it with another part; at intermediate stages there is a well-defined incomplete system rather than an ill-defined complete system. (p. 157)

In effect, the choice becomes one of modeling the problem domain so that one may compose the system from that model or modeling the system while using decomposition to manage the details. Our subjective conceptual models are problem oriented. They define and organize ideas so that they can be transformed into a formal model, and in that sense their use can be considered an outside-in approach. The formal models, on the other hand, establish the objective criteria for the acceptance of the product. Because of their mathematical foundations, they must operate in a top-down fashion in that lower level decisions are constrained by higher level assertions. And this returns us to the fundamental tension within the software process: between the subjective and the objective, between the holistic mental view and the rigorous formal model, between the problem and the product. The first describes what is needed, the second ensures that what was requested is delivered. As the essential model of the software process illustrates, we always begin with the first (i.e., the subjective, descriptive, mental, conceptual model) and end up with the latter (i.e., the objective, prescriptive, rigorous, formal model).

10.5. The Design Method Taxonomy

This section integrates the analysis of the previous two sections in which I established the framework for the taxonomy and identified the principal design methods. Figure 10.2 assigns the principal methods just discussed to one of the four framework categories. Some of these assignments, as already confessed, are debatable. And there are other problems with this categorization as well. Several of the methods are dominated by the representation scheme they support (e.g., there is not a "data abstraction" method, but there are methods for employing data abstraction). Despite the division into conceptual and formal, all methods rely on textual support for explanation (e.g., the process specification in systems analysis and the use of comments in the code for an object). Finally, we must acknowledge that even when a method is formal, its formality does not imply that it will be used formally (e.g., one can use OOP without being rigorous about the consistency of the operations on the objects). Therefore, the display in Figure 10.2 should be seen as a basis for discussion rather than a definitive classification.

	Problem oriented	Product oriented
Conceptual	I Structured analysis Entity-relationship model Logical construction of systems Modern structured analysis Object-oriented analysis	II Structured design Object-oriented design
Formal	III PSL/PSA JSD VDM	IV Levels of abstraction Stepwise refinement Proof of correctness Data abstraction JSP Object-oriented programming

Fig. 10.2. A classification of design methods.

Before analyzing the contents of the figure, some explanation of the assignment strategy is necessary. Quadrant I, problem-oriented conceptual methods, does not require much justification. Most of these methods use a diagrammatic notation to model the application domain and the target system. I have not considered them formal because none is intended to prescribe aspects of the implementation. This assertion can be debated. For example, the entity-relationship model can be used to construct a normalized logical database design, and both structured analysis and object-oriented analysis can establish the major components in the design. I consider them conceptual, however, because the subsequent design *need not* conform to the implications of the conceptual model. Moreover, the models produced in this quadrant normally are used to establish the formal requirements, not to embody the implementation that realizes the requirements.

Both methods shown in Quadrant II, product-oriented conceptual methods, are concerned with the modularization of the implementation. As previously described, two distinct orientations are suggested: first define the processes and then define the data structures that support them, or first define the data structures and then identify the operations on them. I have included object-oriented design as a conceptual model because the resulting design can be implemented in a language that is not an object-oriented programming language (e.g., OOD can be used for languages that only support abstract data types). The design simply guides the implementation but does not mandate it.

Quadrant III includes three examples. No justification for VDM is necessary, but an explanation is needed for the other two. PSL/PSA was included because of its intent, not because of what it accomplished. This intent was to retain key aspects of the system design in a database, which could be checked against the implementation from the time of initial analysis through delivery. Although this database contained only surrogates for the system components, it did represent an early attempt to automate a formal dimension of the software process. The inclusion of JSD in this quadrant is a little more difficult to explain. It was included because (1) it does rely on some formal modeling tools and (2) it is an instance of an operational specification, and there are formal operational specifications that clearly belong in this quadrant.

Quadrant IV, product-oriented formal methods, should arouse little controversy. Each represents a formally based method for constructing modules. These methods are not independent; for example, it would be reasonable to combine levels of abstraction with proof of correctness or stepwise refinement with proof of correctness. Because the formality of JSP is less rigorous than that of, say, object-oriented programming, it is possible that individual designers will apply JSP as if it were an informal method belonging to Quadrant II. In contrast, data abstraction or object-oriented programming reduce to a formal representation (i.e., the source code input to the compiler). Most of the methods in this quadrant are supported by automated tools; in some cases there also are integrated, comprehensive environments that support the methods (either individually or in combination).

The design methods in Figure 10.2 tend to cluster in two quadrants: the Quadrant I problem-oriented conceptual methods that help establish how the software will respond to the need and the Quadrant IV product-oriented formal methods that concentrate on the modular structure of the implementation. This is consistent with the essential model of the software process. There are two categories of model, and this corresponds to the two families of design methods. It also is consistent with the brief history of computing. First, we focused on how to write programs, and then we extended the power of our implementation tools, which, by definition, were formal and product oriented. Starting in the 1970s, we also began to seek methods to establish the requirements and the initial design criteria for the target system. Here we relied on less formal diagrammatic techniques (i.e., conceptual models) to document the problem and its solution.

Although the distribution in Figure 10.2 should not come as a surprise, there is a question of its appropriateness. That is, will progress be served if we continue to improve the methods in these two quadrants, or should we redirect our efforts? It should be clear that I favor a shift to problem-oriented approach that relies on formal models (which must also be conceptual). I believe that every problem-oriented formal method should have the following three properties:

The formalisms used must be able to model the concepts of primary concern during the very early stages of the software process. Here the emphasis is on the ability of the representation scheme to support reasoning about correctness.

The notation must be effective for reasoning about the class of problems under consideration. This implies that the formal notation should communicate application domain concepts clearly among all stakeholders.

These formalisms must be comprehensive in that they can establish the correctness of every behavioral aspect of the system at each level of detail. That is, there should be no discontinuities that break the formal reasoning chain.

Reviewing the three examples in Quadrant III, we see that PSL/PSA does not satisfy fully any of the criteria, that JSD does not satisfy the third criteria, and that VDM satisfies all three criteria for *relatively closed problems*. For *relatively open problems*, however, JSD offers a far more powerful modeling approach. Thus, for certain well-defined problems, a formal specification language, such as that used by VDM, can be very effective. But, as I have pointed out repeatedly, the essential difficulties of software development are associated with open problems. If this is true, then methods closer to those suggested by the JSD example will be favored.

Formal methods such as VDM are, by virtue of their mathematical foundations, top down. When the implications of some early assertion are discovered to be invalid, one must alter that assertion and then reprove everything affected by that change. For this reason, the method depends on stability (e.g., closed problems that can be modeled precisely). JSD, on the other hand, uses an outside-in modeling approach. Each partial model (i.e., each sequential process model of an entity) tends to be extensible in the sense that small changes in the model produce only small changes in the system. This is one of the goals of a composition approach. JSD, however, is not comprehensive. Traditional tools are used for database design, and one may use JSP or any other method for program design. Thus, JSD, despite its formality, also can be used as an informal conceptual modeling method. Nevertheless, its composition orientation suggests the most flexible approach to formally modeling open applications.

In this tension between the openness of the problem and the rigor of a problem-oriented formal method, there is the need to control the feedback necessary to close the problem. Here, the role of automation is critical. PSL/PSA was included in Quadrant III just because it illustrated an early attempt to retain computer-based design artifacts. But, outside of Quadrant IV, we find limited application of automation to the process. For example, many CASE tools support the drawing of JSD diagrams, but their approach tends to be incomplete and partially integrated. Moreover, a common criticism of formal methods, such as VDM, is that they too lack automation support. Without this automated assistance, reasoning must rely on manual methods and personal discipline. Although this rigorous approach has worked with VDM and the cleanroom (Mills, Dyer, and Linger 1987), the method has inherent limitations: Objective decisions will be biased by the designers' misconceptions, and the volume of detail degrades problem-solving efficiency. This suggests a fourth property of a problem-oriented formal method.

> The environment must manage the formal specifications automatically so that lower-level specifications can be verified, system behaviors can be inspected and validated, and documentation can be produced with minimal human intervention.

There is considerable research in this area. For example, the paradigm introduced by Balzer, Cheatham and Green (1983), the program generation techniques of Barstow (1985), and the ongoing work in domain analysis (see Prieto-Diaz and Arango 1991) share this goal. Clearly, unless we can develop comprehensive automated environments, the designers will face substantial challenges in preserving correctness as they move from one formal representation scheme to the next.

Figure 10.3 depicts some alternative roles for automation in analysis and design. The phases of the process are shown on the bottom, and the scale on the left represents the percent of what is known about the application that is available in machine-sensible form. The graphs are not based on real data; they simply illustrate the differences between three development paradigms. The first, the standard paradigm, was used during the period of limited computing resources; only what is necessary for operation is maintained in the computer. As the cost of computer hardware dropped, this necessary core was augmented by tools that maintained information about the project and the product. This is today's tool-enhanced paradigm. Unfortunately, these tools represent a nonintegrated adjunct to the source programs; one may change the programs without affecting the tool database, and vice versa. The third, or fully automated, paradigm collects most of what is known about the application and uses that information to generate the tool databases as well as the final implementation.

I am convinced that the fully automated paradigm is the proper path to process improvement, and my implementation of adaptive design employs this approach. Unfortunately, however, there is no evolutionary

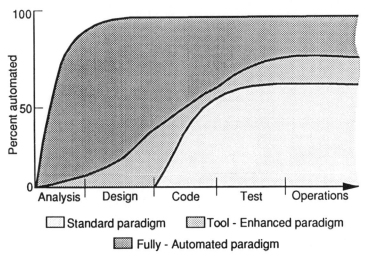

Fig. 10.3 Three paradigms for software development.

transition from the tool-enhanced paradigm to the fully automated paradigm. In my view, there is only a limited benefit to be gained from refining our present methods; consequently, we must be prepared to abandon the traditional solutions we have been pursuing; that is, we must shift to another paradigm. Although such a shift is never an easy, I believe it constitutes the only way in which we can enter into a new era of design.

We now are ready to look to the future of software design—the underlying theme of this book. All that precedes the final two chapters provides a background for what follows. Parts I and II establish a context for software design independent of the software experience. The goal is to provide a foundation for an independent analysis of how software ought to be developed. This and the previous chapter address the software process and software design methods. They describe the essence of process and identify many of the difficulties that I find to be accidental. We come now to the book's conclusion, its resolution of these difficulties. The final two chapters describe and evaluate an alternative paradigm that integrates adaptive design with full automation, one that resolves many of the accidental difficulties of software design. I demonstrate the efficacy of my particular instantiation of adaptive design, but I do not address the complexities of its achieving acceptance. The burden of shifting to that new paradigm is left to the reader.

11

ADAPTIVE DESIGN

11.1. A Personal Preface

Finally, I am about to report on my own research. In the material that preceded this chapter I have tried to present the work of others. My role has been closer to that of a journalist than a scientist. Because I have covered so much ground, my presentations may be criticized as superficial; the chapters left more unanswered than they have answered. Nevertheless, by the time the reader has reached this point, we should have a shared perception of the design process and its rational foundations. Perhaps I could have accomplished this with fewer pages or with greater focus. I did not choose that path because I wanted the reader to build a perspective of her own, a perspective in which my model of adaptive design (as well as many other alternative solutions) would seem reasonable.

The environment for adaptive design that I describe in this chapter is quite old. Work began on the project in 1980, and the environment was frozen in 1982. My software engineering research career began in 1985. Prior to that time I was paid to develop useful software products (i.e., applications that satisfy the sponsor's needs). Since 1985 I have been supported by research funds to deliver research products (i.e., new and relevant knowledge). Of course, there is no clear distinction between my practitioner and research activities, and my research—despite its change in paradigm—has always had a strong pragmatic bias. Many of my software engineering research papers were published when I was developing applications, and my work at the Johns Hopkins Medical Institutions was accepted as research in medical informatics (i.e., how computer technology can assist the practice of medicine and the delivery of care). The approach described in this chapter emerged from attempts to improve the application of computers in medicine, and this is how I finally came to understand software development—from the perspective of complex, life-critical, open interactive information systems.

There is relatively little in this chapter that has not already been published. The chapter integrates what is available in a number of overlapping (and generally unreferenced) papers. I began reporting on my approach before it was fully operational (Blum 1981), but that is not uncommon in this profession. In the year the environment was frozen I described it in an extensive article at an IFIP conference (1982a) and published the first of the evaluations (1982b). I also reported my findings at the NBS FIPS Software Documentation Workshop (1982c), the ACM Workshop on Rapid Prototyping (Blum and Houghton 1982), the National Computer Conference (1983a), COMPSAC (1983b), the International Conference on Software Engineering (1984a), COMPCON (1984b), the Conference on Software Tools (1985a), the Symposium on New Directions in Computing (1985b), and elsewhere.

All this was before I considered myself a researcher in software engineering. In the latter capacity I wrote a book about the environment (1990a) and described my work in papers published in *Software—Practice & Experience* (1986b), *Journal of Systems and Software* (1986c, 1989a, 1993a), *IEEE Transactions on Software Engineering* (1987a), *IEEE Software* (1987b), *Information and Software Technology* (1987c), *Large Scale Systems* (1987d), the IFIP CRIS conference (1988b), *Proceedings of the IEEE* (1989b), *Information and Decision Technologies* (1989c, 1992b, 1994b), *Software Engineering Journal* (1991a), *International Journal of Software Engineering and Knowledge Engineering* (1991b), *Journal of Systems Integration* (1991c), *Information and Decision Technologies* (1992b), *International Journal of Intelligent and Cooperative Information Systems* (1992c), *IEEE Transactions on Systems, Man, and Cybernetics* (1993b), and *Journal of Software Maintenance* (1995). In addition, I presented papers at conferences and (along with others) reported on the products developed with the environment. In fact, in the mid 1980s there were more papers published about applications developed with the environment than there were about the environment itself.

What a long and hard-to-read paragraph! Am I bragging about my skills in writing publishable papers? Hardly. The point I wish to make is that, despite all this effort, my work is hardly referenced and seldom understood. Therefore, the above paragraph is only an acceptance of failed communications; an honest admission of my contribution to deforestation. Cole and Cole (1972) did a study on the value of published research in physics and concluded "that roughly 50 percent of all scientific papers are produced by approximately 10 percent of the scientists" (p. 369). This simply suggests that the distribution follows Pareto's Law, and the reader can figure out where I fit. They go on to reference a citation analysis and report that "about one-half of all the papers published in the more than 2100 source journals abstracted in the SCI [*Science Citation Index*] do not receive a single citation during the year after it is published" (p. 372). I already have told the reader where I fit.

I believe that my work has never been accepted within the mainstream because it employs an alternative paradigm and therefore is outside the mainstream. True, there are many other approaches that also exist within alternative paradigms, but that work is undertaken by communities of researchers who share their work and mutually promote their findings. Given the volume of new reports produced each year, it is not surprising that researchers marshall their time, read selectively, and focus their energies on the topics of principal interest to them. This is not sour grapes; it simply is an acceptance of reality. A reality that may explain why have structured the book in its current form.

If I were to follow my original plan and make this another book about my environment, TEDIUM,[*] it might only be added to the above list of neglected documents. And if I had organized this book so that it produced a logical path with TEDIUM as the obvious destination (my second plan), it still would be a narrow description of one alternative to technological design. By structuring the book in its present form (an organization that evolved as I wrote), I have let the reader assimilate his own understanding of the software design process and the many ways in which it may be altered to meet the demands of the next century. I am certain that few readers will accept all of what I have said; neither I do not expect these final two chapters to "convince" them in any way. Rather, I only hope that a common understanding of software design's complexities will have emerged from the cauldron of ideas that precedes these words and that this new perspective will provide a context for interpreting the final two chapters.

I now turn to the question of how to design and implement software with the one-step, problem-oriented model. In this chapter I describe an environment that has been in production use since 1980. The final chapter reviews the 14-year history of a million-line clinical application that operates in a life-critical setting. Productivity in this project has averaged one production program per effort day, growth in functionality has approximated 10% per year, and the system has been built and maintained by a small number of non-computer scientists who were trained on the job. Of course, if by the time the reader comes across this book that already is the state of the practice, then what follows will be of historical interest only.

11.2. Exploiting Software's Unique Capabilities

As we have seen, there are some unavoidable tensions in the two-step process of technological design. When we work with concrete materials,

---

[*] TEDIUM is a registered trademark of Tedious Enterprises, Inc.

we must determine what we are to build before we begin its construction. Without this planning and analysis, there would be no interchangeable parts, no mass production, no standard components. All our products would have to be custom built, each distinct within a shared style. This is how we produce art. We acknowledge that a work of art is an expression of an individual's vision and that its value is related to that personal expression. In contrast, we want our everyday artifacts to be economical. Industrial designers and architects provide the aesthetic, and we are content to select from among styles and products. We allow cost to limit the number of unique products we own. That is the price of efficiency, a price we accept as quite natural.

It is the concreteness of the artifacts that limits their flexibility; they are expensive to make, and—once made—difficult to change. So society has learned to adjust to its physical surroundings. But the world in which we exist is dynamic, and change is a universal certainty. Without adaptation to change, life might never exist, and—if it did—it could not have evolved into *Homo sapiens*. Our economic, political, and social organizations are constantly changing, and we would like our automated tools, which are intended to serve humanity in-the-world, to evolve with these changes. This, then, is our dilemma. Our tools and equipment exist in the fixed, stable, long-lived, modular, world of the physical objects, while our needs are defined in the ephemeral, dynamic, variable, holistic world of humanity. We begin with artifacts that respond to our needs, but frustration comes as change distorts the object's ability to satisfy the needs. Fortunately, the unique capabilities of software free us from the restrictions of the physical world; they permit a shift from the technological design model to an adaptive model in which artifacts evolve along with the institutions that use them.

The technological design model materialized out of our experience with hardware products, and software engineering brought order to the process by imposing that model on software projects. If we now take a different tack for software and switch to adaptive design, with its emphasis on taking advantage of software's unique features, how then might we characterize the conduct of the process?

Problem orientation. Rather than starting with a specification that states the requirements for a specific response to a real-world problem (i.e., hardware's *product orientation*), the designers would be able to model alternative responses to the need. Using formalized knowledge from previous projects, each response could be refined until either the desired software has been produced or it is recognized that the intent cannot be realized safely and efficiently. Through the use of formal models, all inferences would be proved, and implementation errors would be eliminated.

Immediate feedback. Rather than trying to anticipate all the implications of a set of requirements or a design (i.e., hardware's *forward looking* perspective), the designers would concentrate on the accuracy of their interpretation of the requirements and design. The environment would support the analysis, and the designer—instead of having to think about the implications of the design—would focus on how well the response satisfies the identified need.

Unified realization. Rather than trying to maintain the design separate from the product (i.e., hardware's *dual realization*), the design also would be the product. Automation would provide a trace from objectives to responses; the product and the justification for its creation would exist as an integrated whole.

Thus, the software-based model would be problem oriented, feedback driven, and employ a unified (as-built) specification.

The approach also would exhibit the four properties of a problem-oriented, formal-model environment identified in Chapter 10:

Concept formalization. The model captures the concepts of primary interest in a scheme that permits automatic transformations and reasoning about correctness. For the domain of interactive information systems, these concepts include the description, manipulation, storage, and display of surrogates for items in the domain of use.

Concept expression. All concepts are expressed in a form that facilitates reasoning about the validity of the surrogate representations and their use. Because the evaluations must engage all of the stakeholders, no single mode of expression will suffice.

Concept comprehensiveness. Given a representation scheme that is both formal and expressive, every property of the system can be representable within that scheme. Moreover, the scheme should maintain links that permit reasoning about different items (at different levels of granularity) within the system. (System here is taken to be the as-built specification of the system in-use.)

Concept automation. Because the above three criteria place many demands on the conceptual model, any implementation will require considerable automated support to manage and display the model. That is, the environment will be able to overcome the complexity imposed on it only if it is an instantiation of the fully automated paradigm described in Chapter 10.

Here we have a contrast between how we currently develop software applications—with programs, specifications, modules, and files—and how we might develop them with conceptual models maintained by a support environment. The difference is one of representation, and the shift is from a notion of formality in the form of programs and logical notation to the idea of an as-built specification maintained within an environment. This is the shift that the title, *Beyond Programming*, is meant to imply. It is a shift from a concern for the product (rendered as computational and logical models) to an interest in the response to a problem (organized formally as an expressive and comprehensive model within the computer). Whereas programs (and formal specifications) are inherently top-down and presented as statements within a hierarchy, the components of the conceptual model will be deeply integrated. Whereas the former must conform to a sequential logical analysis, the latter are expected to express concepts from many different perspectives in differing degrees of granularity. Because the new conceptual model will represent the knowledge of the domain of interest, its structure will be as complex as the evolving understanding of that domain.

By way of analogy, a globe represents Earth in three dimensions, but an atlas reduces that surface to planar projections. It is the book medium that forces this choice, and each two-dimensional map abstracts away some of the physical properties of Earth. Yet even the globe itself captures only a small part of our knowledge of the planet as it exists in-the-world. It omits climate, land use, population distributions, ozone densities, and so on. Again, there are limits to what can be expressed with the physical media. Software, however, is free of those restrictions. For example, it is conceptually possible to build a computer model of Earth that captures all of the properties just identified. Of course, it would never be possible to view the entire model; its complexity and the display media defy a single, complete presentation. But one could examine projections and abstractions that suppress what is not of interest as they integrate the properties of principal interest.

This analogy suggests how we might represent the conceptual model. With the problem-oriented approach we are shifting the focus to the capture of what is known about the problem to be solved and our experience in solving problems of this class. This may be characterized as our views of the world. Shifting to the fully automated paradigm, we are committed to representing these views in machine-processable form in what I shall call an *application development environment* (to distinguish it from CASE and SEE, which support the product-oriented approach). In my model of adaptive design, the environment maintains an as-built specification (i.e., conceptual model) represented as *fragments* in an integrated *application database*. The fragments exhibit the following properties.

Atomic independence. Fragments express their characteristics independent of other design dimensions (a concept similar to information hiding). Thus, the designer can view items in the design as properties of the application (or class) being developed without concern for how they are to be used. The representation of the properties should reflect the designer's understanding of their external characteristics without regard for any internal implementation details.

Automatic integration. Because the fragments are maintained in an application database, they are linked either through the explicit specification of associations or the inference of associations resulting from an inspection of a fragment's contents. Segments of the design can be reused wherever appropriate, and consistency checking eliminates redundancy and contradictions.

Holistic perspective. The application design is viewed as a whole rather than a collection of independent units. Because there is neither a top and bottom nor an outside and inside, this holistic organization will be unable to produce displays that capture all the associations among the design objects. Therefore, the environment also must provide local views, which target the immediate concerns as they hide secondary details.

To be effective, the fragments must satisfy the four properties of a problem-oriented, formal-model environment just noted; that is, they must constitute a formal, expressive, comprehensive, and automated conceptual model. Fragments overcome the limitations of programs, modules, and files. Whereas the latter three are text documents that must be integrated by human readers, the fragments are similar to the chunks in a model of human memory. Fragments are composed of fragments such that the sum of all fragments comprises the formal expression of everything that is formally known; no individual fragment is meaningful outside the context of the whole. Fragments also may be described as being similar to operations in activity theory: learned primitives that support actions. In either case, this shift from modules (each of which represents a complete processing unit) to fragments (no one of which will be complete outside the as-built specification) introduces a new computer science that enables a degree of automation not previously possible. The next section provides a concrete illustration of a fragment-based environment that implements adaptive design.

11.3. Introduction to TEDIUM

TEDIUM provides a comprehensive environment for the development and maintenance of interactive information systems (each of which is called an *application*). The basic idea is simple. The environment maintains an *application database* (ADB) that can retain virtually everything known about the application under development (e.g., its formal specification, its descriptive documentation, its computer-generated cross references). The implementation is generated from the ADB, and maintenance is performed at the ADB level. The application designer views the ADB as the repository for all knowledge about the application, and no documentation regarding the application need be retained outside the ADB (i.e., the ADB is an as-built specification in the form of a conceptual model).

The development process with TEDIUM is incremental. The designer enters specifications and descriptions into the ADB. Whenever a portion of the specification in the ADB is sufficiently complete, the program generator is used to create a partial implementation that can be tested (i.e., validated). The designer refines the specifications and regenerates the programs until the partial implementation performs as desired. Because every generated program is functionally complete and efficient, every generated program is also of production quality. Therefore, once a program is validated, it can be accepted for production use. In this way, the production application is composed of the accepted partial implementations.

TEDIUM is tailored to the development of applications with open requirements where an understanding of the necessary functionality evolves with experience and experimentation. Its design method is called *system sculpture*. Using this method, the designer begins by working with the users to understand the need and the appropriate responses to it. There are no diagramming conventions, and communication is informal. Unlike domain analysis, there is no attempt to capture and model domain knowledge. There are no specialists who work with the domain experts. Each designer is expected to learn about the application domain needs and to be aware of the potential benefits of automated support.

The designers, working cooperatively, build a unified conceptual model in the ADB that formalizes knowledge about the target application (i.e., an interactive information system). This knowledge of the information system should not be confused with knowledge about the domain in which the system is used. For example, most TEDIUM applications are used in the medical domain. One function of a clinical information system is the production of daily plans that recommend patient-care activities based on the patient's disease, current therapy, and status. The conceptual model for this plan-generation function would describe how medical knowledge can be organized to make therapeutic recommendations; it also would specify the features necessary to maintain the medical knowledge and to create the plans. However, the therapy knowledge, which is medical domain knowledge, would be viewed as data by the application. The TEDIUM ADB would describe the structure and use of the medical knowledge, but not the knowledge itself.

The representation used for the conceptual model consists of a holistic, integrating framework to which fragments are appended. The framework has no inherent structure; no top, bottom, inside, or outside. As previously noted, fragments are composed of fragments, and fragments are joined within the framework. Fragments describe data model concepts, specify behavior (either procedurally or declaratively), and capture descriptive text. The TEDIUM environment provides tools to enter, edit, peruse, and list fragments at various levels of granularity. There are no complete and independent program listings; instead, TEDIUM provides access to the units of interest to the designers: programs, relations, documents. (The names of these units should not be taken too literally. A TEDIUM *program* is a unit of functionality; one TEDIUM program may be implemented as more than one module or routine in the target language.) In summary, the conceptual model in the ADB is deeply integrated. Although it is possible to print out the entire model, any such listing would obscure many of the associations within the model; effective comprehension depends on interactive access to the holistic, fragment-based specification retained in the ADB.

The method for building a specification in the ADB is very informal. The designers use a composition approach; they identify what is well understood about the application and add that knowledge to the ADB. The designers may begin at any level of abstraction deemed appropriate, and they are free to change levels of abstraction as they pursue their analysis. Usually, designers begin with a brief description followed by a definition of data structures and then the specification of programs that act on the data. But there is nothing in the environment that mandates any sequence of entries.

Although this process may seem chaotic, it must be recognized that the goal is to create a valid, as-built specification for a system that responds to open requirements. Consequently, the environment is designed to encourage opportunistic use. When portions of the conceptual model are complete enough for testing, programs are generated and experimented with. Following the sculptor metaphor, the ADB is modified until the desired behaviors are observed. When this occurs, the generated programs are available for production use. Modifications to a production application are carried out in the same way. Portions of the ADB are altered in response to the changed needs.

Once the modifications are satisfactory, the altered ADB fragments and the generated programs are used to update the production system.

There is only one active ADB model, and it is shared by all the designers. The TEDIUM environment manages the ADB and the generation of products from it. Three categories of knowledge support this process.

Application knowledge. This is knowledge about the need and how automation can provide a response that satisfies or mitigates the need. It already has been pointed out that this knowledge focuses on how automation should be applied in the domain of interest and does not imply deep application domain knowledge. The conceptual model formalizes this knowledge domain with respect to a single application.

Application-class knowledge. This is knowledge about the properties expected of all applications of a particular class. For example, in an interactive information system we expect referential integrity, the testing of inputs, and the availability of a consistent help system; there are other informal standards for real-time systems and large-scale computational applications.

Software-tool knowledge. This is knowledge about software tools, including transformation systems, operating systems, and algorithm development. In a sense, this is the engineering of computer science (i.e., the creation of useful products and concepts through the application of scientific principles).

The application knowledge is retained in the ADB and the application-class and software-tool knowledge are combined in the program generator. Because the TEDIUM environment is a TEDIUM application, there are always at least two ADBs involved. For the application designer, the ADB contains application knowledge—what separates this from all other applications of its class. For the TEDIUM designer, the ADB contains the application-class and software-tool knowledge used to generate the TEDIUM environment used by the application designer.

As will be discussed in the next section, there are strong interactions between the application-class and software-tool knowledge domains, and they are difficult to separate. They are identified as two distinct domains because each domain addresses a different set of issues. Application-class knowledge identifies all of the *implicit* behaviors expected within a particular class of application. Normally, this kind of knowledge is acquired on the job during the first years of employment. It is seldom recorded and almost always learned through experience.

Many common software defects result from the careless omission of this knowledge. The goal of TEDIUM is to formalize the application-class knowledge in a *system style* that can be included automatically in every generated program. In that way, all the behaviors expected of every product in the given application class can be hidden from the designer and included in the generated system by default. In contrast to the application-class knowledge, the software-tool knowledge addresses issues in the preservation of correctness and the improvement of efficiency. Because the technology of interactive information systems is relatively mature, there is sufficient software-tool knowledge to ensure the automatic generation of effective, production-quality programs.

Figure 11.1 presents an overview of the TEDIUM architecture. The designers work with the environment through a standard interface. They maintain the ADB and use the program generator to create programs that can be tested. The program generator has access to the system style. Thus, every generated program incorporates the behaviors specified *explicitly* in the ADB plus those specified *implicitly* in the system style. Therefore, every generated program is functionally complete. Because the technology is mature, every generated program also is efficient. Consequently, the generated programs are of production quality; they are not prototypes that require subsequent refinement. Two categories of program can be generated. Interpretative programs may be exercised in the TEDIUM environment; programs also may be generated in other languages for compilation and execution in other environments. (Except for a set of TEDIUM utility routines, TEDIUM-generated applications are independent of the TEDIUM environment.) There also is a document generator for producing system and user documentation.

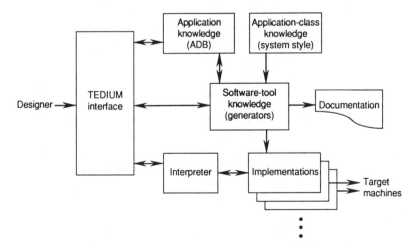

Fig. 11.1. Overview of TEDIUM.

Two versions of TEDIUM exist. The first was frozen in 1982, and it is the system that currently is used in production; all evaluation data (including the project history described in Chapter 12) come from this older system. The second system is under development. Both versions have been implemented as TEDIUM applications. Extensive descriptions and evaluations of the original system are available in a 50-page case study presented at CRIS 88 (Blum 1988b) and *TEDIUM and the Software Process* (Blum 1990a).

Although TEDIUM is an operational environment and these two references and the following chapter document experience with it, this discussion will be far more instructive if I explore adaptive design without the constraint of being faithful to an environment whose essential functionality has not been changed for over a decade. Therefore, in the remainder of this chapter I describe TEDIUM using the idealized (albeit incomplete) constructs of the new system. I first discuss the implementation of TEDIUM from the perspective of its representation of knowledge: application knowledge, TEDIUM knowledge (i.e., the representation of application knowledge in TEDIUM), and the representation of family knowledge. The next section describes the TEDIUM environment, and a final section offers some concluding observations.

11.4. Application Database Representation

The TEDIUM ADB maintains knowledge of the application as fragments. Because TEDIUM is itself a TEDIUM application, these fragments also are specified as fragments. All specifications employ TEDIUM's *uniform representation scheme* (URS) (Blum, 1991b). This scheme is intended to provide great expressive power using a limited number of constructs. Although it is possible to reduce the number of constructs, such a refinement would make some important concepts more difficult to express. Thus, URS is justified on a pragmatic rather than a mathematically pure basis. Indeed, the shift to another application class may uncover concepts that require additional constructs. One final comment before proceeding. We are running out of neutral words. Object, entity, even element all have been spoken for. I have avoided these words because they come burdened with associations I wish to avoid. In searching for alternatives, I chose *item* to denote what a fragment represents. Now to proceed.

URS identifies three levels of abstraction for an item:

Singles. This is the minimal representation of an item at its highest level of abstraction (e.g., a type). The single hides all information about the item's structure while preserving information that is unique to the item (e.g., predicates on its use).

Collections. This is an ordered grouping of singles (e.g., a relation). The collection establishes semantic associations among singles. At the next higher level of abstraction, every collection is a single.

Pairs. This is a special type of collection, composed of two singles such that the second is functionally dependent on the first (e.g., a relation with a key). The pair establishes a unique identifier for certain collections.

All knowledge in TEDIUM (including the procedural knowledge that defines the program generator) is specified with URS. Items within the ADB may be accessed at any of the above-mentioned three levels of abstraction. Because the pair exhibits the least degree of information hiding, it is the notation most frequently used in the TEDIUM listings. The reader should keep in mind, however, that each item in the pair may be expanded as a pair until its specification reduces to primitive singles (i.e., singles that cannot be represented as collections). Although this binding process creates a tree of definitions, the associations among singles are not in any sense hierarchical. The specifications of the items exist in a complex network, which justifies the description of the ADB as a holistic, fragment-based specification.

In the examples that follow, pairs are presented as relations. The complexity of the item structure is masked by information hiding. Each of the "attributes" in the "relation" is itself an item, and many of these items can be represented as pairs. Thus, for example, the slots of a frame constitute the dependent collection of a pair whose independent collection is the frame-slot identifier. The representation of a TEDIUM program as a pair incorporates many more levels of information hiding. By convention, pairs are listed using a functional notation. Thus, the relation

Book (<u>ISBN</u>, Title, Authors, Publisher, City, Year)

would be written

Book (<u>ISBN</u>) = Title, Authors, Publisher, City, Year

where the equal sign separates the independent and dependent collections. (The parentheses for the dependent collection are normally omitted.) The underline in the second notation indicates that the extension of **Book** constitutes the complete set of values for ISBN, that is, **Book** serves as a dictionary for the valid values of ISBN. (Because of the way TEDIUM manages variable names, the dash will not be confused with the minus sign, and it is a valid character in a name.)

If the goal was to develop a library application, one might begin with the above specification of **Book** and, using system sculpture, refine it to produce the following items.

> **Book** (<u>ISBN</u>) = Title, Authors, Publisher, Year
> **Authors** (ISBN, Sequence) = Person
> **Person** (<u>Person-Surrogate</u>) = Name, Affiliation, Address
> **Publisher** (<u>Publisher-Name</u>) = City
> **Affiliation** (<u>Affiliation-Name</u>) = Address

In this extended specification, **Authors** is specified as an ordered list of elements of type Person. (Sequence establishes the order.) The key for **Person** is shown as a surrogate. This implies that the key term has no meaning to the users and therefore should be hidden from them. In this sense, the surrogate is roughly the equivalent of the object identifier as used in an object-oriented database system.

Following the standard practice for the normalization of relational models, **Publisher** contains the publisher's city. The item **Affiliation** has been added to provide addresses so that if one knows a person's affiliation but not his address, then one can direct correspondence to the person using the affiliation address. The need for a person's address, and the use of an affiliation to infer that address, goes beyond what normally is associated with a library system. However, if the requirements are open, and it is believed that the application might be extended to include correspondence with the authors, then the concepts captured in the extended model are valid. The point is that there is a distinction between the semantic validity and the functional utility of the application knowledge. Traditional information system development deliberately ignores everything that is perceived to be, in Jackson's (1982) terminology, *Outside the Model Boundary (OMB)*. Yet, as this example shows, this boundary is artificial; moreover, with an open requirement the boundary is not even static. Thus, the conceptual model should be extensible in the sense that existing concepts may be refined easily with the impact of a change limited to the concepts affected by the refinement.

This objective can be illustrated by a refinement that introduces the concept of a publication as a generalization of a book and that specifies several additional specializations of a publication.

> **Publication** (<u>Publication-Surrogate</u>) = Title, Publication-Type, Authors
> **Book** (Publication-Surrogate, [Publication-Type=Book]) = ISBN, Publisher, Year

Journal (Publication-Surrogate, [Publication-Type=Journal]) = Journal-Id, Volume, Number, Pages, Year.
Proceedings (Publication-Surrogate, [Publication-Type = Proceedings]) = Conference, Location, Pages, Date
Report (Publication-Surrogate, [Publication-Type=Report]) = Organization, Date

In this example I have listed Publication-Surrogate explicitly; because the surrogate contains no information that is meaningful to a user, it is not normally identified. The key ISBN for **Book** has been replaced by the surrogate, and the term has become a dependent item (i.e., a nonkey attribute). The notation also has been extended to include predicates in the keys. Nevertheless, the introduction of the concept of a publication is local to that portion of the ADB that references **Book**. In this case, because the key has been changed, any fragments that set or retrieve ISBN may be affected; otherwise the use of the book item is not altered. Of course, replacing the concept of a book with that of a publication should have a significant impact on the application's specification; indeed, that is why the generalization was specified.

Because the goal of this example is to introduce the underlying mechanisms used in the ADB model, some unimportant (i.e., implementation-oriented) details have been included. The specification would be improved, however, if these details were hidden. This can be done by introducing some standard data structures and listing conventions. For example, the key for **Authors** contains Sequence, which preserves the order in the list (e.g., Sequence=1 for the first author). Inasmuch as the designer already has the concepts of "ordered list," "first element in the list," "next element in the list," and so on, the specification scheme should exploit this fact by employing the concept of an ordered list ([OL]). The list of authors for a publication may then be defined as

Authors [OL, Context: **Publication**] = Person.

Context indicates that the key (i.e., object identifier) for **Authors** is that of **Publication**. The context of an item is its independent collection. In this case, the application cannot identify the authors of a publication unless the context (i.e., publication identifier) is defined in the current state. The fact that there is a surrogate key to **Publication** is hidden. The use of an ordered list, however, should not be considered an implementation constraint. Rather, it represents a way of expressing the semantics upon which the application will build.

The distinction between the semantics of the conceptual model and the implementation of the application is illustrated in this next example.

We know from the specification of **Publication** and **Authors** that there is an inference chain that enables us to establish the name of the authors for a given publication. A similar inference chain shows us how to find the year a book was published. Each of these chains implies that these are useful semantic associations within the application. We recognize that a reverse transversal of these chains also is possible. Given an author, we can find all of his publications, and given a year we can find all of the books published in that year. But our understanding of the application suggests that the former is important and the latter is not. The application specifies that finding the publications of an individual author is an important concept by introducing the item

Author-Publications (Person, **Publication**)

and specifying that **Publication** and **Author-Publications** are related to each other in one-to-one correspondence.

This relationship implies that the two items must always project the same state. The existence of these two items is used by the program generator in improving the efficiency of the queries implied by the items; queries not identified as semantically important (e.g., finding the publications printed in a given year) are processed in an ad hoc manner. Thus, the specifications should not be read too literally. Indeed, if the generated application were to use a relational DBMS, **Author** and **Author-Publications** might be implemented using a common relation; the fact that two items were specified would be used to optimize the definition of the physical data model and its secondary keys.

Notice that the **Author-Publications** item has no dependent collection. This is because the necessary information is already in the independent collection. The two singles in the collection indicates that for each **Person**, there may be more than one **Publication**. In contrast, the item specification

Author-Publications (Person) = Publication

would indicate that for each **Person** there can be only one **Publication**. Such a specification, of course, would not model the real word; I show it only to illustrate the flexibility of the specification notation. Finally, I point out that the definition of **Author-Publications** as a mandatory related item (the default) would indicate that each **Person** in the database must have at least one **Publication** in the database. Individual definitions such as these, when combined with the other information in the ADB, is used by the generator to produce explicit tests that avoid potential database corruptions.

Now to extend the conceptual model to include processes. TEDIUM permits the designers to specify processes as programs. These programs may be specified declaratively or procedurally, and the declarative specifications can be modified using TEDIUM commands. The commands tend to emphasize the semantics of the operation. For example, the command to enter the publisher's city would be

Input Publisher.City.

Implicit in this command are the testing of the input using the validation criteria in the ADB, the processing of requests for help, and the conformance to the standard interaction conventions. All items have an implicit response to the Input command, and the response is determined by the definition of the item. For example, the input for **Publisher** would be a value for Publisher-Name, and the input for **Publication** (which has a surrogate for its key) would be a value for Title. This is illustrated in the slightly more complex sequence that follows.

Consider the command to input a valid value for Person using

Input Person.

As a result of executing this command, the designer expects the state to contain a valid key for the item Person. This is similar to identifying an object within a class; in TEDIUM it is said that the *context* of Person has been set (i.e., a value for Person-Surrogate is defined). Every command has postconditions, and for this command the postcondition will be satisfied if the state contains a valid Person identifier. If no such identifier were found, the Input command would take a default return (called the *abnormal return*) and not proceed to the next command in the sequence. However, the designer is given options for overriding the command defaults. If the *add if not found* option were selected, the generator could use the item definition to produce the following sequence.

```
Input Person-Surrogate
Case abnormal return
    Input Name
    Input Affiliation
    Input Address
End
```

Each of the inputs in the expansion might also be expanded, for example, the specification of Name might cause the generation of inputs for First and Last. Of course, all of these expansions are hidden from the designer; they are detailed here to provide a better understanding of how TEDIUM operates.

Yet, even with this expansion, the input command for **Person-Surrogate** presents a contradiction. By definition, the value set for Person-Surrogate has no meaning to the user, but the user should select a person using values meaningful to the task. For selecting a person, the obvious selection set is that of person names. Because there may be more than one person with the same name, a second item (such as social security number, date of birth, or affiliation) may be necessary to provide uniqueness. There also is a problem with the regularity of the set of names, which may include spaces, punctuation, and alternative capitalizations. To deal with this last issue, we define

Normalized-Name = Normalize(Name)

where Normalize is a TEDIUM program (in this case, a function) that removes punctuation marks and blanks and produces a case-insensitive name string. We then define the item

Person-Name(Normalized-Name, Affiliation) = Person.

The item Affiliation was added to the key to provide uniqueness in the event of identical names. (Person is used in place of Person-Surrogate by convention; in reality, the latter term is never specified.) Finally, we specify **Person** and **Person-Name** to be in one-to-one correspondence and indicate that **Person-Name** should be used as an input for **Person**.

As a result of these definitions, what was shown earlier as Input Person-Surrogate would be replaced by Input Normalized-Name, which a first glance hardly seems an improvement. However, we can define a TEDIUM program that reads in a pattern and then displays all values of Normalized-Name for the item **Person-Name** that match that pattern. This hides from the application user the internal details and provides an interface that will be natural in the context of the application task. The program is specified with the following declarative specification

Prompt-Name *is a* **Prompt** *program*
    using the item Person-Name
    with the input Normalized-Name, Affiliation
    returning Person, Affiliation
    end

The implementation of this program is described in the next section. For the purposes of the current discussion, it will suffice to explain the meaning of the specification. The specification states that a pattern for the first item in the with the input field is to be entered and then matched; for each item in Person-Name that satisfies the match, the values of Normalized-Name and Affiliation are displayed. (Actually, the designer would alter the specification to indicate that Name rather than Normalized-Name should be included in the listing, but I omit this level of detail in the interest of simplicity.) When the matching process is complete, the user either selects a name from the list or indicates that the name is not in the list. Depending on the user's action, the postcondition of the program Prompt-Name is to have the state of Person and Affiliation either defined or undefined; if the state is undefined (i.e., there is no match), the program exits with an abnormal return.

After the program Prompt-Name has been specified, the specification of **Person-Name** can be amended to indicate that Prompt-Name is to be used for input. (Because TEDIUM is designed to work with incomplete specifications, the reference to Prompt-Name can be included in a specification before the program has been defined.) With this overloading of the specification, the expansion of Input Name creates a call to Prompt-Name, which provides a very natural interface for the user. The designer also may specify Prompt-Publication (which uses Title as an input) and Prompt-Publisher and then overload the specifications of **Publication** and **Publisher** so that the selection of a valid value will automatically use these programs.

A similar technique is available for the processing of outputs using the Write command. Each item has a default output format based on its primitive type (e.g., character string, number, date). This default can be overloaded to produce a customized format. For example, the output of Book can be specified as

Book write as: Authors, ", ", [*italics on*], Title, [*italics off*], ", ", Publisher.City, ": ", Publisher, ", ", Year, "."

where Authors has had its Write overloaded using Person, and Person in turn has had its Write overloaded. In this way, the command

Write Book

will produce a standard citation listing. Using system sculpture, the form of that citation listing may be developed incrementally. Using the concept of families (to be discussed in Section 11.6), a selection from alternative customized formats is possible. The next section illustrates how these conceptual modeling constructs are being used to specify TEDIUM.

11.5. Representing Knowledge in TEDIUM

TEDIUM is simply another application developed with TEDIUM. The first version of the system was bootstrapped from a very primitive version of TEDIUM, and the version of the system currently under development is being bootstrapped from the most current operational version. Because of the complexity of the TEDIUM application, it is being organized as a family of applications whose composition comprises TEDIUM. This section describes the knowledge utilized by TEDIUM, and Section 11.6 describes how this knowledge is organized and managed in families.

TEDIUM relies on three categories of knowledge. The application knowledge, maintained in the ADB, specifies the behavior and functionality of the application of interest. The application-class knowledge, maintained as a system style, prescribes all the default behaviors and functions expected in every product of this application class. Finally, the software-tool knowledge, maintained in the program generator, determines how the ADB specification primitives can be implemented efficiently. In the version currently under development, separate applications are being developed for each category of knowledge. These are as follows:

> *ADB Manager* (Meta-ADB). This is the specification of the programs that interface with and manage the ADB contents; it also establishes the representation scheme used for the ADB specifications. It is called meta-ADB because it specifies the ADB used by the TEDIUM designers.

> *System Style* (Meta-style). This is the specification of the system style for the class of interactive information systems (IIS). It identifies all the implicit features of the generated programs, and it also supplies the default actions that may be overloaded. (Meta-style-IIS would be a more accurate name, but there is no ambiguity with only one system style.)

> *Program Generator* (Meta-gen). This is the specification of the program generator used to transform the knowledge in the other two domains into efficient programs. All generated applications operate in a target environment without TEDIUM, but they rely on a library of TEDIUM utility programs written for that environment. Meta-gen is being designed to generate programs in any of several languages (e.g., MUMPS, Ada, and C).

Meta-ADB, meta-style, and meta-gen are but three of the applications that make up the new specification of TEDIUM. Of these three applications, meta-ADB is the most thoroughly understood; it is a direct extension the older version. I therefore begin by presenting the general structure of the ADB. After this introduction to meta-ADB, I explain how meta-gen is organized and conclude with an examination of meta-style. A description of meta-ADB's environment for managing the conceptual model is given in Section 11.7.

Meta-ADB is that portion of TEDIUM that maintains and provides access to the conceptual models stored in the application database. The basic unit within TEDIUM is the *application*, and the ADB is segmented into applications. Each application has a unique identifier, and all items within the specification share that identifier as a *context*. (The multiple uses of "context" will be addressed below.) In the illustration that follows, I begin with the specification of an application and *items* at the *pair* level of abstraction. I omit the collection level of abstraction and reference items within a pair as *singles*. Not shown in this specification is the item **Item**, which establishes a type shared by both pair and single. In effect, the following specification segment suggests how the items specified in Section 11.4 would be represented in the ADB. The following four items establish the general organization.

Application-Names (<u>Application-Id</u>) = Application-Short-Name, Application-Long-Name, Application-Descriptive-Text.

Pair-Names (Application-Id, <u>Pair-Id</u>) = Pair-Short-Name, Pair-Long-Name, Pair-Descriptive-Text.

Pair-Contents (Application-Id, Pair-Id, Key, Sequence) = Single-Id
Pair-Singles (Application-Id, Single-Id, Pair-Id) = Key, Sequence

The last two items are *related* to each other in one-to-one correspondence. They express the concepts that given a pair, one needs to know which singles (i.e., items) are in it, and given a single, one needs to know in which pairs its is used. As with the **Publication - Author-Publication** example of the previous section, this does not imply that the two items will be represented as separate relations.

Items within the specification can be combined as structures. For example, an **Application** structure could be defined to include the four pairs **Application-Id**, **Pair-Names**, **Pair-Contents**, and **Pair-Singles**. Pairs in a structure must share a common context, which is normally one of its highest nodes (in this case **Application-Names**). One also may compose a structure from structures. Meta-ADB uses separate structures for the item definitions in the data model and the program specifications. For instance, here is how the above-mentioned items are extended to produce structures for **Pair** and **Single**, which then are combined in the structure **Item** within the structure **Application**.

Pair-Names (Application-Id, <u>Pair-Id</u>) = Pair-Short-Name, Pair-Long-Name, Pair-Descriptive-Text
Pair-Contents (Application-Id, Pair-Id, Key, Sequence) = Single-Id

Single-Names (Application-Id, <u>Single-Id</u>) = Single-Short-Name, Single-Long-Name, Single-Descriptive-Text
Single-Validation (Application-Id, Single-Id, "Validation") = /* Validation criteria */
Pair-Singles (Application-Id, Single-Id, Pair-Id) = Key, Sequence

Once the context of Application-Id and Pair-Id have been established, the designer can access the name and pair contents of the items bound to that context; similarly, the context of Application-Id and Single-Id defines the names, validation criteria, and pairs within which that item is referenced. This example provides only a portion of the item specification at the single level of abstraction. The key variable "Validation" in **Single-Validation** uniquely identifies the node in the structure that maintains the validity criteria for an item; to simplify the discussion, the form of the criteria is not shown.

The criteria may assume the form of parameters (e.g., length), a predicate, and/or a procedure. Most of the singles used in this example have been in the form of storage-based variables. The exception is the group of items with names ending **Descriptive-Text**. These are blocks of text with embedded commands, and the Input and Write commands for these items generate calls to a text processor. TEDIUM also permits items to be procedures, labels, or any other type that can be processed in the target environment.

Although this example has not shown how structures are specified as items, there is a similarity between structures and objects. A structure is defined as a pair, and its independent collection (i.e., its key) is its context. Thus, the context is similar to the object identifier; once the context exists (i.e., all the variables in the context have been instantiated), the items in the dependent collection are defined. TEDIUM provides default operations, such as Input and Write, for each item. These may be viewed as system-level methods. However, unlike an object-oriented environment, the ADB does not use modules to bind operations to the items. Operations normally are specified as independent programs, and the context for the items the program accesses is specified as a precondition. In this way, an operation may reference more than one class of item, and the associations among items is independent of any inheritance property. For example, **Item** and **Program** both share the same context of **Application**, but they inherit no items from **Application**. Programs (i.e., operations) with the context of **Application** can access items from **Item** and **Program** specified within the same application.

In this explanation, "context" has been used in several different ways. For an item specification, the context is the independent collection in its pair notation (i.e., its key). It also is common to speak of the context for the expansion of items in the dependent collection (i.e., a partial key). For example, there is a pair (which I have not shown) that ties **Pair-Names** to **Application-Names**; consequently, **Pair-Id** is said to have the context Application-Id (i.e., its value has no meaning unless Application-Id has been defined). For programs the context is the state that must be defined either at initiation (preconditions) or at termination (postconditions); more than one set of postconditions (with alternative actions) is allowed (e.g., abnormal return). Because TEDIUM does not restrict programs to operations on a single item, the context of a program may permit it to access or operate on several items. In contrast, with an OOP paradigm methods have the context of only the item for which they are defined, and the contexts would be structured as a class hierarchy.

There are two categories of program specification: *generic* programs (such the **Prompt** program in the previous section) and *common* programs. The former may be declarative, the latter always are procedural. Each program specification is organized as a structure consisting of

Name. This includes an identifier and descriptive text.

Context. This is a set of preconditions and postconditions (including the state variables that define output headings and the use of colors in displays). The context also identifies the abnormal states to be recognized and how the program should react to them. The declarative specification of Prompt-Name constitutes the context for that program (i.e., the items are used in the keys of the expansion of that program).

Commands. The TEDIUM commands are organized as an augmented transition network (ATN), with each node having a label, a guard, operator, operand, and a branch to the next node. This is represented externally as a sequence of nodes, with a branch to the next node in the sequence as the default. All procedural specifications must have commands; all declarative specifications include predefined features that can be overloaded by commands (e.g., in the above Prompt-Name program example, a Write Name command would be introduced to replace the default Write Normalized-Name supplied by the generic program).

Support. Support information includes items such as help messages and instructions for the users.

The program structure is, in part,

> **Program-Names** (Application-Id, <u>Program-Id</u>) = Program-Short-Name, Program-Long-Name, Program-Descriptive-Text)
>
> **Program-Command** [OL] (Application-Id, Program-Id, Command-Location) = Label, Guard, Operator, Operand, Branch.

The item Command-Location in **Program-Command** indicates where the command block applies. Common programs have only one command block, but generic programs have several functions that can be overwritten by designer-supplied commands (e.g., using Name instead of Normalized-Name in the listing for Prompt-Name).

The generic programs are specified as common-program patterns. For example, Figure 11.2 contains a specification of the generic prompt program. (In the interest of clarity, the notation does not strictly conform to the ATN structure used by TEDIUM.) The commands for this generic program specify that the first of the items in the *input* field defines a type for a test string (e.g., character string, integer, date) and that, for each instance of the item that matches the input, the desired input and return items are to be stored in a buffer. When the search is complete, the user will be shown the buffer contents and allowed to select an item from the buffer, enter another test string, or abort the processing. The implementation details and the particulars of the user interface have been hidden in this level of specification. It is assumed that the designer is familiar with the system style and desires, at this level of conceptual modeling, to concentrate on the application task.

```
        Generic-Prompt
Begin   Input        Test-String (verify as match pattern on type
                     <head(input)>)
        For Each     <input> in <item> where <head(input)>
                     matches Test-String
            Assign       Buffer = ((<input>), (<returning>))
            End
        List/Select  Buffer (Accept  Retry  Ignore)
        Case
            Return=Accept    Normal return with (<returning>)
            Return=Retry     Resume at Begin
            Return=Ignore    Abnormal return
            End
```

Fig. 11.2. Specification of a generic prompt program.

Before a program can be generated, the environment must produce a common program. In this example, the Prompt-Name specification would be merged with the generic **Prompt** template to produce the following specification:

```
        Prompt-Name-Expanded
Begin   Input       Test-String (verify as match pattern on type
                        Normalized-Name)
        For Each Normalized-Name, Affiliation in Person-Name
                    where Normalized-Name matches Test-String
            Assign      Buffer  =   ((Normalized-Name,   Affiliation),
                            (Person, Affiliation))
            End
        List/Select Buffer (Accept  Retry  Ignore)
        Case
            Return=Accept       Normal return with (Person, Affiliation)
            Return=Retry        Resume at Begin
            Return=Ignore       Abnormal return
            End
```

From the perspective of the program generator, there is nothing to distinguish this specification from a custom-coded common specification.

The task of the program generator is to transform the conceptual model represented in the specification (as augmented by the application knowledge maintained in the ADB) into a string of instructions in some target language. To accomplish this, TEDIUM relies on a collection of transformations (e.g., rewrite rules) that will reduce a command to a set of primitives that then can be mapped into target-language instructions. For example, the Input command can be replaced by a sequence that first prompts for input, then reads the input, and finally validates the input. When this sequence is combined with the implied system style requirements for exception handling, management of help requests, and abort processing, the extended sequence might become:

```
        Input-ready <item>
Read    Input-read Test-String
        Case
            Help-Request  Help-List <item> and resume at Read
            Abort           Abnormal return
            End
        Validate <item-validity>, Test-String
        Case
            Fail            Error-List and resume at Read
            Else            Assign <item> := Test-String
            End
```

In the expansion of this sequence of commands, free variables are bound to items specified in the ADB. Substitutions are permitted; for example, in the Input command of the program Prompt-Name, the operand in the verify as string overloads the default for *item-validity*. Each command shown in this expansion will be expanded until the command reaches a primitive form. These primitives may be a call to a program in the target language (e.g., programs to list out help messages or error statements) or a template for a sequence of statements in the target language (e.g., an in-line test to confirm that the length of the test string does not exceed that of the target item). The technique is similar to that used by Neighbors (1989) for his modeling domains.

By now the reader should understand the functionality expected of the Prompt-Name program. There also should be some sense of how the command statements are transformed into target-language instructions. But no clues have been given regarding either how the program behaves or how the users interact with it. For example, does the program have a pop-up window? Does the user scroll through the list of names that match the input string and use a mouse for selection? How are responses to help messages processed? How are they requested? These are all issues that must be resolved by the system style, which is specified by the meta-style application.

The rationale for the meta-style application is that there is a domain of knowledge that is valid for (and may be reused with) all applications of a given class. The benefit of using this category of knowledge has been explained, but there are some severe barriers to its capture and representation. The application-class knowledge actually is composed of two very different types of application features.

Mandatory features. These are features expected of all applications of the given class. For an IIS these include the testing of all inputs for validity, the abortion of an input process if a valid value has not been input, and the provision of a useful response to all requests for information. No quality IIS application should violate any of these rules unless they are overloaded by intent. In short, the mandatory features constitute a checklist of expected system properties.

Alternative features. These represent alternative *styles* for some application function. They are the standards and conventions that, when followed, ensure consistency and improve ease of use, effectiveness in training, etc. For example, when selecting a name from the list of names matching the input pattern, the user may employ the cursor keys, function keys, a mouse, or a combination of these devices. Whichever style is chosen, a uniform method should be used throughout the application. The number of styles available for an application class should be limited, and each style should hide both the processing and interface details from the conceptual level.

By way of illustration, the Input command incorporates the mandatory features identified above. It enforces the postconditions

On normal return, <*item*> in the context;
On abnormal return, <*item*> not in the context.

There is nothing in the expanded specification of Input, however, to suggest how the interaction is managed. Input-ready and Input-read, for example, rely on some conventions embedded in the system style to guide their interactions with the users. These interactions may employ a command dialogue or selections from a menu; the selections may utilize a mouse, keyboard input, or the cursor keys. Because there is no best style, the designer must be allowed to adapt the style to the task (i.e., overload the style).

From this brief overview, it can be seen that there is no clear division between the alternative features of the application-class knowledge and the primitive transformations of the software-tool knowledge. They are organized into separate applications to help separate the issues of style (i.e., what conventions the finished software should follow) and performance (i.e., how to implement efficient programs that conform to those conventions). There is no attempt, however, to preserve this separation within the program generator. The meta-style application formalizes the transformations for the alternative style features and maintains a checklist of the mandatory features; the meta-gen application formalizes the transformations from the ADB specification to the target language (and ensures that the mandatory features in the checklist are provided). For the development of TEDIUM, the meta-style and meta-gen applications separate the stylistic concerns from those of the implementation. It is a conceptual device, and the division between the two applications is fuzzy.

In summary, the version of TEDIUM now under development is composed of many cooperating applications. These applications share all or part of their specifications, and they may generate programs that interact with the programs of other applications. (For example, the program generator is composed of programs and data from meta-style and meta-gen.) TEDIUM-generated applications may use one of several target languages, and these applications may operate in a variety of environments. Each application, independent of its target language, will utilize one or more styles that are compatible with the target environment. The conceptual models for the applications developed with this new version of TEDIUM will be independent of the system style and target language used for their implementation. By altering the context of the TEDIUM environment, an application (i.e., ADB specification) can be realized as a product that employs one of several alternative styles and that operates in one of several different target environments. The accomplishment of this objective builds on the idea of family knowledge, which is the topic of the next section.

11.6. Family Knowledge

This section describes how TEDIUM manages its families of knowledge. The notion of families is derived from the work of Parnas (1976). He observed that the recognition of a program as a member of some larger family leads to a concern for the family's properties rather than those of the individual members. The idea of a family is central to the concept of an inheritance lattice. With TEDIUM, the organization as families is holistic, and membership is defined by a context. This can be illustrated by extending the publication application introduced in Section 11.4.

Each of the following three publication applications has specialized objectives, but their specifications can be organized as a family derived from the existing publication application. The first specialization is for a researcher; it integrates a personal list of references with a correspondence system for postal and electronic mail. For these objectives, the family member's ADB must be extended to include knowledge about postal and electronic mail. The second application is designed for a research library. Here, the member's ADB must include knowledge about publishers, journals, costs, and acquisition; it also must introduce a level of granularity to distinguish among different copies of the same book. The third application is for a specialized research group that uses electronic data forms as a media for reporting or exchanging results. This member's ADB must contain knowledge of the data formats and transfer procedures.

In this illustration, there is a family of "publication applications," each member of which shares some common knowledge. Not every application uses all the knowledge available in the family (e.g., the library has little need for the author's affiliation). Some members augment the common structures to capture added concepts (e.g., address may be modified to include e-mail addresses, and book descriptions may contain a copy number); other members introduce new structures (e.g., book-ordering knowledge, electronic-data-sharing knowledge).

Each of these three applications can be developed as a specialization (i.e., member) of the publication application family specified by the nine publication items (i.e., **Publication, Book, Journal, Proceedings, Report, Authors, Person, Publisher,** and **Affiliation**). Although the item definitions used by the applications will vary with the application, much of the knowledge can be shared. For example, **Publication** will be the same for all three applications, a new item (called **Address**) will be needed in the mail system to record the e-mail addresses, the library application will extend the definition of **Publisher**, and the electronic data exchange may use relatively little from these nine item specifications. Of course, changes to a specification should not endanger the integrity and independence of specifications elsewhere in the ADB. (In this sense, managing the items within a family is similar to the problem confronted by a code-management system.)

To understand how TEDIUM manages this, consider the **Single-Names** structure defined in Section 11.5. Its context is Application-Id, and the extension of this structure contains the specifications of every item in the selected application. The value of Application-Id establishes which set of items can be accessed, and changing the value provides access to a different set of item definitions. It is this context-change mechanism that is used to select members from families. For instance, let us name the four application domains: "Publications", "Pubs-Personal", "Pubs-Library", and "Pubs-Electronic". If Publications is defined to be the family root, then every item definition in Publications will be available to every member of that family *except when it is overridden by a definition within the member context*. A designer, working on Pubs-Personal, for example, may reference the root application, Publications, and modify any of its definitions. These changes, however, will not affect the root; instead, new definitions will be created in the Pubs-Personal application. TEDIUM will look first for definitions in the given context (Pubs-Personal). If the items are not defined at this level, then TEDIUM substitutes different contexts within the family organization until it finds the intended definition.

At first glance, this mechanism looks like that used with a hierarchical file system; if the desired file is not found at the current node, then the next alternative node in the list is searched. There are two major differences in the TEDIUM approach. First, the granularity is much finer than that of a file. Designers operate on fragments in the ADB (e.g., item definitions or help message statements). Second, the organization of families is not restricted to hierarchies. For example, the context for **Pair** is specified by

Pair-Context (Application-Id, Pair-Id) = Application-Context

This item allows the designer to assign an arbitrary context for each instance in **Pair**. If no entry for the given context exists, then TEDIUM references a family hierarchy defined in the ordered list

Family-Hierarchy [OL] (Application-Id, Application-Context).

If the item still is not found in the current context and both pairs are null (which is the case on initialization), then the item has not yet been specified. Notice that this mechanism allows more than one member to have local specifications of an item as well as the sharing of items among different families.

In contrast to the ADB families, families in the system style and program generator are application independent. Variations in the system style are used to select the implicit functions and default behaviors to be incorporated into the generated programs. For example, the environment establishes a predetermined set of actions whenever an invalid input has been identified (e.g., display the error in reverse video, sound the bell, record the error in a history file). A set of alternative responses for each class of situation also is available in the system style. The designer may elect to have the TEDIUM generator infer the default, or he may override the default with a response better suited to the application task. The set of all system style actions constitutes a family, and its members consist of compatible subsets of actions available to an application. The default system style is a member of this family.

To illustrate how the system style selections determine the behavior of a generated program, consider the following PRompt command (which is part of the expansion of the List/Select Buffer command in the Generic-**Prompt** program):

PRompt   Accept Retry Ignore

At one level, this statement simply establishes the postcondition

State' =   State $\wedge$ (Last-Read = "A" $\vee$ Last-Read = "R" $\vee$ Last-Read ="I");

it provides no information about the generated program's interaction with the user. The same command specification could be transformed into a pull-down menu, a pop-up menu, a line in a dialogue window, or a formatted pop-up box. The system style determines which option is the default, and—as in the case of the input testing—the designer can replace the default by explicitly selecting an alternative style more appropriate to the task. Similar options are available for the target language and operating environment. Thus, for each application, the designer identifies the ADB family members and selects members from the predefined system style and program generator families. The choices are limited, and only compatible selections are permitted (e.g., the designer can access only a subset of the possible interaction styles, all the programs in a target product must be generated for the same operating system). Decisions regarding the default family members and allowable member alternatives are normally made at the TEDIUM level.

The PRompt command is expanded by meta-gen as the following sequence of operators (i.e., as an [OL] of TEDIUM commands):

```
Prepare
Display-Menu  Accept  Retry  Ignore
Set-Help      <Optional help message>
Input-String  Last-Read = "A" V Last-Read = "R" V Last-Read
              = "I"
Conclude
```

The Display-Menu command processes the interaction, and its operation is a function of both the system style and the target language. The TEDIUM interpreter uses its own windowing mechanism, but the generated programs use the standard windowing conventions and styles of the target environment.   Thus, there must be more than one generator program for Display-Menu, and the selection of the appropriate generating program is established by the context of the program generator. In some cases, the generator uses a table look-up to select the appropriate action. More frequently, the following pair is used to select the generator program with a faceted look-up:

Gen-Select (System-Style-Id, Target-System-Id, Primitive-Command) = Generator-Program

The values for System-Style also can be modified as a function of the primitive command options using

Style-Option (System-Style-Id, Primitive-Command, Primitive-Option) = Alternative-System-Style

Because the system style options are bound to the generator programs, distinctions between the system style and program generator knowledge are somewhat artificial.   Certainly, both categories of knowledge are integrated in the generated programs that comprise the TEDIUM program generator. The separate knowledge families help distinguish between the concepts of knowing what the generated program should do and knowing how the generated program must function. These families also comprise the larger family of applications whose root value of Application-Id is "TEDIUM".

11.7. The TEDIUM Window into Design

I have described my approach to adaptive design as being conceptual on the outside but formal on the inside. Much of the discussion of the previous three sections has focused on the internal representations, an orientation that obscures the conceptual nature of the specification. It is difficult to convey how the designers interact with TEDIUM for two reasons. First, TEDIUM is used for complex problems, and to understand how TEDIUM operates one must understand the problem and its solution-in-the-making. For example, to go beyond the superficial library example used here, we would have to delve into how libraries meet their information needs. Once we understand that, the representations would seem more natural. Secondly, TEDIUM is used interactively, and its interface hides the internal structures from view. Lacking this interaction and the syntactic sugar of the display, the reader is forced to make sense of abstract representations. It is somewhat analogous to describing a paint program to someone who has never seen one. By way of illustration, Bødker, Greenbaum, and Kyng (1991) found that the operators in the UTOPIA project could not comprehend a WYSIWYG interface through verbal descriptions alone; special mockups had to be built to convey this idea (pp. 141-42).

Even though the internal representations are difficult to describe in the abstract, they actually tend to be quite easy to understand in an active project. There are two reasons for this. First, the project provides a context for the interpretation of the conceptual model, and secondly, the ADB displays place a minimal demand on short-term memory. This second feature is derived from the ADB specification's use of fragments rather than the formal, program-language orientation used with the traditional computer science forms. This change in representation bypasses the physical limitations of the paper medium and takes advantage of software's special properties. In so doing, the representation scheme shifts the burden from the reader to the environment. The environment now must compose displays from fragments to accommodate the designers' needs; no longer will the designer be expected to retrieve and assimilate the information stored in numerous, diverse sources. Because the granularity of the fragments will be considerably lower than that of any display that combines them, the environment can easily organize the information to present multiple views, orientations, and degrees of hiding. I call this feature of the TEDIUM environment its *window into design*. The phrase implies that the as-built specification is holistic (i.e., deeply integrated with no apparent external structure); it may be examined from differing perspectives in various levels of granularity. Moreover, because the examination of the displays often is performed interactively, the window also serves as a frame through which the designers can navigate within a complete specification.

Because the TEDIUM environment is a TEDIUM-generated application, the environment generated by TEDIUM normally employs the same system style that it will use in the applications it generates.

For instance, both the TEDIUM environment and the application described in Chapter 12 use a scrolling dialogue style. Alternatively, one could use a standard Windows/Macintosh style. The system style I personally prefer is the "function-key" style documented in Blum (1990a). There is an obvious advantage in keeping the system style of the environment identical to that used in the generated application. The designers become familiar with the style and can anticipate potential problems; that is, their use of the style helps them to become expert in its application.

Designers typically use the environment for four activities: to alter the specification in the ADB, to generate programs and documentation from the ADB, to peruse the ADB, and to exercise applications generated from the ADB. Normally, the designer jumps from one activity to another throughout the session. Therefore, the interface is set up to facilitate this branching and to store checkpoints that enable the resumption of previous activities. From the designer's perspective, the ADB is divided into objective specifications and subjective descriptions. Although objective and subjective fragments are intermixed, the window into design organizes access by concepts deemed natural to designers. Thus, the specifications are grouped into three classes of item:

Schema. This is the data model, and there are several subviews available. The designer may view relations, relationships, types, complex types, and structures. The displays include both the formal (e.g., type is double-precision real and the default listing format is F10.2) and descriptive (e.g., the help message for an attribute).

Programs. These are the processes. There are declarative specifications (which are defined and edited in a dialogue/fill-in-the-blank mode) and procedural specifications (which are written using the TEDIUM command language).

Contexts. All programs have contexts associated with them. Some contexts serve as preconditions and postconditions, others are used to define window attributes and report headings. Because some contexts are shared among many programs, facilities are provided to define and edit contexts separately and reference them by name (e.g., the TEDIUM context with the default TEDIUM definitions).

Notice that the descriptions of the internal representations in the previous sections have concentrated on how the fragments are defined; in contrast, the window into design presents the material in formats considered most helpful to the designer.

When editing the ADB, the interface provides access to all item definitions. Designers may select an existing item by pointing or typing; they also may define a new item by supplying all or part of the necessary information. Whenever a reference is made to an item that has not yet been defined completely, that fact is recorded by the environment; the environment maintains lists of yet-to-be-defined fragments and offers the designer an opportunity to complete any open specification items at the beginning and end of each session. In this, way, the designer need not break her chain of reasoning during a session.

In addition to the descriptive fragments that are appended to the objective items (e.g., in-line program comments), the environment also records the following descriptive (subjective) groups of items:

Objectives, or what functions the application is to provide.

Processes, or the processing flow for the required functions.

Data, or the data to be represented within the system.

Notice that each group represents a different projection of the application's requirements: what should be done, how should it work, and what should it operate on. As part of an as-built requirement, these descriptions explain what the product does. Thus, they tend to be documented at a relatively high level so that small changes to the specifications will not require changes to the descriptions. Users' manuals can be generated from these views.

Appended to the designer-defined items in the ADB are the generator-created fragments (e.g., cross-reference lists) and the artifacts of the design activity (e.g., traces and lists of incomplete definitions). Because the ADB is organized by application, each designer working on the application has access to its full and current specification. Whenever designers query the ADB—a request that may be made during an edit, generation, or review activity—the following six query functions are made available.

Type. This is used for all schema types as determined by the context of the query. The query responds with the definition of the type. By placing the cursor on an item in that definition and then selecting the Next function, the screen is replaced by the definition of that item. (Other standard options include a Last function to retrace the sequence, a Mark to retain the state for later listing by the Trace function, and an escape to return to the original state at the start of the query. These functions are available for all classes of items.) Other query options include viewing the descriptions of the data groups linked to this type, the cross references of the types that use this type, and the programs that use this type.

Program. One can list the identifying information, portions of the program specification, cross references and call trees, and the linked process descriptions. When the TEDIUM commands are displayed, one may position the cursor on any item and use the Next function.

Context. One can list the context definition, contexts used in its definition, and cross references to the programs that use the context. Using the cursor, one may query the definition of both types and programs.

Descriptions. One first must select the kind of description to be displayed (i.e., objectives, processes, or data). The description then can be listed in outline or full-text form (with or without the lowest levels suppressed). One may navigate by using the links between nodes of different kinds of description or between descriptive nodes and programs or types. Where programs or types are referenced, the cursor can be used to select items to be displayed (and possibly marked).

Cross references. The options here include call trees, descriptive links, and objective cross references between programs and types, types and types, and programs and contexts. The cursor can be used to display (and mark) items.

Trace. The trace function lists all items marked in the session. Selecting one of the marked items displays that item and permits the query to continue from that state. Items may be added to or deleted from the trace list.

Each of the above-described displays is produced by a fixed program that is part of the TEDIUM environment. In addition to these tools, TEDIUM will provide an ad hoc query capability. The tense of the last sentence implies that this feature is not yet a part of the baseline TEDIUM version I have just described (i.e., the ad hoc search facility constitutes a refinement of a refinement). Nevertheless, the approach is worth discussing briefly. The richness and complexity of TEDIUM's data model suggests that it will be very difficult to construct a query language that relies on simple structures (such as SQL); on the other hand, there is a great deal of knowledge in the ADB that can be used to infer queries from less structured input (e.g., one should be able to identify the attributes of interest without knowing the relation bindings).

Such a query language was developed for the original version of TEDIUM (Blum 1985c). The users specified the search by selecting attributes from a controlled vocabulary and then adding selection criteria; these inputs were then used to generate the search and report programs. The algorithm was rather simple, and I will use a relational nomenclature to describe it. Given a set of attributes, the program searches through the data model to identify which relations contain the desired attributes. Whenever an attribute is contained in only one relation, then we know that relation must be used in the query. If there are no relations that are unique for the set of attributes, then another algorithm is used to select a set of seed relations. Once these seed relations have been identified, the algorithm tests to see if (a) all the attributes necessary for the query are included and (b) if the set of seed relations will support a network of joins that constitutes a logical whole. If not, the process continues by inferring which relations or attributes should be added to the set. The assembly process is complete when a network of relations exists that covers the requested attributes.

For example, the query

List author and address where publisher city = "Oxford"

would first identify relations in which the attributes author, address, and publisher city appeared. It then would look for a logical link to join these relations. By tracing through the data model introduced in Section 11.4, the algorithm would discover that the relation Book, with its key attribute of ISBN, could be used to join Authors to Publisher and that Person (and perhaps Affiliation) are needed to provide the authors' addresses. Indeed, if the search mechanism were sufficiently powerful, the same algorithm could be used to generate a query for the request, "List all authors whose city is the same as that of their publishers." Clearly, all the knowledge necessary to construct such a query is available in the ADB.

The first query system was built, and it worked reasonably well for small queries, but it exhibited problems as the queries become more complex. In a deeply integrated data model, there are many different networks that will cover a set of requested attributes, and the question then shifts to one of selecting the most semantically correct search (i.e., the one that most probably provides the user with exactly the information requested). Without anyone anxious to use the query feature, the problem was not pursued. Several years later, however, we were faced with a similar problem, and our approach was based on the technique just described. In this project the goal was to create SQL queries for a relational database management system. We called the system the Intelligent Navigational Assistant (Blum et al. 1987; also described in Blum 1990a), and it performed quite well as a prototype interfacing with a very large database.

Semmel continued this line of research and expanded the information available for query resolution to include the entity-relationship model (Semmel 1991). He disambiguates his queries by organizing the relations into contexts that prescribe how the attributes may be combined to produce semantically correct responses. An implementation is being used in a production setting, and the data model it uses has been extended to include additional knowledge of the schema (Semmel and Silberberg 1993). Therefore, I reason, the richness of the TEDIUM ADB should provide an even more powerful resource for generating responses to ad hoc queries, but I leave the proof to the reader.

11.8. Some Final Observations

I am certain that the reader has found this a difficult chapter. Throughout much of the second half of this book I have held out the hope that adaptive design would be an answer to our problems. It would permit designers to adapt their products as the needs evolved, it would focus on the problem and not the product, it would take advantage of the special properties of software, and ... several other good things. I then told the reader how one instantiation of adaptive design worked. For this explanation I invented a new vocabulary so that the reader wouldn't be confused. (Did it help?) I also violated the first principle of conceptual modeling: I described the model rather than the concepts being modeled. Therefore, I'm sure I this has been a less than satisfying description of how TEDIUM achieves its objectives. It is similar to the situations my wife and I found ourselves in when our daughters were in their teens. After being told a "very funny story" to which we failed to respond, we were informed, "Well, you had to be there!" Perhaps you have to work with TEDIUM to get to know it.

Fortunately, my goal never was one of selling TEDIUM. The objective of this and the following chapter is to demonstrate that an environment for adaptive design exists and that it has been used for complex applications for more than a decade. That is, it is real. I begin by accepting the following assertions.

Applications that exist in-the-world are subject to uncertainty with respect to the system objectives. As a result, there will be continuing demand for change as the needs become better understood and as the organization adjusts to the changes in its environment.

All computer-based systems rely on formal models, but those models can be effective only in the domains in which important concepts are directly expressible in the available representation scheme.

During much of the early history of computing, there has been an emphasis on overcoming the difficulties of implementation and its management. Our present methods reflect this early orientation, an orientation that maturing technology has rendered inappropriate.

I therefore conclude that application development environments for the next century must address three principal deficiencies of our present approach. In short,

We need as-built, adaptable specifications.   The use of fixed specifications results in the design of what can be built rather than what is needed; it also constrains the extent of change to what can be changed rather than what needs to be changed.

We must learn to model concepts in the world.   If a representation scheme is to be effective for applications in-the-world, then it must be able to model application concepts. Because concepts vary from one application class to another, two levels of conceptual modeling are needed: one that provides a general, domain-independent framework, and a second (normally built on the first) that is application-class specific.

We need to move beyond programming.   Although there are many domains in which the formalisms of programming are appropriate, most are within the disciplines of computer science and computer engineering. This is too narrow a base for the applications of the 21st century.

My instantiation of adaptive design builds on the essential software process model. Recall that the model consists of iterations of a basic process that begins with the identification of a need and concludes with an implementation that responds to that need.   TEDIUM uses a conceptual model (the ADB, an as-built specification) to define a response to the need. Although the model is conceptual on the outside, it is formal on the inside (i.e., in terms of the essential model, the conceptual and formal models are isomorphic). Finally, because the domain of interactive information systems is relatively mature, it is possible to transform automatically the formal specification in the ADB into a production-quality implementation. In this way, the environment reduces the entire software process to one of conceptual modeling. The window into design provides access to all the information necessary to respond to the need. And knowledge about the implementation process is hidden from the application designer; it is made explicit, however, in the specification of the TEDIUM application that generates the designers' TEDIUM environment.

I like to think of TEDIUM's accomplishment in this way. Assume that a sponsor has provided a specification of what is needed together with a style document that describes the conventions and standards to be followed during the implementation. If the developer can take those materials and, without asking a single question of the sponsor, deliver the requested product, then—at the design level—there has been no value added. Indeed, because the implementation process uses only available knowledge, it can be automated. That, of course, is exactly what TEDIUM does. Moreover, by exploiting the unique features of software to maintain its holistic, fragment-based specification, TEDIUM also eliminates the need for static requirements, and the implementation exhibits the specification's behavior. In short, TEDIUM satisfies the principal objective of adaptive design: It adapts the product as the in-the-world needs change. How well does it work? That is the subject of the next, and final, chapter.

12

A CASE STUDY

12.1. Issues in Evaluation

The purpose of this chapter is to evaluate TEDIUM. Evaluation is similar to correctness in that both are always with respect to some external criteria. What criteria should be used for evaluating an environment that develops and maintains software applications using a new paradigm? Clearly, the criteria of the old paradigm (e.g., lines of code, measures of complexity, effort distributed among phases) are irrelevant. In the early days of medical computing, Barnett playfully suggested the following three criteria for evaluating automated medical systems:

Will people use it?
Will people pay for it?
Will people steal it?

At the time, the answers to first two questions frequently were negative, and Barnett's pragmatic approach was intended to prod the field from theory to practice. TEDIUM is used and paid for, but its techniques have not been transported to other environments (i.e., it has not yet been stolen). I console myself by observing that a lack of recognition need not imply an absence of value. The transfer of ideas often is a product of the marketplace, where acceptance depends more on perception than on quantification. As we have seen throughout this book, there can be vast differences between what we care about and what is measurable. Real projects tend to be large, difficult to structure for comparative studies, and highly dependent on local conditions. In contrast, toy studies are easy to control and analyze, but they seldom scale up or have much creditability.

How then should I evaluate TEDIUM? I have tried a number of strategies. I have analyzed small projects in detail, I have reported on standard problems comparing TEDIUM data with published results, I have presented and interpreted summary data taken from large projects, I have extracted evaluation criteria from other sources, and I have examined how TEDIUM alters the software process. All of this was summed up in *TEDIUM and the Software Process* (1990a). In addition, each descriptive paper contains evaluation data (1986b, 1987a, 1987b, 1987c, 1988b, 1993b), and there are papers that concentrate on evaluation issues only (1986c, 1987d, 1987e, 1989b, 1989e, 1991a, 1993a, 1995). In this chapter I use the case study technique and analyze the most recent project data from the largest system developed with TEDIUM. This is but one of the applications developed with TEDIUM, and there is much about this project that makes it unique. Nevertheless, I believe that these data provide useful insight into adaptive design and illustrate how that approach (as implemented with TEDIUM) affects the software process.

12.2. The Oncology Clinical Information System

The conceptualization and development of TEDIUM grew out of the need to reengineer the Oncology Clinical Information System (OCIS) for the Johns Hopkins Oncology Center. A one-computer configuration of OCIS had been in use since 1976. When funds for a second computer became available, the language used by that system (MUMPS-11) was no longer being supported, and it was clear OCIS would have to be reprogrammed for the two-computer configuration. Although there was much about MUMPS that we liked, we found that the effort to maintain OCIS had come to absorb most of the available labor. Therefore, we sought a better and more rational way to develop and maintain the new system. And this was how I decided to build a comprehensive environment for the software process, an ambitious—and perhaps foolish—undertaking.

Independent of the soundness of our decisions, in 1980 we found ourselves engaged in the implementation of TEDIUM, the conversion of OCIS, the maintenance of the operational version of OCIS, and the development of new systems for the Johns Hopkins Medical Institutions using TEDIUM. It was a tense period, but, fortunately, we were successful. TEDIUM was deemed complete enough to be frozen in 1982, and the two-computer OCIS configuration became operational in 1983. Enterline, Lenhard, an Blum (1989) have edited a book that contains the most complete description of OCIS; it also provides a history of both OCIS and TEDIUM. There is a recent paper by Enterline, et al. (1994) that updates the book and describes the system's current status. Finally, there are papers about new system functions (e.g., chemotherapy and treatment scheduling in Majidi et al. (1993)). Versions of the system have been installed in Australia (Hannan 1991, 1994) and Ohio (McColligan 1989).

The OCIS mission is to support the patient-care needs of the Johns Hopkins Oncology Center. The center has over 200,000 square feet of space consisting of 84 single-bed inpatient rooms, large outpatient and radiation therapy facilities, several ancillary ambulatory care clinics, and basic research laboratories. There are 725 full-time employees including 80 clinical and research faculty, 20 fellows, and 125 nurses. The inpatient component of the center admits more than 800 individual patients per year, with an average of 2.1 admissions per patient, and an average length of stay of 25 days. The outpatient component of the center has 50,000 visits to its Medical Oncology and Radiation Oncology units each year. OCIS is generally considered to be one of the most complete and comprehensive clinical information systems available for this type of tertiary care setting.

The current system, which has evolved from the two-computer configuration of 1983, operates on five networked computers with a distributed database connected to 500 terminals and personal computers located throughout the center. The network is being expanded by replacing several of the minicomputers with less-expensive personal computers, which will permit the number of peak users to exceed 200. The system provides online access to 25 million data points, which represent a half-million days of care for the 20,000 patients treated at the center. (Because of the research mission, there is no data archiving.) OCIS supports the center's clinical activities and complements the services available from the other Johns Hopkins Hospital computers (e.g., admission-discharge-transfer, inpatient and outpatient billing, the clinical laboratory, and radiology reporting).

There are some 550 online users of OCIS, and the system produces an average of 1600 reports daily. It provides the following functions.

Clinical data display. OCIS collects and manages virtually all clinical data that can be displayed in a table or plot. Inputs come from various hospital and center laboratories; some are transferred automatically across the network, and others are entered manually.

Transfusion services. Because the toxicity of the antitumor therapy may result in very low platelet and white blood cell counts, the center maintains its own transfusion services. This involves HLA typing, matching the available products to the patients in need, and evaluating the effect of each transfusion. (Over time, the patient will build up antibodies that reject transfused cells except for those with a close HLA type match.)

Daily care plans. Because most patients are treated using well-established plans (or protocols), OCIS was designed to produce daily care plans that would identify the tests, therapies, and actions for the current day based on previous patient history, current patient status, and general therapy plan. Functionally, this is similar to the service provided by the ONCOCIN expert system (Hickman et al. 1985).

Pharmacy. OCIS includes a pharmacy system for inpatients that supports the special needs of medical oncology.

Clinical research and the Tumor Registry. In addition to maintaining and exchanging data for internal and external clinical trials, OCIS incorporates a registry of all hospital patients diagnosed as having cancer. The registry contains 50,000 patient abstracts, of which 20,000 are for center patients. The data are used as a summary medical record for the center patients.

Administrative functions. Although OCIS was designed to augment the functions provided by the hospital systems, it is used for a variety of administrative purposes, including scheduling, planning, and auditing.

The integrated database is distributed among the network processors and is shared by all functions; a security system prevents unauthorized access to both data and functions (Blum 1991d).

In keeping with the system sculpture method, the approach to specification, production, and evaluation can be characterized as one of collaborative adaptation. The users have needs and perceptions of how automation can be helpful, and the developers have technical skills and perceptions of what the users need. The objective of the development environment is to provide a responsive, collaborative setting in which the participants (i.e., users and developers) can explore and refine their perceptions. This requires discussion, knowledge of similar applications, and operational feedback. Restating this, the users and developers learn by gaining experience, and that experience alters their understanding of their initial goals and their evaluation of the current system. As the experience accumulates, performance potential improves.

There are, however, three barriers to the effectiveness of system sculpture. The first barrier is that of hardware capability. If the system cannot support all the users, they cannot learn how it can help them. There also is a second obstacle: the difficulty in implementing a requested feature. When confronted by this impediment, the users hesitate to make requests because they believe that the request will not be acted on promptly; thus they tend to ask for only what they think they can get, never what they really need. These two constraints are independent of each other, and—depending on the environment— improvements in one area may expose deficiencies in the other. When both barriers are removed, however, then the only hindrances to progress are those of (a) learning what is needed and (b) adjusting to change. It turns out that both of these last activities require more time than expected, and both create a sense of frustration: Development always seems to take longer than it should. Nevertheless, there is no way to overcome these final two restraints.

The history of the OCIS project can be described as one of barrier removal. In the period up to 1983, the principal barrier was the limitation of the equipment. Only a few users and user stations could be supported by the one computer, and round-the-clock service could not be guaranteed. During the conversion to the two-computer configuration, the functionality of OCIS was frozen, and a backlog of requests accumulated. Thus, when the new system became operational in 1983, there was a burst of activity in which new features were introduced and obsolescent features removed. Although the development environment permitted rapid development, the new programs soon saturated the equipment's ability to support the system. Once again, the hardware barrier became dominant. In 1986 a new operating system was installed, and soon the system could support as many users as necessary. By this time, the designers had become expert in the use of TEDIUM, and so—from about 1987 to the present—the only constraint on progress has been the organization's ability to define and adopt the improvements. Thus, when we examine the project data, we should keep in mind that the development activity is divided into two periods: seven years of constrained design (1980-1986) and seven years of mature, adaptive design (1987-1993).

Throughout both these periods there have been surveys to measure users' satisfaction with OCIS. Enterline (1989) reported that "it appears that the user perception, utilization, and understanding of OCIS have improved dramatically between the 1984 and 1988 surveys. Further, if the types of additional functions required by users are any indication, the sophistication level of the OCIS user has increased dramatically during this time period" (p. 227). This comment may be taken as evidence of the users' shift from passively requesting what is deemed reasonable to proactively participating in the design process. The most recent survey, conducted in March 1993, was designed to measure the critical nature of OCIS to both patient care and job responsibilities. Given a scale of 1 to 10, where 10 indicated an absolute dependency on OCIS, 49% reported a dependency rating of 10, and 92% reported a rating of 8 or higher. Ninety-four percent indicated that OCIS was critical in meeting health care needs, and 96% indicated that OCIS was critical in carrying out their job responsibilities; 58% reported that patient care would be impacted if OCIS were down for two or more hours.

In summary, we find that OCIS is a large, comprehensive, and complex system whose users perceive it to be essential to the conduct of their clinical activities. The following sections take these facts for granted as they concentrate on the software development aspects of the OCIS project.

12.3. Characterizing the Project

There are two ways to analyze the data from a TEDIUM project. For small projects I normally describe the project dynamics in the context of the changing needs as they unfold during the process. For a large project, such as OCIS, the needs are far too complex to take that approach. Therefore, the analysis comes to rely on periodic system snapshots that provide static descriptions with limited explanatory power. In what follows, I use a snapshot of OCIS taken at the end of 1993 that describes the baseline specification of the 1994 version of OCIS. The snapshot focuses on the status of three principal items in the ADB: programs, tables (i.e., relations), and elements (i.e., attributes).

Programs are units of functionality. A program may manage a menu, support a prompt (as in the Chapter 11 examples), print a report, manage a dialogue, etc. The length of a program in "lines of specification" will depend on the how well the TEDIUM command language can express the intended concept. For well understood concepts (e.g., a generic file management facility), there can be an 1:80 ratio between the sizes of the specification and the generated programs; for other concepts (e.g., computation), the TEDIUM language may offer no advantages, and the ratio may be 1:2. The snapshots also treat the data model as if it were a relational model; the relationships and structures are ignored. (Of course, the version of TEDIUM reported on here does not permit the deep nesting of fragments described in Chapter 11.) For each of the three primary items the snapshot records the date of initial design, the date of last modification, the designers for those activities, the links among items (e.g., which programs read or write which tables, and which elements are shared among which tables), and some item-specific information (e.g., how many times a program has been generated from a specification).

Table 12.1 compares the most recent snapshot with earlier snapshots. The 1982 snapshot shows the system size when the first component of the two-computer system was installed, and the 1983 line contains the dimensions of the initial two-computer system. The next two snapshots show how system growth rose rapidly to about 5000 programs as the developers responded to the backlog of requests. Growth soon was constrained by the ability of the equipment to support

Table 12.1. Growth of OCIS

Date	Programs	Tables	Elements	Effort	P/ED
Dec. 1982	2,177	456	1,251	14	.61
Aug. 1983	3,662	848	2,025	19	.86
Dec. 1984	5,024	1,045	2,398	24	.93
Sep. 1986	5,541	1,375	2,613	33	.75
Jun. 1988	6,605	1,635	2,924	40	.73
Dec. 1989	7,695	1,920	3,281	48	.71
Feb. 1992	9,257	2,273	3,823	59	.70
Dec. 1993	11,575	2,597	4,253	71	.72

the user demand. To add new features to the system, older features had to be removed. The snapshots indicate only the size of the production system at the time. This might suggest that the size of the application stabilized at 5000-plus programs, but this is misleading. A separate analysis has shown that during this period 1200 production programs were retired. Thus, the period from 1984 to 1986 was one of active development, albeit constrained by the ability to support all of the desired facilities. In 1986, the hardware barrier was removed, and from that point on growth in product size averages 10% per year. This growth represents a measure of improvement in functionality as the users identify new features and the designers become more effective in anticipating user needs.

The final snapshot characterizes the 1994 OCIS specification. It contains 11,575 programs. To relate this to a system implemented in a traditional language, the specifications for TEDIUM programs average 15 lines, and the generated programs average 120 lines of MUMPS (or M) code (Lewkowicz 1989). When translating from TEDIUM to MUMPS, a single specification can generate many routines. In an earlier analysis, it was estimated that one TEDIUM program produced the same functionality as a custom-coded 60-line routine or a 200-line COBOL program (Blum 1982b). Thus, the OCIS application runs as a million-line MUMPS system. If coded in COBOL, it would be much larger; if custom coded in MUMPS, it probably would be less than a million lines. Of course, what is important is the size of the specification, and not the size of the generated product. The data model for OCIS contains 2597 tables with 4253 elements. Because TEDIUM employs fragment-based specifications, none of the schema definitions are counted as part of the program specifications. Thus, the 1994 specification of OCIS is quite large; it contains 18,425 design items. Fortunately, the specifications comprise a conceptual model in which each item can be displayed in one or two screens, all items are connected by numerous links, and the environment supports navigation throughout the specification.

The last two columns of Table 12.1 report on productivity within the OCIS project. The effort column counts the cumulative number of effort years assigned to the project prior to the snapshot. Not all developers worked full time, and only the proportion of time expended on OCIS is counted. The figures include design, maintenance, training, and management. The system manager, responsible for the day-to-day operation of the system, is counted as a half-time developer. The final column computes the number of programs in the production system divided by the cumulative number of effort days expended on the project (P/ED, or programs per effort day). The P/ED figure does not account for programs retired from the production system. As the table shows, net productivity is 0.7 programs per effort day; gross productivity (which includes retired programs) is about a program a day. Given that the program specifications average 15 lines, such a productivity rate is compatible with experience using other languages.

Tables 12.2 and 12.3 summarize designer productivity for both programs and tables. Each table counts the number of items within the 1994 production system. The rows identify the designers and the columns are organized by the year of initial design. The initial group of developers was composed of members from the Department of Biomedical Engineering (BME) and the Oncology Center (OC). During development of the two-computer system, there was little distinction between members of the two groups in terms of background, assignment, or supervision. As soon as the two-computer system was installed, however, most of the BME staff members moved on to other projects; the maintenance of their designs became the responsibility of the OC staff.

As the tables illustrate, the staffing was very stable during the period from 1984 to 1991. The supervisor of development (Sup Dev), the system manager (Sys Mgr), and two developers (OC-1, OC-2) provided the basic continuity as three developers contributed part time (OC-3, OC-4, OC-5), an operator was trained to work as a full-time developer (OC-6), and the staff grew slightly (OC-7, OC-8, OC-9, OC-10). In the early 1990s, however, retirements and staff turnover changed the nature of the project, and in 1993 half the staff was learning both TEDIUM and OCIS. Of the designers added to the staff in the 1990s, two began as computer operators, one had experience with the target language, and the others had some programming experience but required on-the-job training. Despite this need for learning, the data in Table 12.1 do not show any impact on productivity.

The data in Tables 12.2 and 12.3 show when the components of the production system were first designed. Many of these components have been modified since that time, and Tables 12.4 and 12.5 characterize the

Table 12.2. Count of programs defined by designer by year

Designer	1980	1981	1982	1983	1984	1985	1986	1987	1988	1989	1990	1991	1992	1993
BME-1	5	174	182	7	*	*	*	*	*	*	*	*	*	*
BME-2	3	49	232	105	41	*	*	*	*	*	*	*	*	*
BME-3	13	22	*	*	*	*	*	*	*	*	*	*	*	*
BME-4		46	15	*	*	*	*	*	*	*	*	*	*	*
BME-5		92	15	*	*	*	*	*	*	*	*	*	*	*
BME-6		33	*	*	*	*	*	*	*	*	*	*	*	*
BME-7		32	83	*	*	*	*	*	*	*	*	*	*	*
Sys Mgr	1	2	20	25	41	12	14	30	3	4	11	1	12	44
Sup Dev	*	*	208	252	224	162	230	184	57	105	46	95	120	164
OC-1	*	13	215	304	405	206	360	256	141	184	142	95	6	*
OC-2	*	24	59	62	277	212	196	138	166	271	288	256	406	446
OC-3	*	19	24	40	47	1	*	*	*	*	*	*	*	*
OC-4	D	D	1	47	154	*	*	*	9	25	*	*	*	*
OC-5	D	D	33	5	3	*	*	*	*	*	*	*	*	*
OC-6	*	*	*	O		139	91	67	25	33	15	*	*	*
OC-7	*	*	*	O	O	O	O	1	*		196	182	112	22
OC-8	*	*	*	*	*	*	*	*	*	73	81	71	64	*
OC-9	*	*	*	*	*	*	*	*	*	*	*	62	402	380
OC-10	*	*	*	*	*	*	*	*	*	*	*	117	191	191
OC-11	*	*	*	*	*	*	*	*	*	*	*	*	5	56
OC-12	*	*	*	*	*	*	*	*	*	*	*	*	*	78
OC-13	*	*	*	*	*	*	*	*	*	*	*	*	*	40
Other	0	23	23	3	33	0	5	2	9	3	0	8	5	16
Effort	-	7.0	7.0	5.5	4.5	4.5	4.5	4.5	4.5	6.0	5.5	5.5	6.0	6.0

* Not with the Oncology Center; D, clinical data coordinator; O, computer operator.

update history. They show, for both programs and tables, a distribution by the date of initial design and last edit. For example, Table 12.4 shows that 1437 programs were added to the system in 1993 and that 4881 programs were edited during that year (i.e., in 1993 the total number of programs increased by 12%, and 42% of the OCIS programs were new or edited). Not shown in the table are the facts that of the programs and tables actually edited in 1993, 48% of the programs and 27% of the tables were edited by someone other than the original designer. Table 12.4 also indicates that only 390 programs in the 1994 production system were defined on or before 1982 and never were edited after 1982. Thus, Table 12.4 suggests a deeply integrated system in

Table 12.3. Count of tables defined by designer by year

Designer	1980	1981	1982	1983	1984	1985	1986	1987	1988	1989	1990	1991	1992	1993
BME-1	8	74	53		*	*	*	*	*	*	*	*	*	*
BME-2		21	37	15	12	*	*	*	*	*	*	*	*	*
BME-3		1	*	*	*	*	*	*	*	*	*	*	*	*
BME-4		19	12	6	*	*	*	*	*	*	*	*	*	*
BME-5		15	1	*	*	*	*	*	*	*	*	*	*	*
BME-6		29	*	*	*	*	*	*	*	*	*	*	*	*
BME-7	6	6	14	*	*	*	*	*	*	*	*	*	*	*
Sys Mgr	2		8	13	10	3	1	25	8		4	1	8	15
Sup Dev	*	*	37	49	61	56	50	44	11	28	28	35	29	44
OC-1	*	1	20	63	57	63	66	74	42	75	56	30	1	*
OC-2	*	4	6	21	52	39	47	37	42	70	32	40	65	87
OC-3	*	1	15	53	18	2	*	*	*	*	*	*	*	*
OC-4	D	D	21	20	*	*	*	3	3	*	*	*	*	*
OC-5	D	D	10	4	4	*	*	*	*	*	*	*	*	*
OC-6	*	*	*	O	2	46	52	38	18	21	3	*	*	*
OC-7	*	*	*	O	O	O	O	1	*	3	40	34	8	3
OC-8	*	*	*	*	*	*	*	*	*	26	16	21	15	*
OC-9	*	*	*	*	*	*	*	*	*	*	*	12	60	58
OC-10	*	*	*	*	*	*	*	*	*	*	*	45	49	24
OC-11	*	*	*	*	*	*	*	*	*	*	*	*		8
OC-12	*	*	*	*	*	*	*	*	*	*	*	*	*	36
OC-13	*	*	*	*	*	*	*	*	*	*	*	*	*	4
Other	0	5	7	0	1	0	4	0	1	2	0	2	0	4
Effort	-	7.0	7.0	5.5	4.5	4.5	4.5	4.5	4.5	6.0	5.5	5.5	6.0	6.0

* Not with the Oncology Center; D, clinical data coordinator; O, computer operator.

which old programs are constantly being brought to the editor.

The data for table edits, shown in Table 12.5, are less dramatic. They show that in 1993 only 277 tables were added, and only a total of 411 were edited (i.e., in 1993 the total number of tables increased by 11%, but only 16% of the OCIS tables were new or edited). There are two explanations for this difference between program and table updates. First, there is a system artifact. The snapshot records the last date that a specification was brought into the editor and not the fact that the program actually was edited and generated; because the designer sometimes uses the editor to list program specifications, the data may imply more change than may actually exists. In contrast, designers

Table 12.4 Programs by year defined and year last edited

Year Defined	Year of last update												Total
	1982	1983	1984	1985	1986	1987	1988	1989	1990	1991	1992	1993	
To 1982	390	155	56	47	87	25	85	46	52	105	213	386	1,647
1983		182	107	58	48	34	39	26	50	52	72	197	865
1984			331	45	60	76	56	41	52	87	137	340	1,225
1985				91	68	32	21	19	26	79	104	292	732
1986					196	90	65	32	59	87	133	234	896
1987						123	53	39	28	70	119	246	678
1988							100	21	40	37	99	113	410
1989								131	55	88	150	274	698
1990									174	156	217	232	779
1991										256	253	376	885
1992											569	754	1,323
1993												1,437	1,437
Total	390	337	494	241	459	380	419	355	536	1,017	2,066	4,881	11,575

Table 12.5. Tables by year defined and year last edited

Year Defined	Year of last update												Total
	1982	1983	1984	1985	1986	1987	1988	1989	1990	1991	1992	1993	
To 1982	251	48	8	8	12	17	7	3	10	13	15	18	410
1983		154	17	14	11	9	1	1	2	4	10	12	235
1984			167	6	7	5	3	1	2	6	12	14	223
1985				132	7	10	6	0	4	5	13	4	181
1986					151	14	11	2	8	3	4	1	194
1987						139	6	6	3	6	8	12	180
1988							76	9	8	10	5	7	115
1989								113	22	37	9	21	202
1990									130	20	10	5	165
1991										152	25	13	190
1992											198	27	225
1993												277	277
Total	251	202	192	160	188	194	110	135	189	256	309	411	2,597

seldom use the editor to list tables. Second, there is a natural tendency for the tables to be more stable. They model external entities and are subject to less change; designers can also can create a new table for added attributes rather than insert them into an existing table.

Programs, on the other hand, describe how the information in the tables is used. This is a far more dynamic process. As the database expands, designers find new uses for the data; as the users work with the system, new applications for the available data are discovered. The

Table 12.6. Overview of program and table development activity

Year Defined	Count Pgms	Avg Gens	Activity[1] (%) 1<	1-2	>2	Count Tbls	Activity[1] (%) 1<	1-2	>2	Continuity[2] Pgms	Tbls
1980	22	29.2	13	22	63	16	6	25	68	0	6
1981	483	28.9	21	05	73	176	57	8	33	19	48
1982	1,141	22.3	28	8	63	218	69	7	22	39	71
1983	865	19.4	24	12	62	235	70	6	22	58	77
1984	1,225	22.3	28	4	66	223	76	2	21	57	85
1985	732	24.2	17	6	76	181	74	4	20	54	86
1986	896	18.5	28	8	63	194	83	6	9	57	93
1987	678	17.4	23	7	69	180	78	4	16	53	88
1988	410	18.6	28	5	65	115	72	7	20	60	94
1989	698	20.0	24	11	64	202	65	18	15	57	83
1990	779	22.0	32	25	42	165	89	4	6	66	87
1991	885	19.2	46	31	21	190	87	8	3	66	85
1992	1,323	16.3	71	28	0	225	95	4	0	71	91
1993	1,437	11.9	100	0	0	277	100	0	0	86	91
Total	11,575	19.5	42	12	45	2,597	78	6	14	60	83

1. Activity groups the specifications according to their last change: (a) within one year of definition, (b) between the first and second year after definition, and (c) two or more years after definition.
2. Continuity is the percentage of specifications whose last edit was by the original designer.

effect is to add new functionality and to modify existing features, both of which require modifications to the database. The extent of these changes is discussed in further detail in Section 12.8.

Table 12.6 summarizes the development activity for programs and tables. Each snapshot contains the dates of the initial design and the most recent edit together with the identifier of the designer. In addition, for programs the snapshot also contains the number of times the program was generated (i.e., the number of times the edited changes actually were used). The total counts for programs and tables are similar to the total columns in Tables 12.4 and 12.5, except that here the data are given for the years 1980, 1981, and 1982. These two count columns provide a sense of the age of the items in the system.

In the analysis of other systems developed with TEDIUM there seems to be a core of programs that are used throughout the system lifetime; new features are added to the core and existing features. This pattern is consistent with the OCIS data. The average number of generations for the programs increases with the age of the program. This is to be expected, as the older the program is, the more likely it will be modified.

The value for the average number of generations has grown considerably in this most recent snapshot; this most likely is a reflection of the change in staffing and the associated inefficiencies during learning. The activity columns measure the time interval between the initial design and the most recent edit. Note that about one fourth of the older (pre-1990) programs are never modified after 12 months of their design, but that some two thirds of the programs are edited two or more years after they are defined; for tables these figures are closer to three fourths and one fifth. This is consistent with the data presented in Tables 12.4 and 12.5. The final two columns provide a measure of designer continuity (i.e., what percent of the items were last edited by the person who was the original designer). The figure tends to be higher for tables than for programs, and older programs tend to be edited by a designer different from the initial designer—a fact easily explained by the turnover in designers.

The final table in this section, Table 12.7, displays some of the system properties in percentiles. First, it contains the number of generations. Note that whereas the average number of generations is 19.5, the median number is 14. This means that half the program specifications have been modified and generated 13 times or fewer. (Each specification must have an initial generation before it can be modified.) The median number of generations has been rising in recent snapshots; it was 11 in the 1989 snapshot and 13 in the 1992 snapshot. The next two columns show the age distribution of the specification items, and the final two columns give the active age (i.e., the years since the initial definition and the last edit). Both pairs of columns offer a sense of the system components' age and stability. For example, the age distributions of the program and table components are roughly the same;

Table 12.7. Percentile distributions of activity

Percentile	Gen- erations	Actual Age (Years)		Active Age (Years)	
		Programs	Tables	Programs	Tables
10	4	0.9	0.8	0.0	0.0
20	6	2.0	1.7	0.1	0.1
30	8	3.5	2.8	0.3	0.2
40	11	4.8	4.3	0.9	0.3
50	14	6.7	6.5	1.6	0.3
60	17	8.1	7.8	2.8	0.4
70	21	9.5	9.3	4.6	0.5
80	28	10.7	10.3	6.8	1.2
90	42	11.7	11.5	9.0	3.8
Average	19.5	6.4	6.1	3.2	1.0

half the programs and tables in the 1994 system were defined more than six years earlier, and about a quarter are ten years old. The tables, however, are quite stable and have not changed over time. For example, only 30% of the tables have been edited 6 or more months after the initial design. In contrast, the programs tend to be dynamic; 30% of the programs have been edited 4.6 years after their initial design. The fact that only 60% of the programs in the system are at least 4.8 years old implies that half the programs are subject to continuing modification, a pattern that is visible in Table 12.4.

The following sections interpret the data presented in these seven tables. In each of the next three sections I establish some criteria for the evaluation, justify the selection of the criteria, and then employ the above-mentioned data to determine how well TEDIUM satisfies the criteria. My selection of the criteria, of course, is biased. All of my choices are predicated upon a positive outcome. Moreover, I ignore criteria that are deeply committed to a paradigm I do not use. The final two evaluation sections examine the data from the perspective of the process and the product.

12.4. Evaluating the Environment

This section evaluates TEDIUM with respect to its operation as a software support environment. To provide a context for what follows, note that a support environment, as defined by the Software Engineering Planning Group (Musa 1983), is the lowest level in the Software Engineering Hierarchy:

In this structure, methods and practices are chosen to support process descriptions (i.e., process or life cycle models), tools are used to carry out tasks defined by the methods and practices, and the support environment (or software environment) is an integrated set of tools, methods, and practices that enable a specific process model.

The Software Engineering Hierarchy, which really defines a network, illustrates two essential characteristics of a software environment. First, every environment is restricted to a family of process models, and the utility of that environment (and its features) can be evaluated only with respect to how well it supports its process model. The second feature highlighted by this hierarchy is the fact that a support environment must be an integrated collection of automated and non-automated tools, methods, and practices. In the most general sense, all software is developed within a support environment. One goal in software engineering is to extend the role of automation in the software process. In that context, Osterweil (1981) identifies five necessary properties for an automated support environment:

> breadth of scope and applicability, user friendliness, reusability
> of internal components, tight integration of capabilities, and use
> of a central information repository. (pp. 36-37)

If one accepts these criteria, then any environment evaluation must demonstrate that the subject environment possesses these characteristics. Of course, this is a necessary condition, which does not address the basic issues of the scope of process support (i.e., degree of process automation) and effect of use (i.e., outcome measures such as productivity or quality comparisons within a process model).

Because the TEDIUM environment provides comprehensive automated support to all aspects of the software process using a process model distinct from those in general use, an analysis of its individual functions (e.g., how it supports editing, how it maintains files) would offer little insight into its overall utility. Similarly, comparisons with the evaluations of environments designed for other process models (e.g., Moreau 1987, Weiderman et al. 1987, Graham and Miller 1988) would have little validity. However, simply demonstrating that it satisfies Osterweil's necessary conditions for an environment adds nothing to our knowledge regarding the value of the environment (or the process model it supports). Consequently, if we are to evaluate this (or any atypical) software environment, then we ought to begin at the level of the software process that it supports and ask the following three questions:

> Does the environment support the process model as intended, and does it incorporate Osterweil's five characteristics?

> Is the environment (and process model) applicable to a range of software situations, and is it, therefore, worthy of further consideration?

> Is there evidence that the use of the environment (and process model) represents an improvement over other approaches with respect to productivity, quality, maintainability, and so on?

From the description in the previous chapter, it should be clear that TEDIUM supports the fully automated paradigm for the essential software process. The complete conceptual model (except for any text and diagrams too inconvenient to enter) is maintained in the ADB; there is no formal representation other than that of the conceptual model; and the transformation from the conceptual model to the implementation is completely automated. Further, the environment is used from requirements analysis until product retirement. To demonstrate satisfaction of the first requirement, I need only describe how TEDIUM satisfies the five characteristics of an automated support environment with respect to its process model and automation goals.

Breadth of scope and applicability. TEDIUM supports the entire life cycle without recourse to any tools not available in the environment. Its generated programs are treated as object code and never modified.

User friendliness. Although the operational version was frozen in 1982 and therefore does not incorporate features that now have wide acceptance, the interfaces have proven relatively easy to learn and use.

Reusability of internal components. All explicit application knowledge is preserved in an integrated ADB without replication. Thus, knowledge is shared among programs, and text fragments are shared among documents. Facilities also are available to share definitions among applications.

Tight integration of capabilities. TEDIUM was implemented as a closed environment intended to meet all of the users' needs.

Use of a central information repository. All knowledge of the application is maintained in the ADB and is available during all design activities. Validation during system sculpture takes place in an interpretative environment that provides access to both state and specifications.

Thus, TEDIUM satisfies the first evaluation requirement: It supports the process model as intended and incorporates the five characteristics. Its use in the domains of medical informatics (e.g., OCIS) and software engineering (e.g., TEDIUM) indicates that it is applicable to a range of software situations, and the productivity and growth data already cited are evidence of its impact on quality. Thus, I assert that TEDIUM satisfies the criteria of being an effective software development environment.

12.5. The Representation as a Specification

I now examine the TEDIUM specifications. Although there are no standard evaluation criteria for a specification, several guidelines introduced in the 1970s identify some important criteria for the effectiveness of any representation scheme. Parnas (1972b) stated that the specification scheme must provide to both the intended user and the implementer all the information needed by each, but nothing more (i.e., information hiding). He also asserted that the specification must be formal so that it can conceivably be machine tested, and it must "discuss the program in the terms used by user and implementer alike (i.e., not some abstract formalism)" (p. 330). Liskov and Zilles (1975) extended the criteria as follows.

Formality. It should be written in a notation that is mathematically sound. This is a mandatory criterion.

Constructibility. One should be able to construct specifications without undo difficulty.

Comprehensibility. A trained person should be able to reconstruct the concept by reading the specification.

Minimality. The specification should contain the interesting properties of the concept and *nothing more*.

Wide range of applicability. The technique should be able to describe a large number of concept classes easily.

Extensibility. A small change in the concept should produce only a small change to the specification.

Both sets of specification criteria were demonstrated with a concrete concept (i.e., the stack), and this section extends these concepts to large-scale systems. The question is twofold. Do the criteria scale up for the specification of a large system (e.g., one whose implementation constitutes a million lines of code), and, if yes, does the fragment-based specification of TEDIUM satisfy the criteria? The following evaluation assumes that the criteria do scale up and considers only the second issue.

There is no need to prove that TEDIUM's fragment-based specification is mathematically sound; the fact that it is used to generate complete and correct implementations demonstrates that it is sound. Therefore, only the remaining five properties are considered. The discussion begins with the properties of applicability and minimality, and it then uses OCIS project data to characterize constructibility, comprehensibility, and extensibility.

Wide Range of Applicability.   One desirable property of a representation scheme is that it apply to a wide range of concepts. TEDIUM has been optimized for interactive information systems, but there is nothing in its architecture that restricts it to this class of application. The basic design recognizes that requirements engineering is domain oriented, and no one environment (or specification language) will suffice for all domains. TEDIUM uses application-class knowledge to tailor the system to a particular class of needs, and the architecture permits the introduction of system styles for new domains (e.g., real-time and embedded systems). Even though the problem-oriented paradigm implemented by TEDIUM may be employed with multiple application classes, it has only been demonstrated in the domain of interactive information systems. This domain, however, is itself quite broad; and TEDIUM has been used to develop clinical information systems, many software tools, and some AI applications. Clearly, then, the range of applicability for TEDIUM's fragment-based specifications is far broader than that demonstrated with 4GLs and most research specification schemes.

Minimality.   Liskov and Zilles defined minimality in the sense that Parnas defined information hiding. The specification should provide only the necessary information and nothing more. In the 1970s, the concepts of interest were modules (actually, data abstractions, which in an object-based environment become modules). In the TEDIUM environment the concepts to be specified are computer-supported responses to a need. Nevertheless, the goal remains the same: to have the implementer specify the interesting properties of the concept and *nothing more.* TEDIUM addresses this challenge by providing (a) a holistic ADB in which all concepts are shared within an application, (b) a specification command language that reduces housekeeping concerns, and (c) a system style that details (and hides) the implicit and default properties expected in the implementation. Within the ADB the interesting properties are specified in the form of a schema and program specifications, and the goal of the TEDIUM representation scheme is to employ the most-compact representations (i.e., they should be housekeeping free). The productivity reported in the previous section is a consequence of the fragment-based specification's minimality.

Constructibility.   This is defined as the ability to construct specifications without undo difficulty. The fact that net productivity in OCIS over a fourteen-year period is 0.7 production programs per effort day is a clear demonstration that the fragment-based specifications facilitate construction. Several studies have shown that individual differences are within a factor of two with respect to two measures of performance (i.e., number of programs developed and number of edits required). In general, knowledge of the application is a better predictor of performance than training in computer science; many in the current Oncology Center staff began their careers as computer operators. Thus, it is not difficult to teach designers to use TEDIUM effectively.

In addition to this general evidence of productivity, constructibility can be demonstrated by the ease with which designers create and maintain program specifications. One measure of the ability of a designer to express his computational intent is the number of times a program is edited. If this number is low, then it can be concluded that the designer has had little difficulty in expressing his intent. (A high number, on the other hand, can have many causes, such as improper training, poor problem understanding, or a clumsy development environment.) The most recent median number of edits is 14. This count includes all changes to a specification for debugging and maintenance—corrective, adaptive, and perfective—throughout the program's active lifetime. Such a total number of edits over a 14-year period clearly suggests that the representation scheme offers an effective description of the interesting properties of the item specified.

Comprehensibility. This requires that a trained person be able to reconstruct the concept by reading the specification. In TEDIUM, the conceptual model in the ADB is viewed as a statement of the problem and its solution; it should be "close" to the designers' mental models. Thus, comprehensibility can be demonstrated if it can be shown that a designer who understands the problems being addressed (i.e., the Oncology Center's needs) and the specification language (i.e., TEDIUM's ADB interface) has little difficulty in creating and revising the specifications. The fact that almost half of all edits in 1993 were performed by a designer other than the initial developer is a sure indication of the specification's comprehensibility.

Extensibility. The final criterion concerns the ability of the environment to have small changes in the requirements produce only a small change to the specification. With TEDIUM, the specification is maintained holistically, and it models a response to a set of needs in the application domain. Because those needs are deeply integrated, the specification in the ADB should reflect that degree of integration. Therefore, to demonstrate extensibility, the degree of integration within the ADB is examined (i.e., small changes external to OCIS should lead to small changes to OCIS, and the new and changed fragments should be integrated with the unchanged fragments). By way of demonstrating the deep integration of the OCIS application, I note that in 1993 42% of the 11,575 programs were brought into the editor, which implies that relatively few modifications or additions to the system were in any sense "local." That is, the changes to the system in one year affected 42% of the entire system. A further discussion of the integration of the OCIS specification is given in Section 12.8. Nevertheless, the data presented in Section 12.3 provide a clear demonstration that the specification of OCIS is highly dynamic and deeply integrated, which illustrates the extensibility of the TEDIUM representation scheme.

12.6. The Representation as a Conceptual Model

Finally, I use some published criteria to evaluate TEDIUM's conceptual model. With TEDIUM, I claim, the software process reduces to a conceptual modeling activity. What a conceptual model is, of course, will vary with the environment and process model used. Most conceptual models are defined within the two-step problem-oriented model, where its goal is to improve the understanding of the need prior to the documentation of the requirements specification. Lindland, Sindre, and Sølvberg (1994) propose a framework for characterizing the quality of a conceptual modeling scheme. They begin with this definition:

> A conceptual model—any collection of specification statements relevant to some problem—is an important part of early development. Within the scope of conceptual modeling is the requirements specification, as well as any additional knowledge not in the form of requirements. (p. 42)

Clearly, a conceptual model in this sense has no analogue in the problem-oriented paradigm of adaptive design. In the two-step process, where the implementation of the product is seen as the major activity, extra effort in deciding what that product should be is effort well invested. But, on the other hand, when the effort reduces to only conceptual modeling itself (as it does with adaptive design), then the model becomes the end rather than a means to an end. Nevertheless, a brief analysis of their framework will be instructive. They build their quality criteria on linguistic concepts.

> *Syntactic quality.* The more closely the model adheres to the language rules, the higher the syntactic quality.... There is only one syntactic goal, syntactic correctness, which means that all statements in the model are according to the syntax....

> *Semantic quality.* The model can lack something that the domain contains, or it can include something the domain doesn't have. The more similar the model and the domain, the better the semantic quality.... There are two semantic goals: validity and completeness. Validity means that all statements made by the model are correct and relevant to the problem....

Completeness means that the model contains all the statements about the domain that are correct and relevant....

Pragmatic quality.   While semantic quality affects choices between models with alternative meanings, pragmatics affects how to choose from among the many ways to express a single meaning.... There is one pragmatic goal: comprehension.... An important point in making the model understandable is that you must ensure that all concerned parties understand it, not just select groups. (pp. 46-47)

Obviously, the TEDIUM environment processes only syntactically correct statements, so that quality is high.   The model also is as complete and as valid as the product itself (by identity). The only issue to be examined, therefore, is the pragmatic quality. In technological design the conceptual model is separate from the product, and its pragmatics rely upon shared interpretations. With adaptive design, the pragmatics of the conceptual model are demonstrated in the execution of the product.   Thus, the participants in design do not work with model's representations; rather, they work with system's representations. Although this does not eliminate misunderstanding and the development of naive theories, it clearly changes the pragmatic qualities of the conceptual model.

12.7. Characterizing the Software Process

Having used the OCIS project data to focus on TEDIUM as an environment, a specification scheme, and a conceptual model, I now turn outward and examine the context in which TEDIUM is used. I begin with the assertion that TEDIUM employs the essential software process (as do all other development approaches). When TEDIUM uses its own process model and leaves out certain steps and adds in others, how does it change the way the software process behaves? Does it violate any standard assumptions? Does it identify process artifacts that we assume are essential but that, in reality, are accidental?   That is, does the experience with TEDIUM offer new insights about the software process that are valid independent of the use of TEDIUM?   This is the motivation for the examination that follows.

I begin by contrasting once more the problem-oriented model (used by TEDIUM) and the product-oriented model (which is the primary source of all our experience). The software process with a problem-oriented model is a series of conceptual modeling iterations—a process of evolution.   In contrast, the product-oriented model divides the development into requirements analysis and implementation; moreover, maintenance follows installation as a separate activity. Thus, the first distinction is one of a continuous versus a phased process. With the TEDIUM environment there is only the conceptual model in the ADB; it contains everything known about the application, and it always is up to date. In the more traditional process models, much of what is known is maintained in a hierarchy of materials, many of which exhibit both temporal and logical inconsistencies. Here the distinction is between a single, unified design record and an arbitrary set of materials. Finally, with TEDIUM there is no delay between completion of the specification and the availability of an executable product. In a product-oriented model extended delays are expected between the formulation of a concept and the availability of an executable product.

As noted, virtually all of our experience has been with variations of the product-oriented model. The tools developed for that model were intended to overcome the difficulties in its conduct (e.g., for managing phases, integrating diverse collections of documents, and supporting implementation activities). TEDIUM, however, employs an alternative approach that is not plagued by the primary difficulties that have so engaged software engineers. In a TEDIUM project:

There is no prescribed sequence of activities.

The descriptions and specifications are always timely and accurate.

The fabrication of operational products requires no effort.

Obviously, many of the tools proven to be so effective in the product-oriented model will have no value in the problem-oriented model. The question is, therefore, what happens when we eliminate the three principal difficulties of the product-oriented approach? How does the process behave? I divide the answer into two parts. The first examines product evolution, and the second deals with designer performance.

We know, by definition, that a software product with open requirements must evolve. I already have referred to the E-Type program, which, once installed, alters its environment, thereby invalidating its initial requirements specification and causing requests for change (Lehman 1980). It has been known for quite some time that the cost for software maintenance generally exceeds the cost for software development and that most software maintenance is actually product enhancement (Lientz and Swanson 1980). The study by Dekieva (1992) suggests that the ability to accommodate change places a ceiling on how much change will be attempted. In effect, the ability to implement change biases the process because it determines how much change is attempted. Martin (1982) writes of invisible backlogs composed of requests that are never made because they would not be acted on in a timely manner.   How, then, does adaptive design affect product evolution?   I consider product growth, component stability, and the extent of change.

Product Growth.   In a setting such as the Oncology Center there is an unbounded set of needs to which OCIS can respond. Thus, each increment of functionality does not satisfy the center's needs; rather, it stimulates the identification of new needs and the recognition of new functions that can support them. Therefore, one can expect a pressure for change that is beyond the organization's ability to respond. As we have seen in the case of OCIS, the barrier to change has shifted over time. Since 1987 the limits to growth shifted to (a) the ability of the designers to build the conceptual models and (b) the ease with which users could clarify their needs and assimilate new products. The result, shown in Table 12.1, is that the system has grown in size (and hence functionality) by 10% per year during the past 7 years. Although this rate of growth may not satisfy all the open demands, it is clear that (a) an open system is not stable and (b) an organization can respond to only a limited amount of change within a given time period.

Component Stability.   Proponents of data-structured design and composition techniques (including object-oriented design) assert that if one models portions of the real world, then the software will be more stable and easier to maintain. The alternative is data-flow design and decomposition, which emphasizes the division of the system into components or modules that, in turn, may be decomposed. Whereas the former models aspects of the problem domain, the latter models the architecture of the implementation.   One would expect the former methods to be more flexible in making software changes that reflect changes in the external environment. And this is what experience with OCIS demonstrates. The ratio between programs and tables remains constant at 4:1 throughout the life of the project, but the tables require less editing than the processes. In part this is because the entities for which surrogates are maintained in the system are relatively static; in part this is because new uses for the available information require procedural changes rather than data model changes.

Extent of Change.   The product-oriented model is derived from experience with hardware development, and that model places a great emphasis on the target system's architecture. Decomposition allocates functions and maintains a modular structure; this modularity is viewed as a powerful technique for improving quality and controlling change. However, as previously noted, the module is rarely found in-the-world. Although we speak of a circulatory and respiratory system in the human body, we know that they are not modules.   We use the "system" metaphor to abstract complexity; indeed, what is most often of interest is found at the "system" interface. In adaptive design the conceptual model is holistic; it is not modular.   The data from the TEDIUM projects suggest that the products themselves also are deeply integrated and, therefore, that modularity is an accidental, and not an essential, property of a software system. The organization that uses a system is seldom modular, and if the system is to reflect the structure of the organization that it serves, then perhaps modularity can be a barrier to flexibility.   Of course, modularity is essential for the effective management of product development *in a product-oriented model*. Unfortunately, its use constrains the type of projects that will be undertaken and the extent to which requests for changes will be accepted.

I now turn to the second issue, that of designer performance. In "No Silver Bullet" Brooks (1987) observes that most "hopes for the silver" (e.g., Ada, OOP, AI, and graphical interfaces) address the task components of the software process, and therefore they can have only limited benefit. His four promising attacks on the conceptual essence emphasize the cognitive aspects of design.   "Buy versus build" (the ultimate in reuse), "requirements refinement and rapid prototyping," "incremental development—grow, don't build software" (two methods for closing the requirements by learning), and "great designers" (by which he means the nurturing of the individual designers).

> Great designs come from great designers. Software construction
> is a *creative* process.   Sound methodology can empower and
> liberate the creative mind; it cannot inflame or inspire the
> drudge. (p. 18)

The following paragraphs examine the upper bounds on the performance of empowered and liberated designers. I consider overall productivity, ease of expression, and individual differences.

Overall Productivity. Productivity normally is measured in lines of code. In a product-oriented model, the project plan focuses on the attributes of the *product* to be built and not the *problem* to be solved. For example, most cost and schedule estimation tools rely on product size (Boehm 1981). Function points, which measure aspects of the problem solution, were intended to provide a better estimate of product size (Albrecht 1979). Despite its potential for providing a measure for the problem complexity, research into extending function points (Verner and Tate 1987) or using other system-level measures (Bourque and Côté 1991) continue to be evaluated with respect to their accuracy in predicting product size. Yet, as I have discussed elsewhere (1989a), the size of the project is determined, to a very large extent, by the implementation techniques used. For instance, Albrecht and Gaffney (1983) have shown that the number of lines of code to produce a function point varies with the programming language.

It is widely held that productivity as measured in lines of code is roughly independent of the language used (Brooks 1975; Wasserman and

Gatz 1982), and it follows that more compact and expressive representation schemes should lead to improved productivity. When estimating productivity for a moderate-size project, one guideline is two lines per hour for a well-documented system; Cusumano reports that the Japanese software factory creates 500 lines of new code per person month (see Myers 1992b). Because the ADB program specifications average 15 lines, it is reasonable to expect TEDIUM productivity to be on the order of one production program per effort day. And this, of course, is the case.

The compactness of the specification is one productivity factor. What of the skills of the designers? For example, some proponents of formal methods assert that specialized training is a prerequisite for software engineers (Tanik and Chan 1991). As described earlier, three basic groups of people have been responsible for developing OCIS: the initial designers, who were mostly software professionals; the OCIS team, who grew with the system and its environment; and the new hires of the 1990s, who had to learn the system on the job. Few staff members have a formal background in computer science, and many began as computer operators or data technicians within the Oncology Center. Nevertheless, the staff is very skilled in the domain represented within the ADB (i.e., how automation can improve the center's operations), and, in this sense, they are "great designers." Although their expertise is limited to one development environment and one type of application, that is sufficient for the Oncology Center. Anecdotal evidence suggests that an understanding of the application domain is the hardest thing to teach, and, without that knowledge, it is impossible to build the conceptual construct.

Ease of Expression. Designer efficiency improves with the designer's understanding of the intended solution and her ability to represent that solution precisely and easily. With TEDIUM, the ADB constitutes a conceptual model of the desired solution. We can assess the "closeness" of this conceptual model to the designers' mental models by examining the difficulty they have in creating and maintaining this model. One measure of expressiveness (i.e., the ability of a designer to express his computational intent) is the number of times a program is edited prior to its use. We already have seen that this number is low. A second measure of expressiveness is the difficulty that designers have in modifying portions of the conceptual model that they did not create initially. We also have seen that half the pre-1990 programs are maintained by designers who were not their original developers. These data suggest that when the designers have a sound understanding of what the application should do, TEDIUM's fragment-based, holistic conceptual model provides an effective means of expressing that understanding while hiding the unnecessary implementation details.

Individual Differences. Although it is obvious that there are differences among individuals, the extent of that difference is clouded by myth. Ranges of 28:1 and 23:1 have been reported and repeated (Sackman et al. 1968; Curtis 1981); at the 1989 International Conference on Software Engineering Curtis stated that individual differences were on the order of 8:1. Although I have not included all the data in Section 12.3, one can examine individual productivity with respect to both the number of programs produced per unit of time (Tables 12.2 and 12.3) and the number of edits per program (data not supplied). In OCIS, the range of individual differences for trained designers is under 2:1.

As observers of track and swimming events will attest, marked differences in performance will produce relatively small differences in time. Thus, it would seem that individual differences that exceed 2:1 are most likely an indication of a training deficit rather than an inherent cognitive variation range. That is, most motivated and disciplined designers can become great designers, if only within a specialized domain. Moreover, unless there is domain-specific training, then significant differences will persist. Finally, I have found no evidence that expertise in programming skills correlates with effectiveness in system development.

Concluding Observations. In this section, I examine the TEDIUM/OCIS project from the perspective of the perceptions growing out of experience with the technological design process. We find that many of the long-accepted properties associated with the product-oriented model are really accidental rather than essential properties of the process. For instance, when Lehman and Belady (1985) conducted their analysis of OS/360 evolution reported in Lehman (1980), an increasing number of modules affected was used as a marker for structural degradation caused by maintenance. However, with module-free adaptive design, the same ripple effect is taken as evidence of the system's integration. Clearly, if there is integration in-the-world, then integration in-the-computer constitutes a good model.

Yet modularization is an established principle, and it has many advocates. Indeed, Meyer (1988) describes object orientation as a way of achieving of modularization. Thus, if we give up modules, must we give up objects as well? And if we do, where will we end up? With fragments? Obviously, I've shared my biases. But whether or not I am correct, it should be clear from the TEDIUM project data that the conduct of software design within the two-step, product-oriented model introduces artifacts that are not part of the essence of software design. This section suggests what those aberrant artifacts might be; experience with different paradigms should identify others.

12.8. Characterizing the Product

The claim I make about TEDIUM's specifications is that they are holistic and fragment based. Although the representation scheme used with the OCIS specification does not exhibit the degree of nesting implied in Chapter 11, the design is deeply integrated and non-modular. In this section I examine the specification of the OCIS conceptual model. The description is of interest because OCIS operates as a million-line application that is easily maintained and used in life-threatening situations. That is, it is a real system, it is dynamic, and it demonstrates that adaptive design works. Thus, an analysis of its internal structure constitutes a rare opportunity to explore how a system developed with adaptive design differs from one implemented with technological design. The OCIS design, however, is only an instance of the possible, not a description of the ideal; it is interesting only because it has been around for more than a decade and it is used.

Unfortunately, as in much of the analysis in this chapter, there are no external baselines to guide a comparison. Although many AI applications (e.g., expert systems) employ a holistic organization for their knowledge, most papers report only the number of rules used and not their integration, links, or maintainability. Similarly, because the fragment-based approach is intended avoid the restrictions of modularization, one would not expect any correspondence between the OCIS specification and the design of a system in which modularization is a prerequisite. Therefore, it is best to view OCIS as a one-of-a-kind specimen.

I begin by describing the data model. In OCIS this consists of tables (relations), related tables (i.e., secondary tables in one-to-one correspondence), structures, and elements (attributes). As shown in Table 12.1, the specification contains 2597 tables with 4253 elements. Fifty-one of these tables are secondary tables. For example, the table that identifies the patient (indexed by the patient's history number) has a related table indexed by patient name. One table is used for look up by history number, the other for look up by name. The program generator ensures that these two tables will be kept in one-to-one correspondence. In the MUMPS implementation, two separate structures are used for the related tables, but that decision was based on the efficiencies for the target language. For the designer, the critical fact is that he can specify a rapid selection of patient by either history number or name as being important without a concern for how that feature will be implemented.

Many of the OCIS relations are organized into structures with a common context (i.e., root of the key). This may be thought of as a specialized kind of fragment nesting. In effect, the structure creates a hierarchy, and the tables serve as templates for the different nodes in that hierarchy. There are 279 structures of 2 or more tables. The advantage of the structure in the 1982 version of TEDIUM is that there are operators for editing or deleting an entire structure. Of the OCIS structures, most contain relatively few tables (e.g., 154 of the structures have only two tables, 42 three tables, and 36 four tables). The largest structure contains 53 tables; it is used to manage the OCIS network. Other large structures are used to maintain patient data, pharmacy orders, and treatment plans. Of the 2597 tables in the specification, 401 are temporary tables used for internal processing (e.g., sorting) and 185 are center dictionaries (e.g., names of drugs and tests).

The tables are normally written as functions with the key terms shown as the independent variables and the non-key terms shown as the dependent variables. Multiple key terms are permitted, and the number in the OCIS specification ranges from one to 12. The key elements in a table define a hierarchy, and all keys to the left of a given key constitute its context. The fact that there is a large number of key terms is seldom a problem because the context of the program normally fixes the values of all but the lowest order key elements.

For example, the commands in a TEDIUM program specification have 5 key elements with all except the lowest—line number—established by the program context; thus, in entering and editing specification commands, the program treats the table as if it had only one key term. In the OCIS data model, the number of non-key terms ranges from 0 to 55. For many tables, all the information is in the key (e.g., lists of repeating groups) or the designer is concerned only with the fact that an entry exists in the table (patient appointment scheduled for the given date); in these situations no non-key elements are necessary. The fact that there is a table with 55 non-key terms indicates that there is no logical limit to the number of key or non-key terms in a table. The TEDIUM command language makes it easy to access individual elements in a large string, and the table with 55 non-key elements serves as a temporary table for storing search variables. The distribution of tables by the number of key and non-key elements is shown in Table 12.8. As can be seen, the vast majority of the tables have fewer than 6 key and 6 non-key elements.

Table 12.9 displays the elements by their roles in a table (i.e., as a key or as a non-key). Of the 4253 elements in the specification, 477 are not used in any table. These elements normally are type definitions for input data used in computations but not stored in the database. Table 12.9 accounts for the remaining 3776 elements. The first row in that table lists the number of elements that are never used as keys (i.e., in the role of a key). Notice that 1172 elements are used in only one table and that a total of 2039 (or 54% of the elements used in the tables) are never used as a key. Most non-key elements are used in several tables; for instance, 51 of those elements not used as a key are used in a non-

Table 12.8. Distribution of tables by number of elements

Non-Key Elements	Key Elements											
	1	2	3	4	5	6	7	8	9	10	11	12
0	52	138	130	94	76	26	18	9	6	3		
1	174	204	155	159	75	50	12	5	1		4	
2	66	69	62	54	37	11	8	1			2	
3	32	58	29	30	17	15	12	2		1		
4	20	36	21	21	15	5	1	2		3		
5	11	28	36	15	16	6	1			2		
6	17	34	19	6	10	3	1	1	1			
7	8	26	19	9	4	7	2					
8	2	21	13	7	14	6	1					
9	7	8	8	14	3	2	1					
10	8	10		3	1	3	2					1
11-20	20	35	21	25	6	1	5	3	2	2	1	
21-30	7	21	2	1		2						
31-55		3	1									

Table 12.9. Distribution of elements by role in table

Non-Key Roles	Key Roles								
	0	1	2	3-4	5-10	11-25	26-50	51-100	>200
0		328	131	91	54	28	5	1	
1	1172	118	31	25	31	6	3	1	
2	434	25	18	19	13	6	2	1	
3	132	11	12	4	6	2	2		
4	100	7	2	9	2	4	2	1	
5	47	4	5	2	1	1			
6	26	3	1	1	1	7	1		
7	14	1	3	2	3	3	2	1	
8	32		2	5	2	1	2	1	
9	14	3	2	2	3	1			
10	17		2		1				
11-25	40	3	4	3	5	11	7	2	5
>26	11	1	3	2			1	1	4
Total	2039	504	216	165	122	70	27	9	9

key role in 11 or more tables. The top row in the table counts the elements that are used only in a key role; there are 638 of such elements (or 17% of the total). A considerable number of the key elements are used in a large number of tables. The patient history number is used in 1064 tables (959 times as a key, 105 times as a non-key element). Other frequently used elements are patient name (283 tables), clinical category (262 tables), appointment date (185 tables), current hospital location (175 tables), treatment protocol identifier (118 tables), and provider (e.g., physician, nurse) identifier (112 tables).

As can be seen from the previous two tables, the OCIS data model contains a large number of tables and elements with a limited number of elements used very frequently. The majority of the tables have three or more keys, and some tables have a very large number of non-key elements. Lacking any standard reference models for a relational data model, it is difficult to see how this compares with data models of other systems. One might consider, however, how effectively the OCIS data model could be represented as an entity-relationship model (ERM). We begin by observing that the large size of the model would make an overview representation impractical. For example, there are a thousand tables linked to the patient (history number) entity; even if we grouped the tables as structures to reduce the number of relationships, we still would have too large a number to depict in an intelligible diagram.

Also, we should note that each OCIS table with more than one key element is a weak relationship in the ERM. Again, the size of the data model would make the diagram unmanageable. Yet, when stored as fragments and supported by a window into design, all the necessary information is available and maintainable. Thus, we may conclude that it would be impractical to represent the OCIS data model as an ERM. There is also a complementary question. If we started with an ERM, could we derive the OCIS data model? I personally think not. The diagrammatic conventions do not support the complexity we have found in the OCIS data model, and the limited automated support of CASE tools could not manage the 6000+ items that comprise the data model. As a result, the designers would be forced to develop a data model for what they could implement and not one for what is needed (i.e., they would take a product-oriented rather than a problem-oriented approach).

I now examine the 11,575 program specifications in the OCIS conceptual model. Four types of specifications are used. The *Common* specifications are written using only the TEDIUM command language. There also are three types of generic (declarative) specification: *Menu* for preparing menus, *Entry* for performing the standard file management functions for one or more tables, and *Prompt* for generating a prompt and table lookup.

The Prompt program was illustrated in Chapter 11. All of the generic programs may be modified through the use of the TEDIUM command language. Table 12.10 gives the distribution of the specifications by type of program and the number of TEDIUM command statements within each type. The total size of a program specification is the number of TEDIUM commands plus two statements for specification identification plus any additional statements to define the context. Generic programs also have mandatory declarative statements. As can be seen from the table, the average length of the TEDIUM specifications for OCIS is about 18 statements. (The previously cited figure of 15 lines per program specification is based on the data reported in Blum 1990a.)

The size and number of the specifications is consistent with the idea of a conceptual model composed of many fragments. Three fourths of all programs explicitly access the database, and one fourth access process user inputs. The general style adapted with TEDIUM is to avoid the use of input commands with report programs. By following this convention, all reports may be listed either on-line or printed off-line. (The TEDIUM generated programs recognize the mode of use and format the reports accordingly.) Of the 10,452 common routines, 45% print all or part of a report. The printing of off-line reports normally is initiated by entering the request onto the stacker (i.e., spawning a task); 7% of all calls are initiated by this mechanism.

A sense of the system's integration can be seen in Table 12.11. It presents the fan in, fan out, and database access for the 11,575 programs in the system. Eleven percent of the programs (1302) have no fan in. These normally are utility routines accessed directly or from the

Table 12.10. Distribution of command statements by program type

| Percentile | Program Type | | | |
	Common	Menu	Entry	Prompt
10	4	0	0	0
20	9	2	2	0
30	10	4	4	0
40	12	8	6	0
50	13	13	9	0
60	16	20	13	0
70	20	29	20	2
80	24	38	33	3
90	31	56	53	7
Avg.	16.1	22.3	18.6	1.8
Count	10,452	326	665	132

TEDIUM menu. (For instance, all the programs used to compute the tables in this section have zero fan in.) Of course, some of the programs with a zero fan in also are probably obsolete artifacts that have not been deleted. The vast majority of the programs have only one fan in (7204 programs), and 88% of the programs have at most two fan ins.

This suggests a structure in which processes are decomposed into strings of sequences such that most programs are designed to perform operations within only one flow sequence. There are, naturally, some utility programs with a large fan in. For example, the program to prompt for a patient by either name of history number is called from 344 different programs. In all, however, there are only 15 utility programs with a fan in of 30 or more.

The analysis of fan out is similar to that of fan in. Forty-five percent of all programs (5185) have no fan out; that is, they are terminal nodes in the processing trees. Eighty percent of the programs (9288) have a fan out of 2 or less. The fan out distribution is biased by the menu programs, whose primary function is one of fanning out. Thus, the table also divides the fan out distributions into menu and non-menu tables. The final column in Table 12.11 displays the distribution of programs that access the database. One fourth of the programs (2526) never access the database. Of those programs that access the database, 39% access only one table, 25% two tables, 15% three tables, and 20% access four or more tables. There are 81 programs that access between 10 and 31 tables. Most of the programs accessing a very large number of tables are menu programs; these can be quite large and often use the table contents to validate inputs and guide branching.

Table 12.11. Program structural characteristics

| Percentile | Fan In | ------ | Fan Out ------ | | Database |
	All	All	Menus	Non-Menus	Accesses
10	0	0	2	0	0
20	0	0	4	0	0
30	1	0	6	0	1
40	1	0	7	0	1
50	1	1	10	0	1
60	1	1	11	1	2
70	1	1	15	1	2
80	1	2	17	1	3
90	3	4	22	3	4
Avg.	1.6	1.7	11.0	1.4	1.9

Table 12.12. Matrix of frequency of table use by programs

Read Table	Write to Table												
	0	1	2	3	4	5	6	7	8	9	10	11-20	21-30	>30
0		209	102	51	29	15	4	4	3	2	5	1		
1	174	222	155	98	55	13	18	7	6	3		4		
2	76	95	84	44	26	21	11	4	2	2	2	7		2
3	38	37	42	19	12	11	10	5	3		1	2	1	
4	27	24	22	14	13	12	8	6	2	1		4		
5	21	28	14	21	10	2	7	3	1	3	2	6		
6	11	20	12	8	7	7	5	4	1	3	1	4	1	2
7	16	9	5	6	5	4		1	4			6		
8	10	7	8	7	8	1	3	2		1		4	1	
9	6	3	4	2	3	4			3	1	2			
10	9	6	3	1	4	1		1	2		3	1		
11-20	14	19	8	7	11	9	2	8	7	3	3	15	2	
21-30	5	7	6	4	3	3	2	1	1			7	1	1
31-50	1	2	1			3	3	1	2		3	4	1	1
51-99	4	2	2		1	1	2	1	4		1	8	5	3
>99	3	1		1			1	1	2		1	5	4	2

The structure suggested by the data in Table 12.11 is one in which there are many small and relatively independent processes operating on a large and integrated database. Most of the functions supported by the programs tend to be independent of each other. There is a small number of utility programs that are used widely, but the vast majority of the programs seem to have unique objectives. There is little evidence of reuse or generality at the program level. There also is no indication of modularity. Externally—in the OCIS documentation—the functions are presented as a hierarchy, for example, the clinical data displays, the pharmacy system, the hemapheresis system (for blood products), the daily-care plan system, etc. But this is only a consequence of the need to organize the ideas so they may be examined serially.

Internally, the programs are independent and too small to be considered modules; if groups of linked programs were to be organized as modules, the cohesion would be coincidental. For example, there are programs in the pharmacy system that manage the processing of orders, the accounting for drugs in the orders, the administration of drugs, the reporting of drug therapies in the clinical displays, and the inclusion of drug therapies in the daily care plans. Each of the first three functions, but none of the last three, are considered part of the pharmacy system. Moreover, of the three functions in the pharmacy system, each is different, and, consequently, each function's programs also will be

Table 12.13. Relative ages of associated OCIS items, 1992 subset

	Years Before			Months			Years After		
	2 <	2-1	1-½	6-1	±1	1-6	½-1	1-2	> 2
Called Program[1]	18	5	5	7	35	7	5	6	12
Read Table[1]	35	9	7	6	15	6	3	4	16
Written Table[1]	13	7	7	8	29	6	5	7	18
Programs[2]	37	15	13	15	48	14	9	12	25
Tables[3]	48	23	18	24	64	16	9	10	12

1. Period between the date of program definition and the date of the referenced item's definition. Shown are the percent of the total number of references (8957 programs first defined before 1991; 15,234 calls to other programs, 11,576 reads of tables, and 4649 writes to tables).
2. Percentage of the 8957 programs defined before 1991 with at least one interaction with an item defined in the relative time period.
3. Of the 2028 tables defined before 1991, this shows the percentage of all tables accessed by a program defined before or after the table's definition.

different.

What the programs have in common is the database, and that is shared throughout OCIS. Table 12.12 presents a matrix that shows the interactions between the programs and the tables that they read (i.e., read only) and write (i.e., write only or read-and-write). Each table is counted once in the matrix. The table shows that most OCIS tables are both read and written to by a relatively large number of tables. In fact, 55% of the tables have 3 or more programs that read or write to them. This provides a picture of the OCIS system as a highly integrated database that supports a very large number of small and relatively simple operations. Structurally, OCIS can be characterized as a model of the real world (represented by surrogates in the database) surrounded by a collection of many small, specialized, function-specific programs. Furthermore, there appears to be no natural way in which to divide the whole into modules or subsystems.

The discussion so far has concentrated in the *spatial* integration of OCIS. Table 12.13 provides evidence that OCIS also is *temporally* integrated. That is, as the system evolves, the changes are not localized; they ripple throughout the system. We already have seen evidence of the temporal integration of OCIS in the fact that 42% of the programs in the 1994 baseline had been edited in the previous 12 months. Table 12.13 categorizes the relative age of each program with respect to the programs it calls, the tables it reads, and the tables to which it writes.

In the standard, modular approach to design, programs normally interface only with previously defined items or items defined at the same time; an effort is made to constrain changes within modules. Interactions with items that were defined after a program was defined can be seen as a measure of how well the program is integrated into the system. A large number of such interactions implies that, as new features are added, existing features are modified to interface with them. A trivial example is the modification of a menu to enable the execution of a new feature. A more complex illustration is the revision of an existing program to update the elements in a newly defined table.

Table 12.13 analyzes the subset of the 1994 baseline that was in operational use prior to 1992 (i.e., items that have been defined for at least two years), and it includes three kinds of data. First, it shows for each type of interface (i.e., call, read, or write) the relative ages of the program and the interfaced item. The time periods are organized as nine discrete time periods. Interactions with items defined *before* the initial definition of the program are shown to the left; those interactions with items defined *after* the program are indicated on the right. The table shows that 12% of the program calls are to programs defined two or more years after the calling program—a clear indication that the calling programs must have been edited two or more years subsequent to their definition. As one might expect, 35% of the program reads are to tables defined two or more years before the definition of the reading program (i.e., the program reads available data). Surprisingly, however, the table shows that there are more writes to tables defined two or more years after the program's definition (18%) than there are writes to tables defined two or more years earlier (13%). This implies that as new tables are defined, older programs are modified to update them.

The fourth line in Table 12.13 classifies the percentage of all programs in the 1992 subset having at least one interaction in the given time frame. Notice that 37% of the programs have been modified to interact with items defined one or more years after their initial definition, and 25% are modified two or more years afterward. The final line in the table presents similar data for the tables. It shows that 12% of all references to the table come from programs that were defined two or more years prior to the definition of the table (i.e., the programs were edited to process the data in the new table). Clearly, OCIS is both spatially and temporally integrated.

Thus, we may conclude that the structure of the OCIS application is very different from what one might expect with a traditional product orientation. It is composed of many small fragments, it is deeply integrated, and it is highly dynamic. If it were not for the facts that the system is of high quality (as judged by its users), high reliability (as judged by its life-critical mission), high complexity (as judged by comparison to other clinical information systems), and high adaptability (as demonstrated by this chapter), then any experienced software engineer would be forced to characterize the project as unstructured, undisciplined, and chaotic (i.e., clearly a model of what should be avoided).

Here, once more, is the dilemma of a paradigm shift. If we retain the product-oriented approach, then we would have to define OCIS in a modular way using an ERM data model. We would have to specify what we needed even before we understood the needs, and we obviously would never end up with a system such as OCIS—certainly not with the limited resources available. The alternative, however, is of high risk; it implies that we cannot rely on prior experience. This is not an easy either-or choice. Nevertheless, I would hope that the reader will recognize the OCIS experience as an existence proof that there is at least one proven alternative. Moreover, this alternative offers a kind of gold standard: every new paradigm should be subjected to an extended operational text, and it ought to perform at least as well as TEDIUM.

12.9. What the Case Study Tells Us

These final two chapters have been devoted to adaptive design and the recognition that design is a continuing process supportable by the special properties of software. Chapter 11 describes an environment for implementing the fully automated paradigm, and this chapter provides a case study that shows how that environment works in practice. The evaluation in this chapter has been divided into two parts. First, there was the evaluation of the environment itself; as a support environment, a specification scheme, and a conceptual model. Then there were characterizations of how the use of this environment affects both the process and the product. These last two sections were intended to demonstrate that software engineering experience is based on one particular model for design and implementation, and that shifts in the model can render some of its axiomatic principles irrelevant.

The system used for the case study, OCIS, is a large system. It is fully paid for out of patient-care funds and is justified only on the basis of its contribution to the Oncology Center mission: patient care, cancer research, and education. Its development history always was motivated by the goal of creating a system for the Oncology Center. There was a great deal of frustration in the period prior to 1986 because the users could not get the changes they desired. Today, it seen as the users's system, and the designers view themselves as the agents for expanding the system's functionality.

Progress is never as rapid as one would hope, but at least the designers and users are working on the right problems. They do not concern themselves with implementation details; they navigate through the conceptual model to see what is there to be used; and they have a formal specification language that allows them to express their concepts concisely and accurately. They use TEDIUM to address the problems to be solved; they ignore the products it generates. TEDIUM captures the application-class and software tool knowledge for reuse; it hides the implementation details from the designers. Thus, as the 1957 description of FORTRAN showed how a 1000-line program could be reduced to 47 statements, TEDIUM illustrates how a million-line system implementation can be reduced to 200,000 statements in a conceptual model.

This is what this long book has been about: an appeal to reexamine our foundations and first principles. Just as there are many logics and geometries, there are many computer sciences. I believe we currently have too strong a commitment to the computer science that gave us FORTRAN. Therefore, I urge the computer science community to move *beyond programming* in the sense of abandoning the fixation with programs and programming notations.

We must learn to look outside the computer and ask,

> What are the best representations for formally expressing problem solutions?

For each domain (or application class) we may come up with a different set of answers. We also must reassess our focus in the area of internal representations. We should ask,

> How can we best capture (and hide) what we have come to know about implementing solutions so that we can transform problem solutions into implementations automatically?

Finding answers to these questions, it seems to me, is the appropriate goal for a computer science of the early 21st century.

EPILOGUE

We have come to the end of the my part of the story, the story of how to develop software. My exposition has not been direct. I have treated learning as an activity of expansion and not one of knowledge transfer. In the process I have examined contemporary software design theory from many different perspectives; I have used a wide-angle lens that distorts the periphery and sacrifices the fine details. Nevertheless, if we have done our jobs right—you as the reader and I as the author—then we should each have a better idea of what it means to design software, what the inherent limits to design are, and where the opportunities for improvement can be found. As the result of reading this book, we should each find a set of answers. These answers will differ, and the feedback from trying to apply those answers will change them further. Perhaps that is the principal lesson of this book: Ideas change and there are few fixed truths. Science is not about finding truth; it is about finding hypotheses that can be demonstrated to be consistent with reality. Computer science does not exist as a beacon to guide us; it is a tool to aid us in the creation of software products. As a tool, therefore, computer science must take its direction from the process it supports.

I use some literary analogies to summarize the central lessons of this book. The first is from *One Hundred Years of Solitude* by Gabriel Garcia Marquez.

> In March the gypsies returned. This time they brought a telescope and a magnifying glass the size of a drum,... They placed a gypsy woman at one end of the village and set up the telescope at the entrance to the tent. For the price of five reales, people could look into the telescope and see the gypsy woman an arm's length away. "Science has eliminated distance," Melquiades proclaimed. "In a short time, man will be able to see what is happening in any place in the world without leaving his own house." (Garcia Marquez 1967/1970, p. 12)

The humor in this extract comes from our knowledge of optics, its power, and its limitations. Yet, Melquiades's conclusions are correct; only a different technology has been used. The way we now look at software design may—for some later generation of designers—be seen as comically naive. Regardless, our goals may still be met.

How do we now see computers? As a tool that brings us into the age of information? As a source of intelligent agents? As an alternative to repetitive human activity? There are many possible answers, and none will be completely correct. In this book I have suggested one more answer. Computing provides a mechanism for developing and altering the artifacts in our environment, a mechanism that moves us from the plan-and-build paradigm to the build-and-evolve paradigm. As we learn to automate manufacture, hardware will differ from software only in the cost of the materials. One-of-a-kind products will become common, and production will consider design change a process-control variable. The availability of deep knowledge structures will also change what we now call information processing. Automation will eliminate the need for many traditional records (the motivation for much of today's design), and the rationalization of knowledge-oriented work will place a premium on the ability to react quickly. I do not think that this is all necessarily for the good, but I do not see where we will have much of a choice.

Toulmin (1990) writes of a transition away from modernity with its underlying faith in science and progress. I see, within the context of that greater revolution, a change in the way we approach design. To understand this dynamic, the first half of this book explored the intellectual foundations of design. The relationships between science and technology, and the limitations of scientific knowledge; the ability to solve problems using rules and the automaticity of expertise; alternative views of human activity and the role of reflection. My conclusion is that design is a human activity that builds on prior knowledge. The second half of the book examined design in architecture, manufacturing, and software. It was seen to be a complex human process, subjected to continuing change (which often is controlled artificially), and deeply dependent on experience and knowledge. The final two chapters, of course, illustrated how adaptive design employs change to improve satisfaction. With this approach, design no longer is considered a phase to be completed before implementation begins; it becomes a continuing, forward-looking process nurtured by the feedback of product use. In short, it reintegrates the activity of design with the task of doing. This altered vision is comparable to a shift from the telescope to television.

The second literary extract comes from *Jurgen* by James Branch Cabell. In his travels, Jurgen is given a cantrap containing 32 of the Master Philologist's own words. Here is one of Jurgen's attempts to use that cantrap.

"O most unrighteous judges," says Jurgen, sternly, "now hear and tremble! 'At the death of Adrian the Fifth, Pedro Juliani, who should be named John the Twentieth, was through an error in the reckoning elevated to the papal chair as John the Twenty-first!'"

"Hah, and what have we to do with that?" inquired the priest of Vel-Tyno ... And Jurgen perceived that either he had not employed the cantrap correctly or else that its magic was unappreciated by the leaders of Philistia. (Cabell 1919/1977, pp. 214-15)

On his third use of the cantrap, Jurgen enters Heaven as John the Twentieth. Obviously, he discovers, it is the cantrap's content—and not its form—that is important.

What does Jurgen's cantrap have to do with software design? I believe that the current interest of computer science centers around formal representations and the correctness of a program with respect to its specifications (i.e., the form of the product). In contrast, I assert we need to find ways of representing and validating the concepts of interest to the users (i.e., the content of the problem solution). We have been successful in doing this in the domains of drawing programs, CAD interfaces, and virtual reality. In each case we rely on internal formality, but we hide it. This is the move *beyond programming* that is implied in the title. A shift from how to represent the product's implementation to one of finding problem solutions. Or, using the Jurgen analogy, a shift from the Master Philologist's words to their meaning. I have used TEDIUM and the OCIS project to illustrate what can be done in the domain of interactive information systems. The same principles can be applied in other domains, but it requires a new vision for computer science.

As I remarked earlier in the book, computer science is a form of mathematics. It begins with axioms and constructs a set of consistent theories and rules from these axioms. Early interest focused on programming languages and programming, and here the discipline of formality provides obvious benefits. Other elements of computer science drew from different mathematical models (e.g., relational database, computational complexity); at the same time, much of what was called computer science turned to the engineering of computer systems (e.g., operating systems, communications). All of this work is necessary, but it is not sufficient. Some suggest that a discipline of systems architecture is needed to fill the void not covered by either traditional computer science or software engineering, but I do not agree. For me, this implies that a new discipline will be layered on top of the established disciplines. In contrast, I argue that a shift to adaptive design introduces a new set of issues that defines a new computer science. If we do not shift the focus of computer science, these issues will never be considered.

Here are some of the new problems to be addressed. How do we represent problems in-the-world? How does this vary with interactive information systems, real-time systems, manufacturing systems, etc.? What is general, and what is domain specific? How do we write holistic specifications that abandon traditional forms to take advantage of software's unique capabilities? How do we provide deep linkage and automatic consistency checking? How do we capture (for automatic reuse) the knowledge used to create efficient implementations? What transformations for generating programs should we use and how much of the process can be automated?

These questions fall into two categories:

Those that relate to the formal representation of problem domains in-the-world.

Those that relate to transforming the above representations into computations in-the-computer.

These two sets of questions now are marginal concerns within today's computer science mission. In effect, the questions define two new subdisciplines that will push computer science away from the *programs* and toward the *problem solutions* for which the programs have been created. They broaden the scope of computer science, and they also go far in resolving the central design tension that we have seen throughout this book: the tension between what we care about and what we can study, between the concept and its formal expression, between the subjective and the objective. By creating a environment for describing concepts formally, we move design to the boundary between human reasoning and mathematical logic. The designer documents her understanding, the environment automatically creates the product, and the designer experiments with and refines that understanding. The concern is for how the computer is used, not with how it operates.

Notice that a new computer science will have a profound effect on research in computer science. Much of the current work is carried out in what Potts (1993) describes as a "research-then-transfer" mode. Ideas are developed as separate, sequential activities, and the results are reported for adoption by others. Virtually all this work is conducted within the existing programming paradigm, and therefore (in the sense of Kuhn) it constitutes mopping up. It builds on available mathematical concepts, and its relevancy is justified by the dominant paradigms.

Tichy, et al. (1995) has conducted an informal literature search and concluded that about two thirds of the software engineering papers encountered were theory papers of this sort. Potts proposes the alternative of "industry-as-laboratory." "In this approach, researchers identify problems through close involvement with industrial projects, and

[they] create and evaluate solutions in an almost indivisible research activity" (pp. 19-20). Although this approach corrects many of the deficiencies of computer science/software engineering research as it is being currently conducted, Potts admits that there are problems. There is an overemphasis on the short term, and "industry-as-laboratory research sacrifices revolutionary discoveries in favor of evolutionary improvements" (p. 26). He continues, however, by observing that "many talented researchers will continue to look for revolutionary advances by researching and then transferring" (p. 27). Yet, if revolutionary advances can come only at the expense of breaking out of the present paradigm, (a) will that work even be undertaken, and (b) can it be transferred?

Glass (1995) observes that computer science research lacks a solid framework—a well-understood selection of methods and phases through which research activities might pass. He identifies four fundamental methods:

Scientific method. This is based on observations of the world. In my interpretation, computer science is mathematically abstract and therefore not in-the-world. Thus, I believe, there can be no scientific methods in the sense of classical physics.

Engineering method. Here one begins by observing existing solutions and proposing improvements. This is an effective approach whenever we have instances of an alternative paradigm such as TEDIUM.

Empirical method. This is what Potts refers to as industry-as-laboratory. It refines the existing paradigm as it is carried out in practice.

Analytical method. This is the research-then-transfer approach. The operative paradigm establishes the relevancy of what is to be researched, and I claim that new criteria for relevancy are needed.

If we are to shift the paradigm, therefore, we must begin by analyzing the right questions and then engineering and testing our answers. Both steps are needed, and analysis alone will never suffice.

And so I bring this work to an end. In Chapter 1 introduced the role of science in software engineering by quoting Shaw (1990), who observed that professional engineering emerges after there is a "sufficient scientific basis to enable a core of educated professionals so they can apply the theory to analysis of problems and synthesis of solutions" (p. 17). Yet, the argument of this book concludes that there is no scientific basis for computer science. The problems to be researched are socially determined, and the "science" of computer science is its logical rigor. By definition, the theories that computer scientists research establish what computer science is. Computer science models no external reality, and design—the creation of artifacts to improve the human condition—is iterative, subjective, and not formally representable. We can choose to ignore these facts and define computer science to be what it already is. In that case, we will have to develop new disciplines to fill the voids left by computer science. Or, we can rethink what we expect computer science to do.

Clearly, I favor the second path. That is why this book has examined the assumptions upon which we have constructed computer science, questioned many of the findings we have come to accept as truths, and offered and evaluated an alternative—one that introduces new areas for computer science to research. But I will not argue my case any further; rather, I shall close this work by repeating the final paragraph of *TEDIUM and the Software Process*:

> This is all so simple and obvious. It reminds me of the story of the emperor's new clothes. Of course, I don't know if I am the child or the emperor. At least, I hope I'm not the tailor. (p. 238)

REFERENCES

Abdel-Hamid, Tarek K. and S. E. Madnick (1986), Impact of Schedule Estimation on Software Project Behavior, *IEEE Software*, pp. 70-75, July.

Abrahamsen, Adele A. (1987), Bridging Boundaries Versus Breaking Boundaries: Psychololinguistics in Perspective, *Synthese*, 72:355-388.

Ackermann, D. and M. J. Tauber, eds. (1990), *Mental Models and Human-Computer Interaction I*, Amsterdam: North-Holland.

Adler, Paul S. and Terry A. Winograd, eds. (1992b), *Usability. Turning Technology into Tools*, New York: Oxford.

Adler, Paul S. and Terry A. Winograd (1992b), The Usability Challenge, in Paul S. Adler and Terry A. Winograd, eds., *Usability. Turning Technology into Tools*, New York: Oxford, pp. 3-14.

Aiken, Henry D. (1956), *The Age of Ideology*, New York: New American Library.

Alba, Joseph W. and Lynn Hasher (1983), Is Memory Schematic?, *Psychological Bulletin*, 93:203-231.

Albrecht, A. J. (1979), Measuring Application Development Productivity, *Proceedings IBM Application Development Symposium*, pp. 14-17.

Albrecht, A. J. and J. E. Gaffney (1983), Software Function, Source Lines of Code, and Development Effort Prediction: A Software Science Validation, *IEEE Transactions on Software Engineering*, SE-9:639-648.

Alexander, Christopher (1964/1971), *Notes on the Synthesis of Form*, Cambridge, MA: Harvard University Press.

Allen, Robert B. (1990), User Models: Theory, Method, and Practice, *International Journal of Man-Machine Studies*, 32:511-543.

Astley, W. Graham (1984), Subjectivity, Sophistry and Symbolism in Management Science, *Journal of Management Studies*, 21:259-272.

Astley, W. Graham (1985), Administrative Science as Socially Constructed Truth, *Administrative Science Quarterly*, 30:497-513.

Attewell, Paul (1994), Information Technology and the Productivity Paradox, in Douglas Harris and Paul Goodman, eds., *Understanding the Productivity Paradox: The Role of Organizational Linkages and Productivity*, National Academy of Sciences Press.

Baars, Bernard J. (1986), *The Cognitive Revolution in Psychology*, New York: The Guilford Press.

Baecker, Ronald M. and William A. S. Buxton, eds. (1987), *Readings in Human-Computer Interaction*, Morgan Kaufmann Publishers.

Ballay, Joseph M. (1987), An Experimental View of the Design Process, in William B. Rouse and Kenneth R. Boff (1987a), *System Design*, Amsterdam: North-Holland, pp. 65-82.

Balzer, Robert, Thomas E. Cheatham, Jr., and Cordell Green (1983), Software Technology in the 1990's: Using a New Paradigm, *Computer*, (16,11):39-45.

Bannon, Liam J. (1986), Issues in Design: Some Notes, in Donald A. Norman and Stephen W. Draper, eds., *User Centered System Design*, Hillsdale, NJ: Lawrence Erlbaum Associates, pp. 35-30.

Bansler, Jørgen P. and Keld Bødker (1993), A Reappraisal of Structured Analysis: Design in an Organizational Context, *ACM Transactions on Information Systems*, 11:165-193.

Banville, Claude and Maurice Landry (1989), Can the Field of MIS be Disciplined?, *Communications ACM*, 32:48-60.

Barber, Bernard (1952), *Science and the Social Order*, Glencoe, IL: Free Press.

Barnes, Barry (1982), A Science-Technology Relationship: A Model and a Query, *Social Studies of Science*, 12:166-72.

Barnes, Barry (1983), On the Conventional Character of Knowledge and Cognition, in Karen Knorr-Cetina and Michael Mulkay, eds., *Science Observed: Perspectives on the Social Study of Science*, London: Sage, pp. 19-52.

Barstow, David R. (1985), Domain-Specific Automatic Programming, *IEEE Transactions on Software Engineering*, SE-11:1321-1336.

Bartlett, F. C. (1932), *Remembering*, Cambridge: Cambridge University Press.

Barwise, Jon (1989), Mathematical Proofs of Computer System Correctness, *Notices of the American Mathematical Society*, 36:844-851.

Barwise, Jon and John Perry (1983), *Situations and Attitudes*, Cambridge, MA: MIT Press.

Bechtel, William (1988a), *Philosophy of Science: An Overview for Cognitive Science*, Hillsdale, NJ: Lawrence Erlbaum Associates.

Bechtel, William (1988b), *Philosophy of Mind: An Overview for Cognitive Science*, Hillsdale, NJ: Lawrence Erlbaum Associates.

Beirne, Martin and Harvie Ramsay (1992), A Creative Offensive? Participative Systems Design and the Question of Control, in Martin Beirne and Harvie Ramsay, eds., *Information Technology and Workplace Democracy*, London: Routledge, pp. 93-120.

Belady, L. A. (1991), From Software Engineering to Knowledge Engineering: The Shape of the Software Industry in the 1990's, *International Journal of Software Engineering and Knowledge Engineering*, 1:1-8.

Bernstein, J. (1966), *The Analytical Engine*, New York: Random House.

Berreman, G. (1966), Anemic and emetic analyses in social anthropology, *American Anthropologist*, 68:346-54.

Biggerstaff, T. J. and A. J. Perlis (1989), *Software Reusability*, 2 v., New York: ACM Press.

Bjørner, D. et al., eds. (1987), *VDM'87: VDM—A Formal Method at Work*, Berlin: Springer-Verlag.

Bloomfield, Brian P. (1992), Understanding the Social Practices of Systems Developers, *Journal of Information Systems*, 2:189-206.

Bloor, David (1976), *Knowledge and Social Imagery*, London: Routledge and Kegan Paul.

Bloor, David (1981), The Strengths of the Strong Programme, *Philosophy and the Social Sciences*, 11:199-213.

Blum, B. I. (1981), Program Generation with TEDIUM, An Illustration. *Trends and Applications*, National Bureau of Standards, Gaithersburg, Maryland, May 18.

Blum, B. I. (1982a), A Tool for Developing Information Systems, in H. J. Schneider and A. I. Wasserman, eds., *Automated Tools for Information Systems Design*, North-Holland Publishing, pp. 215-235.

Blum, B. I. (1982b), MUMPS, TEDIUM and Productivity. *Proceedings of the First IEEE Computer Society International Conference on Medical Computer Science/Computational Medicine (MEDCOMP)*, pp. 200-209.

Blum, B. I. (1982c), An Approach to Computer Maintained Software Documentation. *NBS FIPS Software Documentation Workshop*, NBS SP 500-94, ed., A. J. Neumann, October, pp. 110-118.

Blum, B. I. (1983a), An Information System for Developing Information Systems. *1983 National Computer Conference*, Anaheim, California, pp. 743-752.

Blum, B. I. (1983b), A Workstation for Information Systems Development, *COMPSAC '83*, IEEE Computer Society Press, pp. 116-120.

Blum, B. I. (1984a), Three Paradigms for Developing Information Systems, *Seventh International Conference on Software Engineering*, IEEE Computer Society Press, pp. 534-543.

Blum, B. I., (1984b) The Small Computer as a Solution to the Software Crisis, *Fall COMPCON*, IEEE Computer Society Press, pp. 96-100.

Blum, B. I. (1985a), A Life Cycle Environment for Interactive Information Systems, *Conference on Software Tools*, pp. 198-206.

Blum, B. I. (1985b), Experience with an Automated Generator of Information Systems, *Symposium on New Directions in Computing*, pp. 138-147.

Blum, B. I. (1985c), TEQUILA: An Intoxicating Query System, *14th MUMPS Users' Group*, pp. 87-94.

Blum, B. I. (1986a), *Clinical Information Systems*, Springer-Verlag, New York, 1986.

Blum, B. I. (1986b), Iterative Development of Information Systems: A Case Study, *Software-Practice & Experience*, 6:503-515.

Blum, B. I. (1986c), Four Years' Experience with an Environment for Implementing Information Systems, *Journal of Systems and Software* 6:261-271.

Blum, B. I. (1987a), A Paradigm for Developing Information Systems, *IEEE Transactions on Software Engineering*, SE-13:432-439.

Blum, B. I. (1987b), The TEDIUM Development Environment for Information Systems, *IEEE Software*, (4,2):25-34, March.

Blum, B. I. (1987c), An Overview of TEDIUM, *Information and Software Technology*, 29:475-496.

Blum, B. I. (1987d), Evaluating Alternative Paradigms: A Case Study, *Large Scale Systems*, 12:189-199.

Blum, B. I. (1987e), Evolution with System Sculpture: Some Empirical Results, *Conference on Software Maintenance*, pp. 45-56.

Blum, B. I. (1988a), Documentation for Maintenance: A Hypertext Design, *Conference on Software Maintenance - 1988*, October 24-27, pp. 23-31.

Blum, B. I. (1988b), An Illustration of the Integrated Analysis, Design and Construction of an Information System with TEDIUM, in T.W. Olle and A.A. Verrijn-Stuart, eds., *Proceedings of the IFIP WG 8.1 Conference on Computerized Assistance During the Information System Life Cycle (CRIS 88)*, Egham Surrey, UK, September 19-22, 1988, Amsterdam: Elsevier, pp. 287-336.

Blum, B. I. (1989a), Volume, Distance and Productivity, *Journal of Systems and Software*, 10:217-226.

Blum, B. I. (1989b), Improving Software Maintenance by Learning From the Past: A Case Study, *Proceedings of IEEE*, 77:596-606.

Blum, B. I. (1989c), Formalism and Prototyping in the Software Process, *Information and Decision Technologies*, 15:327-341. Reprinted in Timothy R. Colburn et al. (eds.), *Program Verification*, Boston, MA: Kluwer Academic Publishers, 1993, pp. 213-238.

Blum, B. I. (1989d), On the Cognitive Journey to the What and How, *28th Annual Technical Symposium of the Washington, DC Chapter of ACM*, pp. 87-94.

Blum, B. I. (1989e), A Paradigm for the 1990s Validated in the 1980s, *AIAA Computers in Aerospace VII*, pp. 502-511.

Blum, B. I. (1989f), Toward a Paperless Development Environment, *Tools for AI*, pp. 495-498.

Blum, B. I. (1990a), *TEDIUM and the Software Process*, Cambridge, MA: MIT Press.

Blum, B. I. (1990b), Knowledge-Based Systems for Software Development, *COMPSAC 90*, p. 27.

Blum, B. I. (1991a), A Ten-Year Evaluation of an Atypical Software Environment, *Software Engineering Journal*, 6:347-354.

Blum, B. I. (1991b), Towards a Uniform Structured Representation for Application Generation, *International Journal of Software Engineering and Knowledge Engineering*, 1:39-55.

Blum, B. I. (1991c), Integration Issues Elucidated in Large-Scale Information System Development, *Journal of Systems Integration*, 1:35-53.

Blum, B. I. (1991d), Computer Security in a Clinical Environment, in S. Jajodia and C. E. Lanwehr (eds), *Database Security, IV Status and Prospects*, Amsterdam: North-Holland, pp. 1-12.

Blum, B. I. (1992a), *Software Engineering: A Holistic View*, New York: Oxford University Press.

Blum, B. I. (1992b), On the Development of Hardware and Software, *Information and Decision Technologies*, 18:375-394.

Blum, B. I. (1992c), The Fourth Decade of Software Engineering: Some Issues in Knowledge Management, *International Journal of Intelligent and Cooperative Information Systems*, 1:475-514.

Blum, B. I. (1992d), A Multidimensional Approach to Application Development, *Computer Applications and Design Abstractions*, PD-Vol. 43, ASME Press, pp. 87-90.

Blum, B. I. (1992e), The Dynamics of a Clinical Information System, *MEDINFO 92*, pp. 168-173.

Blum, B. I. (1992f), TEDIUM's Window into Design, *4th International Conference on Software Engineering and Knowledge Engineering*, pp. 200-205.

Blum, B. I. (1993a), The Economics of Adaptive Design, *Journal of Systems and Software*, 21:117-128.

Blum, B. I. (1993b), Representing Open Requirements with a Fragment-Based Specification, *IEEE Transactions on Systems, Man, and Cybernetics*, 23:724-736.

Blum, B. I. (1993c), On the Engineering of Open Software Systems, *International Symposium on Engineered Software Systems 1993*, World Scientific, pp. 43-56.

Blum, B. I. (1993d), Knowledge Representation in Current Design Methods, in V. Ambriola and G. Tortora, eds., *Advances in Software Engineering and Knowledge Engineering*, Volume I, World Scientific Publishing Company, pp. 73-94.

Blum, B. I. (1994a), The Evolving Role of Hospital Information Systems, *Proceedings, Medical Informatics in Europe '94*, pp. 23-26.

Blum, B. I. (1994b), Characterizing the Software Process, *Information and Decision Technologies*, 19:215-232.

Blum, B. I. (1995), Resolving the Software Maintenance Paradox, *Journal of Software Maintenance: Research and Practice*, 7:3-26.

Blum, B. I. and K. Duncan, eds. (1990), *A History of Medical Informatics*, Reading, MA: Addison-Wesley.

Blum, B. I. and Raymond C. Houghton, Jr. (1982), Rapid Prototyping of Information Management Systems. *ACM SIGSOFT Software Engineering Notes*, (7,5):35-38.

Blum, B. I. and T. Moore (1993), Representing Navy Tactical Computer System Knowledge for Reengineering and Integration, *Journal of Systems Integration*, 3:331-349.

Blum, B. I., S. D. Diamond, M. G. Hammond, M. E. Perkins, and R. D. Semmel (1987), An Intelligent Navigational Assistant for a Decision Resource Database, *Expert Systems in Government*, pp. 19-25.

Bobrow, D. G. and D. A. Norman (1975), Some Principles of Memory Schemata, in D. Bobrow and A. Collins, eds., *Representation and Understanding: Studies in Cognitive Science*, New York: Academic Press.

Boehm, Barry W. (1976), Software Engineering, *IEEE Transactions on Computers*, C-25:1226-1241.

Boehm, Barry W. (1981), *Software Engineering Economics*, Englewood Cliffs: Prentice-Hall.

Boehm, Barry W. (1984), Verifying and Validating Software Requirements and Design Specifications, *IEEE Software*, pp. (17,1):75-88.

Boehm, Barry W. (1988), A Spiral Model of Software Development and Enhancement, *Computer*, (21,5):61-72.

Boehm-Davis, Deborah A., Robert W. Holt, Matthew Koll, Gloria Yastrop, and Robert Peters (1989), Effects of Different Data Base Formats on Information Retrieval, *Human Factors*, 31:579-592.

Bødker, Susanne (1991a), Activity Theory as a Challenge to Systems Design, in H.-E. Nisson, H. K. Klein, and R. Hirschheim, eds., *Information Systems Research*, Amsterdam: North Holland, pp. 551-564.

Bødker, Susanne (1991b), *Through the Interface: A Human Activity Approach to User Interface design*, Hillsdale, NJ: Lawrence Erlbaum Associates.

Bødker, Susanne, Joan Greenbaum, and Morten Kyng (1991), Setting the Stage for Design as Action, in Joan Greenbaum and Morten Kyng (1991), eds., *Design at Work: Cooperative Design of Computer Systems*, Hillsdale, NJ: Lawrence Erlbaum Associates, pp. 139-154.

Booch, Grady (1986), Object-Oriented Development, *IEEE Transaction on Software Engineering*, SE-12:211-221.

388   References

Booch, Grady (1983), *Software Engineering with Ada*, Menlo Park, CA: Benjamin/Cummings.

Booch, Grady (1991), *Object-Oriented Design with Applications*, Menlo Park, CA: Benjamin/Cummings.

Boring, E. G. (1930), A New Ambiguous Figure, *American Journal of Psychology*, 42:444-445.

Bourque, P. and V. Côté (1991), An Experiment in Software Sizing with Structured Analysis Metrics, *Journal of Systems and Software*, 15:159-172.

Braverman, H. (1974), *Labor and Monopoly Capital—The Degradation of Work in the Twentieth Century*, New York: Monthly Review Press.

Brehmer, Berndt (1980), In One Word: Not from Experience, *Acta Psychologica*, 45:223-241.

Brehmer, Berndt (1987), Development of Mental Models for Decision in Technological Systems, in Jens Rasmussen, Keith Duncan and Jacques Leplat, eds., *New Technology and Human Error*, New York: John Wiley & Sons, pp. 111-120.

Broad, William and Nicholas Wade (1982), *Betrayers of the Truth*, New York: Simon and Schuster.

Brooks, Frederick P. Jr. (1975), *The Mythical Man-Month*, Reading, MA: Addison-Wesley.

Brooks, Frederick P. Jr. (1987), No Silver Bullet, *Computer*, (20,4):10-19.

Brooks, Ruven (1993), The Case for the Specialized Interface, *IEEE Software*, pp. (10,2):86-88.

Brown, John Seely and Susan E. Newman (1985), Issues in Cognitive and Social Ergonomics: From Our House to Bauhaus, *Human-Computer Interaction*, 1:359-391.

Brown, John Seely and Paul Duguid (1992), Enacting Design for the Workplace, in Paul S. Adler and Terry A. Winograd, eds., *Usability: Turning Technologies into Tools*, New York: Oxford University Press, pp. 164-197.

Bruce, Darryl (1985), The How and Why of Ecological Memory, *Journal of Experimental Psychology, General*, 114:78-90.

Bruner, Jerome (1986), *Actual Minds, Possible Worlds*, Cambridge, MA: Harvard University Press.

Bruner, J. S., J. J. Goodnow, and G. A. Austin (1956), *A Study of Thinking*, New York: John Wiley & Sons.

Bucciarelli, Louis L. (1988), Engineering Design Process, in Frank A. Dubinskas, ed., *Making Time. Ethnographies of High-Technology Organizations*, Philadelphia: Temple University Press, pp. 92-122.

Bush, Vannevar (1945), As We May Think, *Atlantic Monthly*, (176,1):101-108.

Bush, Vannevar (1947), *Endless Horizons*, New York.

Buxton, J. N., and B. Randell eds. (1970), *Software Engineering Techniques: Report on a Conference Sponsored by the NATO Science Committee, Rome, Italy, 27th to 31st October 1969*, Brussels: Scientific Affairs Division, NATO.

Cabell, James Branch (1919/1977), *Jurgen*, New York: Dover Publications.

Callebaut, Werner (1993), *Taking the Natuaralistic Turn*, Chicago: University of Chicago Press.

Cambrosio, Alberto and Peter Keating (1988), "Going Monoclonal": Art, Science, and Magic in Day-to-Day Use of Hybridoma Technology, *Social Problems*, 35:244-260.

Camerer, Colin, George Loewenstein, and Martin Weber (1989), The Curse of Knowledge in Economic Settings: An Experimental Analysis, *Journal of Political Economy*, 97:1232-1254.

Cameron, John R. (1986), An Overview of JSD, *IEEE Transactions on Software Engineering*, SE-12:222-240.

Campbell, Donald T. (1960), Blind Variation and Selective Retention in Creative Thought as in Other Knowledge Processes, *The Psychological Review*, 67:380-400, reprinted in Gerard Radnitsky and W. W. Bartley II, eds., *Evolutionary Epistemology, Rationality, and the Sociology of Knowledge*, LaSalle, IL: Open Court (1987), pp. 91-114.

Campbell, Donald T. (1969), Ethnocentrism of Disciplines and the Fish-Scale Model of Omniscience, in Muzafer Sherif and Carolyn W. Sherif, eds., *Interdisciplinary Relationships in the Social Sciences*, Chicago: Aldine Publishing, pp. 329-48.

Campbell, Donald T. (1974/1987), Evolutionary Epistemology, in Paul A. Schilpp, ed., *The Philosophy of Karl Popper*, LaSalle, IL: Open Court (1974), pp. 413-463, reprinted in Gerard Radnitsky and W. W. Bartley II, eds., *Evolutionary Epistemology, Rationality, and the Sociology of Knowledge*, LaSalle, IL: Open Court (1987), pp. 47-89.

Card, Stuart K., Thomas P. Moran, and Allen Newell (1983), *The Psychology of Human-Computer Interaction*, Hillsdale, NJ: Lawrence Erlbaum Associates.

Carraher, Ronald G. and Jacqueline B. Thurston (1966), *Optical Illusions and the Visual Arts*, New York: Reinhold Publishing Co.

Carroll, John M. (1989a), Evaluation, Description and Invention: Paradigms for Human-Computer Interaction, in Marshall C. Yovits, ed., *Advances in Computers*, Boston: Academic Press, Vol. 29, pp. 47-77.

Carroll, John M. (1989b), Taking Artifacts Seriously, *Software-Ergonomie '89*, Stuttgart: B. G. Teubner.

Carroll, John M., ed. (1991a), *Designing Interaction: Psychology at the Human-Computer Interface*, Cambridge: Cambridge University Press.

Carroll, John M. (1991b), Introduction: The Kittle House Manifesto, in John M. Carroll, ed., *Designing Interaction: Psychology at the Human-Computer Interface*, Cambridge: Cambridge University Press, pp. 1-16.

Carroll, John M. and Robert L. Campbell (1989), Artifacts as Psychological Theories: The Case of Human-Computer Interaction, *Behavior and Information Technology*, 8:247-256.

Cerns, A. B. (1977), Can Behavioral Science Help Design Organizations? *Organizational Dynamics*, 5, Spring, 44-64.

Chalmers, A. F. (1982), *What Is This Thing Called Science?*, 2nd ed., St. Lucia: University of Queensland Press.

Chase, W. G. and H. A. Simon (1973), Perception in Chess, *Cognitive Psychology*, 4:55-81.

Checkland, P. B. (1981), *Systems Thinking, Systems Practice*, Chichester: John Wiley & Sons.

Checkland, P. B. and J. Scholes (1990), *Soft Systems Methodology in Action*, Chichester: John Wiley and Sons.

Chen, Peter S. (1976), The Entity-Relationship Model: Toward a Unifying View of Data, *ACM Transactions on Database Systems*, 1:9-36.

Cheng, Patricia W. and Keith J. Holyoak (1985), Pragmatic Reasoning Schemas, *Cognitive Psychology*, 17:391-446.

Cherns, Albert B. (1977), Can Behavioral Science Help Design Organizations?, *Organizational Dynamics*, Spring:44-57.

Chi, Michelene T. H., Robert Glaser, and M. J. Farr, eds. (1988), *The Nature of Expertise*, Hillsdale, NJ: Lawrence Erlbaum Associates.

Chomsky, A. N. (1957), *Syntactic Structures*, The Hague: Mouton.

Churchman, C. West (1971), *The Design of Inquiring Systems*, New York: Basic Books.

Clancey, William J. (1993), Situated Action: A Neuropsychological Interpretation Response to Vera and Simon, *Cognitive Science*, 17:87-116.

Coad, Peter and Edward Yourdon (1991), *Object-Oriented Analysis*, 2nd ed., Yourdon Press, Englewood Cliffs, NJ: Prentice-Hall.

Codd, Edgar E. (1990), *The Relational Model for Database Management: Version 2*, Reading, MA: Addison-Wesley Publishing Co.

Coffey, R. M. (1980), How a Medical Information System Affects Hospital Costs: The EL Camino Hospital Experience, Washington, DC: U.S. Government Printing Office, DHEW (PHS) 80-3255.

Cohen, B., W. T. Harwood, and M. I. Jackson (1986), *The Specification of Complex Systems*, Reading, MA: Addison Wesley.

Cohen, Gillian (1989), *Memory in the Real World*, Hillsdale, NJ: Lawrence Erlbaum Associates.

Cohen, L. Jonathan (1981), Can Human Irrationality be Experimentally Demonstrated?, *The Behavioral and Brain Sciences*, 4:317-370.

Cole, Jonathan R. and Stephen Cole (1972), The Ortega Hypothesis, *Science*, 178:368-375.

Cole, Michael (1991), Conclusion, in Lauren B. Resnick, John M. Levine, and Stephanie D. Teasley, eds., *Perspectives on Socially Shared Cognition*, Washington, DC: American Psychological Association, pp. 398-417.

Coll, Richard A., Joan H. Coll, and Ganesh Thakur (1994), Graphs and Tables, A Four-Factor Experiment, *Communications of the ACM*, (37,4):77-86.

Collins, Harry M. (1985), *Changing Order: Replication and Induction in Scientific Practice*, London: Sage.

Computer Science and Technology Board (1992), Computing the Future, *Communications of the ACM*, (35,11):30-40.

Constant, Edward (1980), *Origins of the Turbojet Revolution*, Baltimore, MD: Johns Hopkins University Press.

Cooley, Mike J. E. (1987), *Architect or Bee? The Human Price of Technology*, London: Hogarth Press.

Cooley, Mike (1988), From Brunelleschi to CAD-CAM, in John Thackara, ed., *Design After Modernism. Beyond the Object*, New York: Thames and Hudson, pp. 197-207.

Corbett, J. Martin (1992), Work at the Interface: Advanced Manufacturing Technology and Job Design, in Paul S. Adler and Terry A. Winograd, eds., *Usability. Turning Technology into Tools*, New York: Oxford, pp. 133-163).

Couger, J. Daniel (1990), Ensuring Creative Approaches in Information System Design, *Managerial and Decision Economics*, 11:281-295.

Crevier, Daniel (1993), *AI The Tumultuous History of the Search for Artificial Intelligence*, New York: Basic Books.

Cuff, Dana (1991), *Architecture: The Story of Practice*, Cambridge, MA: MIT Press.

Curtis, Bill (1981), Substantiating Programmer Variability, *Proceedings of the IEEE*, 69:846.

Curtis, Bill (1985), *Tutorial: Human Factors in Software Development*, 2nd ed., Washington, DC: Computer Society Press.

Curtis, Bill and Bill Hefley (1994), A WIMP No More, *Interactions*, 1:22-34.

Curtis, Bill, Herb Krasner, Vincent Shen, and Neil Iscoe (1987), On Building Software Process Models Under the Lamppost, *ACM National Conference*, pp. 96-103.

Dalbom, Bo (1986), Computer and Human Values, in Hans-Eric Nissen and Gunhild Sandström, eds., *Quality of Work Versus Quality of Information Systems*, Lund: University of Lund, pp. 16-34.

Darden, Lindley and Nancy Maull (1977), Interfield Theories, *Philosophy of Science*, 44:43-64.

Dasgupta, Subrata (1991), *Design Theory and Computer Science*, Cambridge: Cambridge University Press.

Davies, Simon P. (1991), Characterizing the Program Design Activity: Neither Strictly Top-Down nor Globally Opportunistic, *Behavior & Information Technology*, 10:173-190.

Davis, Alan, M. (1988), A Taxonomy for the Early Stages of the Software Development Cycle, *Journal of Systems and Software*, (8,4).

Davis, Alan M. (1993), *Software Requirements: Objects, Functions and States*, Englewood Cliffs, NJ: Prentice Hall.

Davis, Randall, Howard Shrobe, and Peter Szolovits (1993), What is a Knowledge Representation, *AI Magazine*, (14,1):17-33.

Day, Mary Carrol and Susan J. Boyce (1993), Human Factors in Human-Computer System Design, in Marshall C. Yovits, ed., *Advances in Computers*, Vol. 36, Boston: Academic Press, pp. 334-430.

Dekieva, Sasa M. (1992), The Influence of the Information Systems Development Approach on Maintenance, *MIS Quarterly*, 16:355-372.

DeMarco, Tom (1978), *Structured Analysis and System Specification*, New York: Yourdon Press.

Denning, Peter J. (1991), Beyond Formalism, *American Scientist*, 79:8-9.

Denning, Peter J. (1992a), Educating a New Engineer, *Communications of the ACM*, (35,12):83-97.

Denning, Peter J. (1992b), Work is a Closed-Loop Process, *American Scientist*, 80:314-317.

Denning, Peter J. (1992c), What is Software Quality?, *Communications of the ACM*, (35,1):13-15.

Denning, Peter J. and Pamela A. Dargan (1994), A Discipline of Software Architecture, *Interactions*, (1,1):55-65.

Denning, Peter J. (Chairman), Douglas E. Comer, David Gries, Michael Mulder, Allen Tucker, A. Joe Turner, and Paul R. Young (1989), Computing as a Discipline, *Communications of the ACM*, 32:9-23.

Deregowski, Jan B. (1972), Pictorial Perception and Culture, *Scientific American*, (227,11):82-88.

Dijkstra, Edgser W. (1968a), The Structure of "THE"-Multiprogramming System, *Communications of the ACM*, 11:341-346.

Dijkstra, Edsger W. (1968b), Go To Statement Considered Harmful, *Communications of the ACM*, 11:147-148.

Dijkstra, Edsger W. (1989), On the Cruelty of Really Teaching Computing Science, *Communications of the ACM*, (32):1398-1404.

Dreyfus, Hubert L. (1972/1992), *What Computers* Still *Can't Do*, Cambridge, MA: MIT Press.

Dreyfus, Hubert L. (1991), *Being-in-the-World: A Commentary on Heidegger's* Being and Time, *Division I*, Cambridge, MA: MIT Press.

Dreyfus, Hubert L. and Stuart E. Dreyfus (1986), *Mind Over Machine*, New York: The Free Press.

Donovan, Arthur (1986), Thinking about Engineering, *Technology & Culture*, 27:674-79.

Dubinskas, Frank A., ed. (1988a), *Making Time. Ethnographies of High-Technology Organizations*, Philadelphia: Temple University Press.

Dubinskas, Frank A., (1988b), Cultural Constructions: The Many Faces of Time, in Ffrank A. Dubinskas, ed., *Making Time. Ethnographies of High-Technology Organizations*, Philadelphia: Temple University Press, pp. 3-38.

Dunlop, Charles and Rob Kling, eds. (1991), *Computerization and Controversy*, Boston: Academic Press.

Dyson, Freeman (1979), *Disturbing the Universe*, New York.

Ehn, Pelle (1989), *Work-Oriented Design of Computer Artifacts*, 2nd ed., Hillsdale, NJ: Lawrence Erlbaum Associates.

Ehn, Pelle (1992), Scandinavian Design: On Participation and Skill, in Paul S. Adler and Terry A. Winograd, eds., *Usability: Turning Technologies into Tools*, New York: Oxford University Press, pp. 96-132.

Elstein, A., L. Shulman, and S. Sprafka (1978), *Medical Problem Solving*, Cambridge, MA: Harvard University Press.

Engelbart, D. and W. English (1968), A Research Center for Augmenting Human Intellect, *Proceedings of the Fall Joint Computer Conference*, pp. 395-410.

Engeström, Vrjö (1987), *Learning by Expanding: An Activity-Theoretical Approach to Developmental Research*, Helsinki: Orienta-Konsultit Oy.

Enterline, J. P. (1989), Evaluation and Future Directions, in J. P. Enterline, R. E. Lenhard, and B. I. Blum, eds., *A Clinical Information System for Oncology*, New York: Springer-Verlag, pp. 217-240.

Enterline, J. P., R. E. Lenhard, and B. I. Blum, eds. (1989), *A Clinical Information System for Oncology*, New York: Springer-Verlag.

Enterline, J. P., R. E. Lenhard, Jr., B. I. Blum, F. M. Majidi, and G. J. Stuart (1994), OCIS: 15 Years' Experience with Patient-Centered Computing, *M. D. Computing*, (11,2):83-91.

Erickson, J. David (1993), Beyond Systems: Better Understanding the User's World, *Computer Language*, (10,3):51-64.

Evans, Jonathan St. B. T., ed. (1983), *Thinking and Reasoning*, London: Routledge & Kegan Paul.

Evans, Jonathan St. B. T. (1989), *Bias in Human Reasoning: Causes and Consequences*, Hillsdale, NJ: Lawrence Erlbaum Associates.

Farhoomand, Ali F. (1987), Scientific Progress of Management Information Systems, *Data Base*, Summer:48-56.

Fenton, Norman (1993), How Effective Are Software Engineering Methods?, *Journal of Systems and Software*, 22:141-146.

Ferguson, Eugene S. (1977), The Mind's Eye: Nonverbal Thought in Technology, *Science*, 197:827-836.

Ferguson, Eugene S. (1992), *Engineering and the Mind's Eye*, Cambridge, MA: MIT Press.

Feyerabend, Paul K. (1970), Philosophy of Science: A Subject with a Great Past, in R. H. Stuewer, ed., *Historical and Philosophical Perspectives of Science*, Minneapolis: University of Minnesota Press, pp. 172-183.

Feyerabend, Paul K. (1975), *Against Method: Outline of an Anarchistic Theory of Knowledge*, London: New Left Books.

Feynman, Richard P. (1988), *What Do You Care What Other People Think?*, New York: W. W. Norton & Co.

Flores, Fernando, Michael Graves, Brad Hartfield, and Terry Winograd (1988), Computer Systems and the Design or Organizational Interaction, *ACM Transactions on Office Information Systems*, 6:153-172.

Floyd, Christiane (1991), Software Development as Reality Construction, in Floyd, Christiane, Heinz Züllighoven, Reinhard Budde, and Reinhard Keil-Slawik, eds. (1991), *Software Development and Reality Construction*, Berlin: Springer-Verlag, pp. 86-100.

Floyd, Christiane, Wold-Michael Mehl, Fanny-Michaela Reisin, Gerhard Schmidt, and Gregor Wolf (1989), Out of Scandinavia: Alternative Approaches to Software Design and System Development, *Human-Computer Interaction*, 4:253-349.

Floyd, Christiane, Heinz Züllighoven, Reinhard Budde, and Reinhard Keil-Slawik, eds. (1991), *Software Development and Reality Construction*, Berlin: Springer-Verlag.

Fodor, J. A. (1987), A Situated Grandmother? Some Remarks on Proposals by Barwise and Perry, *Mind & Language*, 2:64-81.

Frankl, Viktor E. (1985), *The Doctor and the Soul*, 3rd edition, New York: Vintage Books.

Fraser, Jane M., Philip J. Smith, and Jack W. Smith (1992), A Catalog of Errors, *International Journal of Man-Machine Studies*, 37:265-307.

Freeman, Peter (1980), The Central Role of Design in Software Engineering: Implications for Research, in H. Freeman and P. M. Lewis II, eds., *Software Engineering*, New York: Academic Press.

Friedman, Andrew (1989), *Computer Systems Development: History, Organization and Implementation*, Chichester: John Wiley & Sons.

Friedman, Batya and Peter H. Kahn, Jr. (1994), Educating Computer Scientists: Linking the Social and the Technical, *Communications of the ACM*, (37,1):64-70.

Fuller, Steve (1994), Underlaborers for Science [review of Callebaut (1993)], *Science*, 264:982-983.

Funke, Joachim (1991), Solving Complex Problems: Exploration and Control of Complex Social Systems, in Robert J. Sternberg and Peter A. Frensch, eds. (1991), *Complex Problem Solving*, Hillsdale, NJ: Lawrence Erlbaum Associates, pp. 185-222.

Gane, C. and T. Sarson (1979), *Structured Systems Analysis*, Englewood Cliffs, NJ: Prentice-Hall.

Garcia Marquez, Gabriel (1967/1970), *One Hundred Years of Solitude*, New York: Avon Books.

Gardner, Howard (1985), *The Mind's New Science*, New York: Basic Books.

Geertz, Clifford (1973), *The Interpretation of Cultures*, New York: Basic Books.

Gentner, Dedre and Albert L. Stevens, eds. (1983), *Mental Models*, Hillsdale, NJ: Lawrence Erlbaum Associates.

Getzels, J. and M. Csikszentmihalyi (1976), *The Creative Vision: A Longitudinal Study of Problem Finding in Art*, New York: John Wiley & Sons.

Gibson, James J. (1979), *The Ecological Approach to Visual Perception*, Dallas: Houghton Mifflin, republished Hillsdale, NJ: Lawrence Erlbaum, 1986.

Gilb, Tom (1988), *Principles of Software Engineering Management*, Reading, MA: Addison Wesley.

Gilhooly, K. J. (1988), *Thinking: Undirected, Undirected and Creative*, 2nd ed., London: Academic Press.

Glaser, Robert and Michelene T. H. Chi (1988), Overview, in Michelene T. H. Chi, Robert Glaser, and M. J. Farr, eds. (1988), *The Nature of Expertise*, Hillsdale, NJ: Lawrence Erlbaum Associates, pp. xv-xxxvi.

Glass, Robert L. (1994), In the Year 2020, The Computing and Software Research Crisis, *IEEE Software*, November.

Glass, Robert L. (1995), Research Phases in Software Engineering: An Analysis of What is Needed and What is Missing, *Journal of Systems and Software*, 28:3-7.

Glass, Robert L. and Iris Vessey (1992), Toward a Taxonomy of Software Application Domains: History, *Journal of Systems and Software*, 17: 189-199.

Glass, Robert L., Iris Vessey, and Sue A. Conger (1992), Software Tasks, Intellectual or Social? *Information & Management*, 23:183-191.

Goel, Vinod and Peter Pirolli (1989), Motivating the Notion of Generic Design within Information-Processing Theory: The Design Problem Space, *AI Magazine*, (10,1):18-36.

Goldman, Alvin I. (1993), *Readings in Philosophy and Cognitive Science*, Cambridge, MA: MIT Press.

Goldstein, Sheldon (1994), Review of Peter R. Holland, *The Quantum Theory of Motion*, *Science*, 263:254-255.

Gooding, David (1990), Mapping Experiment as a Learning Process: How the First Electromagnetic Motor Was Invented, *Science, Technology, and Human Values*, 15:165-201.

Goodman, Nelson (1984), *Of Mind and Other Matters*, Cambridge, MA: Harvard University Press.

van den Goor, Gilbert, Shuguang Hong, and Sjaak Brinkkemper (1992), *A Comparison of Six Object-Oriented Analysis and Design Methods*, Method Engineering Institute, University of Twente, Enschede, The Netherlands.

Gorman, Michael E. and W. Bernard Carlson (1990), Interpreting Invention as a Cognitive Process: The Case of Alexander Graham Bell, Thomas Edison, and the Telephone, *Science, Technology, and Human Values*, 15:131-164.

Graham, M. H. and D. H. Miller (1988), *ISTAR Evaluation*, Technical Report CMU/SEI-88-TR-3, Software Engineering Institute.

Grandjean, E. (1985), *Fitting the Task to the Man*, London: Taylor & Francis.

Green, T. R. G., M. Petre, and R. Bellamy (1991), Comprehensibility of Visual and Textual Programs: A Test of Superlativism Against the "Match-Mismatch" Conjecture, in J. Koenemann-Belliveau, T. Moher, and S. Robertson, eds., *Empirical Studies of Programmers: Fourth Workshop*, Norwood, NJ: Ablex, pp. 121-146.

Greenbaum, Joan and Morten Kyng, eds. (1991a), *Design at Work: Cooperative Design of Computer Systems*, Hillsdale, NJ: Lawrence Erlbaum Associates.

Greenbaum, Joan and Morten Kyng, eds. (1991b), Introduction: Situated Design, in Joan Greenbaum and Morten Kyng, eds., *Design at Work: Cooperative Design of Computer Systems*, Hillsdale, NJ: Lawrence Erlbaum Associates, pp. 1-24.

Greenbaum, Joan and Lars Mathiassen (1987), Zen and the Art of Teaching Systems Development, Computer Science Department Report DAIMI-238, Aarhus University, Aarhus Denmark.

Gregory, S. A., ed. (1966), *The Design Method*, New York: Plenum Press.

Greif, Irene, ed. (1988), *Computer Supported Cooperative Work: A Book of Readings*, San Mateo, CA: Morgan Kaufmann.

Gries, David (1981), *The Science of Programming*, New York: Springer-Verlag

Grudin, Jonathan (1989a), The Case Against User Interface Consistency, *Communications of the ACM*, 32:1164-1173.

Grudin, Jonathan (1989b), Why Groupware Applications Fail: Problems in Design and Evaluation, *Office Technology and People*, 4:245-264.

Grudin, Jonathan (1993), Interface: An Evolving Concept, *Communications ACM*, 36:110-119.

Guindon, Raymonde (1990), Designing the Design Process: Exploiting Opportunistic Thought, *Human-Computer Interaction*, 5:305-344.

Gutting, Gary (1984), Paradigms, Revolutions, and Technology, in Rachel Laudan, ed., *The Nature of Technological Knowledge. Are Models of Scientific Change Relevant?*, Boston: D. Reidel Publishing, 1984, pp. 47-65.

Hannan, Terry, (1991), Medical Informatics - An Australian Perspective, *Australian and New Zealand Journal of Medicine*, 21, 363-378.

Hannan, Terry (1994), International Transfer of the Johns Hopkins Oncology Center Clinical Information System, *M. D. Computing*, (11,2):92-99.

Harel, D. (1992), Biting the Silver Bullet, *Computer*, January, pp. 8-20.

Harel, D., H. Lachover, A. Naamad, A. Pnueli, M. Politi, R. Sherman, A. Shtull-Trauring, and M. Trakhtenrot (1990), STATEMATE: A Working Environment for the Development of Complex Reactive Systems, *IEEE Trans. S. E.*, SE-16:403-414.

Harmon, Willis W. (1970), *Alternative Futures and Educational Policy*, Stanford Research Institute, Eric #6747-6, February.

Hartmanis, Juris (1994), On Computational Complexity and the Nature of Computer Science, *Communications of the ACM*, (37, 10):37-43.

Hayes-Roth, Barbara and Fredrick Hayes-Roth (1979), A Cognitive Model of Planning, *Cognitive Science*, 3:275-310.

Hayes-Roth, B., K. Pfleger, P. Lalanda, P. Morignot, and M. Balabanovic (in press), A Domain-Specific Software Architecture for Adaptive Intelligent Systems, *IEEE Transactions on Software Engineering*.

Hayes-Roth, Fredrick (1994), Architecture-Based Acquisition and Development of Software: Guidelines and Recommendations from the ARPA Domain-Specific Software Architecture (DSSA) Program V.1.01, Teknowledge Technical Report.

Hayes-Roth, Fredrick, Lee D. Erman, A. Terry, and Barbara Hayes Roth (1992), Domain-Specific Software Architectures: Distributed Intelligent Control and

Management, *Proceedings IEEE Symposium on Computer-Aided Control System Design*, pp. 117-128.

Henderson, Kathryn (1991), Flexible Sketches and Invisible Data Bases: Visual Communication, Conscription Devices, and Boundary Objects in Design Engineering, *Science, Technology, & Human Values*, 16:448-473.

Henle, Mary (1962), On the Relation Between Logic and Thinking, *Psychological Review*, 69:366-378.

Hesse, Mary (1974), *The Structure of Scientific Inference*, London: Macmillian.

Hesse, Mary (1980), *Revolutions and Reconstructions in the Philosophy of Science*, Brighton, England: Harvester Press.

Hickman, D. H., E. H. Shortliffe, M. B. Bischoff, A. C. Scott, and C. D. Jacobs, (1985), A Study of the Treatment Advice of a Computer-Based Chemotherapy Protocol Advisor, *Annals of Internal Medicine*, 101:928.

Hindle, Brooke (1981), *Emulation and Invention*, New York: New York University Press.

Hirschheim, R., H. K. Klein, and M. Newman (1991), Information Systems Development as Social Action: Theoretical Perspective and Practice, *OMEGA International Journal of Management Science*, 19:587-608.

Hirschhorn, Larry (1982), The Soul of a New Worker, *Working Papers Magazine*, (9,1):42-47.

Hix, Deborah, H. Rex Hartson, Antonio C. Siochi, and David Ruppert (1994), Customer Responsibility for Ensuring Usability: Requirements on the User Interface Development Process, *Journal of Systems and Software*, 25:241-255.

Hornby, P., C. W. Clegg, J. I. Robson, C. R. R. MacLaren, S. C. S. Richardson, and P. O'Brien (1992), Human and Organizational Issues in Information Systems Development, *Behavior & Information Technology*, 11:160-174.

Horton, Robin (1967), African Traditional Thought and Western Science, *Africa*, 38:50-71, 155-187.

Horton, Robin (1982), Tradition and Modernity Revisited, in M. Hollis and S. Lukes, eds., *Rationality and Relativism*, Cambridge, MA: MIT Press.

Hoyningen-Huene, Paul (1993), *Reconstructing Scientific Revolutions: Thomas S. Kuhn's Philosophy of Science*, Chicago: University of Chicago Press.

Hudson, Liam (1966), *Contrary Imaginations*, New York: Schocken Books.

Hughes, Thomas P. (1979), Emerging Themes in the History of Technology, *Technology and Culture*, 23:697-711.

Hull, R. and R. King (1987), Semantic Database Modeling: Survey, Applications, and Research Issues, *ACM Computer Surveys*, 19:201-260.

Humphrey, Watts S. (1989), *Managing the Software Process*, Reading, MA: Addison-Wesley.

Hunt, Earl (1991), Some Comments on the Study of Complexity, in Robert J. Sternberg and Peter A. Frensch, eds. (1991), *Complex Problem Solving*, Hillsdale, NJ: Lawrence Erlbaum Associates, pp. 383-395.

Hutchins, Edwin L., James D. Hollan, and Donald A. Norman (1985), Direct Manipulation Interfaces, *Human-Computer Interaction*, 1:311-338.

IIT (1968), *Technology in Retrospect And Critical Events in Science (TRACES)*, Jacksonville, IL: Illinois Institute of Technology Research Institute, under Contract NSF-C535.

Jackson, Michael A. (1975), *Principles of Program Design*, New York: Academic Press.

Jackson, Michael A. (1982), *System Development*, Englewood Cliffs, NJ: Prentice-Hall.

Jensen, R. W. and C. C. Tonies (1979), *Software Engineering*, Englewood Cliffs, NJ: Prentice-Hall.

Jirotka, Marina, Nigel Gilbert, and Paul Luff (1992), On the Social Organization of Organizations, *Computer Supported Cooperative Work (CSWC)*, 1:95-118.

Johnson-Laird, Philip N. (1983a), *Mental Models*, Cambridge: Cambridge University Press.

Johnson-Laird, Philip N. (1983b), Thinking as a Skill, in Jonathan St. B. T. Evans, ed, *Thinking and Reasoning*, London: Routledge & Kegan Paul, pp. 164-196.

Jones, C. B. (1980), *Software Development, A Rigorous Approach*, Englewood Cliffs, NJ: Prentice-Hall.

Jones, Edward E. (1986), Interpreting Interpersonal Behavior: The Effects of Expectancies, *Science*, 234:41-46.

Jones, John Christopher (1963), A Method of Systematic Design, *Conference on Design Methods*, Oxford: Pergamon, reprinted in *Developments in Design Methodology* for which I have no citation.

Jones, John Chris (1988), Softecnica, in John Thackara, ed., *Design After Modernism. Beyond the Object*, New York: Thames and Hudson, pp. 11-34.

Jydstrup, R. A. amd M. J. Gross (1966), Cost of Information Handling in Hospitals, *Health Services Research*, Winter:235-271.

Kahneman, Daniel, Pail Slovic, and Amos Tversky (1982), *Judgment Under Uncertainty: Heuristics and Biases*, Cambridge: Cambridge University Press.

Kaplan, Abraham (1964), *The Conduct of Inquiry: Methodology for Behavioral Science*, San Francisco: Chandler Publishing Co.

Kaplan, Craig A. and Herbert A. Simon (1990), In Search of Insight, *Cognitive Psychology*, 22:374-419.

Kaufmann, Geir, (1979), *Visual Imagery and its Relation to Problem Solving*, Bergen: Universitetsforlaget.

Kihlstrom, John F. (1987), The Cognitive Unconscious, *Science*, 237:1446-1451.

Kitcher, Philip (1993), *The Advancement of Science*, New York: Oxford University Press.

Kitching, Gavin (1988), *Karl Marx and the Philosophy of Praxis*, London: Routledge.

Klein, Gary A. (1987), Analytical Versus Recognitional Approaches to Design Decision Making, in William B. Rouse and Kenneth R. Boff, 3eds., *System Design*, Amsterdam: North-Holland, pp. 175-188.

Kline, Stephen J. (1985), Innovation Is Not a Linear Process, *Research Management*, Jul-Aug:36-45.

Kling, Rob (1980), Social Analyses of Computing: Theoretical Perspectives in Recent Empirical Research, *Computing Surveys*, 12:61-110.

Knorr-Cetina, Karen (1983), The Ethonographic Study of Scientific Work: Towards a Constructivist Interpretation of Science, in Karen Knorr-Cetina and Michael Mulkay, eds., *Science Observed: Perspectives on the Social Study of Science*, London: Sage, pp. 115-140.

Knorr-Cetina, Karin and Klaus Amann (1990), Image Dissection in Natural Scientific Inquiry, *Science, Technology, and Human Values*, 15:259-283.

Knorr-Cetina, Karen and Michael Mulkay (1983), Introduction: Emerging Principles in Social Studies of Science, in Karen Knorr-Cetina and Michael

Mulkay, eds., *Science Observed: Perspectives on the Social Study of Science*, London: Sage, pp. 1-18.

Knuth, Donald E. (1989), The Errors of TEX, *Software Practice and Experience*, 19:607-685.

Kobsa, Alfred and Wolfgang Wahlster, eds. (1989), *User Models in Dialogue Systems*, Berlin: Springer-Verlag.

Kuhn, Deanna (1989), Children and Adults as Intuitive Scientists, *Psychological Review*, 96:674-688.

Kuhn, Deanna, Eric Amsel, and Michael O'Loughlin, (1988), *The Development of Scientific Thinking Skills*, San Diego, CA: Academic Press.

Kuhn, Thomas S. (1970), *The Structure of Scientific Revolutions*, Second Edition, Urbana: University of Chicago Press, (originally published in 1962).

Kumar, Kuldeep and Niels Bjørn-Anderson (1990), A Cross-Cultural Comparison of IS Designer Values, *Communications of the ACM*, 33:528-538.

Kurtz, Paul (1992), *The New Skepticism*, Buffalo, NY: Prometheus Books.

Kuutti, Kari (1991), Activity Theory and Its Applications to Information Systems Research and Development, in H. E. Nissen, H.K. Klein, and R. Hirschheim, eds., *Information Systems Research*, Amsterdam: North Holland, pp. 529-549.

Kuutti, Kari (in press), Activity Theory, Transformation of Work and Information System Design, in Y. Engeström and R.-L. Punamäki, eds, *Perspectives on Activity Theory*, Cambridge: Cambridge University Press.

Kuutti, Kari and Tuula Arvonen (1992), Identifying Potential CSWC Applications by Means of Activity Theory Concepts: A Case Example, *CSWC 92 Proceedings*, pp. 233-240.

Lakatos, Imre (1970), Falsification and the Methodology of Scientific Research Programmes, in I. Lakatos and A. Musgrave, eds., *Criticism and the Growth of Knowledge*, Cambridge: Cambridge University Press, pp. 91-196.

Lakatos, Imre (1978), History of Science and Its Rational Reconstructions, in J. Warrall and G. Currie, eds., *The Methodology of Scientific Programmes. Philosophic Papers of Imre Lakatos*, Cambridge: Cambridge University Press.

Land, Edwin H. (1959), Experiments in Color Vision, *Scientific American*, 52:247-264 (84-99).

Lang, Kathy Lynn (1990), *Understanding Errors in Human-Computer Interaction*, Ph.D. Dissertation, Memphis State University.

Langefors, B. (1966), *Theoretical Analysis of Information Systems*, 1st ed., Lund: Studentlitteratur.

Langley, Pat and Herbert A. Simon (1981), The Central Role of Learning in Cognition, in J. R. Anderson, ed., *Cognitive Skills and Their Acquisition*, Hillsdale, NJ: Lawrence Erlbaum Associates.

Langley, Pat, Herbert A. Simon, Gary L. Bradshaw, and Jan M. Zytkow (1987), *Scientific Discovery, Computational Explorations of the Creative Process*, Cambridge, MA: MIT Press.

Latour, Bruno (1986), Visualization and Cognition: Thinking with Eyes and Hands, *Knowledge and Society*, 6:1-40.

Latour, Bruno (1987), *Science in Action*, Cambridge, MA: Harvard University Press.

Latour, Bruno and Steve Woolgar (1986), *Laboratory Life: The Construction of Scientific Facts*, 2nd ed., Princeton, NJ: Princeton University Press.

Laudan, Larry (1981), The Pseudo-Science of Science?, *Philosophy of the Social Sciences*, 11:173-198.

Laudan, Larry, Arthur Donovan, Rachel Laudan, Peter Barker, Harold Brown, Jarrett Leflin, Paul Thagard, and Steve Wykstra (1986), Scientific Change: Philosophical Models and Historical Research, *Synthese*, 69:141-223.

Laudan, Rachel (1984a), Introduction, in Rachel Laudan, ed. *The Nature of Technological Knowledge. Are Models of Scientific Change Relevant?*, Boston: D. Reidel Publishing, 1984, pp. 1-26.

Laudan, Rachel (1984b), Cognitive Change in Technology and Science, in Rachel Laudan, ed., *The Nature of Technological Knowledge. Are Models of Scientific Change Relevant?*, Boston: D. Reidel Publishing Co., 1984, pp. 83-104.

Laurel, Brenda, ed. (1990), *The Art of Human-Computer Interface Design*, Reading, MA: Addison-Wesley.

Lave, Jean (1988), *Cognition in Practice*, Cambridge: Cambridge University Press.

Lave, Jean (1991), Situated Learning in Communities of Practice, in Lauren B. Resnick, John M. Levine, and Stephanie D. Teasley, eds., *Perspectives on Socially Shared Cognition*, Washington, DC: American Psychological Association, pp. 63-82.

Law, John and Michel Callon (1988), Engineering and Sociology in a Military Aircraft Project: A Network Analysis of Technological Change, *Social Problems*, 35:284-297.

Layton, Edwin T., Jr. (1971), Mirror-Image Twins: The Communities of Science and Technology in 19th-Century America, *Technology and Culture*, 12:567-580.

Layton, Edwin T., Jr. (1974), Technology as Knowledge, *Technology and Culture*, Jan., 15:31-41.

Layton, Edwin T., Jr. (1984), Science and Engineering Design, *Annals of the New York Academy of Science*, 424:173-81.

Lederman, Leon M. (1984), The Value of Fundamental Science, *Scientific American*, November:40-47.

Lee, Kang W., Frank A. Tillman, and James J. Higgins (1988), A Literature Survey of the Human Reliability Component in a Man-Machine System, *IEEE Transactions on Reliability*, 37:24-34.

Lehman, Meir M. (1980), Life Cycles and Laws of Program Evolution, *Proceedings of the IEEE*, 68:1060-1076.

Lehman, Meir M (1991), Software Engineering, the Software Process and Their Support, *Software Engineering Journal*, 6:243-256.

Lehman, Meir M. (1994), Introduction to FEAST, *FEAST Workshop*, Department of Computer Science, Imperial College of Science, Technology and Medicine, pp. 6-10.

Lehman, Meir M. and Laszlo A. Belady (1985), *Program Evolution—Processes of Software Change*, London: Academic Press.

Lehman, M. M., V. Stenning and W. M. Turski (1984), Another Look at Software Design Methodology, *ACM SIGSOFT SEN*, (9,3).

Leontyev, A. N. (1972/1979), The Problem of Activity in Psychology, *Voprosy filosofii*, 9:95-108, translated in James V. Wertsch, ed., *The Concept of Activity in Soviet Psychology*, Armonk, NY: M. E. Sharpe, pp. 37-71.

Leontyev, A. N. (1981), *Problems of the Development of the Mind*, Moscow: Progress Publishers.

Lewkowicz, John (1989), *The Complete MUMPS*, Englewood Cliffs, NJ: Prentice Hall.

Lientz, B. P., and E. G. Swanson (1980), *Software Maintenance Management*, Addison Wesley, Reading, MA.

Likins, Peter (1992), Viewpoint: A Breach of the Social Contract, *Communications of the ACM*, (35,11):17-18,111.

Lindland, Odd Ivar, Guttorm Sindre, and Arne Sølvberg (1994), Understanding Quality in Conceptual Modeling, *IEEE Software*, (11,2):42-49.

Lindley, David (1993), *The End of Physics: The Myth of a Unified Theory*, New York: Basic Books.

Liskov, B. H., and S. N. Zilles (1975), Specification Techniques for Data Abstraction, *IEEE Transactions on Software Engineering*, SE-1:7-19.

Lynch, Michael (1985), *Art and Artifact in Laboratory Science*, London: Routledge & Kegan Paul.

Lynch, Michael and Steve Woolgar (1988), Introduction: Sociological Orientation to Representational Practice in Science, *Human Studies*, 11:99-116.

Machlup, Fritz (1983), Semantic Quirks in Studies of Information, in Fritz Machlup and Una Mansfield, eds., *The Study of Information*, New York: John Wiley & Sons, pp. 641-671.

Mahoney, Michael J. (1976), *Scientist as Subject: The Psychological Imperative*, Cambridge, MA: Ballinger Publishing.

Mahoney, Michael S. (1988), The History of Computing in the History of Technology, *Annals of the History of Computing*, 10:113-125.

Majidi, Farideh, John P. Enterline, Barbara Ashley, Mary E. Fowler, Lisa Lattal Ogorzalek, Raymond Gaudette, Gloria J. Stuart, Monica Fulton, and David S. Ettinger (1993), Chemotherapy and Treatment Scheduling: The Johns Hopkins Oncology Center Outpatient Department, *SCAMC '93*, pp. 154-158.

Marca, David A. and Clement L. McGowan (1993), Specification Approaches Express Different World Hypotheses, *Proceedings, 7th International Workshop on Software Specification and Design*, pp. 214-223.

Martin, C. Dianne (1993), The Myth of the Awesome Thinking Machine, *Communications of the ACM*, (36, 4):121-133.

Martin, James (1982), *Application Development without Programmers*, Englewood Cliffs, NJ: Prentice-Hall.

Masterman, Margaret (1970), The Nature of a Paradigm, in I. Lakatos and A. Musgrove (eds), *Criticism and the Growth of Knowledge*, Cambridge: Cambridge University Press, pp. 59-89.

Matousek, Robert (1963), *Engineering Design*, New York: John Wiley & Sons.

Matson, Floyd W. (1964), *The Broken Image: Man, Science and Society*, New York: George Braziller.

Mayer, Richard E. (1983), *Thinking, Problem Solving, Cognition*, New York: W. H. Freeman.

McCloskey, Michael (1983), Intuitive Physics, *Scientific American*, (248,4):122-130.

McColligan, Elizabeth E (1989), Implementing OCIS at the Ohio State University, in J. P. Enterline, R. E. Lenhard, Jr., and B. I. Blum, eds., *A Clinical Information System for Oncology*, New York: Springer-Verlag, 1989, pp. 241-259.

McDonald, Clement J. (1976), Protocol-Based Reminders, the Quality of Care, and the Non-Perfectibility of Man, *New England Journal of Medicine*, 295:1351-3555.

Medina-Mora, Raúl, Terry Winograd, Rodrigo Flores, and Fernando Flores (1992), The Action Workflow Approach to Workflow Management Technology, *CSCW 92 Proceedings*, pp 281-288.

Meister, David (1987), A Cognitive Theory of Design and Requirements for a Behavioral Design Aid, in Willaim B. Rouse and Kenneth R. Boff, eds., (1987a), *System Design*, Amsterdam: North-Holland, pp. 7-18.

Mey, Jacob L. (1994), Adaptability, *Encyclopedia of Language and Linguistics*, Oxford: Pergamon/Elsevier, pp. 25-27.

Meyer, Bertrand (1988), *Object-Oriented Software Construction*, New York: Prentice-Hall.

Miles, R. K. (1985), Computer Systems Analysis: The Constraint of the Hard Systems Paradigm, *Journal of Advanced Systems Analysis*, 12:55-65.

Miller, George A. (1956), The Magical Number Seven, Plus or Minus Two, *Psychological Review*, 63:81-97.

Mills, H. D., M. Dyer, and R. Linger (1987), Cleanroom Software Engineering, *IEEE Software*, (4,5):19-25.

Mills, H. D., R. C. Linger, M. Dyer and R. E. Quinnan (1980), The Management of Software Engineering, *IBM Systems J.*, (24,2):414-77.

Minsky, Marvin (1975), A Framework for Representing Knowledge, reprinted in J. Haugeland, ed., *Mind Design*, Cambridge, MA: MIT Press, 1981, pp. 95-128.

Mitchell, Tom (1988), The Product as Illusion, in John Thackara, ed., *Design After Modernism. Beyond the Object*, New York: Thames and Hudson, p. 11-34.

Mitcham, Carl (1978), Types of Technology, *Research in Philosophy & Technology*, 1:229-294.

Mitroff, Ian I. (1972), The Myth of Objectivity or Why Science Needs a New Psychology of Science, *Management Science*, 18:B-613-618.

Mitroff, Ian I. (1983), Archetypical Social Systems Analysis: On the Deeper Structure of Human Systems, *Academy of Management Review*, 8:387-397.

Mitroff, Ian I. and Richard O. Mason (1981), Dialectical Pragmatism, *Synthese*, 47:29-42.

Moreau, D. R. (1987), *A Programming Environment Evaluation Methodology for Object-Oriented Systems*, PhD dissertation, U. of Southwestern Louisiana.

Mowshowitz, Abbe (1981), On Approaches to the Study of Social Issues in Computing, *Communications of the ACM*, 24:146-155.

Mowshowitz, Abbe (1985), On the Social Relations of Computers, *Human Systems Management*, 5:99-110.

Muller, Michael J., Daniel M. Wildman, and Ellen A. White (1993), Introduction [to the Special Edition on Participatory Design], *Communications of the ACM*, (36, 4):24-28.

Mumford, Enid (1993), The Participation of Users in Systems Design: An Account of the Origin, Evolution, and Use of the ETHICS Method, in Douglas Schuler and Aki Namioka, eds., *Participatory Design: Principles and Practices*, Hillsdale, NJ: Lawrence Erlbaum Associates, pp. 257-270.

Mumford, Lewis (1964), Authoritarian and Democratic Technics, *Technology & Culture*, 5:1-9.

Murata, T. (1989), Petri Nets: Properties, Analysis and Applications, *Proceedings of the IEEE*, 77:541-580.

Musa, John, ed. (1983), Stimulating Software Engineering Progress, A Report of the Software Engineering Planning Group, *ACM SIGSOFT, SEN*, (8,2):29-54).

Myers, Brad A. (1989), Introduction to Visual Programming and Program Visualization, *Proceedings CHI '89*.

Myers, Brad A., ed. (1992a), *Languages for Developing User Interfaces*, London: Jones and Bartlett.

Myers, Brad A. (1992b), "Factory" Concept Challenges Software Management, *Computer*, (25-8):97-98.

Nadler, Gerald (1986), The Role of Design Processes in Engineering, Unpublished lecture.

Nadler, Gerald and Gordon Robinson (1987), Planning, Designing, and Implementing Advanced Manufacturing Technology, in T. D. Wall, C. W. Clegg, and N. J. Kemp, eds., *The Human Side of Advanced Manufacturing Technology*, pp. 15-36.

Nardi, Bonnie A. (1993), *A Small Matter of Programming*, Cambridge, MA: MIT Press.

Naur, Peter (1985/1992), Programs as Theory Building, in Peter Naur, *Computing: A Human Activity*, New York: ACM Press, pp. 37-48.

Naur, Peter (1990/1992), Computing and the So-Called Foundations of the So-Called Sciences, in Peter Naur, *Computing: A Human Activity*, New York: ACM Press, pp. 49-63.

Naur, Peter and Brian Randell, eds., (1969), *Software Engineering: Report on a conference sponsored by the NATO Science Committee, Garmisch, Germany, 7th to 11th October 1968*, Scientific Affairs Division, NATO, Brussels.

Naylor, Gillian (1990), Swedish Grace ...or the Acceptable Face of Modernism?, in Paul Greenhalgh, ed., *Modernism in Design*, London: Reaktion Books, pp. 164-183.

Neighbors, James M. (1989), DRACO: A Method for Engineering Reusable Software Systems, in T. J. Biggerstaff and A. J. Perlis (eds.), *Software Reusability*, New York: ACM Press, 1989, Vol. 1, pp. 295-319.

Nelson, Holm (1990), The Right Way to Think about Software Design, in Brenda Laurel, ed., *The Art of Human-Computer Interface Design*, Reading, MA: Addison-Wesley.

Newell, Allen (1990), *Unified Theories of Cognition*, Cambridge, MA: Harvard University Press.

Newell, Allen and Herbert A. Simon (1972), *Human Problem Solving*, Englewood Cliffs, NJ: Prentice-Hall.

Nickerson, Raymond S., David N. Perkins, and Edward E. Smith (1985), *The Teaching of Thinking*, Hillsdale, NJ: Lawrence Erlbaum Associates.

Nielsen, Jakob and Johathan Levy (1994), Measuring Usibility, *Communications of the ACM*, (37,4):67-75.

Nisbett, Richard E., Geoffrey T. Fong, Darrin R. Lehman, and Patricia W. Cheng (1987), Teaching Reasoning, *Science* 238:625-631.

Norman, Donald A. (1982), *Learning and Memory*, New York: W. H. Freeman and Co.

Norman, Donald A. (1983), Some Observations on Mental Models, in Dedre Gentner and Albert L. Stevens, eds., *Mental Models*, Hillsdale, NJ: Lawrence Erlbaum Associates, pp. 7-14.

Norman, Donald A. (1986), Cognitive Engineering, in Donald A. Norman and Stephen W. Draper, eds., *User Centered System Design*, Lawrence Erlbaum Associates, pp. 31-61.

Norman, Donald A. (1988), *The Psychology of Everyday Things*, New York, Basic Books.

Norman, Donald A. (1991), Cognitive Artifacts, in John M. Carroll, John M., ed., *Designing Interaction: Psychology at the Human-Computer Interface*, Cambridge: Cambridge University Press, pp. 17-38.

Norman, Donald A. (1993), *Things that Make Us Smart*, Reading, MA: Addison-Wesley Publishing Co.

Norman, Donald A. and Stephen W. Draper, eds. (1986), *User Centered System Design*, Hillsdale, NJ: Lawrence Erlbaum Associates.

Nurminen, Markku I. (1986), Information System Quality versus Quality of Work. Is there any Difference?, in Hans-Erik Nissen and Gunhild Sandström, eds., *Quality of Work Versus Quality of Information Systems*, Lund: University of Lund.

Nurminen, Markku I. (1988), *People or Computers: Three Ways of Looking at Information Systems*, Lund: Studentlitteratur.

Nyce, James M. and William Graves III (1990), The Construction of Knowledge in Neurology: Implications for Hypermedia System Development, *Artificial Intelligence in Medicine*, 2:315-322.

Nygaard, Kristen (1991), How Many Choices De We Make? How Many Are Difficult?, in Christiane Floyd, Heinz Züllighoven, Reinhard Budde, and Reinhard Keil-Slawik, eds., *Software Development and Reality Construction*, Berlin: Springer-Verlag, pp. 52-59.

Olerup, A. (1991), Design Approaches: A Comparative Study of Information System Design and Architectural Design, *The Computer Journal*, 34:215-224.

Olton, Robert M. (1979), Experimental Studies of Incubation: Searching for the Elusive, *Journal of Creative Behavior*, 13:9-22.

Olton, Robert M. and David M. Johnson (1976), Mechanisms of Incubation in Creative Problem Solving, *American Journal of Psychology*, 89:617-630.

Osterweil, Leon (1981), Software Environment Research: Directions for the Next Five Years, *Computer*,(April):35-43.

Osterweil, Leon (1987), Software Processes are Software Too, *Proceedings, 9th International Conference on Software Engineering*, pp. 2-13.

Palmer, Richard E. (1969), *Hermeneutics*, Evanston, IL: Northwestern University Press.

Palvia, Shailendra C. and Steven R. Gordon (1992), Tables, Trees and Formulas in Decision Analysis, *Communications of the ACM*, (35,10):104-113.

Parnas, David Lorge (1972a), On Criteria to Be Used in Decomposing Systems into Modules, *Communication of the ACM*, 15:1053-1058.

Parnas, David Lorge (1972b), A Technique for Software Module Specification with Examples, *Communications of the ACM*, 15:330-336.

Parnas, David Lorge (1976), On the Design and Development of Program Families, *IEEE Transactions on Software Engineering*, 2:1-9.

Parnas, David Lorge (1990), Education for Computing Professionals, *Computer*, January:17-22.

Peckham, J. and F. Maryanski (1988), Semantic Data Models, *ACM Computer Surveys*, 20:153-189.

Pepper, Stephen C. (1942), *World Hypotheses: A Study in Evidence*, Berkeley, CA: University of California Press.

Perrolle, Judith A. (1986), Intellectual Assembly Lines: The Rationalization of Managerial, Professional and Technical Work, *Computers and the Social Sciences*, 2:111-122.

Petroski, Henry (1982), *To Engineer is Human*, New York: St. Martins Press.

Polson, P. G. and D. E. Kieras (1985), A Quantitative Model of the Learning and Performance of Text Editing Knowledge, *Proceedings of CHI'85*, pp. 207-212.

Popper, Karl R. (1959), *The Logic of Scientific Discovery*, 2nd ed., New York: Harper & Row. (Originally published in 1934.)

Popper, Karl R. (1965), *Conjectures and Refutations: The Growth of Scientific Knowledge*, Second Edition, New York: Basic Books. (Originally published in 1963.)

Popper, Karl R (1974/1987), Campbell on the Evolutionary Theory of Knowledge, in Paul A. Schilpp, ed., *The Philosophy of Karl Popper*, LaSalle, IL: Open Court (1974), pp. 1059-65, reprinted in Gerard Radnitsky and W. W. Bartley II, eds., *Evolutionary Epistemology, Rationality, and the Sociology of Knowledge*, LaSalle, IL: Open Court (1987), pp. 115-120.

Potts, Colin (1993), Software-Engineering Research Revisited, *IEEE Software*, September:19-28.

Prieto-Diaz, Ruben and Guillermo Arango (1991), *Tutorial: Domain Analysis and Software Systems Modeling*, Silver Spring, MD: IEEE Computer Society Press.

Price, William J. and Lawrence W. Bass (1969), Scientific Research and the Innovative Process, *Science*, 164:802-806.

Prigogine, Ilya (1980), *From Being to Becoming: Time and Complexity in the Physical Sciences*, San Francisco.

Pye, David (1978), *The Nature and Aesthetics of Design*, New York: Van Nostrand Reinhold.

Quine, W. V. O. (1961), Two Dogmas of Empiricism, in W. V. O. Quine, ed., *From a Logical Point of View*, Second Edition, New York: Harper and Row, pp. 20-46 (originally published in 1953).

Quine, W. V. O. (1969), *Ontological Relativity and Other Essays*, New York: Columbia University Press.

Quine, W. V. O. (1975), The Nature of Natural Knowledge, in Samuel Guttenplan, ed., *Mind and Language*, Oxford: Clarendon Press, pp. 67-81.

Raeithel, Arne (1991), Activity Theory as a Foundation for Design, in Christiane Floyd, Heinz Züllighoven, Reinhard Budde, and Reinhard Keil-Slawik, eds., *Software Development and Reality Construction*, Berlin: Springer-Verlag, pp 391-415..

Rasmussen, Jens (1983), Skills, Rules, Knowledge: Signals, Signs and Symbols and Other Distinctions in Human Performance Models, *IEEE Transactions on Systems, Man and Cybernetics*, 13:257-267.

Rasmussen, Jens, Keith Duncan, and Jacques Leplat, eds. (1987), *New Technology and Human Error*, New York: John Wiley & Sons.

Reason, James (1990), *Human Error*, Cambridge: Cambridge University Press.

Redwine, Samuel T. and William E. Riddle (1985), Software Technology Maturation, *Proceedings, International Conference on Software Engineering*, 189-200.

Reitman, W. (1965), *Cognition and Thought*, New York: John Wiley & Sons.

Resnick, B. (1983), Mathematics and Science Learning: A New Conception, *Science*, 220:477-478.

Resnick, Lauren B. (1991), Shared Cognition: Thinking as Social Practice, in Lauren B. Resnick, John M. Levine, and Stephanie D. Teasley, eds., *Perspectives on Socially Shared Cognition*, Washington, DC: American Psychological Association, pp. 1-20.

Rey, Georges (1983), Concepts and Stereotypes, *Cognition*, 15:237-262.

Rheinfrank, John J., William R. Hartman, and Arnold Wasserman (1992), Design for Usability: Crafting a Strategy for the Design of a New Generation of Xerox Copiers, in Paul S. Adler and Terry A. Winograd, eds., *Usability. Turning Technology into Tools*, New York: Oxford, pp. 15-40.

Rich, Elaine and Kevin Knight (1991), *Artificial Intelligence*, 2nd ed., New York: McGraw-Hill.

Richardson, John T. E. (1983), Mental Imagery in Thinking and Problem Solving, in Jonathan St B. T. Evans, ed., *Thinking and Reasoning, Psychological Approaches*, London: Routledge & Kegan Paul, pp. 197-226.

Rittel, Horst W. J. and Melvin M. Webber (1973), Dilemmas in a General Theory of Planning, *Policy Sciences* 4:155-69, reprinted (1984) as Planning Problems are Wicked Problems in *Developments in Design Methodology*, New York: John Wiley & Sons.

Rosaldo, Michelle (1984), Toward an Anthropology of Self and Feeling, in R. Schroeder and R. Le Vine, eds., *Culture Theory: Essays on Mind, Self, and Emotion*, Cambridge: Cambridge University Press, pp. 137-158.

Rosenberg, Victor (1974), The Scientific Premises of Information Science, *Journal of the American Society for Information Science*, July-August, pp. 263-269.

Ross, D. T. and K. E. Schoman, Jr. (1977), Structured Analysis for Requirements Definition, *IEEE Transactions on Software Engineering*, SE-3:6-15.

Rouse, Willaim B. and Kenneth R. Boff (1987a) eds., *System Design*, Amsterdam: North-Holland.

Rouse, Willaim B. and Kenneth R. Boff (1987b), Designers, Tools, and Environments: State of Knowledge, Unresolved Issues, and Potential Directions, in Willaim B. Rouse and Kenneth R. Boff (1987a), eds., *System Design*, Amsterdam: North-Holland, pp. 43-64.

Royce, W. W. (1970), Managing the Development of Large Software Systems, *IEEE WESCON*, pp. 1-9.

Royce, W. (1990), TRW's Ada Process Model for Incremental Development of Large Software Systems, *International Conference on Software Engineering*

Rumelhart, David E., James L. McClelland, and the PDP Research Group (1986), *Parallel Distributed Processing, Explorations in the Microstructures of Cognition*, 2 vols., Cambridge, MA: MIT Press.

Rumelhart, David E. and Donald Norman (1981), Accretion, Tuning, and Restructuring: Three Modes of Learning, in J. W. Cotton and R. Klatzky, eds., *Semantic Factors in Cognition*, Hillsdale, NJ: Lawrence Erlbaum Associates.

Runkle, Donald L. (1991), SMR Forum: Taught in America, *Sloan Management Review*, Fall, pp. 67-72.

Russell, Bertrand (1903), *Principles of Mathematics*, Cambridge: Cambridge University Press.

Sackman, H., W. J. Erickson, and E. E. Grant (1968), Exploratory Experimental Studies Comparing Online and Offline Programmers, *Communications of the ACM*, 11:3-11.

Sacks, Oliver (1993), To See and Not See, *The New Yorker*, May 10, pp. 59-73.

Sage, Andrew P. (1990a), *Concise Encyclopedia of Information Processing in Systems and Organizations*, Oxford: Pergamon Press.

Sage, Andrew P. (1990b), Design and Evaluation of Systems, in Andrew P. Sage, *Concise Encyclopedia of Information Processing in Systems and Organizations*, Oxford: Pergamon Press.

Sage, Andrew P. (1992), *Systems Engineering*, New York: John Wiley & Sons.

Salzman, Harold (1989), Computer-Aided Design: Limitations in Automating Design and Drafting, *IEEE Transactions on Engineering Management*, 36:252-261.

Salzman, Harold (1992), Skill-Based Design: Productivity, Learning, and Organizational Effectiveness, in Paul S. Adler and Terry A. Winograd, eds., *Usability. Turning Technology into Tools*, New York: Oxford, pp. 66-96.

Schön, Donald A. (1983), *The Reflective Practitioner: How Professionals Think in Action*, New York: Basic Books.

Schuler, Douglas and Aki Namioka, eds. (1993), *Participatory Design: Principles and Practices*, Hillsdale, NJ: Lawrence Erlbaum Associates.

Schwartz, Steven and Timothy Griffin (1986), *Medical Thinking: The Psychology of Medical Judgment and Decision Making*, New York: Springer-Verlag.

Seabrook, John (1994), My First Flame, *The New Yorker*, June 6, pp. 70-79.

Searle, John R. (1969), *Speech Acts*, Cambridge: Cambridge University Press.

Segall, Marshall H., Donald T. Campbell, and Melville J. Herskovits (1966), *The Influence of Culture on Visual Perception*, New York: Bobbs-Merrill.

Semmel, Ralph D. (1991), *A Knowledge-Based Approach to Automated Query Formulation*, Ph. D. Dissertation, University of Maryland, Baltimore.

Semmel, R. D. and D. P. Silberberg (1993), Extended Entity-Relationship Model for Automatic Query Generation, *Telematics and Informatics*, 10:301-317.

Senders, John W. and Neville P. Moray (1991), *Human Error: Cause, Prediction, and Reduction*, Hillsdale, NJ: Lawrence Erlbaum Associates.

Shapin, Steven (1982), History of Science and Its Sociological Reconstruction, *History of Science*, 20:157-211.

Shaw, Mary (1990), Prospects for an Engineering Discipline of Software, *IEEE Software*, November:15-24.

Sheppard, S. B., B. Curtis, P. Milman, and T. Love (1979), Modern Coding Practices and Programmer Performance, *Computer*, (12,12):41-49.

Sherwin, Charles W. and Raymond S. Isenson (1967), Project Hindsight, *Science*, 156:1571-77.

Shneiderman, Ben (1980), *Software Psychology: Human Factors in Computer and Information Systems*, Cambridge, MA: Winthrop Publishers.

Shneiderman, Ben (1983), Direct Manipulation: A Step Beyond Programming Languages, *Computer*, (16,8):57-69.

Shneiderman, Ben (1987), *Designing the User Interface: Strategies for Effective Human-Computer Interaction*, Reading, MA: Addison-Wesley Publishing Co.

Shu, N. (1988), A Visual Programming Language Designed for Automatic Programming, *21st Hawaii International Conference on System Sciences*.

Silverman, Barry G. and Toufic M. Mezher (1992), Expert Critics in Engineering Design: Lessons Learned in Research Needs, *AI Magazine*, Spring, pp. 45-62.

Simon, Herbert A. (1957), *Models of Man: Social and Rational*, New York: John Wiley & Sons.

Simon, Herbert A. (1969/1981), *The Sciences of the Artificial*, 2nd ed., Cambridge, MA: The MIT Press (originally published in 1969).

Simon, Herbert A. (1973), The Structure of Ill-Structured Problems, *Artificial Intelligence*, 4:181-201.

Sission, J. C., E. B. Schoomaker, and J. C. Ross (1976), Clinical Decision Analysis: The Hazard of Using Additional Data, *Journal of the American Medical Association*, 236:1259-1263.

Skinner, Wickham (1986), The Productivity Paradox, *Harvard Business Review*, July-August, pp. 55-59.

Smith, C. S. (1970), The Cover Design: Art, Technology, and Science: Notes on their Historical interaction, *Technology and Culture*, 11:493-549.

Soloway, Elliot and Kate Ehrlich (1984), Empirical Studies of Programming Knowledge, *IEEE Transactions on Software Engineering*, 10:595-609.

Sonnenwald, Diane H. (1992), Developing a Theory to Guide the Process of Designing Information Retrieval Systems, *ACM SIGIR '92*, pp. 310-317.

Sperling, G. (1960), The Information Available in Brief Visual Presentations, *Psychological Monographs*, 74:1-29.

Staudenmaier, John M. (1985), *Technology's Storytellers: Reweaving the Human Fabric*, Cambridge, MA: MIT Press.

Sternberg, Robert J. and Peter A. Frensch, eds. (1991), *Complex Problem Solving*, Hillsdale, NJ: Lawrence Erlbaum Associates.

Stevens, Albert and Patty Coupe (1987), Distortions in Judged Spatial Relations, *Cognitive Psychology*, 10:422-437.

Stevens, W., G. Myers and L. Constantine (1974), Structured Design, *IBM Systems Journal*, 13:115-139.

Suchman, Lucy A. (1987), *Plans and Situated Actions*, Cambridge: Cambridge University Press.

Suchman, Lucy A. (1988), Representing Practice in Cognitive Science, *Human Studies*, 11:305-325.

Sullivan, Joseph W. and Sherman W. Tyler, eds. (1991), *Intelligent User Interfaces*, New York: ACM Press.

Suppe, Frederick (1974), The Search for Philosophic Understanding of Scientific Theories, pp. 3-241 in F. Suppe, ed., *The Structure of Scientific Theories*, Urbana, IL: University of Chicago Press.

Sutherland, I. E. (1963), Sketchpad: A Man-Machine Graphical Communication System, *Proceedings of the Spring Joint Computer Conference*, pp. 329-346.

Tanik, M. M. and E. S. Chan (1991), *Fundamentals of Computing for Software Engineers*, Van Nostrand Reinhold, New York.

Tauber, M. J. and D. Ackermann, eds. (1991), *Mental Models and Human-Computer Interaction II*, Amsterdam: North-Holland.

Teichroew, D. and E. A. Hershey III (1977), PSL/PSA: A Computer-Aided Technique for Structured Documentation and Analysis of Information Processing Systems, *IEEE Transactions on Software Engineering*, SE-3:41-48.

Thackara, John, ed. (1988a), *Design After Modernism. Beyond the Object*, New York: Thames and Hudson.

Thackara, John (1988b), Beyond the Object in Design, in John Thackara, ed., *Design After Modernism. Beyond the Object*, New York: Thames and Hudson, p. 11-34.

Thomas, Kenneth W. and Walter G. Tymon, Jr. (1982), Necessary Properties of Relevant Research: Lessons from Recent Criticisms of the Organizational Sciences, *Academy of Management Review*, 7:345-352.

Thompson, Peter (1985), Visual Perception: An Intelligent System with Limited Bandwith, in Andrew Monk, ed., *Fundamentals of Human-Computer Interaction*, New York: Academic Press.

Tichy, Walter F., Paul Lukowicz, Lutz Prechelt, and Ernst A. Heinz (1995), Experimental Evaluation in Computer Science: A Quantitative Study, *Journal of Systems and Software*, 28:9-18.

Timmers, T. and B. I. Blum, eds. (1991), *Software Engineering in Medical Informatics*, Amsterdam: North Holland.

Timpka, T., P. Hedblom, and H. Holmgren (1991), ACTION DESIGN: Using an Object-Oriented Environment for Group Process Development of Medical Software, in Timmers, T. and B. I. Blum, eds., *Software Engineering in Medical Informatics*, Amsterdam: North Holland, pp. 151-166.

Timpka, T. and Nyce, J. (1992), Towards a Pragmatics for Medical Hypermedia Systems, *Proceedings MEDINFO '92*, Amsterdam: North-Holland, pp. 1254-1260.

Toulmin, Stephen (1953), *The Philosophy of Science*, London: Hutchinson.

Toulmin, Stephen (1961), *Foresight and Understanding*, London: Hutchinson.

Toulmin, Stephen (1990), *Cosmopolis: The Hidden Agenda of Modernity*, Chicago: University of Chicago Press.

Tracz, Will (1994), Domain-Specific Software Architecture (DSSA) Frequently Asked Questions (FAQ), *ACM Software Engineering Notes*, April, pp. 52-56.

Tulving, Endel and Daniel L. Schacter (1990), Priming and Human Memory Systems, *Science*, 247:301-306.

Turski, W. M. (1985), The Role of Logic in Software Enterprise, *Proceedings, International Conference on Software Engineering*, p. 400.

Tversky, Amos and Daniel Kahneman (1974), Judgment Under Uncertainty: Heuristics and Biases, *Science*, 185:1124-1131.

Tweney, Ryan D., Michael E. Doherty, and Clifford R. Mynatt (1981), *On Scientific Thinking*, New York: Columbia University Press.

Vera, Alonso H. and Herbert A. Simon (1993), Situated Action: Reply to Reviewers, *Cognitive Science*, 17:77-86.

Verner, J. M. and G. Tate (1987), A Model for Software Sizing, *Journal of Systems and Software*, 7:173-177.

Vessey, Iris (1991), Cognitive Fit: A Theory-Based Analysis of the Graphs Versus Tables Literature, *Decision Sciences*, 22:219-240.

Vessey, Iris and Dennis Galletta (1991), Cognitive Fit: An Empirical Study of Information Acquisition, *Information Systems Research*, 2:63-84.

Vincenti, Walter G. (1984), Technological Knowledge without Science: The Innovation of Flush Rivetting in American Airplanes, ca. 1930-ca. 1950, *Technology and Culture*, 3:540-576.

Vincenti, Walter G. (1990), *What Engineers Know and How They Know It*, Baltimore, MD: Johns Hopkins University Press.

Visser, Willemien (1990), More or Less Following a Plan During Design: Opportunistic Deviations in Specification, *International Journal of Man-Machine Studies*, 33:247-278.

Voss, James F. and Timothy Post (1988), On the Solving of Ill-Structured Problems, in Michelene T. H. Chi, Robert Glaser and M. J. Farr, eds. (1988), *The Nature of Expertise*, Hillsdale, NJ: Lawrence Erlbaum Associates, pp. 261-285.

Vygotsky, Lev (1962), *Thought and Language*, Cambridge, MA: MIT Press.

Vygotsky, Lev (1981a), The Instrumental Method in Psychology, in James V. Wertsch, ed., *The Concept of Activity in Soviet Psychology*, Armonk, NY: M. E. Sharpe, pp. 134-143.

Vygotsky, Lev (1981b), The Genesis of Higher Mental Functions, in James V. Wertsch, ed., *The Concept of Activity in Soviet Psychology*, Armonk, NY: M. E. Sharpe, pp. 144-188.

Waldrop, M. Michael (1987), *Man-Made Minds*, New York: Walker and Co.

Wallas, Graham (1926), *The Art of Thought*, New York: Harcourt, Brace, and Co.

Ward, P. T., and S. J. Mellor (1985, 1986), *Structured Development for Real-Time Systems*, 3 Vols., Englewood Cliffs, NJ: Yourdon Press, vols. 1 and 2, 1985, vol. 3, 1986.

Warnier, J. D. (1975), *Logical Construction of Programs*, New York: Van Nostrand.

Warnier, J. D. (1981), *Logical Construction of Systems*, New York: Van Nostrand.

Wason, Peter C. (1960), On the Failure to Eliminate Hypotheses in a Conceptual Task, *Quarterly Journal of Experimental Psychology*, 12:129-140.

Wason, Peter C. (1966), Reasoning, in B. M. Foss, ed., *New Horizons in Psychology I*, Harmandsworth: Penguin.

Wason, Peter C. (1983), Realism and Rationality in The Selection Task, in Jonathan St. B. T. Evans, ed, *Thinking and Reasoning*, London: Routledge & Kegan Paul, pp. 44-75.

Wasserman, A. I. and S. Gatz (1982), The Future of Programming, *Communications of the ACM*, 25:196-206.

Weiderman, N. et al. (1987), *Evaluation of Ada Environments*, Technical Report CMU/SEI-87-TR-1, Software Engineering Institute.

Weinberg, G. M. and E. L. Schulman (1974), Goals, and Performance in Computer Programming, *Human Factors*, 16:70-77.

Weisberg, Robert W. (1980), *Memory, Thought, and Behavior*, New York: Oxford University Press.

Weisberg, Robert W. (1986), *Creativity: Genius and Other Myths*, New York: W. H. Freeman.

Weizenbaum, Joseph (1976), *Computer Power and Human Reason*, San Francisco: W. H. Freeman.

Wertsch, James V., ed. (1981a), *The Concept of Activity in Soviet Psychology*, Armonk, NY: M. E. Sharpe.

Wertsch, James V. (1981b), The Concept of Activity in Soviet Psychology, An Introduction, in James V. Wertsch, ed., *The Concept of Activity in Soviet Psychology*, Armonk, NY: M. E. Sharpe, pp. 3-36.

Wertsch, James V. (1991), A Sociocultural Approach to Socially Shared Cognition, in Lauren B. Resnick, John M. Levine, and Stephanie D. Teasley, eds., *Perspectives on Socially Shared Cognition*, Washington, DC: American Psychological Association, pp. 85-100.

Whitley, Richard (1984), *The Intellectual and Social Organization of the Sciences*, Oxford: Clarendon.

Wickens, Christopher D. (1984), *Engineering Psychology and Human Performance*, Glenview, IL: Scott, Foresman.

Wiederhold, G., P. Wegner, and S. Ceri (1992), A Paradigm for Component-Based Programming, *Communications of the ACM*, 35:89-99.

Wilkes, M. V., D. J. Wheeler, and S. Gill (1951), *The Preparation of Programs for an Electronic Digital Computer*, Reading, MA: Addison-Wesley.

Willcocks, Leslie and David Mason, *Computerizing Work: People, Systems Design and Workplace Relations*, London: Paradigm.

Williges, Robert C. (1987), The Use of Models in Human-Computer Interface, *Ergonomics*, 30:491-502.

Winograd, Terry and Fernando Flores (1986), *Understanding Computers and Cognition*, Norwood, NJ: Ablex Publishing Corp.

Wirth, Niklaus E. (1971), Program Development by Stepwise Refinement, *Communications of the ACM*, 14:221-227.

Wise, George (1985), Science and Technology, *OSIRIS*, 2nd series, 1:229-246.

Wittgenstein, Ludwig (1953), *Philosophical Investigations*, New York: Macmillian Publishing.

Woodworth, R. S. (1938) *Experimental Psychology*, New York: Holt.

Wright, Patricia (1978), Feeding the Information Eaters: Suggestions for Integrating Pure and Applied Research on Language Comprehension, *Instructional Science*, 7:249-312.

Yeh, Raymond T. (1991), System Development as a Wicked Problem, *International Journal of Software Engineering and Knowledge Engineering*, 1:117-130.

Yourdon, Edward (1989), *Modern Structured Analysis*, Englewood Cliffs, NJ: Prentice Hall.

Zave, Pamela (1984), The Operational versus the Conventional Approach to Software Development, *Communications of the ACM*, 27:104-118.

Zave. P. and W. Schell (1986), Salient Features of an Executable Language and its Environment, *IEEE Transactions on Software Engineering*, SE-12:312-325.

Zuboff, Shoshana (1988), *In the Age of the Smart Machine*, New York: Basic Books.

Zukier, Henri and Albert Pepitone (1984), Social Roles and Strategies in Prediction: Some Determinants of the Use of Base Rate Information, *Journal of Personality and Social Psychology*, (47,2).

INDEX

Abnormal return 317
Abrahamsen, A. A. 47, 74
Abstract data types 288-89
Abstractions 139
Accretion 117
Ackermann, D. 211
Activity theory 146-48, 224
Ad hoc query 336-37
Ada 292-93
Adaptability 233-34
Adaptive design 16, 258
Adaptivity 233-34
Add ketchup 208
Adjustment and anchoring 165
Adler, P. S. 173, 213
Advanced manufacturing technology
    230-32
Aesthetics and design 173-74
Affordance 127
Against Method 42
Alba, J. W. 108
Albrecht, A. J. 363
Alexander, C. 178-81, 196, 199, 279
Algebraic specification 289
ALGOL 245
Alienation 142
Allen, R. B. 211
Alternative features 326
Amann, K. 129
Amsel, E. 117
Analytic approach 192
Analytic statements 32-33
Annapurna 251
Anything goes 42
Application database 306, 308
Application development environment
    306
Application knowledge 310
Application-class knowledge 310
Arango, G. 299
Arationality 124

Architecture, process of 152-53
Aristotle 74, 265
Artificial intelligence 11, 107-09, 112-13
Artificial world 175
As-built specification 261-62, 338
Assimilation 226
Astley, W. G. 78, 82-83, 85
ATM 230-232
Atomic independence 307
Attewell, P. 232
Austin, G. A. 106
Automacticy (in experts) 123
Automatic integration 307
Availability 164
Availableness 98

Baars, B. J. 107
Backus, J. 245
Baecker, R. M. 208-09
Ballay, J. M. 195-96
Balzer, R. 299
Bannon, L. J. 209
Bansler, J. P. 275
Banville, C. 79-80
Barber, B. 17
Barnes, B. 59-60, 129
Barnett, O. 340
Barstow, D. R. 299
Bartlett, F. C. 116
Barwise, J. 64, 71, 75, 102
Basic research 55
Bass, L. W. 18, 54, 56-57
Bayes Theorem 161, 165-66
Bechtel, W. 23-28, 66, 108
Behavior gap 230
Being and Time 95
Being-in-the-world 96
Beirne, M. 224-25
Belady, L. A. 266-67, 365
Belief, justified true 23
Bell, A. 121